Identities and Politics in Germany

HARRINGTON PARK PRESS

NEW YORK, NY • USA   YORK, NORTH YORKSHIRE • UK

Queer Identities and Politics in Germany

A HISTORY
1880–1945

Clayton J. Whisnant

Harrington Park Press
Box 331
9 East Eighth Street
New York, NY 10003

Library of Congress Cataloging-in-Publication Data

Names: Whisnant, Clayton John, 1971—author.
Title: Queer identities and politics in Germany : a history, 1880–1945 /
    Clayton J. Whisnant.
Description: New York, NY : Harrington Park Press, 2016. | Includes
    bibliographical references and index.
Identifiers: LCCN 2016002615 (print) | LCCN 2016010510 (ebook) | ISBN
    9781939594099 (pbk. : alk. paper) | ISBN 9781939594082 (hardcover : alk.
    paper) | ISBN 9781939594105 (ebook)
Subjects: LCSH: Gays—Germany—History. | Gay rights—Germany—History.
Classification: LCC HQ76.2.G4 W463 2016 (print) | LCC HQ76.2.G4 (ebook) |
    DDC 306.76/60943—dc23
LC record available at http://lccn.loc.gov/2016002615

Manufactured in the United States of America

10 9 8 7 6 5 4 3 2 1

For all my Rice friends

CONTENTS

ILLUSTRATIONS

ABBREVIATIONS

BfM	Federation for Human Rights (*Bund für Menschenrecht*)
DFV	German Friendship Alliance (*Deutsche Freundschafts-Verband*)
GdE	Community of the Special (*Gemeinschaft der Eigenen*)
SPD	Social Democratic Party of Germany (*Sozialdemokratische Partei Deutschlands*)
WhK	Scientific-Humanitarian Committee (*Wissenschaftlich-humanitäres Komitee*)
WLSR	World League for Sexual Reform (*Weltliga für Sexualreform*)

ACKNOWLEDGMENTS

First order of thanks goes to Bill Cohen, who had the idea for this book and has been a faithful shepherd through the whole process. Also thanks to the editor Steven Rigolosi for all his help and encouragement, to Ann Twombly for her careful reading of the manuscript, and to Patrick Ciano for his work with the various images and the design of this book. Marti Lybeck and Alison Guenther-Pal both kindly sent me copies of their dissertation so that I could take advantage of their insights; Laurie Marhoefer and Andrew Wackerfuss generously forwarded me advance copies of their new books well before these books were out so I could work their challenging new interpretations into my own work. Geoffrey Giles and Jennifer Evans have always been very encouraging of my research and writing, and for this book they read the entire manuscript and gave me some absolutely invaluable comments and advice. I want also to thank Moritz Föllmer for his reading of the manuscript and his many cogent remarks and useful critiques. Finally, two friends at Wofford gave me important assistance: Karen Goodchild in the Art History Department, who read chapter 4 and offered her perspective, and Chris Dinkins, who did the vital work of editing the book during the last stages.

Some of the research for this book was done many years ago while I was working on my dissertation, and so I should again thank the German Academic Exchange Service (DAAD) for the research funding that they gave me in 1998–99. Most of the writing was done during my sabbatical semester of fall 2014, for which I owe Wofford much gratitude. I cannot imagine having finished it on time without the semester to read, reflect, and compose in a systematic way. I also owe a great debt to several individuals who helped me with the images in this book: Tim Benoit-Ledoux at the University of New Hampshire, Jens Dobler at the Schwules Museum, Harald Lützenkirchen with the Kurt Hiller Gesellschaft, Cornelia Pastelak-Price with the Jeanne Mammen Stiftung, Gunter Schmidt in Hamburg, Rick Watson at the Harry Ransom Center, and my father, David Whisnant, who helped digitally enhance the image resolution of several pictures. Last, but not least, I thank my family for their love and encouragement during the entire project.

I would like to thank Harry Oosterhuis and the University of Chicago Press for permission to include a lengthy and detailed summary of Oosterhuis's important book *Stepchildren of Nature: Krafft-Ebing, Psychiatry, and the Making of Sexual Identity* (Chicago: University of Chicago Press, 2000). All rights reserved.

Queer Identities and Politics in Germany

INTRODUCTION

Why Study Queer German History?

CHAPTER SUMMARY

Queer Identities and Politics in Germany: A History, 1880–1945 offers a useful and readable account of the history of homosexuality in Germany between the end of the nineteenth century and 1945, and a short epilogue suggests the ways that the long history of LGBTQ life and politics in Germany continued to be felt after 1945. It looks not only at the individuals, events, and movements of the era, but also briefly surveys some of the scholarly debates that have defined the historical literature.

OVERVIEW

Queer German history has a great deal of relevance for any reader interested in LGBTQ issues. Unfortunately for English-language readers, though, much of the recent work has been written in German and is therefore inaccessible to those who do not read this language. Even looking for primary sources can be hard. Many historians still find themselves regularly citing James Steakley's *The Homosexual Emancipation Movement in Germany*—a pathbreaking book, but one published in 1975, at the very beginning of research into German LGBTQ history. Robert Beachy's recent work, *Gay Berlin: Birthplace of a Modern Identity,* very good in so many ways, focuses only on Berlin, largely neglects lesbian life, and stops at the beginning of the Nazi era.

Queer Identities and Politics in Germany: A History, 1880–1945 offers a useful and readable account of the history of homosexuality in Germany between the end of the nineteenth century, when the homosexual movement formed, and 1945, when the Allies finally defeated the Nazi state. The conclusion looks forward to the present, suggesting the ways that the long history of LGBTQ life and politics in Germany continued to be felt after 1945: in the gay scenes that reemerged after the war, in the various political movements that eventually reappeared, in the scientific theories of sexuality that continued to evolve, and in the different sexual identities that LGBTQ individuals have adopted. *Queer Identities and Politics in Germany* not only looks at the individuals, events, and movements of the era, but also briefly surveys some of the scholarly debates that have defined the historical literature. This book offers opportunities to consider important issues still facing lesbians, gay men, bisexuals, transgender individuals, and others within the larger queer community—issues of identity, language, community building, and political strategizing.

KEY TERMS
German gay history; queer German history; German gay political history; Foucault in gay German history

Whisnant, Clayton J.
Queer Identities and Politics in Germany: A History 1880–1945
dx.doi.org/10.17312/harringtonparkpress/2016.08.qipg.00a
© Harrington Park Press, LLC, New York, NY 10011

FIGURE 1 **TRANSVESTITES IN THE ELDORADO CLUB, 1929**

Cross-dressing acts became popular attractions in Berlin and many other major European cities in the
era between the two world wars, certainly in some of the best-known gay clubs, but also in cabarets,
which attracted a mixed gay and straight audience. Source: Bundesarchiv, Bild 146-1976-141-25.
Photograph by Herbert Hoffmann

Tracing the history of the contemporary lesbian, gay, bisexual, transgender, and queer (LGBTQ) community can take you in many directions.[1] The Stonewall Riots on the streets of New York City on June 28, 1969, obviously looms large in LGBTQ consciousness, as evidenced by the many pride events that take place worldwide in June. Popular films such as *Milk* (2008) and the *Dallas Buyers Club* (2013) help maintain an awareness of important moments in 1970s gay politics and the 1980s AIDS crisis. For those willing to dig deeper, there are now good histories of gay and lesbian life in major cities around the world, major accounts of the prejudices against homosexuality and modern efforts to regulate sexuality, and important examinations of the roles that same-sex relations could play in ancient and non-Western cultures.[2] For men and women who identify as transgender, many of these studies offer glimpses of their own history for the simple reason that gender transgression has so often been linked in people's mind with sexual transgression. For those who want a more focused study, there is a fascinating history of transsexuality in the United States as well as a couple of surveys of transgender (or queer, broadly defined) history.[3]

So many of these lines of inquiry will take you to Germany if you follow them long enough. The first homosexual activists were German; the first writer to coin the term *homosexual* was a German-speaking Hungarian who moved from one German city to another for much of his adult life. Berlin's gay life became internationally renowned (or infamous, depending on your point of view) by the 1920s (Figure 1). The first periodicals addressed to gay men, lesbians, and transgender people were all German. A German scientist coined the term *transvestism,* paving the way for the distinction that we make between homosexual and transgender. The first step toward something like rights for cross-dressers came when the Berlin police agreed to issue "transvestite passes." The first sex reassignment operation was done by a German doctor in 1920. And, of course, the pink triangle attached to the inmate uniforms of homosexual men in the Nazi concentration camps has been transformed since the 1970s into one of the internationally recognized symbols of LGBTQ politics.

This historical background suggests that queer German history has a great deal of relevance for American readers. Much of this work has been written in German, however, and is therefore inaccessible to those who do not read this language. Even looking for primary sources can be hard. Slowly, some of the key works have been translated, thanks to the tireless work of Michael Lombardi-Nash and Hubert Kennedy. Nevertheless, there are many others that are still available only in German. What overviews are available are very old at this point. Many of us still find ourselves regularly citing James

Steakley's *The Homosexual Emancipation Movement*, a pathbreaking book no doubt, but one published in 1975, at the very beginning of research into German LGBTQ history. Richard Plant's *The Pink Triangle: The Nazi War against Homosexuals* came out in 1986 and is not considered entirely reliable by professional historians. More recent overviews tend to be short chapters in larger collections, and most often focus on Nazi persecution, ignoring the turn-of-the-century movement entirely. Robert Beachy's recent book, very good in so many ways, focuses only on Berlin, largely neglects lesbian life, and stops at the beginning of the Nazi era. On the other hand, Laurie Marhoefer's recent book offers several important new perspectives on the Weimar and Nazi eras but does not highlight the many continuities that link the Weimar period with the late nineteenth century that are important for readers to understand.[4]

In this book I offer what I hope is a useful and readable account of the history of homosexuality in Germany between the end of the nineteenth century, when the homosexual movement formed, and 1945, when the Nazi state was finally defeated by the Allies. My intention is to reach a general audience interested in LGBTQ history or the history of sexuality more broadly. Consequently, I will try to steer clear of a lot of the jargon and theory that, despite often giving important insights, can make a study of sexuality difficult to appreciate for the average reader. Instead, I focus on the people, organizations, political philosophies, and events of the period. I certainly do not ignore key academic debates—for example, debates about the role of science in shaping conceptions of sexuality at the turn of the century, or research into the motives behind Nazi persecution. I do try to introduce them in a quick and accessible way so that they can easily be read and used as the basis for discussion and perhaps further research.

The material presented in this book should offer opportunities to consider important issues still facing lesbians, gay men, bisexuals, transgender individuals, and others within the larger queer community, including:

- gender and sexual identity
- defining the nature of LGBTQ relationships
- the roots of social and political persecution
- the social conditions that allow real progress to be made
- building institutions to serve the LGBTQ community
- political strategies for winning political rights, gaining social acceptance, and contributing toward larger social change
- the significance of which language we choose to work with for queer politics
- the role of commercialization in gay life and politics.

A QUICK SURVEY OF QUEER GERMAN HISTORY

The study of Germany's queer history has come a long way since its meager beginnings in the 1970s. Drawing vitality from the gay and lesbian liberation movement that sprang to life in West Germany at the beginning of the 1970s, the study of LGBTQ history was driven forward by a relatively small cadre of devoted historians. Some of them were academically trained, but most were admirably self-taught. A group of women connected with the autonomous feminist movement founded the Spinnboden archive as a location dedicated to "the Discovery and Protection of Women's Love" in 1973.[5] In 1985 Manfred Baumgardt, Manfred Herzer, Andreas Sternweiler, and Wolfgang Theis opened the Gay Museum (*Schwules Museum*) in Berlin. Since then, as one visitor noted, "the museum has produced fabulous exhibitions and publications of the highest aesthetic and intellectual quality, without ever neglecting witty and erotic content."[6] Over the years, the two institutions have nurtured scholars interested in German gay and lesbian history, both by providing central locations for pursuing and sharing ideas and by compiling large archives and libraries. Berlin, not surprisingly, has been the center for much of the work, but scholars elsewhere have made their own invaluable contributions: Wolfgang Voigt and Hans-Georg Stümke in Hamburg, Rüdiger Lautmann at the University of Bremen, Rainer Hoffschildt in Hannover, Burkhard Jellonnek in Saarbrücken, and Günter Grau at the University of Bremen, to name but a few. Scholars from outside Germany have also made significant contributions: the U.S. historians James Steakley, Geoffrey Giles, and John Fout, for example, as well as Harry Oosterhuis, from the Netherlands.

Gay and lesbian history in Germany, as elsewhere, initially pursued two major themes: one tragic and the second heroic. For the first generation of gay and lesbian activists, an important part of confronting hostility to homosexuality in the contemporary world was uncovering its roots in the past. This research could take them deep into the Middle Ages to uncover the origins of social prejudice and legal persecution against same-sex desire.[7] The bulk of the scholarship, though, quickly became focused on the fate of homosexuals under Hitler's regime. This research has grown quite large since it began in the early 1970s, taking on an increasingly local character in the past decade or so.[8] The second theme at the center of much research has been writing the history of the first homosexual rights movement, from its origins with mid-nineteenth-century writers such as Karl Heinrich Ulrichs to its flourishing in the Weimar Republic and ultimate demise at the hands of the Nazis in 1933.[9] Dr. Magnus Hirschfeld and his Scientific-Humanitarian Committee (*Wissenschaftlich-humanitäres Komitee*, hereafter cited as WhK) has garnered much attention; so too has Hirschfeld's chief rival, Adolf Brand—publisher of the world's first gay periodical, *The Special One* (*Der Eigene*), and founder of his own group, the Community of the Special (*Die Gemeinschaft der Eigenen*, hereafter cited as GdE).[10]

In the course of the 1980s new research directions emerged. One strand of study, very much influenced by the social history that had grown in strength during the previous two decades, examined the homosexual milieu that surfaced at the end of the nineteenth century in several large cities and would survive until today, despite a severe contraction during the Nazi era and World War II. With concepts and research strategies borrowed from anthropology and the subcultural school of sociology, these researchers were able to map out city areas that served as locations for gay men to meet and have sex. They also traced a range of linguistic, symbolic, and material strategies that provided gay men and women with ways to resist the hegemony of the dominant heterosexual culture.[11]

The other direction, often closely connected with previous efforts to research the early homosexual movement, was greatly influenced by Michel Foucault's work. This body of scholarship set Hirschfeld's efforts as a scientist and activist into a much larger context of writers, doctors, psychologists, and scientists who at the end of the nineteenth century and the beginning of the twentieth debated the nature of same-sex desire.[12] The scholars involved interrogated the very idea of the homosexual identity instead of seeing it as a given; they asked questions about its formation and its implications for the politics of same-sex desire. Unlike the first generation of scholars of the 1970s, they were more likely to approach Hirschfeld's hopes for scientific enlightenment with a heavy dose of skepticism.[13] Indeed, scholars began at this stage to see continuity between fin-de-siècle research into homosexuality and the Nazis' later misuse of science to "purify" the German race of homosexuality.[14] Furthermore, lesbian scholars were likely to view the obsessive classifications pursued by nineteenth-century sexology as rooted at least in part in the male desire to control female sexuality.[15]

The effect of Foucault on the practice of gay and lesbian history has gradually opened this field up to the "discursive turn." Although it took longer for the discursive turn to come to the historical profession in Germany than it did in the Anglo-American world, when its influence did become noticeable in the 1990s, gay and lesbian history was exposed to a range of methods and ideas stemming from psychoanalysis, literary and film studies, anthropology, queer theory, and gender studies.[16] One effect has been to move away from focusing specifically on notions of homosexual identity and toward talking about how these identities formed in relation to the category of "the heterosexual." Under the influence of gender history, which itself experienced a major burst of activity in the 1980s and 1990s, historians of sexuality have increasingly asked questions about the gendered aspects of homosexuality as well as the relationship between homosexuality and the gender norms established by the dominant culture.[17] In this way, they have reconnected gay men and lesbians with their heterosexual counterparts. Queer theory of the 1990s also played no small part here in blurring the division between gay and straight.[18] Queer theory, along with the seminal works of George Mosse, served to widen gay and lesbian scholarship's gaze away from focusing specifically on same-sex-desiring individuals (and the groups they formed) and toward analyzing and critiquing the broader culture and society of Germany.[19]

Over time, there has been a noticeable tendency of many historians of sexuality to distance themselves from various aspects of Foucault's argument. Beginning with some early efforts in the 1980s to revise Foucault's choice of 1870 as the date when the "modern homosexual" was born, the trend gathered momentum after George Chauncey's suggestion that "sexual inversion" (based on a notion of gender reversal) should be more carefully distinguished from modern homosexuality (based on an independent sexual orientation).[20] Eve Kosofsky Sedgwick and other queer theorists gradually made us aware of the problems of talking about a single "modern homosexual" identity at all.[21] And since roughly 2000, historians of medieval and early modern Europe, as well as scholars working on premodern Asia, Latin America, and Africa, have raised questions about whether we can safely draw a clear line between modern and premodern sexualities. As Helmut Puff writes, "If deployed indiscriminately, the premodern-modern divide . . . risks flattening the complexities of so-called traditional and modern societies alike."[22]

Others have raised fundamental problems with even writing queer history. In slightly different ways, many scholars have asked about our ability to legitimately connect past configurations of gender, sexual desire, and identity with our own. Judith Halberstam's *Female Masculinities* drew our attention to the "perverse presentism" of much contemporary lesbian history: "Many contemporary lesbian historians cannot extricate themselves from contemporary understandings of lesbian identity long enough to interpret the vagaries of early same-sex desire."[23] David Halperin wrestled with a similar problem in *How to Do the History of Homosexuality*. As a kind of solution to the issues of "continuity and discontinuity, identity and difference," he suggested a kind of "genealogical approach" that tears apart various notions connected with modern homosexuality and traces their history.[24] Laura Doan's *Disturbing Practices* highlights even more fundamental disciplinary differences with regard to standards and expectations between historians of sexuality and many queer theorists. Instead of despairing, though, Doan proposes a kind of productive dialogue between the two fields, one that encourages a kind of "hybrid practice" that can produce insights for both fields.[25]

Historians of sexuality have responded in different ways to these many challenges, as the essays collected recently in the anthology *After the History of Sexuality: German Genealogies with and Beyond Foucault* suggest.[26] Many grew less antagonistic toward science as they became aware of the multiple ways that it can be read and used. Others turned away from the "heterosexual/homosexual binary as a tool for understanding erotic cultures and identities in the past," in the words of Marti Lybeck, an approach that has the advantage for historians of allowing them to "consider a wider range of voices, choices, and meanings."[27] A few have taken a "detour to other kinds of thinking about sexuality and subjects, including particularly psychoanalysis, critical theory, and Marxism," or they have gone back to reread Foucault, being attentive to the ways that he might have been misunderstood in the past or might have offered insights that have been neglected.[28]

PURPOSE AND GUIDING QUESTIONS

Besides offering a useful survey of German LGBTQ history, this book should also serve as an easy reference for those people who want to dig deeper into the debates on their own. With this in mind, I generally cite English translations of German works when they are available. In the text, I chose to translate German titles of book, journals, magazines, and films, since I know from my experience as a teacher of undergraduate students that those who do not read German will remember scarcely anything that is presented in a foreign language. This may be frustrating for teachers and scholars, however, so I offer the original titles in parentheses for easy reference.

In the following chapters, I examine several guiding questions that have been important for LGBTQ historians of German history:

- How did German gays and lesbians look for love and relationships in an era in which homosexuality was suppressed socially and legally?
- Why did the world's first homosexual rights movement appear in Germany?
- Why is 1920s Berlin still remembered as such an amazing place for LGBTQ persons?
- Why did the Nazis throw homosexuals and many whom we would identify as transgender men and women into concentration camps

along with Jews, prostitutes, communists, Jehovah's Witnesses, Gypsies, and other asocials?

- What happened to those gay men and lesbians who eluded the SS and police or in other ways survived Nazi persecution?
- How have men and women who desired to have sex with members of the same sex understood themselves and their sexuality?

The theme of identity runs through the entire book. The first chapter introduces two distinct versions of this identity, one put forward by homosexuals influenced by scientific debate about sexuality, another influenced more by classical imagery and texts. The second considers several turn-of-the-century scandals that in many ways hinged on the issue of identity. The third chapter examines the gay scenes that, many historians have argued, were important social spaces for helping such identities coalesce. Cruising the streets, public parks, and the hallways of train stations, men at some level began to habitually sort other men into those interested in same-sex encounters and those who were not. In the gay and lesbian nightclubs, bars, and social organizations of Berlin, men and women interested in such relationships acquired a sense of belonging and were given an opportunity to perform their identities through the clothes they wore, the language they spoke, the stories they told, the songs they sang, and the people with whom they danced.

Identity is most explicitly dealt with in chapter 4, where it is treated alongside other popular representations of same-sex-desiring men and women. By treating identities and representations together, I do not mean to conflate the two. Popular representations were never easily or uncritically absorbed by gay men and lesbians as they formulated understandings about their sexuality. I also hope, however, to demonstrate that the two things cannot be entirely distinguished from one another. Forming an identity is inevitably a social process and so necessarily involves some interaction with the wider culture. In this chapter I show the ways that scholars, under the influence of queer theory, have gradually been moving away from the dual-model approach that was put forward in the 1980s and 1990s. Gay men and lesbians living in Germany in the late nineteenth and early twentieth centuries cannot be so easily divided into those who accepted a model of same-sex desire that was based on scientific theories of gender inversion and those who did not. There were many individuals who liked some aspects of the theory but not others. And as they worked through this problem, they had other cultural traditions to draw from—not simply the classical images of Greek and Rome, but also late nineteenth-century Romanticism and more novel images of modern life in the city.

I hope to highlight the range of identities by opening each chapter with a brief introduction to a different person. Each individual will be important for the topic of that chapter, of course, but each one also has his or her own approach to what it means to be homosexual. About the issue of gender, the poet and philosopher Denise Riley once wrote, "Any attention to the life of a woman, if traced out carefully, must admit the degree to which the effects of lived gender are at least sometimes unpredictable, and fleeting."[29] The same can be said about sexuality, I think.

TERMINOLOGY

A quick note about terminology is needed. I use the term *scene* instead of *subculture,* which is more prevalent in academic scholarship.[30] I think *subculture*—which was developed by the Birmingham School to think about a particular subset of a class—does not apply very well to the networks of gays and lesbians that have developed in modern cities. I also prefer *scene* since it tends to foreground the importance of space, thereby avoiding a certain ambiguity of *subculture.* The latter is often used to denote specific locations (gay bars, parks, public bathrooms, and so on), but also could suggest the distinct symbolic interactions that take place between gay men or lesbians. *Subculture* might also imply that the rest of the heterosexual culture is a monolithic whole, although few historians would see it that way today. The problem is that once you start chipping off other pieces—a working-class subculture, various ethnic subcultures, a youth subculture, and the like—it is not always clear what you have left. Finally, *scene* emphasizes the importance of a central interest in drawing men and women together into a series of social interactions. In the twentieth century, a number of scenes have emerged over time, yielding the complex, ever-changing landscape of the modern world. Like the individuals who gathered together to enjoy jazz in the 1920s or drugs in the 1960s, gay men and lesbians created distinct locations and interactions to facilitate a common love.[31]

I generally use the terms *homosexual, gay,* and *lesbian* to refer to men and women who experience sexual desire for members of the same sex to some considerable degree. I also regularly apply these terms to the relationships, associations, social networks, and institutions that they built in the course of the period covered by this book. No scholar of LGBTQ history today can use such language without some misgivings. I certainly accept the arguments made by queer studies that sexuality is fluid and sexual identities are inherently unstable. As we will see, there were indeed many debates in the late nineteenth and early twentieth centuries about the nature of sexual desire and the proper language to apply to same-sex desire. There is an argument to be made, however, for the pragmatic use of language. Both *homosexual* and *lesbian* were used frequently by Germans at the time in a way that is not too different from the way that I employ them. *Gay* or, rather, its German equivalent, *schwul*, is more problematic because it was a deeply pejorative slang term that would never have been employed by homosexual men at that time to refer to themselves. Its meaning was transformed in the course of the 1970s, however, and today it is used proudly by many. The largest problem with *homosexual, lesbian,* and *gay* is that these terms often blur together sexual and gender transgression. Many people at the time whom today we would identify as transgender were grouped with homosexual men and lesbians, both by the emerging gay and lesbian community and by society at large. It is a weakness that readers will need to be mindful of as they move forward.

CHAPTER 1

The Birth of Homosexual Politics

CHAPTER SUMMARY

This chapter examines the emergence of the early LGBTQ rights movement in Germany, in which Magnus Hirschfeld played an important role. It also considers the complicated interplay that developed among science, same-sex identities, and LGBTQ politics at the end of the nineteenth century.

OVERVIEW

The world's first homosexual movement was launched in Germany in the 1890s. Magnus Hirschfeld organized the Scientific-Humanitarian Committee (WhK). The committee's goals were to use the latest scientific research to repeal the country's sodomy law, Paragraph 175, and to promote wider tolerance for homosexuals. A magazine founded in the same decade by the anarchist and independent publisher Adolf Brand advocated for a revival of "Greek love." This magazine served as the focal point for a group of men who championed a return to the "manly culture" of the classical era, which the group's chief intellectual, Benedict Friedlaender, believed would revitalize all of Western civilization. This chapter discusses the history of this homosexual movement: Enlightenment-era criticism of the sodomy laws; writers such as Heinrich Hössli and Karl Heinrich Ulrichs, who paved the way; and nineteenth-century scientific research that gave Hirschfeld and others ideas about how Paragraph 175 could be challenged. This chapter also considers the complicated interplay that developed among science, same-sex identities, and LGBTQ politics at the end of the nineteenth century. It relates the emergence of the homosexual movement to the wider political context, considering its connection with the socialist politics of the 1890s and the appearance of the life reform movement.

KEY TERMS

Magnus Hirschfeld; Adolf Brand; Scientific-Humanitarian Committee; *Der Eigene*; Karl Heinrich Ulrichs; Richard von Krafft-Ebing; Paragraph 175

Whisnant, Clayton J.
Queer Identities and Politics in Germany: A History 1880–1945
dx.doi.org/10.17312/harringtonparkpress/2016.08.qipg.001
© Harrington Park Press, LLC, New York, NY 10011

FIGURE 2 **MAGNUS HIRSCHFELD**

The German-Jewish physician and sexologist Magnus Hirschfeld emerged as the most important face of homosexual activism in the early twentieth century. From 1897 until 1929 he served as the chair of the Scientific-Humanitarian Committee (WhK). This chapter examines the emergence of the early LGBTQ rights movement in Germany, in which Hirschfeld played an important role. It also considers the complicated interplay that developed among science, same-sex identities, and LGBTQ politics at the end of the nine-teenth century. Source: Schwules Museum, Berlin

In 1897 Magnus Hirschfeld (Figure 2) was a twenty-nine-year-old physician, himself the son of another physician, born and raised "on the shores of the Baltic." Both of his parents were Jewish, and if Hirschfeld's memories are any indication, they were prime examples of the modern, assimilated Jewish population that had emerged in the country by the second half of the nineteenth century. Little is known about his mother except that Hirschfeld remembered her as forgiving and affectionate. About his father, though, Hirschfeld had a great deal to say. In 1848 his father had been chosen by his fellow citizens of Kolberg as "the man for freedom and progress." He worked very hard for his patients, often taking no fee from those who could not afford it. He was politically engaged, writing a weekly column for the local newspaper for nearly thirty years, and working to push through a modernization of the local sewage and water supply system. In short, Hirschfeld's father left a lasting mark on his son, who would later remember, "My father was a doctor of high reputation, to whom we children looked up as to a higher being."[1]

In 1887 Hirschfeld began his university studies, soon committing to medicine. As one of his biographers notes, however, he was "possessed by an inner restlessness," becoming quickly "frustrated by the routine of academic life."[2] He studied in Breslau, moved to Strasbourg and then on to Berlin, only to end up in Munich, where he finally passed his intermediate exams in medicine. In Munich, which at the turn of the century was the artistic focus for the country, he made the acquaintance of the writers Henrik Ibsen and Frank Wedekind. But Munich could not keep him. Soon he was off to Heidelberg to do his six months of military service, and then back to Berlin at the end of 1891, where he would finally write his thesis for his medical degree. Next he went to Würzburg, where he successfully passed his final medical examination. And after all this work, he decided to try journalism! With a friend, he took a ship from Hamburg to New York, eventually ending up in Chicago to report on the Columbian World Exhibition in 1893. He loved traveling and writing, but journalism ultimately proved not to his taste. So by 1896 he found himself back in Berlin, ready to take up a new medical practice.

It is not clear when exactly Hirschfeld realized that he was homosexual. He never publicly admitted it, though his eventual political involvement for the cause would make it an open secret by the turn of the century. It is probably safe to say that he understood his sexual orientation by the time he arrived in Berlin, since he was clearly deeply affected by the suicide of one of his new patients. The young man, an officer in the German army, had been pressured to get married, but at the last minute, on the eve of his wedding, he shot himself in the head. The day after the young man's death Hirschfeld received a letter from the man relating the story leading up to his suicide. The strain of living a double life had proved to be too much for the man, who lived, in his own words, under this "curse" against human nature. The letter provoked Hirschfeld to write his first work about homosexuality, a thirty-four-page booklet entitled *Sappho and Socrates: How Can One Explain the Love of Men and Women for People of Their Own Sex?* It was published with the help of Max Spohr, the owner of a publishing house in Leipzig who originally specialized in the subjects of homeopathic medicine and the occult, but who had also started to explore the market for material on homosexuality beginning in 1893.[3]

The appearance of the booklet was timely. Only a year beforehand, Oscar Wilde had been sentenced to two years in prison because of his homosexuality. This infamous trial had provoked a great deal of public discussion about the "love that dares not speak its name," and Hirschfeld hoped injecting science into the debate might finally lead to some progress in popular attitudes and legal treatment. As one recent study of Hirschfeld notes, "Hirschfeld did not believe in practicing science for science's sake. For Hirschfeld, science not only increased knowledge but was a tool against injustice."[4] In this early work, he relied heavily on a theory of homosexuality developed by psychiatrists and a few other writers since the 1850s that argued that homosexuality was rooted in an individual's biological makeup. He supported this theory with more recent evidence presented by the embryologist and early Darwinian supporter Ernst Haeckel. Hirschfeld added his own ingredient to the theory, namely an emphasis on the strength of the sex drive. This strength played a large role, Hirschfeld argued, in explaining certain character differences that inevitably emerge among homosexuals. More important, though, it was further evidence of the congenital nature of sexuality. It could "neither be acquired through environmental factors or suggestions, nor extinguished through medical treatment or psychological conditioning."[5] Legally and morally, then, the only rational conclusion was to repeal all the laws against homosexuality.

His first book was published under a pseudonym, but by the following year Hirschfeld was ready to take a more public stance. On May 15, 1897, he invited Max Spohr and Eduard Oberg, a railroad official from the northern city of Hannover, to his home in the fashionable, middle-class Berlin suburb of Charlottenburg. Together, the three of them wrote the articles of association for the world's first homosexual organization, the Scientific-Humanitarian Committee (WhK).[6] Relying initially on the financial support of several wealthy donors, the WhK gradually picked up members and supporters, including doctors, lawyers, writers, and other professionals. The group met initially in Hirschfeld's apartment, but within a few years it had grown enough to justify renting rooms in the Prinz Albrecht, one of the city's fanciest hotels. The WhK drew on both enlightenment ideas and scientific perspectives in its campaign against Paragraph 175, Germany's sodomy law. It also pursued a wide range of related activities, from promoting scientific research on homosexuality to combating prevailing social prejudices against the "vice."

The WhK was soon joined by other individuals and groups that wanted to change the country's attitudes and perhaps in the process lay the groundwork for a more thorough transformation of German culture. Together, these many people, organizations, and publications formed a vibrant and dynamic movement. As in any political movement, there were disagreements and tensions, personality conflicts and power struggles. Nevertheless, the growth of the movement and, perhaps equally important, the way that the movement was able to interact with wider social and political transformations boded well for its future.

EARLY HOMOSEXUAL ACTIVISTS

Although Paragraph 175 had been created only recently, the criminalization of male homosexuality in Germany dated back centuries. Several nineteenth-century writers traced a history of persecution stretching back to Roman tribes. According to Tacitus, the German tribes at the time punished sodomites by drowning them in swamps. The early Christian church repeatedly issued proclamations against male-male love. And the Roman emperors Justinian and Theodosius both wrote legal codes with strict punishments against adultery that were broadly defined to include homosexual acts. The death sentence for male homosexuality was then picked up by the first major criminal code of the Holy Roman Empire, the *Constitutio Criminalis Carolina* issued by Emperor Charles V in 1532, which called for such criminals to be burned at the stake.

We should point out that this story of unswerving persecution has been undermined over the years. More recent historians have raised doubts about how rigidly and consistently any of these laws were actually enforced. And, famously, John Boswell's book *Christianity, Social Tolerance, and Homosexuality* opened up questions about how unequivocal the early Christian condemnation of homosexuality actually was.[7] There were certainly moments of "moral panic" set off by epidemics or other disasters that sent the rulers looking for scapegoats; however, most same-sex acts probably never came to the attention of the authorities, and even Christian clerics gave out relatively minor penances when such acts were confessed to them. Still, the death sentence remained the official rule, and some historians have argued that the persecution of "sodomites" was stepped up in the eleventh and twelfth centuries—an effect of the growing power of state institutions and a growing obsession with social and sexual "pollution."[8] Boswell also cited the possible influence of natural law theory, which was revived around this time and provided a justification for calling same-sex desire unnatural. The Protestant Reformation of the sixteenth century, in turn, created many opportunities to seek moral scapegoats and to brand many Catholic priests and monks as sodomites. Moral panics were rampant in this era of religious turbulence, creating the backdrop for the death penalty's being maintained by the emerging absolutist states of seventeenth-century central Europe.[9]

In the course of the eighteenth century, however, several Enlightenment thinkers began to raise questions about criminalizing sexual behavior. The general admiration that philosophes felt for ancient Greek culture, as well as their suspicion of state and church involvement in private life, tended to push many of them in the direction of official toleration—even when the very same people could still express disgust toward this "unnatural" behavior.[10] The Napoleonic conquests of central Europe paved the way for a series of legal reforms in the first half of the nineteenth century that either decriminalized same-sex contact between men (in Bavaria, Hannover, Württemberg, and Brunswick) or more commonly lessened the penalty to imprisonment (most in notably in Prussia). The decriminalization that occurred in a few cases was unfortunately undercut by public hostility to the reform as well as the continued existence of numerous police codes that, in contrast to the penal codes, could punish "sodomites" with prison sentences and fines.[11] Most important, though, the repeal of the laws against homosexuality did not last long. In 1871 Prussia united Germany under a single government, which caused its own sodomy law to become valid for the entire nation. Paragraph 175, as the law would be known from this point on, declared that "the unnatural vice [*widernatürliche Unzucht*] committed between men or between humans and animals" was to be punished by imprisonment.

Nevertheless, enlightenment criticisms of sodomy laws were not forgotten. Furthermore, science was raising new questions about the origins or same-sex desire, which itself caused some people to wonder if this sexual preference was really so unnatural after all. Even before 1871, several individuals had written works attacking the criminalization of sexual contact between men. One of the earliest was the Swiss author Heinrich Hössli, who in the course of the 1830s published two volumes of his work *Eros: The Greek Love of Men, Its Relationship to History, Education, Literature, and Legislation of All Ages (Eros: Die Männerliebe der Griechen, ihre Beziehung zur Geschichte, Erziehung, Literatur und Gesetzgebung aller Zeiten)*. Inspired by French Enlightenment thinkers such as Charles de Montesquieu and the liberal Swiss writer Heinrich Zschokke, Hössli fashioned a fascinating argument against the persecution of homosexuality out of anti–witch trial rhetoric, pleas for the legal emancipation of Jews, and the admiration for Greek society then fashionable among German literati.[12]

Another major writer was the Hungarian Karl Maria Kertbeny. From Austria, he lived much of his adult life in Germany. Reacting to the growing influence of Prussia in north Germany and the possibility that the Prussian law might become the law of the land, Kertbeny anonymously wrote two small political tracts. These works have attracted some attention over the years, since in them he coined the word *homosexual,* a term that by the mid-1880s would begin to circulate as a popular alternative to other, more pejorative terms widely used at the time. In other ways, though, his arguments drew on an older, Enlightenment tradition. He argued that modern notions of justice "necessarily proceeding from human justice through acknowledgment of the subjectivity of human nature" required a radical rethinking of old laws.[13] Modernization of social and political conditions called for a state that no longer played "the role of guardian, which is, anyhow, a thankless and irritating role." Instead, it needed to recognize the right to "one's own life, with which one may do as one pleases, fully free from the start to finish as long as the rights of other individuals of society or of the state are not injured by these actions."[14] History, he argued, had proved that all efforts to suppress homosexuality had had little to no effect on its practice. Moreover, it was time to rectify the hypocrisy and logical contradiction of a state that imprisoned two consenting adult males for engaging in harmless sexual activity while at the same time doing little to stop public prostitution, solitary masturbation, or various "unnatural acts" that were committed between husband and wife.

Much more influential than either Hössli or Kertbeny was Karl Heinrich Ulrichs, a lawyer from Hannover who emerged in the 1860s as the most prominent critic of the laws against homosexuality. Ulrichs was also a powerful voice in the emerging scientific debate about how same-sex desire should be understood. His studies of the topic began in 1850s, shortly after he resigned his position as a civil servant, perhaps forced out owing to a homosexual incident. In 1862 he began the process of what we would today call coming out by writing several letters to his family in which he revealed his sexual preferences. Although his family reacted hostilely to the news, he persisted on his course. He wrote five small booklets in 1864 and 1865 under the pseudonym Numa Numantius. In them he explored the laws of different eras and lands, speculated on the biological origins of "man-manly love," discussed the various dilemmas of living with such desire amid persecution and prejudice, and examined various philosophical problems connected with the issue. He then published seven more booklets under his own name, the final one in 1879. During these years he was extraordinarily active, giving public speeches on the topic and carrying on correspondence with doctors, scientists, lawyers, allies, and rivals. In Munich he even tried to present a petition to the national convention of the Association for German Jurists, only to be booed off the stage.[15]

Besides offering an early compendium of arguments against the German homosexuality laws, Ulrichs gradually developed a series of theories about the roots of same-sex desire. Beginning with a rather primitive idea based on Friedrich Anton Mesmer's theories of "animal magnetism," he gradually developed a much more complex construction rooted in classical philosophy but buttressed with recently acquired knowledge about human embryo development.[16] In his first published work, he introduced the term *Uranian* (*Urning*) to describe men who loved other men. The Uranian was "not a complete man" but, rather, should be called a "would-be man . . . a kind of feminine being when it concerns not only his entire organism, but also his sexual feelings of love, his entire natural temperament, and his talents."[17] In subsequent books, he argued that this hybrid could be traced to embryonic development: "Each person without exception is neither a boy nor a girl during the first three to four months of its life in the mother's body, but rather a hermaphroditic intermediate individual with sexual organs that are half male, half female."[18] In the case of heterosexuals (or *Dioninge,* as he called them), "Mother Nature" reshapes the "primitive hermaphrodite" into a boy or girl with the usual sexual markers. In the case of Uranians (or *Urninden,* which he used to describe women who loved other women), though, traces of the original hermaphroditic quality persist. Some Uranians will be mostly masculine, he noted, except for "the direction of the yearning toward the male sex." In many others, though, their "movements, gestures, manners, behavior, and gait are unmistakably feminine."[19] Such development was not an abnormality but simply a natural variation. Quoting the Roman writer Petronius, he observed, "Nature is not satisfied with only one rule; it favors alternatives much more."[20]

Ulrichs's concept of the Uranian was met initially by some skepticism. Even Kertbeny, who very early on had been inspired by Ulrichs's writings and during the 1860s entered into an excited letter exchange with the author, came to have doubts. Though Kertbeny never published his own study of sexuality, privately he developed a more complicated schema that would include not only the preferred sexual object but also the preferred mode of sexual interaction.[21] He accepted that sexual preferences were inborn but told

Ulrichs in a letter that he thought this particular argument would be ineffective at best with lawmakers and counterproductive at worst. "Legislators do not care a rap about the hereditary factors of a drive," he insisted, "but rather only about the drive's personal or social danger." And, what was more, insisting on homosexuality's hereditary nature might only reinforce popular prejudices: it potentially "makes them into special natures, into sinister, abnormal, unfortunate people, changeable creatures, into hermaphrodites, who are not organized as fully as other people."[22]

SCIENTIFIC DEBATE ABOUT HOMOSEXUALITY

Ulrichs's theory of the Uranian gradually gained ground, though, in part because his works were timely. By the 1860s a wider medical and scientific debate had started to emerge about the nature of same-sex desire. Historians usually trace this debate to the eighteenth century, when Enlightenment thinkers began to think in fundamentally different ways about the nature of sexual difference, the legitimacy of traditional sexual mores, and the foundations of human society. Enlightenment thinkers were by no means of a single mind when it came to deciding whether sexual pleasure was something to be valued as promoting procreation and harmonious family life or feared as an essentially irrational and egoistic drive. Nevertheless, debate on the topic helped spur medical research on sexuality in general.[23]

The Swiss physician Samuel-Auguste Tissot was the chief pioneer, famous for his 1760 work on masturbation, which argued that it weakened the nervous system and might lead to dangerous "antisocial" forms of sexuality such as "sodomy" and "tribadism."[24] Other contributions were made by less famous researchers doing biomedical work on ovulation, menstruation, fertilization, and eventually endocrinology in the mid-nineteenth century. Just as important for doctors, though, was the growing prestige that the field of medicine commanded socially. "More and more," notes the historian Harry Oosterhuis, "physicians, acting as mediators between science and the vexing problems of everyday life, succeeded in convincing the public of the indispensability of their expertise, and gradually they began to replace the clergy as authoritative personal consultants in the realm of sexuality."[25] Unfortunately, not all doctors really understood very much about sexuality. The result was that many of them dispensed advice that was not much better than folk medicine. What medical literature was out there could give radically different opinions and information, but the main leitmotifs of the literature when it came to healthy sexual behavior were "ordered living, moderation, and willpower."[26]

Before the mid-nineteenth century, most of the doctors who dealt specifically with homosexuality and other "sexual disorders" were forensic experts whose main role was to give court testimony about physical evidence of anal intercourse or rape. In Germany most of them referred to a seventeenth-century book by Paul Zacchias that gave doctors instructions about how to examine the anuses of passive sodomites for signs of anal intercourse.[27] The French professor of forensic medicine Ambrose Tardieu was still working in this tradition in the 1850s, when he claimed that his own experience of giving medical examinations indicated that repeated anal intercourse caused the penises of sodomites to become tapered like a dog's.[28] By this time, though, psychiatrists had started to deal with same-sex acts. When these medical practitioners had first turned to the subject of homosexuality in the 1820s, they generally linked it with masturbation. Influenced by Tissot, they argued that it could lead to physical weakness and mental insanity. Not until around 1850 did two doctors working independently—the psychiatrist Claude-François Michéa in France and the forensic doctor Johann Ludwig Casper in Germany—suggest that biological differences might actually be the *cause* of homosexuality. Although these doctors were not the first people in history to suggest that sexual taste was innate somehow, their work initiated a growing obsession in psychiatry with finding a somatic cause (that is, a physical, bodily origin) for same-sex desire.[29] Interestingly, both linked male homosexuality to effeminate physical characteristics. This connection was later repeated by Carl Westphal in his 1869 study of the "contrary sexual feeling."[30] By this time, a growing number of psychiatrists were also following Wilhelm Griesinger in believing that pederasty was at its root a constitutional nervous disease.

Not all medical experts went with such a diagnosis. A sizable section of the psychiatric profession still continued to be influenced by the older "philosophical-idealist" school, which saw homosexuality as the product of bad habits, seduction, or an immoral social environment.[31] By the 1860s, however, evolutionary theories were attracting a lot of public and professional attention, and humans' advanced mental faculties were increasingly understood as merely a recent acquisition in the long march of evolution. In this context, it was easy to connect mental illness with ideas about hereditary degeneration. As early as 1857, two years before Darwin's first book was published, the French psychiatrist Bénédict Augustin Morel had argued that the demands of modern civilization were leading to strains on the nervous system, yielding a kind of retrograde evolution. Detrimental behaviors adopted as a response to a high-stress environment ultimately left their mark on heredity, sometimes leading to the reemergence of primitive or animal-like traits in families. In the last decades of the nineteenth century, degeneration theory found many advocates, in part because it accounted for so much. The Italian criminologist Cesare Lombroso used it to explain crime. The Austrian-Jewish physician Max Nordau blamed it for producing the warped perception of modern art. And the French psychiatrist Valentin Magnan argued that degeneration could be used to explain many sexual disturbances.[32]

Among German-speaking psychiatrists, one of the most influential advocates of degeneration theory was Richard von Krafft-Ebing, a towering figure in Austrian psychiatry and one of the founders of modern sexology. His life mirrors in many ways the growing professionalization of psychiatry in the last three decades of the century. Beginning his psychiatric training in the Illenau asylum in southwest Germany in 1864 and then receiving an adjunct position at the Austrian University of Graz in 1873, he eventually moved up to take a full professorship in psychiatry at the University of Vienna in 1889. He made a name for himself as an author of about ninety books (often in numerous editions) and even more articles. He was an effective lecturer, though he was sometimes criticized as "showy" and sensational. By reaching out beyond academia, he did much to expand the reputation of his field in the wider community and, he hoped, to fight ignorance and prejudice in the name of science and humanitarianism.[33] He also ran a private practice through which he gradually acquired a huge catalog of cases from which to draw his information. As many of these patients were not ill enough to be incarcerated in an asylum, his study of them did much to expand psychiatric understanding of the mind and to blur the once-strict divide between normal and abnormal.

In many ways, Krafft-Ebing embodied what might be called the biological (or somatic) school of psychiatry, a school that sought explanations for mental illnesses in the biological makeup of the individual. At the beginning of his career Krafft-Ebing, like Griesinger, traced mental disorder to problems of the nervous system, and especially of the brain. Krafft-Ebing was also inspired by Morel's degeneration theory, publishing numerous papers on the influence of family and other hereditary factors on mental illness. In his works on neurasthenia and the neurological effects of syphilis, he highlighted the various risks and instabilities associated with modern society in either causing or accentuating these maladies. And in his magnum opus, *Psychopathia Sexualis,* his massive taxonomy of different kinds and varieties of sexual disorders, he traced everything from masochism to pedophilia to homosexuality to a degenerative disorder.[34]

Not surprisingly, Krafft-Ebing has been demonized over the years as the chief contributor to the scientific pathologization of homosexuality in the nineteenth century. Recently, however, the historian Harry Oosterhuis has painted a much more complicated view of Krafft-Ebing's work and legacy in his book *The Stepchildren of Nature*. First of all, we need to acknowledge that Krafft-Ebing's views on homosexuality changed dramatically over the years. Though he began with a simple view of "contrary sexual feeling" influenced by Westphal's and Ulrichs's theories of inverted gender identity, by the fourth edition of his book, published in 1889, he was differentiating between inborn and acquired forms of the "perversion," each of which was further subdivided into four forms on the basis of the level of gender inversion involved. He acknowledged that there were men and women who desired only members of the same sex but otherwise exhibited no signs of psychic or physical "inversion" (diagnosed as "simple reversal of sexual feeling" if it was acquired, "homosexuality" if it was congenital). He also had one category for bisexuals, which he called "psychic hermaphroditism."[35]

While consistently insisting that homosexuality had roots in the physical nervous system, he was forced to admit that examinations of the brain had failed to turn up any significant signs of sickness or even abnormality. He firmly believed that one day such evidence might be found, but in the meantime he developed a clinical practice based largely on a description and analysis of behavior and psychological symptoms. He listened to his patients, working up detailed histories of the men and women he worked with. He paid attention not only to physique and physiognomy but also to more subjective information such as moods, dreams, fantasies, moral awareness, and perceptions.[36] In developing a treatment plan for his patients, he was eclectic, using a range of options that included hydrotherapy, hypnosis, and "psychical therapy," which could resemble Freud's talking method.[37]

Krafft-Ebing's methods sometimes made him a target of criticism from other psychiatrists from the biological school who were focused on pure research. His response was both pragmatic and moral. Clinical practitioners needed some method of handling troubled patients until the biological side of the science could catch up. More important, though, the rigid materialism of some researchers was wrong-minded. Symptoms of mental illness, he argued, were not "mathematic variables, physical phenomena, or chemical solutions. On the contrary, appearing as feelings, perceptions, and aspirations, they form a class of their own."[38] Such an attitude toward the mind led him to conclude that willpower and moral judgment could play some role in treatment.

Krafft-Ebing's willingness to listen explains his popularity. He was sought out by many seeking help with various sexual disorders, and beyond that he received many letters from appreciative readers who hoped that by detailing their own sexual histories they might make some contribution to his scientific work. His *Psychopathia Sexualis* includes lengthy excerpts from these case histories, drawn not only from existing work and legal sources, but also from a growing number of cases assembled on his own. Eventually 440 distinct case histories were used in one work or another.[39] For readers struggling with their sexuality, such stories could be invaluable. "By publishing his patients' letters and autobiographies and by quoting their statements verbatim," writes Oosterhuis, "Krafft-Ebing enabled voices to be heard that were usually silenced." Just to learn that they were not alone could be immensely comforting for many. And such voices sometimes left a real mark on Krafft-Ebing as well. He took what his patients said seriously and reported their accounts honestly, even when they contradicted his own ideas. Moreover, in several key respects his own theories were clearly changed as a response to listening to his patients talk about their own sexuality.

Perhaps the best example of this process of give-and-take can be seen in Krafft-Ebing's relationship with Karl Heinrich Ulrichs. Having sent copies of his pamphlets to Krafft-Ebing in 1866, when the psychiatrist was at the very beginning of his career, Ulrichs decided to visit Krafft-Ebing as a patient in 1869. They developed a long relationship. They wrote many letters to one another, and Ulrichs forwarded copies of his new works to Krafft-Ebing as they were published.[40] As we have seen, Ulrichs was not the only author in the 1860s and 1870s who was arguing that homosexuality was a form of hermaphroditism, so it is impossible to say that Krafft-Ebing's own belief that homosexuality represented a form of gender inversion was directly inspired by Ulrichs. The relationship, however, clearly stimulated Krafft-Ebing's interest in "contrary sexual feeling." Years later, Krafft-Ebing would tell Ulrichs in a letter that it was "knowledge of your writings alone which led to my studies of this highly important field."[41]

Just as important for Krafft-Ebing's changing notions of homosexuality was Ulrichs's insistence that his sexuality was a natural variation. Over time, as Krafft-Ebing listened to more and more men and women, this idea gradually took root. Ulrichs was not the only one of his patients who believed that his or her sexuality was not "painful or immoral." A few even suggested that their sexuality was not different in any substantial way from that of heterosexuals.[42] By the mid-1890s Krafft-Ebing was clearly coming around to the belief that homosexuality should not be legally penalized. By the end of his life, in 1902, he accepted that "contrary sexual feeling" was not even a psychic degeneracy or a disease but rather simply a biological and psychological condition.[43] As he backed away from degeneration theory, he increasingly relied on embryonic research that investigated how sexual differentiation takes places in the very early stages of life. By suggesting that masculinity and femininity were in fact malleable properties, this research potentially offered a very different perspective on same-sex desire from that of degeneration theory. Instead of being a sign of modern illness and immorality, it might in fact be simply a natural variation produced by a complicated process of life that had many possible outcomes.[44]

Krafft-Ebing's influence at the turn of the century is hard to exaggerate. His *Textbook of Psychiatry* (*Lehrbuch der Psychiatrie*) was commonly used in university classes across Germany. His *Psychopathia Sexualis* was a best seller, and translations of it were published in French, Italian, English, Russian, Japanese, Hungarian, and Dutch. New editions continued to appear regularly even after Krafft-Ebing's death; the thirteenth came out in 1937. It popularized the notion of fetishism and coined the terms *sadism, masochism,* and *pedophilia.* More fundamentally, Oosterhuis argues, it was one of several books that during the 1890s transformed our notion of sexuality by suggesting that it could have other psychic and social purposes besides simply reproduction.[45]

Through his research, Krafft-Ebing laid the groundwork for the emerging field of sexology. Today we Americans tend to associate this field with Alfred Kinsey and the Masters and Johnson team. Around the turn of the century, this field was first being defined by names such as Albert Moll, Havelock Ellis, and Iwan Bloch. Moll's 1891 book, *Contrary Sexual Feeling* (*Conträre Sexualempfindung*), was considered a definitive work on the topic, and his 1897 *Libido Sexualis* (*Untersuchungen über die Libido Sexualis*) was even more important for suggesting that sexuality was actually constructed from two discrete instincts, one for discharge and a second for physical contact. Only the first had anything to do with procreation: the second was the foundation for many social relationships.[46] Havelock Ellis's *Sexual Inversion* (originally published in German in 1896 as *Conträre Sexualempfindung*) compiled a number of case histories to suggest that homosexuality was in most cases inborn.[47] Iwan Bloch's 1906 book, *The Sexual Life of Our Times and Its Relations to Modern Culture* (*Das Sexualleben unserer Zeit in seinen Beziehungen zur modernen Kultur*), presented a social and cultural overview of modern sexuality. In this massive tome, he covered everything from sexuality in marriage and art to more illicit subjects such as pornography, prostitution, and homosexuality.[48]

HIRSCHFELD'S THEORY OF SEXUAL INTERMEDIARIES

It was in this German world, with its growing academic debate about the nature of homosexuality, that Magnus Hirschfeld appeared, hoping that the debate might eventually lead to a major reconsideration of Paragraph 175. Although initially his work would borrow very heavily from Ulrichs's publications, Hirschfeld's conceptualization of homosexuality would continue to develop over the years and would gradually become more refined and complex. In 1905 he published a new study, *Sexual Transitions* (*Geschlechtsübergänge*), which was based on his own observations as a physician of the differences between men and women.[49] Filled with clinical photographs and sketches, *Sexual Transitions* made the argument that "taken in very strong scientific terms, one is not able in this sense to speak of man and woman, but on the contrary only of people that are for the most part male or for the most part female."[50] The book gave visual examples of male bodies with rounded hips and female bodies with small breasts. It further developed Hirschfeld's guiding idea that we all began life as one asexual creature, only then to develop various sexual characteristics after being exposed to hormones and physical maturation. Everyone experiences this development in unique ways, though. Consequently, we all represent slightly different mixtures of these various sexual characteristics. In other words, we are all "sexual intermediaries." As the historian Elena Mancini put it, absolute male and absolute female were only "abstractions that occupied extreme positions on a male-female identity continuum."[51]

The notion of "sexual intermediaries" was apparently in the air at the turn of the century. Another important writer to develop this idea was the Austrian philosopher Otto Weininger. In his important 1903 book, *Sex and Character*, Weininger argued that "masculine" and "feminine" were psychological ideals, perhaps Platonic "forms," that became embodied as imbalanced mixtures in human beings. Femininity, he argued, was an unconscious force, saturated by sexuality and emotion and concerned only with reproduction; masculinity, on the other hand, was a rational agent, thoughtful and fully conscious of itself and the world around it.[52] The former was a principle of chaos, the root of all destructive tendencies in history, whereas the latter was the origin of all the positive achievements in human history. Connecting his view of the sexes with the Chinese yin and yang, he suggested that both are bound together intimately in history and in every single individual. Our psyche contains masculine and feminine aspects together—though some people (women, of course, but also Jews and homosexuals) are dominated by the feminine. In love, we seek individuals who will allow us to balance the two principles within our lives.[53]

Despite Weininger's and Hirschfeld's shared belief in intersexuality, there were many important differences between them. Hirschfeld did not share Weininger's anti-Semitism (which was complicated, since Weininger himself was an Austrian Jew), homophobia, or blatant misogyny. In addition, Weininger's conception of sexuality was metaphysical; he saw the two sexual principles as affecting every turn of world history. And although the early portion of his study used language such as "intermediate forms" and suggested that everyone possessed a "permanent double sexuality," the latter portion reestablished a much clearer gender division between men and women. In the end, the "spiritual" character of women overwhelmed them, suppressing the masculine within them.[54] In contrast, Hirschfeld's understanding was rooted in the biological sciences. And when it came to the sexual intermediaries, he was interested mostly in the large and blurry range in the middle rather than the two abstractions at either end.

In a later work, *Transvestites: The Erotic Drive to Cross-Dress* (*Die Transvestiten: Eine Untersuchung über den erotischen Verkleidungstrieb*), Hirschfeld further refined his theory of sexual intermediaries. This 1910 book coined the term *transvestite* while offering the first major empirical study of the topic. Having befriended a number of cross-dressers during his study, he argued that transvestism was a sexual variation distinct from homosexuality. Around a third of the men and women that he studied were homosexual, but another third were clearly not. A smaller fraction of the sample exhibited bisexual characteristics, and the remainder appeared to get sexual satisfaction in a narcissistic fashion simply by dressing in clothes of the opposite sex.[55] He still insisted that all gender characteristics and sexual orientations had their root in biological development; in fact, in this book he went so far as to argue that sex character left a trace on every single cell of an organism's body. Ultimately, however, it manifested itself in four distinct ways: the sex organs, sexual orientation, emotional characteristics, and secondary sexual characteristics such as voice and facial hair.[56] These four distinct levels of sexual characteristics supplied the theoretical basis for what is often considered his most important work, *The Homosexuality of Men and Women,* published in 1914. A large portion of this later book is dedicated to a discussion of how to diagnose homosexuality on the basis of these sexual characteristics and, most important, how to differentiate it from other kinds of sexual intermediaries.[57]

Hirschfeld's research was just one facet of his life at this stage. In the early years of the twentieth century, he increasingly found himself called as an expert medical witness in trials involving homosexuality. The political culture and court system of Germany were changing rapidly at the time, which created an opening for more and more psychiatrists and criminologists to be called to give witness to the social environment or mental state that might serve as mitigating circumstances in a case. The German court system had long been highly dependent on expert witness testimony, and around the turn of the century, under pressure from the Social Democratic and left-liberal press, the courts increasingly listened seriously to the opinions of psychiatrists.[58] Hirschfeld was happy to offer his opinion in any case involving homosexuality, and in many cases he managed at least to get reduced sentences for defendants, and occasionally even an acquittal.[59]

In other ways, he took on the role of defending the interests of "sexual intermediaries." In 1909 Hirschfeld convinced local authorities in Berlin to experiment with "transvestite passes" (*Transvestitenschein*) that enabled men and women to cross-dress in public without worry of being arrested for disorderly conduct or being harassed by the police in other ways. In making his case, he discovered that there was some public sympathy for these individuals since a series of newspaper reports and books had recently reported on the difficulties that they faced.[60] When he was not in court or meeting with public representatives, he devoted much time to public speaking, seeking financial support for the WhK and serving as the organization's first chairman. Under Hirschfeld's leadership, the WhK gradually matured. It established an annual publication in 1899, *The Yearbook for Sexual Intermediaries* (*Jahrbuch für sexuelle Zwischenstufen*), devoted to the study of homosexuality; in 1901 the group also began to put out a newsletter, *The Monthly Report* (*Monatsbericht des wissenschaftlich-humanitären Komitees*). Branch groups were established in a number of other cities, including Hamburg and Hannover, that helped organize activity in the local area. Back in Berlin, the committee developed a kind of club life that included not only scientific conferences but also more informal meetings on a regular basis. At these meetings discussions, scientific presentations, and art exhibits were held. To manage all these activities, the WhK developed a more formal organizational structure headed by a board of seven men.[61] One of the main goals of this committee was to draft and circulate a petition for the repeal of Paragraph 175, which attained over 900 signatures by the time it was first presented to the Reichstag (or parliament) in 1898. The petition found little support within the Reichstag, but it continued to circulate and by 1914 had received signatures from more than 3,000 doctors, 750 university professors, and thousands of others. The signatories included such prominent individuals as the poet Rainer Maria Rilke, the sexologist Krafft-Ebing, and several prominent leaders of the Social Democratic Party (SPD).[62]

HIRSCHFELD AND TURN-OF-THE-CENTURY POLITICS

Hirschfeld's lobbying effort was very much typical of what one influential historian has called the "politics in a new key" that emerged at the end of the century.[63] In fact, the WhK was just one of the many new political groups that emerged in this time of political ferment. The radical expansion of the franchise, the growing population of cities, advancements in literacy, and the appearance of large-scale newspapers that addressed a mass audience all contributed to the middle and lower classes becoming involved in politics on a regular basis in ways that were unimaginable before these changes. The working class became organized into labor unions, the peasants into farmers' leagues. New political parties appeared, but even old ones were forced to change how they operated. Whereas politics had been rather "discreet and gentlemanly" before the appearance of mass suffrage—the preserve of men from the German aristocracy and upper middle class—the new style of politics became more dynamic and professional. As one historian observes, "Paid officials, party newspapers, auxiliary organizations and energetic campaigning became the norm."[64]

Economic interests and politics became intertwined as unions, monopoly cartels, businessmen's associations, local chambers of commerce, professional organizations, and other interest groups increasingly vied for influence over laws and policies.[65] And many other pressure groups appeared with quite a diverse range of goals and concerns. There were groups devoted to expanding women's rights and right-wing organizations like the racial hygiene movement and the Navy League. In between these extremes, there were numerous groups that aimed at the transformation of society and everyday life. This loose coalition was known as the life reform movement (*Lebensreformbewegung*) and included activists interested in natural health, natural living, nutritional reform, nudism, and even clothing reform.

Like many in the life reform movement, Hirschfeld embraced a broad philosophy that emphasized living in accordance with nature. According to this philosophy, exercise, healthy eating, and time spent outdoors could produce a better harmony between mind and body and ultimately heal many physical illnesses and mental ailments that were the result of modern living.[66] Although too scientific-minded to accept all the Romantic baggage that often came with naturalism, he still held an ideal of living according to certain natural standards. He was an advocate of natural healing medicine, and in the 1890s he edited a weekly magazine that championed healthy lifestyles and natural therapies. In particular he took on alcoholism and tobacco consumption, two practices that were common among the working class and accepted uncritically by most leaders of the labor movement.[67] During the 1920s he also took up nude sunbathing as a pastime.

The goal of eventually transforming the lifestyle and basic attitudes of the masses fitted in well with his socialist sympathies. Although Hirschfeld did not join the SPD until 1923, his socialist inclination dated to his student years. As a twenty-year-old medical student, he had encountered the book *Woman and Socialism* (*Die Frau und der Sozialismus,* 1879) by the towering figure of German socialism and undisputed leader of the party, August Bebel. "I was very influenced by this book," Hirschfeld later remembered. Its tightly reasoned argument, its insight into the challenges that women faced, and above all its unswerving instinct for justice made Hirschfeld seek out the author when he eventually moved to Berlin in the 1890s. The two soon struck up a friendship. Although back in 1879 Bebel had denounced "boy- and male-love" as an unnatural by-product of the subjection of women in *Woman and Socialism,* in the course of the 1890s his position gradually changed. He became one of the first four individuals to sign the WhK's petition. In 1898—in the context of the considerable debate about the proposed *Lex Heinze,* a law that sharpened several provisions of the criminal code dealing with sexual vices—Bebel took the opportunity to denounce Paragraph 175 in the German Reichstag. The prevalence of homosexuality at every level of society, he argued, suggested how badly this law had failed in its basic goal. He guessed that even the number of homosexuals in Berlin alone would quickly fill the nation's prisons. The inconstancy and arbitrariness of Paragraph 175's enforcement was the only thing that allowed the law even to function. But this inconsistent application of the law allowed class bias to enter into the equation. The Berlin police, he had been told, tended to overlook the sexual predilections of many wealthy and powerful men in the city while simultaneously arresting less fortunate men.[68]

Bebel's turn against Paragraph 175 might have been influenced somewhat by his relationship with Hirschfeld, but the position taken by Eduard Bernstein was more decisive. Today Bernstein is remembered mostly as a socialist maverick—the most important advocate of revisionism within German Marxism and an opponent of those who thought that violent revolution was necessary to build a socialist world. Shortly before he wrote the book that earned him this reputation, though, Bernstein had been inspired by the Oscar Wilde trial in London to write two essays in 1895 that denounced the criminal persecution of homosexuality. Admittedly, he betrayed some real ambivalence about the matter. In fact, he seems to have seen homosexuality as a symptom of a defective modern world that he very much despised. Wilde's aestheticism was associated in his mind with French decadence, and his sexual activities might even reflect a pathological disturbance. He came down clearly against punishing homosexuals legally, however: they were just as much victims of social conditions as the working class was. Why punish homosexuality for being "unnatural," he asked, when there are so many deeper problems in the world to address? "Our entire cultural life," he wrote, "our way of life from morning until evening is a continual infraction against nature, against the original precondition of our very existence."[69]

Bernstein's arguments seem to have had an effect on many members of the SPD. Besides Bebel, Karl Kautsky—the founder and editor of an important journal of socialist theory—was also persuaded by these arguments, and in 1897 he agreed to sign Hirschfeld's petition. With three of the leading figures of the SPD publicly siding against Paragraph 175, many others in the party came around, though slowly and often without giving up their basic prejudices. Negative attitudes toward homosexuality were just as widespread in the working classes as among other classes, and even such radical thinkers as Karl Marx and Friedrich Engels had privately made disparaging remarks about "pederasts" and "warm brothers" during the 1870s and 1880s.[70] And not everyone in the party was won over by Bernstein's and Bebel's arguments. During a 1905 debate about Paragraph 175 in the Reichstag, one SPD representative rose to criticize another for suggesting all members of the party were of one mind on the issue. He implied that the homosexual question had nothing to do with Social Democracy. He and anyone he spoke for may very well have harbored anxiety that identification with the homosexual cause might make the SPD vulnerable come election time.[71]

As we will see in later chapters, the SPD would not necessarily be above playing off widespread homosexual prejudices when it came to attacking its own enemies. Still, the party would also prove itself to be the most consistent political ally of Hirschfeld's in his fight against Paragraph 175. And Hirschfeld would return the favor. His affinity for the party might have been grounded in the same factors that attracted many modern European Jews to socialism in the second half of the nineteenth century: the movement's universalism, secularism, and defense of social equality and social outsiders. Hirschfeld's own individual character—his "empathic concern for human physical and emotional well-being," his rational outlook, and his optimistic belief in progress—would have also steered him in this direction.[72]

THE MASCULINISTS

Despite Hirschfeld's success with the WhK, he was not embraced as a leader by all gay men at the time. In fact, many homosexual men had issues with Hirschfeld's use of such language as "third sex" and "sexual intermediaries," which they insisted only perpetuated an inaccurate stereotype of the effeminate homosexual. This stereotype was becoming prevalent by the end of the nineteenth century thanks in no small part to the role of sexology in promoting it. Yet, throughout the nineteenth century, some men managed to distance themselves from the stereotype of the effeminate sodomite. Karl Heinrich Ulrichs himself had recognized that in addition to "womanly Uranians," there were also "manly Uranians" (*Mannlings*): "Their physical characteristics, that is, the total expression of movements, gestures and mannerisms, character, the type of erotic yearnings and sexual desires, are completely masculine; only the bare mental sex, the direction of the yearning toward the male sex, is feminine."[73] These men, Ulrichs noted, were generally attracted to "soft and gentle males, beardless, and smooth . . . not solid men, only youths, *pueri.*"

As this description suggests, many educated men of the nineteenth-century European nobility and upper middle class who felt attraction toward males often looked to the civilizations of Greece and Renaissance Italy as a way to understand same-sex desire.[74] Following the notion of "Greek love," they tended to idealize an age-old tradition of sexual relationships between men of different ages, especially adult men and adolescent boys. This allowed them, at least in their own minds, to maintain a feeling of masculine power by putting themselves in a position of authority.

At the turn of the twentieth century, such men became emboldened by Magnus Hirschfeld's efforts and by other groups within Germany's life reform movement. They grew increasingly vocal about the possibility of dressing and behaving in the manner common to "respectable" males while at the same time having sexual desire for men. In effect they did two things. They challenged the notion that effeminacy had anything to do with a man's experiencing love for another man. At the same time, they contested the norms of masculinity that lent credence to the stereotype of the effeminate homosexual. These masculinist homosexuals, as they are sometimes now called, attempted to change public perceptions about both men and homosexuals by demonstrating that dressing, speaking, gesturing, and walking like a "respectable" man of the upper classes did not necessarily mean desiring only women sexually.[75]

One of the earliest figures within this masculinist tradition was Gustav Jäger.[76] In several publications from the 1880s, this professor of zoology and anthropology argued that the primary purpose of sexual desire was not procreation but social bonding. Consequently, homosexuality among men was not simply healthy but also a virtue.[77] Another prominent masculinist was John Henry Mackay, a Scot who had been raised in Germany. Mackay is probably best remembered for his 1898 biography of Max Stirner, whose anarchist book *The Ego and Its Own* (*Der Einzige und sein Eigentum*, 1845) was being rediscovered by many radicals at the end of the century. Beginning in 1905, though, Mackay turned his mind to sexual matters. In a series of books written under the pseudonym Sagitta, he explored the joys of the "nameless love," his term for Greek-style man-boy love.[78]

By far the most influential masculinist was Benedict Friedlaender, a turn-of-the-century polymath who studied mathematics, physics, botany, and physiology. His most important book, *The Renaissance of Uranian Love* (*Die Renaissance des Eros Uranios*, 1904), trumpeted his idealization of the classical world, openly promoting a revival of "chivalric love," by which he meant the "close friendship between youths and even more particularly the bonds between men of unequal ages."[79] He drew on the notion of the male-bonding community (*Männerbund*) proposed recently by the ethnologist Heinrich Schurtz. The male-bonding community, according to Schurtz, was responsible for nearly "all higher social development."[80] Friedlaender agreed, simultaneously connecting it with Jäger's suggestion that sexuality was fundamentally a social instinct. Sexuality formed the basis for "physiological friendships" between men, as Friedlaender described them. It was the emphasis on such friendships in Greek civilization that had supposedly allowed this culture to make such important achievements.

Unlike much of the medical world by this point, Friedlaender believed that all men had a bisexual potential. Men could therefore participate in families, doing their natural part by procreating, and at the same time engage in male-bonding societies, through which they could make social and cultural contributions to their nation and race.[81] Friedlaender was influenced by several writers of the day associated with social Darwinism, German Romantic nationalism, anti-Semitism, and nudism. In line with these intellectual trends, he argued that the neglect of male bonds in modern society had led to the endangerment of the "white race," further threatened at the end of the nineteenth century by the persistent influence of the stifling effects of Christian morality and the appearance of the women's movement. What was needed, Friedlaender insisted, was a revival of "manly culture" (*männliche Kultur*), which would then nourish the strength of the Aryan race. This change would be accompanied by a return to a natural form of society, in which "natural people (who are unclothed people) in a *natural* mood (which is unconstrained happiness) deal with each other in a natural way (which is harmless friendliness)."[82] The basic building block of this natural society would be not the family, which gave too much power to women, but the bond between older and younger males, as modeled by Greek society.[83]

The publication of *The Renaissance of Uranian Love* turned Friedlaender into a person of some note. Having joined the WhK, he was elected to chair its advisory committee. He began to invite other writers interested in Greek man-boy love to have dinner with him at his home and to share their work. One of the regular attendees, Friedrich Dobe, compared these evenings to Plato's *Symposium*. "Whoever had a young friend," he recalled, "brought him along."[84] John Henry Mackay, another person to frequent these dinners, offered his own portrait in his 1926 novel *The Hustler:*

He moved in closed circles of gentlemen who did not cruise the street in order to look for boys to have a good time with. . . . These circles were supplied—one did not exactly know how: one boy just brought another along and all were first carefully examined, to see if they were trustworthy, before they were granted the honor of being accepted. . . . The gentleman who already had a young friend brought him along. Those who had none hoped to find one here. . . . It was like a secret fraternity with unwritten laws, which, however, were all the more strictly observed.[85]

Besides Friedlaender, the other most important masculinist was Adolf Brand (Figure 3). Another fan of Max Stirner's anarchist philosophy, Brand had published since the mid-1890s a magazine called *The Special One*—in German, *Der Eigene*, a term that is difficult to translate because it also resonates with Stirner's anarchist ideas of "self-ownership" (*Eigentum*).[86] The magazine started as a literary publication with a vaguely anarchist slant. In 1896, though, Brand read Hirschfeld's *Sappho and Socrates* and shortly thereafter met Hirschfeld personally, which turned out to be a life-changing moment for him. Two years later, after briefly shutting down operations of *The Special One,* he started up the magazine again, but this time with an entirely different purpose: to promote homosexuality, or what *The Special One* generally called "the love of friends" or "manly culture." The journal appeared only irregularly because of insufficient funds and legal problems. Brand himself was convicted several times by the Berlin authorities for "disseminating immoral material," eventually spending several terms in prison. Brand proved tenacious, returning *The Special One* again and again to publication.[87]

One of Brand's biographers has described him as a "quick-tempered character." His writing was known for its use of abusive language. In person, he could be unpredictable: he once created a scandal by pulling out a dog whip in the German Reichstag and attacking one of the members with it.[88] He was very different from Hirschfeld. Their joint desire to repeal Paragraph 175 led Brand to join the WhK, but over time he became increasingly critical of Hirschfeld. Like Friedlaender, he disagreed from the beginning with Hirschfeld's theory of the Uranian "third sex." At meetings of the WhK, he and Friedlaender often raised questions about the direction that Hirschfeld was giving the group. Brand frequently tried to embolden the group to take aggressive political strategies, such as organizing a mass "self-outing" by prominent individuals; Friedlaender, for his part, raised questions about Hirschfeld's scientific methodology, which generally assumed in this early stage a strict division between homosexuals and heterosexuals.[89]

FIGURE 3 **ADOLF BRAND**

Brand was editor of the pioneering gay magazine *The Special One*
and one of the chief personalities among the gay masculinists.
Source: Schwules Museum, Berlin

In 1903 the two of them joined with a third masculinist, Wilhelm Jansen, to form a new organization called the Community of the Special (*Gemeinschaft der Eigenen,* or GdE). The GdE was not intended originally to be a rival to Hirschfeld's group. "It was in fact more of a literary circle," writes Harry Oosterhuis, an early historian of the group; it was comparable "to a masonic lodge or classical symposium." The all-male group met weekly at Brand's house in one of Berlin's suburbs to recite poems, listen to readings, and discuss matters important to the group. Brand also organized public lectures in Berlin and group excursions into the nearby countryside for enjoyment.[90] Like Brand, some in the group had connections to anarchism, but a much more important influence on the people who wrote for the journal was late nineteenth-century Romanticism, with its emphasis on living according to natural impulses, its embrace of emotion over reason, and its love of traditional national culture.

ACADEMIC VIEWS OF EARLY HOMOSEXUAL ACTIVISM

Historians of the homosexual emancipation movement have been sharply divided over the masculinist wing of the movement associated with Brand and Friedlaender. The generation that came out of the gay liberation movement of the 1970s tended to see them as a reactionary group whose racism, antifeminism, and Romantic nationalism overlapped in dangerous ways with Nazi ideology. In the 1990s, though, a new generation of historians, influenced by critiques of science and modernity, began to view them more sympathetically. The French philosopher Michel Foucault was especially important for this cohort. Foucault had been very suspicious of modern science's tendencies to categorize people, to open our internal mental life to study, and to produce forms of self-identification that are conducive to external controls. With this perspective in mind, Harry Oosterhuis painted the masculinists as rebels who refused to accept the claims of modern medicine. "They criticized some very essential presuppositions," he wrote, "that have determined the conceptualization of homosexuality from the late nineteenth century until the present day."[91] In contrast to Hirschfeld's efforts to define homosexuality as a biological and physical type, masculinists defended an older tradition of "Romantic friendship" between men in which deep, intimate bonds might sometimes grow to involve "passionate and sensual" forms of expression, including long embraces and even kissing.[92] They refused to go along with a culture that tried to fit people firmly into neat boxes.

More recently, though, a third cohort has argued that both sides of the debate have tended to exaggerate the differences between the masculinists and those men associated with Hirschfeld's WhK. Glenn Ramsey suggests that we have retroactively thrown present conceptions of "butch" and "femme" on a feud that perhaps was much more complicated and multifaceted than this.[93] Similarly, Marita Keilson-Lauritz points out that a complicated network of relationships connected individuals from both camps. Authors associated with the WhK published in *The Special One,* just as individuals close to Brand published in Hirschfeld's major journal. And, most important, both camps often relied on a similar core group of literary figures to make their arguments, which suggests that they shared more in terms of their values and perspectives than is normally acknowledged. Perhaps, Keilson-Lauritz argues, the differences between the two had more to do with their opinions on the proper strategies for achieving legal reform.[94]

Academic debates over the masculinist wing should not cause us to overlook significant differences in how Magnus Hirschfeld has been seen over the years. Activists of the 1970s sometimes saw him as a heroic pioneer of their own struggle. The first major biography of him, though—a 1986 book by Charlotte Wolff—portrayed him as a well-meaning but perhaps naive reformer who, in both his hopes and delusions, embodied the tragic fate of the Weimar Republic. Harry Oosterhuis described him as a key contributor to the medicalization of homosexuality that ultimately displaced earlier, more fluid conceptualizations of male-male eroticism. Manfred Herzer portrayed him as a meek reformer: a Social Democrat who never really embraced the socialist cause; a German Jew who did everything he could to deny his heritage; and a sexual progressive whose attachment to biological explanations and Darwinian thinking made his ideas horribly outdated by the second half of the twentieth century. And most recently, Elena Mancini's biography has tried to salvage Hirschfeld's reputation by highlighting aspects of his work that remain relevant today. Hirschfeld's theory of intersexed categories was multifaceted enough, she argues, to point in the direction of modern-day queer theory. The sexual ethnographies of East Asia and the Middle East that he published in the 1930s exhibited "a conscious eschewal of a Euro-centric perspective" that resists "exploitative stances of exoticization or judgment."[95] Last, his attachment to the Enlightenment values of knowledge and freedom should not be written off as naive principles or expressions of middle-class values. Instead, the empiricism of his scientific research was intimately connected with his openness to other people and cultures, Mancini insists, while his commitment to freedom led him to stand up for the rights of homosexuals, women, the working class, and nonwhite people around the world.

Whatever you make of the differences between the two wings of the homosexual movement, what is certainly true is that they were exacerbated by the many homosexual scandals that broke out in Germany around the turn of the century. These scandals raised many substantive issues about the best strategy to achieve legal reform. How might reformers use the judicial system itself to gain needed publicity? How do the personal rights of individuals to some privacy weigh against the needs of the homosexual movement as a whole? What kinds of alliances might be fruitful in the movement's quest to change people's minds about sex between men and sex between women? And, most fundamentally, what behaviors, character traits, and predilections define someone as a homosexual to begin with?

CHAPTER 2

Scandals and Alliances

CHAPTER SUMMARY

This chapter examines the ways in which various high-profile scandals, including the Eulenburg affair, helped raise public awareness of same-sex desire and consequently played a role in shaping same-sex identities. It also looks at the political alliances that various homosexual activists sought with Freudians, feminists, and youth-movement leaders.

OVERVIEW

The pioneering queer theorist Eve Kosofsky Sedgwick has suggested that the turn of the twentieth century was marked by "homosexual panic." At that time we began to acquire the mental habit (familiar to us today) of constantly raising questions about people's sexual preferences. The homosexual panic created a seeping paranoia about same-sex desire that worked its way into the fabric of our culture. It changed how we behaved in public and in private; it fundamentally reorganized the relationships between men and men, women and women, and women and men. This chapter examines several national scandals that played a significant role in Germany in promoting this homosexual panic. One involved a prominent businessman who headed up the nation's principal steel company; a second revolved around a colonial governor in the far-off city of Dar es Salaam, the capital of German East Africa. The most important scandal, the Eulenburg affair of 1907, ended up taking down two central figures in the German Kaiser's court.

These scandals created publicity for the homosexual movement, but not the kind that the movement wanted. In fact, the Eulenburg scandal produced a serious crisis for Hirschfeld's WhK and created a political atmosphere in which the government seriously considered sharpening the law against homosexuality instead of repealing it. To get through this difficult period, homosexual activists tried to build alliances with other movements: feminism, Freudianism, and youth organizations. Not all these alliances would prove productive, but the effort to build them was a critical step in the maturation of the homosexual movement.

KEY TERMS
Friedrich Alfred Krupp; Philip von Eulenburg; Kuno von Moltke; Johanna Elberskirchen; Hans Blüher

Whisnant, Clayton J.
Queer Identities and Politics in Germany: A History 1880–1945
dx.doi.org/10.17312/harringtonparkpress/2016.08.qipg.002
© Harrington Park Press, LLC, New York, NY 10011

FIGURE 4 **JOHANNA ELBERSKIRCHEN**

Elberskirchen was both a feminist author and an early female member of Hirschfeld's WhK. Her most famous book was *The Love of the Third Sex,* published in 1904. Her connection with feminist politics and the WhK suggests some of the complicated political alliances that were being built by homosexual activists around the turn of the century, one of the major focal points of this chapter. This chapter also examines the ways in which various high-profile scandals helped raise public awareness of same-sex desire and consequently played some role in shaping same-sex identities. Source: *Kinderheil* 1 (1905/1906)

One of the first female members of the Scientific-Humanitarian Committee (WhK) was Johanna Elberskirchen (Figure 4), a good example of the "New Woman" that was becoming a topic of much public discussion and political debate in Germany and elsewhere at the end of the century. After making a living in her early twenties as a bookkeeper in her hometown of Bonn, she attended the Universities of Bern and Zurich for a time in the 1890s, during which she undertook a wide-ranging education in the natural sciences, medicine, anatomy, philosophy, and law. Unfortunately, her financial situation kept her from finishing her degree, so she returned to Bonn. She became active in the German women's movement, writing many books on women's emancipation and its relationship to socialism and sexual issues.[1]

The women's movement in Germany, founded in the wake of the Revolution of 1848, had grown in two directions. Some women had found themselves drawn toward the Marxist Social Democratic Party (SPD) by their concern for working-class women, while others who opposed socialism organized the League of German Women's Organizations (*Bund Deutscher Frauenvereine*) in 1894 to focus on issues of education, legal rights, and welfare.[2] Elberskirchen clearly leaned toward the socialist side of the divide, though she was never a major figure in the socialist movement. In Bonn she wrote several books on women's emancipation and its relationship to socialism and sexual issues. Her work to cause the biggest stir, though, was *The Love of the Third Sex* (*Die Liebe des Dritten Geschlechts*), published by Max Spohr's press in 1904. In this piece she argued that the existence of homosexuality in many different cultures across the world and at every point in human history suggests that it was a fully natural phenomenon. Like Karl Heinrich Ulrichs, she posited that its origins lay in the original bisexual nature of the human embryo. And in a manner perhaps influenced by the popularity of Otto Weininger's recent book, she emphasized that this bisexual nature left traces on our character even after physical development was diverted in one direction or another: "There is no absolute man. There is no absolute woman. There are only bisexual varieties."[3]

In the last section of *The Love of the Third Sex,* she argued that homosexuality had a higher spiritual purpose aimed at the generation of society, a position that hints at some familiarity with the arguments made by Benedict Friedlaender.[4] Like many masculinists, she insisted that homosexuality was a kind of higher "soul-love" that was more spiritual than physical. This assertion might easily have been related more to her feminism, however, since the historian Marti Lybeck notes that many turn-of-the-century feminists found the denial of lust an important strategy for claiming political authority.[5] In another book published that same year, *What Has Man Made of Woman,*

Child, and Himself? (Was hat der Mann aus Weib, Kind und sich gemacht?), she clearly attacked male sexual (or better, heterosexual) appetite. Drawing on the anthropologist Johann Bachofen's theory that prehistoric societies were dominated by matriarchy, Elberskirchen argued that women had played a key role both for society and for human evolution. Women had watched over children and chosen mates on the basis of their ability to provide for the family. Under their watch, a culture of "innocence and chastity" had flourished.[6] Only later, as men took control of private property and subjugated women to their own needs, had such evils as prostitution and venereal disease flourished. Implicitly, then, breaking the power that private property had in our society would return the proper gender order, reestablish public morality, and restore evolutionary progress.[7]

Elberskirchen's book was one of the first to connect two distinct meanings of the term *the third sex*. Marti Lybeck's recent book *Desiring Emancipation* is an important reminder that before 1900 this phrase most commonly referred to the "New Woman," not homosexuals. Beginning in the 1880s, a number of women had gone to Zurich to attend the university there. Authors and journalists hostile to the ambition of these women branded them as asexual hermaphrodites. These students were portrayed as unattractive, cigarette-smoking radicals, and their rejection of marriage in favor of study branded them as social outsiders. In fact, many of the German students were anxious about the stereotype and did what they could to maintain an image of respectability. Nevertheless, they perhaps could not entirely help contributing to the stereotype, since they had to guard against the sexual advances of fellow students and professors. Wanting "to be taken seriously as students and intellectuals," female students "consciously created personae that steered between masculine and feminine stereotypes."[8] Keeping men at some emotional distance, a number of them did clearly find love, and sometimes perhaps even physical intimacy, among the other women in their social circle. It would be a mistake, however, Lybeck points out, to see these student circles as a breeding ground for homosexuality. Looking at those novels written later by former students, including Aimée Duc's *Are These Women? A Novel about the Third Sex* (1901), Lybeck finds it significant that the erotic relationship between the chief characters blossomed on vacation or otherwise in a setting *away* from the university.[9]

It was only after 1900 that *the third sex* began to be applied to homosexuals with some regularity. The attention that sexology received by the German reading public in the next decade offered a new perspective on the lives, work, and relationships of independent women. By this time, there were already small networks and groups of women—sometimes working-class, sometimes independent-minded artists or professionals—that were fostering high levels of intimacy among their members and offering opportunities for couples to pair off into longer relationships. Some of these women even experimented with a certain level of masculine dress and behavior, though in the society of pre-1914 Germany, "masculine" might simply mean smoking cigarettes or cutting one's hair short. Lybeck suggests that it was a transitional period for women who loved other women. Some clearly were fascinated by the literature on homosexuality, welcoming the insights that it seemed to give about their lives at many different levels, but also hoping to shape what the term *homosexual* meant. Many others, however, were not happy with the implication that *homosexual* had for their claims to respectable status and their feminist ambitions to shape German politics.[10]

It was an era that Eve Kosofsky Sedgwick suggested was marked by "homosexual panic." Sedgwick, one of the pioneers of what academics now call queer theory, famously wrote that the proliferation of the term *homosexual* around the turn of the twentieth century was closely connected with "the world-mapping by which every given person, just as he or she was necessarily assignable to a male or a female gender, was now considered necessarily assignable as well to a homo- or a hetero-sexuality, a binarized identity that was full of implications, however confusing, for even the ostensibly least sexual aspects of personal existence."[11] The invention and then proliferation of the term *homosexual* in the second half of the nineteenth century did not, of course, mean that there was no sexual activity between men or between women taking place earlier. Nor did it mean that before this time individuals did not sometimes construct identities around a preference for certain kinds of sexual activity. What it did mean is that only around the turn of the twentieth century did this tendency to assign people to one "team" or the other, so to speak, become systematic. Only then did we acquire the mental habit familiar to us today of constantly raising questions in our own mind about the sexual preferences of people. As we did start to acquire this habit, however, it changed us. It transformed how we see ourselves and others. It created what Sedgwick called a "homosexual panic," a seeping paranoia about same-sex desire that worked its way into the fabric of our culture. It changed how we behaved in public and in private; it fundamentally reorganized the relationships between men and men, women and women, and women and men.

A substantial amount of historical work has confirmed Sedgwick's central insight and yet also suggested that the habit of asking questions about sexuality was not acquired instantaneously. Nor did it affect everybody at once, or in the same way. In fact, Sedgwick herself pointed in this direction in a 1990 essay. Rather than seeing modern homosexuality as a "coherent definitional field," perhaps it is better to envision it, she suggested, as "a space of overlapping, contradictory, and conflictual definitional forces."[12] Much research on lesbian culture suggests that "homosexual panic" generally affected women's lives later than it did men's. Different national contexts also seem to make a difference. Laura Doan's research on Englishwomen in her book *Fashioning Sapphism* suggests that they were subjected to "homosexual panic" only after furor about Radclyffe Hall's *Well of Loneliness* broke out in 1928, rather later than in either France or Germany.[13] And then we cannot forget about the important influence of class. George Chauncey's *Gay New York,* for example, suggests that in the United States wealthier, better-educated men were drawing clearer distinctions in their minds between "homosexual" and "heterosexual" by the 1920s, long before most working-class men were.[14] My own research on West Germany suggests that as late as the 1960s working-class men were familiar with the distinction, but they also were able to apply it rather selectively to their own lives.[15] In the transitional period, there were many individuals who resisted both the idea that everyone could be neatly categorized as well as the social implications of this "world-mapping."

In this long and complicated process of instilling these nagging questions about people's sexual desires, the growing body of medical and scientific writing no doubt played a major role, as the philosopher Michel Foucault argued in the introduction to his *History of Sexuality.* But an equally important role was played by a series of public scandals that rocked the European world around the turn of the century. We English-speaking people are generally familiar with the Oscar Wilde trials of 1895, which ultimately led to this brilliant Irish writer's being sent to prison for two years. Less well known to us are the trials involving two central figures in the German Kaiser's court and other scandals involving wealthy steel magnates, a colonial governor, and a youth movement leader.

These scandals created publicity for the homosexual movement, but not the kind that the movement wanted. In fact, the most important of the scandals, the Eulenburg scandal, produced a serious crisis for Hirschfeld's WhK and created a political atmosphere in which the government for a time seriously considered sharpening the law against homosexuality instead of repealing it. To get through this difficult period, homosexual activists tried to build alliances with other movements: feminism, Freudianism, and youth organizations. Not all these alliances would prove productive, and yet the effort to build them would be a critical step in the maturation of the homosexual movement.

In 1902 the socialist newspaper *Forward* (*Vorwärts*) outed Friedrich Alfred Krupp, the head of the largest steel company in Germany, which eventually would make many of the weapons that the country would use in both world wars. Although this millionaire and close friend of the German Kaiser was married and had two children, he was reported to take regular trips to the Italian island of Capri to carry on secret relationships with young Italian men. As the scandal unfolded, it was discovered that there had been so many complaints on the island that the Italian authorities were forced to become involved. An effort to cover up the incident failed. A blackmail letter threatening further allegations was sent to Krupp's wife, who went to Kaiser Wilhelm II for advice. Alas, he was the wrong person to ask, as the Kaiser turned to four influential psychiatrists and asked them to have her committed to a mental institution in Jena. As the uproar in the press continued, Alfred suddenly died, supposedly of a stroke. His body was sealed in a closed casket at the funeral, so suicide was widely suspected.[16] The Kaiser attended Krupp's funeral, where he made a speech striking back at the Social Democratic press for stirring up the scandal that led directly to Krupp's death. The SPD certainly deserved some blame, but for their part they always insisted that their only intention was to reveal the hypocrisy of the government and ultimately force a repeal of Paragraph 175. The effect, though, was certainly counterproductive, as it only stirred up hostility against homosexuality.

Another scandal broke out in Germany's newly acquired colonial lands, a case studied thoroughly by the historian Heike Schmidt. In Dar es Salaam, the capital of German East Africa (today Tanzania), a series of public accusation and court trials gradually accumulated into what is known as the Rechenberg scandal. The instigator of the controversy was Willy von Roy, the owner and managing editor of a local paper, the *German East African Newspaper* (*Deutsch-Ostafrikanische Zeitung*). Beginning in 1907, Roy began to target German East Africa's colonial governor, Georg Albrecht Freiherr von Rechenberg, in a series of increasingly hostile editorials and news columns. Rechenberg was not liked by many German colonists because he was accused of weakening the local military presence and otherwise undermining German interests in the colony after the violent suppression of a native uprising carried out by his predecessor.[17] He was also vulnerable to the accusation of being homosexual since he was a bachelor who liked to socialize in small groups of men, playing cards and drinking good wine. According to Wilhelm Methner, who was Rechenberg's second in command, many young men appreciated "the governor's generous and casual hospitality, which reminded them of Russian fashions and which suited the local Oriental conditions well."

How much Methner, Rechenberg, or others knew about the tendency for some of these men to spend time at a brothel full of African and Arab male sex workers is unclear.[18] What made the accusations explosive, though, was apparently widespread rumors surrounding Eberhardt Freiherr von Waechter, an ex–military officer and senior civil servant working in Rechenberg's office as the head of finances. Waechter was not well liked, and in the small and constricted society that the German colonists inhabited in Dar es Salaam, tensions could escalate quickly and rumors could fly.[19] Some of Waechter's enemies began to spread rumors of his homosexuality; these rumors rapidly circulated through the city and even made it to the city of Moshi, on the northern border of the colony, nearly 350 miles away. Waechter tried to defend himself in court, but without success. His case was not helped by the fact that two African men indicted in a separate court case involving homosexuality mentioned his name during the proceedings.[20]

At roughly the same time as the Waechter trial, three other court cases were being heard, these aimed at Willy von Roy, the editor of the *German East African Newspaper*. Accused of defamation by Rechenberg and two other senior members of the government, Roy was initially convicted and sentenced to four months in prison. Roy appealed, though, which gave him time to gather evidence of Rechenberg's alleged homosexuality. He enlisted the help of a friend, Julius Klein, who owned the printing press that produced Roy's newspaper and, more important, spoke enough Kiswahili to be able to converse with some native Africans who worked at his company. With Klein's help, Roy found an African employee of his newspaper named Theodor who was willing to spend time in the local coffeehouse with an ear open for rumors. He soon came back with stories of late-night encounters between Rechenberg and a servant, as well as a cross-dressing prostitute named Mtoro, who was seen making visits to the governor's palace.[21] How much truth there was behind any of these stories is hard to say. Many of the witnesses had clearly been bribed to give information, and under the pressure of the trial they retracted their stories or gave information that contradicted other accounts. The flimsiness of his evidence did not bode well for Roy's case. The judge for the appeals case upheld Roy's initial conviction in late 1910, and in fact both Roy and Klein were accused and eventually convicted of defamation, slander, and spreading dangerous rumors among the native Africans. One of the judges involved noted how hazardous it was for the entire colony for Germans to involve Africans in the way that Klein and Roy had: "Such conduct is fit to undermine the standing of the white population in general and in particular that of the highest colonial officers in the territory and thus of the imperial government amongst the natives."[22] This type of sedition could not be tolerated, and so the governor gave the order for both Roy and Klein to be deported from the colony.

The Rechenberg affair of 1910 might have created some waves in the German colonies, but its effect paled in comparison to that of the Eulenburg scandal, which had broken out a few years earlier. This one involved a number of individuals right at the center of the German government. At the turn of the century, one of the most powerful people in Germany was Philipp von Eulenburg, a longtime friend of Kaiser Wilhelm II and the chief adviser within the monarch's court. The two of them had met back in 1885 at a shooting party and soon found that they shared a passion for Nordic ballads and Bavarian art. Eulenburg was charming and had a gift for storytelling, and his residence, Liebenberg castle, roughly fifty miles north of Berlin, became a center for much entertaining, musical offerings, and rich conversation about spiritualism and other contemporary topics. Although Eulenburg was not universally liked—Bismarck notoriously had serious doubts about his ability as a diplomat—Wilhelm II came to trust his advice above all others' in the years after he became monarch. Eulenburg demonstrated unusual candor in his conversation with the Kaiser, which the latter no doubt appreciated. Perhaps it was the age difference—Eulenburg was nearly twelve years older—that lent him this confidence.[23]

There had long been rumors about Eulenburg's sexuality. There was talk that he had been forced out of an early position as a diplomat in Vienna when blackmail charges threatened him.[24] Some detected a hint of effeminacy about him. Chlodwig von Hohenlohe, a previous chancellor of Germany, wrote in a letter to his son that Eulenburg "made a thoroughly unfavorable impression on me. I wonder that I did not feel this aversion to him earlier." And a doctor who examined Eulenburg observed his "neurasthenia, brought about by an irregular life, careless diet, effeminization and———," preferring not to openly name the sexual lifestyle of such a prominent member at court.[25] Furthermore, the men in Eulenburg's circle shared a friendship that was highly emotional and intimate, a kind of relationship that seems to have been more common earlier in the century but by the late nineteenth century had increasingly been defined as abnormal and therefore suspicious. And they were aware of their unconventionality. They saw themselves as a group that stood apart from the masses—not only because of their aristocratic background and similar upbringing but, more important, because of their sensitive, artistically inclined characters. They were all devoted to art and music; together they

wrote poems.[26] Within their circle, they used a language that the Germa
call *schwärmerisch:* effusive, lyrical, even gushing. Their nicknames suggested
romantic feelings for one another. One of Eulenburg's best friends, Kuno von
Moltke, was known as "Tutu" and "the Sweet One." For his part, Eulenburg
was referred to as "My Soul," "My Love," and "My Little Puppy."[27]

Besides Eulenburg, the other major target of the scandal was Count Kuno
von Moltke. His family name was well known in late nineteenth-century
Germany, though he was not directly related to the two most famous Moltkes: Helmuth von Moltke, the field marshal and military strategist who led
the Prussian army to victory against the Austrians and French in the wars of
unification, and the field marshal's nephew Helmuth Johann Ludwig von
Moltke, who would become the Prussian chief of staff in 1906 and would
eventually lead the German army in the initial phase of World War I.[28] Still,
his family had a long tradition of sending their males into the military, and so
Kuno joined in 1866 despite showing no obvious disposition for the career.

Kuno von Moltke had a stroke of luck when he met Eulenburg. Moltke
had what everyone acknowledged was a real talent for the piano, and Eulenburg soon took a liking to the young man. Through Eulenburg, Moltke was
introduced to the Kaiser in 1888. He quickly became a permanent fixture
in Wilhelm's camarilla. At Hubertusstock, the monarch's favorite hunting
lodge, he became a regular riding and hunting partner; at Liebenberg castle
he entertained the crowd with his remarkable piano playing. The relationship
jump-started his career. In 1893 Moltke was appointed the Kaiser's on-duty
aide-de-camp.[29] In 1899 he was promoted to colonel within one of Prussia's
elite cavalry regiments, which paved the way for his appointment to the Kaiser's general staff in 1903. His lack of military aptitude was impossible to
conceal, though: jokes circulated about his special office to organize a new
unit of army pianists. So in 1905 he was quietly retired from that position
and made the military commandant of Berlin instead.

Like Eulenburg, Moltke was rumored to be homosexual by gossips in
court circles. Eulenburg and Moltke were both married, and Eulenburg even
had five children, but these circumstances had not entirely stopped the talk.
It was kept largely in the Kaiser's court, though, until November 1906, when
Maximilian Harden wrote an article hinting at some doubts about the morality of those closest to Wilhelm II. Harden—actually a pen name taken by
Felix Ernst Witkowski, a Jewish-German from the Polish regions of Prussia—
was the founder and editor of the prominent Berlin weekly *The Future* (*Die
Zukunft*). He had originally made a name for himself as a theater critic and
a writer of fun, entertaining pieces for the German press. In 1892, however,
he had a chance to meet Bismarck, an encounter that left a deep impression

on him. Bismarck had been forced into retirement two years earlier by Wilhelm II, who did not trust the aging Bismarck's abilities nearly as much as his grandfather, Kaiser Wilhelm I, had. Bismarck did not go quietly, though. He took whatever opportunities he found to criticize the monarch and the policies of his government. Bismarck's crankiness registered with Harden and inspired him to get involved with politics. Soon afterward, Harden established *The Future*. In it he frequently criticized the German Kaiser, other members of the German nobility, and various officials in the government. Much of what he wrote was bitingly satirical, in a style that betrayed more than a hint of his theatrical background. In his own words, Harden hoped to avoid the "pedantic methods" common in much of the press of his day. His "outlandish, unconventional language," notes one historian, soon attracted a wide audience for his paper. It also frequently got him in trouble with the law. During the 1890s Harden was frequently accused of slander, libel, and lèse-majesté. More than once he ended up in prison.[30]

The Eulenburg scandal represented the culmination of a series of escalating attacks against Wilhelm II. Like many nationalists, Harden was concerned about a string of missteps on the part of the monarch—from the Kruger Telegram to the First Moroccan Crisis—that seemed to indicate flawed judgment and, perhaps, a weak character. His articles toward the end of the 1906 Algeçiras Conference criticized Wilhelm for having missed the opportunity to stand up to the British and the French. "Germany is strong and was once feared. And it can be again, if only it will stop being scared by every bluff."[31] In Harden's mind, the homosexuals at the center of the Kaiser's court were directly connected with Germany's feeble foreign policy. Their effeminacy was in Harden's mind "incompatible with public life."[32] Much of the scandal's gendered language betrayed middle-class prejudices about the aristocracy. For a class that defined its status in terms of respectability, ethical behavior, and self-control, the refinement of aristocratic etiquette and the excesses sometimes connected with the court could seem very unmasculine.[33] The closed nature of the Kaiser's court was also incompatible with the modern conception of a government that was transparent to the public, allowing for more democratic influence. Harden was a nationalist, but he also had a liberal side. From this angle, Eulenburg symbolized the difficulties inherent in the Kaiser's "personal rule" whereas Moltke stood as a representative of the army that had arguably excessive weight in government affairs. As the historian Jeffrey Schneider has convincingly shown in his analysis of the scandal, their closeted homosexuality symbolized the secrecy of the court.[34]

The information that Harden had received pointing to Eulenburg's and Moltke's homosexuality offered a prime opportunity to attack what he saw as a very dangerous clique that surrounded the Kaiser, distorting the monarch's judgment and "encouraging him in a new absolutism."[35] It was a timely moment, since the army recently had been rocked by a series of well-publicized courts-martial that were due to homosexual conduct (as well as numerous related suicides). But where did the information come from? This question has prompted much speculation among historians, but no clear answers have emerged. At the time many believed that the source had to be someone with close connections to the court and some considerable social influence.[36] The historian Helmuth Rogge pointed to Friedrich von Holstein, a skillful and successful official in Germany's Foreign Office who had been recently forced to retire after his unfortunate role in the First Moroccan Crisis, in 1905. Establishing many connections between Holstein and Harden, Rogge speculated that Holstein harbored a grudge against Wilhelm II and his entourage for being forced from office and took the opportunity for revenge when he saw it.[37]

Peter Winzen has recently argued in his book *The End of Imperial Glory* (*Das Ende der Kaiserherlichkeit*), however, that Holstein was simply an intermediary between Harden and the real mastermind behind the affair, the government's Chancellor Bernard von Bülow. According to Winzen, Bülow had come to blame Eulenburg for the mismanagement of the Moroccan Crisis and a missed opportunity to stand up to France and potentially drive a wedge between that country and its fresh ally, Britain. He had serious doubts about the wisdom of several royal appointments that could easily be traced to Eulenburg's patronage. Most important, Bülow's government had recently been severely shaken by political crises, parliamentary divisions, and colonial revolts. Greatly worried that his position as chancellor might not be secure, he quickly identified Eulenburg as a potential rival for his position.[38]

No matter who provided him with the information, Harden certainly used it to good effect. Over the next few months, Harden stepped up his attacks, which culminated in his explicit denunciation of Eulenburg as a pervert in April 1907. Hearing about the accusations, Wilhelm II said, "Harden is a damned scoundrel, but he would not have risked attacks like these if he did not have adequate evidence on his hands." He immediately fired Moltke and, a little over a month later, after trying to find a way to safely vindicate his best friend, asked Eulenburg for his resignation as well. He ordered both men to take Harden to court—to protect their own reputations, yes, but also the monarchy's.[39]

Thus began a series of trials, six in all before the affair was over. The first, in which Moltke accused Harden of libel, ended with Moltke's homosexuality being confirmed by the court. Although no direct evidence of sexual relations was offered, his ex-wife, Lily von Elbe, presented what for many was a shocking story of Moltke's kissing a handkerchief left accidentally by Eulenburg at his home while mumbling, "My soul, my love!" The prosecution offered other stories suggesting Moltke's effeminacy and culminated with a startling scientific witness: Magnus Hirschfeld, who gave his expert opinion that the evidence presented in court pointed to Moltke's homosexuality (even if it was perhaps present only at the *unconscious* level).[40] Moltke's conviction was appealed and voided on technical grounds, which set the stage for a retrial.

In the meantime, a second trial occurred, this one involving another leader of the homosexual movement, Adolf Brand. Brand decided during the affair to experiment with a tactic that he had advocated within the WhK, namely, outing (what he grimly called the "path over corpses," referring to the martyrdom that victimized homosexuals might acquire). Within gay circles, there was talk that Chancellor Bülow himself was homosexual and that he had had a long relationship with his private secretary. There were also some who believed that Bülow's nephew was involved with Eulenburg's son-in-law. Brand went public with these rumors in an issue of *The Special One* published in September 1907. After distributing this issue in Berlin, Brand was summoned to court in November 1907 to defend himself against a libel suit. His article, Brand insisted, was never meant as an insult against Bülow, since Brand did not believe there was anything immoral or dishonorable about homosexuality. His only intent was to suggest how widespread homoerotic relationships such as those carried on by Bülow, Eulenburg, and Moltke truly were. Brand, however, had no real evidence to offer besides what he had heard. No one came to his aid. A friend of his who had promised to produce damning material evidence fled Germany. Hirschfeld was called, only to deny ever having heard such stories. Bülow, on other hand, got up in court to defend his reputation, and he had many friends and colleagues who backed him up. Even Bülow's rival, Eulenburg, gave character evidence while taking the opportunity to defend his own close friendships. The court ruled in Bülow's favor, and Brand was sentenced to eighteen months in prison.[41]

The retrial of Moltke's libel suit against Harden took place in December. Moltke's legal team was better prepared this time. The credibility of Moltke's ex-wife was skillfully undermined. Police witnesses (apparently under some official pressure) retracted some of their earlier statements. Hirschfeld, having been blackmailed by Moltke's attorney with evidence of Hirschfeld's own homosexuality, also changed his own testimony.[42] Moltke was vindicated in court, and Harden was convicted. It was a pyrrhic victory, though. Moltke's reputation would not survive the trials. For Harden, defeat brought heavy fines, but they eventually were covered by a fund from the chancellor's office as part of a settlement negotiated by Bülow (a fact that Winzen finds extremely suspicious). More important, the court cases got him closer to his real target: Eulenburg.

During both the trial against Adolf Brand and the second libel trial against Harden, Eulenburg had sworn under oath that he was not homosexual and had never violated Paragraph 175. (We should note that Eulenburg may not technically have been lying about the latter if he had never engaged in anal sex or some similar form of penetration, something that will be discussed a little later.) His testimony opened the door for two more court cases, each of them revolving around Harden's effort to catch his victim in a perjury trap. In Munich, Harden and his friend Anton Städele staged a libel trial in which Harden produced a fisherman and a laborer who both swore under oath that they had had sex with Eulenburg during the late 1880s. "The reaction in Berlin," wrote the historian Isabel Hull in *The Entourage of Kaiser Wilhelm II,* "was immediate and electric." Eulenburg was arrested; the police searched his castle.[43] He was tried for perjury, a process that lasted over two weeks in mid-1908. It eventually produced much damning material: testimony from the Berlin vice squad, men who had observed suspicious goings-on at Eulenburg's castle, a rehashing of the evidence presented in the Munich trial, and a new story involving a sailor on the Kaiser's yacht who claimed that he had been hit on by Eulenburg. Eulenburg denied up and down that he had ever done anything "dirty," but the trial was clearly going against him.[44] Then, suddenly, Eulenburg collapsed—a sign of the strain that he was under. The judge tried to carry on with the case by moving the entire proceedings to the hospital. After Eulenburg was brought in on a stretcher still dressed in his nightgown, however, the court yielded to the doctors' pleas and postponed the trial. More than a year later, on July 7, 1909, it resumed under Eulenburg's protestation that he was still too ill. The process was barely under way when Eulenburg complained of heart pains. The court doctor examined him and, fearing that Eulenburg had had a heart attack, postponed the trial again, indefinitely.[45] It never resumed. Twice a year until he died in 1919, Eulenburg was examined by doctors who declared him too ill to stand trial.

The prestige of the monarchy and the ruling class of Germany was deeply shaken. Many were left with the impression that the German aristocracy as a whole lived a "squalid and effete" life.[46] The scandal acquired international attention. One Italian cartoonist depicted the Kaiser struggling to get free from a pig in military costume, which was sitting on the Kaiser's coat and apparently soiling it badly. This was a clear allusion to *Schweinereien,* a common way of referring to homosexual acts in German. The French, still smarting from their humiliating military defeat during the 1870 Franco-Prussian war, gleefully joked about the "German vice." In Austria, the anti-Semitic press raised questions about the health of a monarchy that could lay itself open to attacks by the Jew Harden. Back in Germany, not a few even began to have doubts about the Kaiser's sexuality.[47]

For the instigators of the scandal, the results were mixed. Chancellor Bülow, if he was indeed the source of the information being supplied to Harden, might have benefited temporarily from having a rival removed, but it did not save his job. Ultimately the debate about Eulenburg in the Reichstag eroded the ties that held his coalition together. By July 1909 it was clear that Bülow had lost the ability to get major laws passed, and he was replaced by Theobald von Bethmann Hollweg. Harden might have been happier with the results. His paper had made quite a profit during the affair. His name had become known internationally. And like David taking on Goliath, he had gone against the mightiest in the land and won, despite his lower-middle-class background and Jewish heritage. Bismarck himself had thought it impossible. Harden fully believed that "the results were healthy for the empire and the Kaiser."[48] We might judge otherwise, though. Very quickly, Eulenburg was replaced by a new favorite, Prince Max Egon zu Fürstenburg, who did nothing to promote transparency in the court. And hard-liners in the German military found their hands strengthened by the public revulsion against national "effeminization," which contributed to an increasingly aggressive style in the German government. These hard-liners would play an important role in egging the Kaiser on to a war that they saw as inevitable in the years leading up to World War I.[49]

From the perspective of the homosexual movement, the Eulenburg scandal was a disaster. It unleashed a wave of articles, editorials, and cartoons in the press that took full advantage of public prejudices (Figure 5).[50] It also established a stereotype of the homosexual as somebody whose sexual proclivities and character weakness endangered the state—a stereotype that would be revived by both Nazis in the 1930s and Cold Warriors in the 1950s.[51] Harden himself always insisted that he had nothing in particular against homosexuals, and some evidence even suggests that he might have had a homosexual past during his days in the theater. In the midst of the scandal, however, with passions running high, his tone shifted in a noticeably pejorative direction when talking about male-male desire. "In our Germany, politics is much too soft and sweet," he wrote in his paper *The Future*. "The German Kaiser should and must have healthy men around him."[52]

Why had Magnus Hirschfeld volunteered to help Harden in his attacks against Eulenburg? He seems to have hoped that by revealing homosexuals at the center of the government, he might make Paragraph 175 look all the more hypocritical. Moreover, he assumed that the controversy would bring

(Redaktionsschluss: 28. Oktober 1907)   JUGEND 1907 Nr. 45

Meues preußisches Wappen
(Liebenberger Entwurf)

A. Weisgerber (München)

Herausgeb.: Dr. GEORG HIRTH; Redakt.: F. v. OSTINI, Dr. S. SINZHEIMER, A. MATTHÄI, P. LANGHEINRICH, K. ETTLINGER. Für die Redaktion verantwortlich: Dr. S. SINZHEIMER, für den Inseratenteil: G. POSSELT, sämtlich in München. Verlag: G. HIRTH's Kunstverlag, München. Druck von KNORR & HIRTH, G. m. b H., München. — Geschäftsstelle für Oesterreich-Ungarn: MORITZ PERLES, Verlagsbuchhandlung Wien I, Seilergasse 4 — Für Oesterreich-Ungarn verantwortlich: JOSEF MAUTNER. — ALLE RECHTE VORBEHALTEN

**FIGURE 5 A NEW PRUSSIAN COAT OF ARMS:
A POLITICAL CARTOON BY ALBERT WEISGERBER**

This cartoon is characteristic of those that appeared internationally during the Eulenburg scandal of 1907. Source: *Jugend* 11, no. 45 (October 28, 1907): 1028. Courtesy of the Harry Ransom Center, Austin, Texas attention to homosexuals and their cause. In this second respect, he was proved correct. Years later he would remark that the word *homosexual* entered into public discourse in an unprecedented way during the media coverage of the scandal. The attention was important in the long run. As the historian James Steakley writes, the scandal "contributed significantly to publicizing and legitimating the embryonic discipline of sexology, which accounts for the grudging respect accorded Dr. Hirschfeld."[53] In the short run, though, his name was dragged through the mud by the press. Right-wing papers painted him as a poison to the nation, and even more moderate, liberal papers joined in the outcry, calling him "a freak who acted for freaks in the name of pseudo-science."[54] More important, he had not anticipated how overwhelming the public condemnations of "effeminacy" would become. Political cartoons depicting naked, bearded Prussian cupids tickling each other and steel-helmeted soldiers wearing dresses could have contributed very little to the "enlightening" of Germany. On the contrary, the moral panic set off by the scandals had unleashed a host of conservative critics who were predicting the death of the German people at the hands of homosexuals.

The organizations of the movement experienced the scandal as traumatic. With Adolf Brand's imprisonment, *The Special One* disappeared and would not be published again until after the First World War. We can probably assume, as well, that the Community of the Special (GdE) also quit meeting, at least until Brand emerged from jail eighteen months later. Censorship was stepped up, as the police cracked down on works by homosexual authors (such as John Henry Mackay's works published under his pseudonym, Sagitta) that were judged to be obscene.[55] Hirschfeld's WhK began to hemorrhage members, and many of its earlier sources of financial support dried up.[56] In 1907 Hirschfeld's journal *The Yearbook for Sexual Intermediaries* failed to appear for the first time since it was initially issued, a sure sign of the stress that Hirschfeld was under.[57] And to add to the crisis, a group of men led by Benedict Friedlaender seceded from the WhK at the beginning of 1907 as a protest against Hirschfeld's leadership and the role that he had played in the Eulenburg scandal.

Friedlaender's secession at this moment might have been purely a coincidence, though, since his conflict with the WhK went back to the previous year, when Friedlaender and his friend Friedrich Dobe had raised questions about Hirschfeld's handling of finances during a meeting of the WhK's advisory board. Hirschfeld, already annoyed by Friedlaender's constant criticisms of his theory of sexual intermediaries, fought back by working with allies to simply eliminate the advisory board. A vote was put to the general assembly at its annual October meeting in 1906. Friedlaender was too sick with dysentery to attend, but his friends Dobe and Mackay were both there, and they were furious. Hirschfeld tried to calm them down, but Mackay screamed, "I'll break the glass in the door if you don't let us out!" The two of them, along with another friend, stormed out and headed down to a local bar to plot their response. In early 1907 Friedlaender published a manifesto for the "Secession of the Scientific-Humanitarian Committee" in one of the last prewar issues of *The Special One*. Later a new name was attached to the group: the League for Manly Culture (*Bund für männliche Kultur*).[58]

The splinter group was short-lived. Dependent on the generosity of the independently wealthy Friedlaender for its existence, the League for Manly Culture dissolved after Friedlaender committed suicide in June 1908. The secession, however, might be seen simply as a sign of the hardening line between Hirschfeld's supporters and his masculinist critics, precipitated by the Eulenburg scandal. This polarization would not disappear in 1908 and in fact would remain an enduring feature of the homosexual movement through the 1930s.

FREUDIAN PSYCHOANALYSIS

To recover from the difficult year of 1907, Hirschfeld took a trip to Italy in early 1908. On the way south, he stopped in Vienna, where he made the acquaintance of Sigmund Freud. Freud was a relative newcomer to the field of psychiatry at the time. His first major work, *The Interpretation of Dreams,* had been published in 1899, followed by several other works, most notably his 1905 book, *Three Essays on the Theory of Sexuality.* He began to attract followers, and in 1910 he would establish the International Psychoanalytical Association to spread his ideas, foster further research, and train a new generation of psychoanalysts. Although Freud did not deny the biological foundations of sexuality, his "depth psychology" (*Tiefenpsychologie*), as he called it, challenged the assumption held by the most important psychiatrists of his day that mental disturbances (including "sexual perversions") were ultimately the result of some physical abnormality—brain damage, for example, or neurological degeneration. In contrast to this biological school, Freud's method of psychoanalysis assumed that there was a distinction between the mind and the brain—between the thoughts and emotions that get bound up together through the symbolic networks of our inner life and the gray matter that is the physical location of this inner life.[59]

On a professional level, psychoanalysis represented a revolt against university professors who dominated the psychological profession, with their emphasis on research in mental asylums. It widened the psychiatrist's focus to include not only the serious psychoses of asylum inmates but also the "psychiatric disorders of daily life."[60] On the level of theory, it opposed the biological school's materialism and faith in the scientific method with the very "unscientific" notion of the unconscious; it saw mental illness as caused by dynamic processes of the mind instead of neurological diseases.[61] Treating a number of women who suffered from strange and seemingly incurable maladies, Freud began to interpret their symptoms as "incomprehensible messages from the human inner world," a carefully encoded series of signals from an unconsciousness that was struggling to work through childhood traumas or other difficult experiences.

Gradually, Freud began to imagine the mind as energized by several powerful instinctive drives, which he soon interpreted as different forms of a single impulse, the sexual libido. During infancy, the libido is not yet focused on the genitals but instead finds release through a number of objects (the mother's breast, for example) and autoerotic zones (such as thumb sucking). Over time, though, our potential for "polymorphous perversity" gets shut down as the libido gradually gets channeled toward specific body parts that are critical for various stages of maturation. As we grow up, Freud believed, our sexuality becomes suppressed, its energy driven back into the unconsciousness, where it ultimately seeks satisfaction in a sublimated, symbolic form. Healthy sublimation leads to the passion that we feel for work, play, art, music, and the social relationships that are important to us. Growing up is a difficult process, though, and so it is easy for sexuality to be inadequately sublimated or to accidentally find an outlet in a manner that society finds unacceptable.

From this point of view, homosexuality—or inversion, as Freud called it—might not necessarily be an inborn characteristic, as Krafft-Ebing, Ulrichs, and Hirschfeld argued. Though he did not at first entirely reject the idea that some homosexuals are "absolute" or "amphigenic" inverts whose sexuality is rooted in biological factors, he insisted that there could also be "contingent inverts" whose homosexuality arises in the course of growing up.[62] His assumption that all men and women begin their lives as "polymorphously perverse" led him to believe that everyone has a potential for both heterosexual and homosexual feelings. His psychoanalytic research yielded several possible explanations for why some individuals might not develop into "normal" heterosexuals. They ranged from an extreme identification with one's mother to strongly developed narcissism, to even an inability to deal with the fear of castration evoked by women.[63] And other possibilities were developed by the next generation of psychoanalysts. For Alfred Adler, male homosexuality represented a revolt against an overly strict parent: in the case of the father, by valorizing and adopting unmanly behavior; in the case of the mother, by opting for a male partner to love as a way of dealing with insecurities toward all women. For Carl Jung, homosexuality represented a failure to construct a coherent gender personality, usually as a result of being overly attached to the parent of the opposite sex. This attachment leads male homosexuals to identify with the feminine soul image (or anima, as Jung called it) whereas lesbians identify with the masculine (or animus).[64]

Hirschfeld and others in the WhK were first introduced to Freud's ideas in 1905, shortly after the publication of the *Three Essays on Sexuality* (*Drei Abhandlungen zur Sexualtheorie*).[65] Despite the differences between his and Freud's approaches, he was intrigued. He no doubt appreciated that Freud in his books had referred to his own research and the articles of allied researchers published in the *Yearbook for Sexual Intermediaries*. His visit with Freud was closely connected with an effort to reorient himself slightly; he certainly did not give up his work with the WhK, but beginning in 1908 he increasingly widened his interests to include a broader range of sexological topics. In January the first issue of *The Journal for Sexual Science* (*Die Zeitschrift für Sexualwissenschaft*) appeared.[66] It was printed monthly for a year before financial problems brought publication to a halt. In this brief time, though, it made available important essays on many different topics, including biological studies of the sexual life of plants, psychoanalytic investigations of the erotic origins of the arts, and even empirical observations of the dreams that prostitutes had.

Included in *The Journal for Sexual Science* were numerous articles written by prominent psychoanalysts, including Alfred Adler, Wilhelm Steckel, and Sigmund Freud himself.[67] In the same year, Hirschfeld developed a relationship with Karl Abraham, a physician in Berlin who became an early advocate of Freudian methodology. Hirschfeld and Abraham became founding members of the Berlin Society of Psychoanalysis, established in August 1908, one of only three worldwide at that stage. In March 1910 Hirschfeld attended the second International Psychoanalytic Congress, held in Nuremberg, where he had an opportunity to meet with Freud for a second time. Despite the implicit tensions between Hirschfeld's and Freud's views on sexuality, the relationship was still amicable.

Signs of a growing disagreement were there for anyone looking, however. Hirschfeld's 1910 book, *Transvestites,* may be read as an effort to distinguish between gender identity and sexual orientation (even if inadequately). This distinction implicitly opposed Freud's psychoanalytic theory, which tended to conflate the two. Freud was a little more forthright with his criticism. In 1910 he published the essay "Leonardo da Vinci and a Memory of His Childhood" ("*Eine Kindheitserinnerung des Leonardo da Vinci*"). It is now famous for its psychoanalytic interpretation of one of Leonardo's earliest memories—

namely, of a vulture landing on his cradle when he was still a baby and then striking him "many times with its tail against my lips."[68] Suggesting that Leonardo's so-called memory is really a kind of disguised homosexual fantasy, in which the wing takes the place of a penis, Freud weaved this memory together with Leonardo's longing for a missing father, ambivalent memories of his biological mother, and other evidence of a pronounced autoerotic fixation to produce a remarkably complicated picture of this artist's inner life. In the process, he raised serious doubts about those doctors who described homosexuals as "a distinct species, as an intermediate sexual stage, as a 'third sex.'" "What is for practical reasons called homosexuality may arise from a variety of psychosexual inhibitory processes," he insisted.[69] Although Hirschfeld was not mentioned by name, it was clear that Freud believed that Hirschfeld's theories were far too simplistic to address this complicated issue.

The simmering conflict came to a boil in 1911 at the Third Congress of the International Psychoanalytical Association. At this meeting, the Hungarian therapist Sándor Ferenczi gave a paper in which he articulated more clearly than any Freudian ever had the assumption that homosexuality was a kind of neurosis that could be healed in many cases. With the battle engaged, Carl Jung jumped in and verbally attacked Hirschfeld in an openly insulting manner. Hirschfeld was outraged and stormed out of the meeting, giving up his membership in the association.[70] Freud was not there, but Karl Abraham wrote him a letter referring to the conflict. "Hirschfeld's defection is no great loss to us; for the work of our group it is, rather, a gain," he insisted. Hirschfeld's approach to the subject was fundamentally different, his knowledge of psychoanalysis shallow. In the end, Abraham concluded, it was "probably only the emphasis on sexuality that made analysis attractive to him, especially at a time when his own sex research met with hostility."[71] Freud soon wrote to Jung, saying that he too felt that Hirschfeld's defection was no tragedy. He was an "unsavory fellow" who was not "in a position to learn anything."[72]

For his part, Hirschfeld did not immediately give up his hope of building a bridge with psychoanalysis, and in 1913 he published an important psychoanalytic-inspired essay by Hans Blüher in his *Yearbook for Sexual Intermediaries* (which will be examined more fully later). In a series of works, however, he tried to sharpen his own criticism of psychoanalysis. He raised questions about whether love and sexual attraction could be easily identified through a singular libido. His critique was hampered, though, by the fact that he had earlier conflated homosexuality and "Platonic love," accepting the assumption that sexual desire could be sublimated into nonsexual relationships. He unfortunately was also forced to admit that he had no better explanation than Freud of such sexual practices as fetishism. This left him trying to defend the biological basis of homosexuality with recent evidence from chemical and biological research into the role of hormones in sexuality.[73]

NEW ALLIANCES: SEXOLOGISTS AND THE WOMEN'S MOVEMENT

Notwithstanding his quarrel with the Freudians, Hirschfeld was no doubt satisfied with the general trend among sexologists and psychiatrists when it came to their views of homosexuality. He was building a good working relationship with the sexologist Iwan Bloch as well as with Albert Eulenburg, a Berlin neurologist who had written a book on masochism and sadism. Both had actually been early opponents of Hirschfeld's ideas, which made Hirschfeld's success at winning them over even more significant. Iwan Bloch had started off his career as a sexologist, believing that most homosexuals had been the victims of seduction. By 1907, however, Bloch had come around to accepting Hirschfeld's argument that in most cases homosexuality was inborn and non-pathological.[74] Eulenburg did not go quite that far. He was still a believer in degeneration theory, and he consequently saw homosexuality and other perversions as fundamentally caused by a weak nervous system, although there might need to be a specific event or environment that triggered the latent condition.[75] He respected Hirschfeld's ability as a researcher, however, and they had a range of mutual friends. In February 1913 he joined Hirschfeld and Bloch to establish the Medical Society for Sexual Science and Eugenics (*Ärtzliche Gesellschaft für Sexualwissenschaft und Eugenik*), which they hoped would grow into an international society that could encourage sexual research and promote sexual reform. The society began to publish *The Journal for Sexual Science* again; Eulenburg and Bloch served as its chief editors.[76] Eulenburg died in 1917, but Bloch continued to be an important supporter of Hirschfeld's professional and political work until Bloch passed away in 1922.

Bloch and Eulenburg were prominent figures in the emerging field of sexology, but they were perhaps not entirely representative. There were lots of conflict and disagreements, and the historian Edward Ross Dickinson has recently argued in *Sex, Freedom, and Power in Imperial Germany* that some of the divisions became more intense around 1908–9 as a wider public debate about sexuality and proper gender roles also heated up.[77] Still, when it came specifically to the question of whether homosexuality is inborn or acquired, an observer of the scientific debate at the time might easily have concluded that experts were moving toward some broad consensus on the issue.[78] There were certainly a few notable advocates of the acquired position besides Freud and his followers. Max Dessoir at the University of Berlin, probably the most important psychiatrist still working in the old philosophic-idealist tradition dominant in the earlier part of the century, argued that individuals typically become sexually differentiated only in the late teens. Before this, sexuality is rather amorphous and can be directed toward both males and females, and even animals.[79] His work had some influence on Freud, who was busy in Vienna working out his own theories of sexual development. And then there was Albert von Schrenck-Notzing, who became well known for his research on hypnotism. Schrenck-Notzing believed that he had some success using hypnotism to reverse his patients' sexual preferences, which led him to conclude that it was caused by environmental factors.[80]

Havelock Ellis, however, summarized the situation well when he observed that the vast majority of researchers had come around to accepting that a "favoring predisposition," or what some were calling a "latent" tendency, had to exist even when there needed to be a series of experiences or environmental factors that turned the predisposition into a reality.[81] Albert Moll, whose *Libido Sexualis* was a pioneering work in arguing that all forms of sexuality were constructed, suggested that there might be a congenital psychological weakness that made it difficult for some to develop normally.[82] Even Schrenck-Notzing admitted by the early twentieth century that homosexuals might possess an inherited weakness of the nervous system that made it difficult to resist "perverted" ideas.[83] And on the other side of the debate, such well-known advocates of the inherited nature of homosexuality as Iwan Bloch and Magnus Hirschfeld did not deny that there were "pseudohomosexuals," as they called them, whose sexual behavior was primarily a response to a particular environment, such as prisons or all-male boarding schools.

The opinions of Schrenck-Notzing and Albert Moll suggest that the emerging consensus was unfortunately due more to the persistent appeal of degeneration theory than to Hirschfeld's powers of persuasion. Krafft-Ebing may have distanced himself from this theory at the turn of the century, but it still had an influential advocate in Emil Kraepelin, whose *Psychiatry* (*Psychiatrie*) had replaced Krafft-Ebing's book as the standard textbook in many German universities by this point. It is interesting, however, that even Kraepelin, who would later emerge as one of Hirschfeld's most powerful professional opponents, did at this time accept the criticisms made by sex reformers regarding Paragraph 175. For Kraepelin and his students, homosexuality might be a "sign of degeneration and possibly a morbid condition," as the historian Florian Mildenberger notes, but it "posed so little danger and was so unimportant that neither punishment nor a deeper analysis of its etiology seemed necessary."[84]

While struggling to forge some consensus in the psychiatric and sexological professions on the need for legal reform, Hirschfeld also worked to develop an alliance with the emerging women's movement. Women in general, though, were slow to take any interest. Few women writers can be found in the pages of Hirschfeld's *Yearbook,* and only slowly did women begin to join the WhK. Elberskirchen, as we have seen, was one of the first, and in the next years she became an advocate for an alliance between the two movements. In 1903, in one of her many works addressed to the women's movement, Elberskirchen bravely declared her homosexuality: "If we women of the emancipation are homosexual—well, this must be allowed! We are homosexual with good right."[85]

Even better known today than Elberskirchen is the name Anna Rüling, a pseudonym taken by Theodora Ana Sprüngli. Born in Hamburg, Sprüngli began a career as a journalist writing for one of Hamburg's newspapers, and by 1904 she was also making contributions to an anarchist paper, *Struggle* (*Kampf*). In 1905 she moved to Berlin, where she went to work for Scherl Publishing, which was responsible for several of the city's biggest newspapers. By the 1920s she was freelancing, her pieces published by newspapers all across Germany. Under her own name she wrote pieces mostly on theater and music. She did try her hand once at short-story writing. A short-story collection of hers, published by Max Spohr's press, stood out for its inclusion of two stories about gay men and three about lesbians. Most of the time, though, she kept references to homosexuality isolated to pieces published under her pseudonym.[86]

As "Anna Rüling," Sprüngli gave one of the most famous speeches advocating lesbian rights, during a meeting of the WhK's 1904 annual assembly in Berlin's Hotel Prinz Albrecht.[87] From our modern perspective, the speech seems very typically nineteenth-century in many ways: she assumes that a heterosexual woman is generally ruled by feeling rather than reason and is "organically by nature determined above all to become a wife and a mother."[88] At the time, though, the speech struck like a bombshell. Arguing that women had a lot of interests in common with homosexuals, she focused much of her speech on lesbians, or "Urninds," as she called them, using Karl Heinrich Ulrichs's term for female homosexuals. There were some tensions and ambiguities in the way that she talked about homosexual women, as Kirsten Leng has recently suggested.[89] The main thrust of her argument, though, was suggesting that Urninds had just as much, or perhaps even more, interest in addressing key women's issues such as education, marriage, and prostitution. Accepting Hirschfeld's position that homosexual women exhibited "a masculine nature and masculine traits," she argued that they were naturally unsuited for marriage, even if many of them did marry, either because of social pressure or because their stunted education left them without a "clear view and understanding of sexuality and sexual life."[90] As women pushed for the expanded rights of women in marriage, they needed to keep in mind those women for whom marriage would be a disaster—for themselves, their husbands, and society as a whole. Such women should be left to lead an independent life, a life that they were well suited for, given what Sprüngli described as their more masculine qualities: energy, rationality, and clarity. They needed access to education and jobs, however.

Homosexual women's desire for independence was one reason that they often played a leading role in the women's movement, according to Sprüngli. "I cannot and will not name anyone," she remarked, for fear of doing harm to the women involved and possibly to the women's movement as a whole, given the negative stereotypes often applied by men who opposed the movement. She asserted, though, that they had played a critical role, being "mostly responsible for activating the movement." Consequently, as those involved in the movement pushed forward toward their goals, it behooved them to give "due consideration to the homosexual question when it discusses sexual, ethical, economic, and general human relationships."[91]

The speech was published in Hirschfeld's *Yearbook* and given again to a meeting of the League for Human Rights, a small anarchist and pacifist group founded in Berlin by the publisher of *The Struggle* (*Der Kampf*), Johannes Holzmann (who normally wrote under his pseudonym, Senna Hoy).[92] Holzmann, who had also come to accept homosexual rights as a logical extension of anarchism, had heard the speech the first time at the WhK's congress and had commented on it favorably in a review for *The New Magazine* (*Das neue Magazin*). The audience, Holzmann wrote, "did not expect such quiet and factual explanations" from Sprüngli, whom they apparently knew of from her pen name. Pleasantly surprised by "the likable speaker," they rewarded her with "much applause." Not everyone liked what she had to say, though. Not surprisingly, at least one conservative writer attacked the "shamelessly cheeky agitations" of such lesbian feminists. And, in turn, several prominent leaders of the moderate wing of the women's movement came to blame her for associating feminism with lesbianism.[93]

More unexpected, though, was the reaction that came from within the WhK. As this was 1904, and many masculinists had not yet followed Benedict Friedlaender in seceding from the organization, several people in the audience listening to the speech at the Hotel Prinz Albrecht found much to object to. Masculinists took issue with her reliance on the language and theory of biologically determined homosexuality. They also did not like the way that she highlighted the cultural character of the women's movement; as Christiane Leidinger has pointed out, this focus contradicted Friedlaender's assumption that "women were unable to accomplish any cultural contribution."[94]

Sprüngli apparently failed to convince many in the women's movement that homosexuality was a major issue for them. Instead, what really made a difference to women's willingness to ally with the homosexual movement was the Eulenburg scandal, which for the first time created a real possibility that lesbianism might be made illegal. The origin of Paragraph 175 in much older sodomy laws meant that the law was oriented to sexual penetration, thereby ruling out lesbian sex. Since 1902, however, there had been some discussion of revising the entire criminal code, which opened up public debate about the future of Paragraph 175. Many police officials at the time found the law difficult to enforce since getting a conviction required proving that someone had committed sex that resembled coitus—in German, *beischlafsähnlich*—normally meaning either anal or oral sex. A great deal of sexual activity was not punishable, including mutual masturbation and having sex between a partner's thighs. The WhK, naturally, argued that the solution was simply to get rid of the law entirely, but in the wake of the Eulenburg affair many public figures became convinced of the dangers of homosexuality. Even some progressive-minded legal experts who had previously signed the WhK's petition now changed their minds.[95] In the process of considering whether to change the language of the law, the possibility was introduced that female homosexuality might also be included. Wolfgang Mittermaier, a law professor at the University of Giessen, insisted that the "danger for family life and youth is the same. Such cases are on the increase in modern times."[96] This announcement quickly got the attention of many women in the German women's movement, and of Dr. Helene Stöcker in particular.[97]

Stöcker was the leader of a relatively new group in the German women's movement, the League for the Protection of Motherhood (*Bund für Mutterschutz*). This organization, founded in 1904, was situated somewhat uncomfortably between the socialist and middle-class wings of the women's movement. The league attracted a lot of supporters from those who did not fit well into either category—too concerned with individual women's rights to feel at home in the League of German Women's Organizations, but also often too independent-minded to fit in with the working-class, male-dominated SPD. Helene Stöcker was a perfect example. One of the first women to enter the University of Berlin, in 1896, and eventually to earn a PhD (from a Swiss university in 1902), Stöcker was influenced by the philosopher Friedrich Nietzsche, from whom she took away a belief in self-determination and personal freedom. She was also a strong supporter of pacifism. In the League for the Protection of Motherhood, she found herself among many other left-liberals—men and women—who wanted to push for legal equality in marriage, easier access to divorce, legalization of "free unions" between unmarried men and women, and improving the status of single women.[98] They were not, however, so radical as to reject the assumption that women had a calling to be mothers. Like many of the more conservative women in the wider movement, they "hailed motherhood as the highest individual fulfillment and the mother-child bond as the most sacred of ties," in the words of one historian, Ann Taylor Allen.[99]

This interest in motherhood led the organization to also develop an interest in sexual behavior more generally. Responding to turn-of-the-century anxiety about declining birth rates and newly available statistics on infant mortality rates, some in the organization turned to eugenics, with its promise of racial health through sexual selection.[100] Even more important, though, was the need to redefine the understanding of motherhood so that it fit the changed conditions of the modern era.[101] The most vulnerable children, they argued, were illegitimate ones, left without proper support by overworked mothers and a hypocritical state that refused to recognize them.[102] What Germany needed to do, then, was to rework the laws that discriminated against single women and their children. This would not be so easy, however, in a country in which traditional Christian attitudes toward sexuality still ruled. Such conventional morality needed to be replaced by a "new ethic" based on the "affirmation of life and all its healthy instincts."[103] This new ethic would affirm all forms of sexuality, even homosexuality, among both married and unmarried partners.

Along with many other male sexologists, Hirschfeld joined the League for the Protection of Motherhood and soon contributed several articles to its chief journal.[104] He also invited Stöcker to make a contribution to his new *Journal of Sexual Science.* Stöcker was not a lesbian, but she was clearly sympathetic with the cause of the homosexual movement. In an article published not long after the Eulenburg scandal, she chastised the German government: "I find it indefensible and hypocritical that seduction to homosexual acts is regarded as criminal, while the seduction of a woman, which can ruin her entire life, is still regarded as honorable."[105]

It was not until 1910 that the two movements began to move toward one another. During this year, the Reichstag agreed to consider a preliminary draft for a suggested new criminal code (known as E1909) put forward by the government. It included a reworded Paragraph 175 that not only made enforcement easier but also broadened the statute to include lesbian acts. In view of what would be a real setback to their movement, the WhK worked consciously to build important bridges with the women's movement. In response to feminist criticism that the leadership of the WhK was entirely male, the organization's general assembly voted on April 30, 1910, to include two women on the executive committee for the first time: the writer Toni Schwabe and the police officer Gertrud Topf.[106] Stöcker did her part as well. In 1911 Stöcker, along with several other women in the League for the Protection of Motherhood, joined the WhK.[107] In February two meetings of the league were held in which Hirschfeld and Stöcker addressed the possible revisions to Paragraph 175. Soon afterward, Stöcker published an article in her magazine, *The New Generation* (*Die neue Generation*), in which she declared Paragraph 175 an absurd law and a social evil. She pointed out that many single women might accidentally find themselves falling victim to the law. Women who failed to find suitable spouses or whose jobs made it impossible to get married often turned to each other for companionship or simply to make ends meet. If Paragraph 175 were revised, such friendships could easily fall under suspicion, the women involved eventually landing in prison.[108]

The partnership was finalized at the League for the Protection of Motherhood's first international congress, held in Dresden in September 1911. Stöcker gave the opening address, and then Hirschfeld spoke to the crowd. As one of Hirschfeld's biographers described, Hirschfeld made a powerful case that the two movements had a common goal: "Love had been misunderstood through the prejudices of the Church, and had been treated only sentimentally by novelists. But science, he said, could put the record straight and give a realistic view of love."[109] The conference was well attended; there were visitors from England, Scandinavia, Italy, France, Russia, and even the United States. Many prominent names were there, including Iwan Bloch. And, appropriately for the occasion, most of the talks were given by women.[110]

The partnership between the WhK and League for the Protection of Motherhood proved to be a successful one, lasting until 1933. In 1911 the two groups carried on an energetic campaign together. They found prominent allies in several legal experts who countered the government's proposal by putting together an alternative draft of the law that punished homosexual acts only when they were committed with minors or prostitutes. They received some assistance from moderates such as the right-liberal politician Wilhelm Kahl, who very much opposed extending the law to women, even if he backed away from abolishing Paragraph 175 altogether at that time. Such moderates worried about the suspicions and even blackmail that innocent single women might fall prey to. There was also some concern about the effect on public morality that talking about the sexual practices of lesbians in court would have, since the proceeding would then be reported on in the newspapers.[111]

The government, for its part, hoped that new elections would secure passage of the E1909 revisions, but in January 1912 the socialist SPD won an enormous victory, gaining control of 34 percent of the votes nationally. In September the Law Reform Commission voted unanimously against the changes, returning the previous language of Paragraph 175 to the draft. It was a victory of sorts, though a strange one for a group of feminists and sex reformers. The law against male homosexuality was maintained, though with the earlier restricted language. The government justified the unequal treatment of men and women as being maintained largely to keep female homosexuality from acquiring an even larger presence in the public sphere.[112]

HOMOSEXUALITY AND THE YOUTH MOVEMENT

The alliance between the women's movement and the critics of Paragraph 175 had found one supporter among the masculinists in Adolf Brand's circle of friends as early as 1903. In the June 1903 issue of *The Special One,* Edwin Bab had suggested that the "women's movement and male culture are not opposites; they are absolutely necessary complements for a practicable solution to the sexual problem. . . . No longer will woman alone control the taste of man and require his love; she will also no longer be his slave, but rather his companion with equal rights, his equal."[113] Bab's sympathy for the feminist movement was unusual for a masculinist, though. Normally, masculinist arguments were littered with misogynist language, and they sometimes explicitly expressed disdain for women's political claims. In his *Renaissance of Uranian Love,* Benedict Friedlaender clearly devalued women and their social roles. The family, portrayed as an environment that was thoroughly saturated by primitive desires and feminine ideals, was defined as a potential danger to men since it distracted them from their critical political duties and cultural calling.[114] Any claim that women might make to equality was laughable at best: "Nothing is so overwhelmingly stupid and such great nonsense."[115]

Rejecting an alliance with the women's movement, many masculinists turned instead to the youth movement, hoping that it might offer a way of disseminating their vision of "manly culture" to the wider German society. The youth movement, beginning with the appearance of the Wandervogel ("Bird of Passage" or "Wandering Bird"), was a relatively new presence in the nation. It started as a small study group of teenage schoolboys around Berlin who took to wandering the German countryside on Sundays and holidays at the end of the 1890s. In 1901 Karl Fischer created a formal structure for the group, and soon other chapters of the Wandervogel began to appear elsewhere in the country. In 1904 the Wandervogel began to split into several rival groups, each with its own slightly different philosophy, policies, and leadership structure. Around 1909 they were joined by a branch of the

British scouting movement. This proliferation would lay the groundwork for the explosion of the youth groups that appeared after the First World War. By the 1920s, the German youth movement would include diverse religious organizations and would represent many different political perspectives.[116]

Even as the German youth movement grew, the various Wandervogel organizations continued to be important, and their philosophy, very much influenced by German nationalism and late nineteenth-century Romanticism, left an imprint on many of the groups. A key role was played by Karl Fischer, a "brooding, overbearing" young man who nevertheless was a "born leader."[117] Under his influence, the youth movement became strongly marked by Romantic themes and attitudes. Fischer portrayed himself as carrying on the legacy of the wandering medieval scholars known as Bacchants. His fascination with medieval imagery and customs quickly spread to other members. Under his leadership, the organizations began to idealize nature and the simple rural life, seeing them as an antidote to the modern, materialistic civilization around them. And like other German Romantics, they were strong supporters of the artistic impulses in humankind. They were especially fond of the musical arts. Indeed, one of the most important contributions of the Wandervogel was in the field of music. Members helped revive an interest in German folksongs, collecting old songs and having them published for a new audience.[118]

Today the interest in folk music reminds us a little of the 1960s student movement. And there were other similarities. The young men in the early Wandervogel were united by a sense of rebellion directed at their parents and the prevailing social norms. As the historian George Mosse once wrote, many members saw the organization as a path to liberation from "school, parents, authoritarianism, and the whole order of bourgeois mores, prejudices, and hypocrisies."[119] Some grew their hair long; others enjoyed the effect that big, flamboyant hats could have. Many chose to flout nineteenth-century norms by simply leaving their knees bare and their heads hatless.[120] In many of the boys, this rebellion could promote independence and the feeling that they were becoming men. They believed, according to the historian Elizabeth Heineman, that the movement "would help them to escape the fate of the men who populated their bourgeois world," generally seen as "weak and pathetic."[121] Ideas about masculinity thus became an important element in the way that boys understood their participation in the movement. They saw the organization as a group of independent spirits who "recognized, admired, challenged and nurtured each other." While strengthening "their bodies and spirits against the harsh natural elements," they "sustained the potency of their souls with intense friendships with each other."[122]

The influence of German Romanticism and the attention paid to male bonding meant that the youth movement had a fair amount in common with the masculinists associated with Benedict Friedlaender and Adolf Brand. The artist Hugo Höppener, better known by his pseudonym, Fidus, was an important connection. A symbolic illustrator whose style was clearly influenced by the ornamentalism and sexuality of the Vienna secession movement and art nouveau more broadly, Fidus hoped to "transmit the quintessence of life" and "communicate that which was beyond the senses," as the historian George Mosse once observed.[123] Fidus was inspired not only by the neopaganism common among many German Romantics of his day, but also by theosophy and Buddhist mysticism. His images appeared in a range of journals around the turn of the century, including nudist magazines, youth movement periodicals, and Brand's *Special One.*

The symbolism and eclectic nature of Fidus's works made it easy for many different groups to see what they wanted in these illustrations.[124] His subjects were often young, and their strength and vitality were clearly attractive to many young people in the Wandervogel. Masculinist homosexuals, on the other hand, appreciated the attention that Fidus paid to the male physique, generally shown nude or seminude. As one author wrote in *The Special One,* "Every line that Fidus draws contains longing, every nude chasteness. . . . He likes to draw juvenile figures with fluttering hair, who longingly storm the peak of a mountain and beseechingly stretch out their hands to the heavens and stammer their burning wishes for recognition. . . . They are ethereal like a lovely scent—like the tender scent of a lily."[125] And both groups found the Romantic implications of the images appealing, since they frequently showed humans in commune with nature, as in his most famous painting, *Prayer to the Light.*[126]

It is not known how many homosexuals became involved with the Wandervogel, but at least two became controversial figures in the decade before the First World War: Willie Jansen and Hans Blüher. In 1906 Jansen became the leader of one of the largest youth organizations in Germany, the Old Wandervogel (*Alt-Wandervogel*). He was also a prominent member of the masculinist GdE and a good friend of Benedict Friedlaender (whom Jansen would join in 1908 in seceding from the WhK). Like other masculinists, Jansen advocated "Hellenic" bonds between older and younger men. Such an attitude fit well, it turned out, with the organization of the Old Wandervogel, which tended to emphasize male beauty, deep friendships among members, and the charismatic role of the leader. Jansen's enthusiasm for Greek ideals and everything modern—which he associated with freedom from Christian dogma and a return to natural living—did run counter to Karl Fischer's love of the Middle

Ages, but by the time Jansen joined, many members were beginning to tire of Fischer's tendency to want to control everything and everybody in the movement. Jansen, on the other hand, "accepted every individual as he was, giving him the right to exist and live his life as his nature demanded." [127]

Jansen's appearance in the Old Wandervogel coincided with a power struggle in the group that yielded a new constitution for the organization and ultimately drove Fischer out. "The youth needed a hero," reflected one of Jansen's devotees, Hans Blüher, and for those looking for a new charismatic figure to take the place of Fischer, Jansen seemed a worthy candidate. [128] His "masterful vitality knocked everybody over, and nothing seemed to get in his way." [129] Having freed himself from his Catholic upbringing and distanced himself from his aristocratic heritage, he became the center of a small circle of free spirits who lived an open-minded, easygoing life. His connections to prominent intellectual figures of the day—Benedict Friedlaender and John Henry Mackay, but also the socialist economist and ethical philosopher Eugen Dühring—helped open many young minds to new ideas. "One can imagine," Hans Blüher would later reminisce, "what an impression it made on a young man of my age, lusting as I was with every fiber of my being for spiritual activity of the mind, to find myself in the presence of such society." [130]

Jansen became deeply involved in a much wider debate about the rules and the character of the youth movement. Should young people be permitted to drink alcohol? Should women be admitted to the group? Within larger discussions about proper behavior, Jansen had his own favorite cause: he passionately advocated the virtues of nude bathing and Greek-style gymnastics. This position raised not a few eyebrows, and soon some of Jansen's opponents were asking questions. Then the Eulenburg scandal hit the country, and the witch hunt began. Jansen, it was pointed out, had a number of friendships with men who were strongly suspected of being homosexual. Journalists caught wind of this, and a press attack began, pointing out that the police suspected that Jansen's studio had been used to make pornographic pictures. The suspicions were never verified, but this did not stop Jansen's enemies from making their own accusations. One came to the Old Wandervogel's board of directors claiming to know about a diary kept by a young member that proved that Jansen had had a sexual encounter with the boy. The leadership of the group began what Blüher described as an "inquisition," looking for boys who had had sex with other members, or for any evidence that there were other homosexuals in the group. [131]

The press did not wait for the results. Within no time, newspapers began to call the Old Wandervogel the "pederasty club"; one even suggested that the entire youth movement had been created by a bunch of grown men who were seeking an opportunity to seduce boys.[132] Jansen was driven out of his leadership post. Even some of his supporters began to abandon him, pointing out that even if Jansen was innocent, his reputation was forever stained, which threatened to leave the entire movement forever mired in controversy. Some boys worried that the scandal might make it difficult to get a job later if it became known that they had connections with Jansen. Jansen was forced to resign from the movement in 1910. The Old Wandervogel, which had previously refused to follow other youth organizations by accepting women into the fold, quickly changed course and began to establish female groups, hoping to play down the stigma of homosexuality.[133]

HANS BLÜHER AND HIS THEORIES OF EROS

Hans Blüher (Figure 6) was intimately involved in the Jansen affair, and his attempt to work through the episode led him to write a book that itself was destined to become the center of much controversy. Blüher had been recruited by Karl Fischer himself into one of the earliest Wandervogel groups in 1902. Fourteen years old at the time, Blüher found the initiation a life-changing moment: "On this day, the happiness of my youth began."[134] He developed many close relationships, gradually rose up through the ranks, and eventually entered into the cadre of Willie Jansen's followers. Under the influence of Fischer and Jansen, he began to understand his activities as a kind of primordial rebellion by which the German nation as a whole might eventually be regenerated and purified.[135] After the Jansen controversy, he left the Old Wandervogel, taking up his studies at the University of Berlin. He remained preoccupied with the organization and the meaning it might have for his country, however, watching sadly as the youth movement was racked by further scandals and divided by controversies. He began to write a history of the movement, which by 1912 had grown to include two volumes.

As he was working through the last of the material, he also happened to get involved with a study group reading Sigmund Freud's theories of sexuality. Freud's views on sexuality left a deep impression on Hans Blüher. In a later autobiography, he remembered "flying through" Freud's *Interpretation of Dreams* and having the whole mysterious relationship between the charismatic leader and his followers become clear to him. He quickly connected Freud's ideas, which seemed to explain so well many of the feelings he had had and the relationships that he had developed in the youth movement, with the ideas of Friedlaender that he had been introduced to by Jansen. In particular, Freud's ideas of sublimation seemed to illuminate Friedlaender's belief that the "men's hero" played a key role in the development of civilization.

FIGURE 6 **HANS BLÜHER**

Blüher was an early member of the Wandervogel youth movement and became famous in 1912 for his book *The Wandervogel Movement as Erotic Phenomenon*, which used Freudian psychoanalytic theories of erotic attraction to explain the success of the movement. In the years leading up to World War I, he became one of the leading masculinist theorists.

Blüher quickly dashed off another book, *The Wandervogel Movement as Erotic Phenomenon* (*Die deutsche Wandervogelbewegung als erotisches Phänomen*). It argued that the strength of relationships formed in the Wandervogel was caused by the sublimated sexuality that infused them. In his first two volumes, he had already speculated about the role of erotic attraction in the movement, especially in the affection felt by many boys for the leaders of the group. Many boys, he insisted, felt a kind of love for the leaders that might be compared to the love between men and women.[136] In the third book on the movement, he developed this kernel of an idea into a full theory. In a sense, he admitted, sexual "inversion" was central to the movement. The group was founded and led by men who were little interested in women and instead had dedicated their lives and energy toward young men and their development.[137] They exhibited an "antique" character—personalities that might have been more at home during the golden age of Greece, when the love of one man for another could be freely expressed. This idea, however, did not mean that they expressed this affection physically. Instead, the Wandervogel allowed for a healthy and necessary suppression and sublimation of male attraction toward one another. In this transformed state, erotic attraction deepened friendships between males and increased group cohesion. The group members would sublimate homosexual desire in the form of surplus energy that would contribute to the immense creativity of the male-bonding community.[138]

In an essay published a year later, Blüher tried to construct a bridge between this Freudian-inspired view of homosexuality and the theories of Magnus Hirschfeld. Inverts, he argued, might be divided into three types: the effeminate homosexual, or "inverted *Weibling*" as he called them; the "men's heroes" (*Männerhelden*) that Benedict Friedlaender had praised as the saviors of civilization; and then a third type, the "latent invert," that was exemplified by many of the members of the Wandervogel movement, who suppressed their feelings and channeled them into other pursuits. Although relying on both Hirschfeld and Freud, Blüher differed from both in believing that inversion was a widespread phenomenon, and that many people fell into one of the three categories. Inversion was not a result of a disturbed maturation, he insisted. And it certainly was not a minority issue, a condition of concern only to an unfortunate few and their doctors. "Men's heroes" played a critical role in civilization, whereas "latent inverts" were some of the most creative scientists and artists in any given culture. Blüher was sympathetic with Hirschfeld's and Weininger's concept that most people might embody a mixture of various gendered characteristics, and that very few fell at the extreme of "all male" or "all female." He insisted, however, that sexual attraction was not a gendered characteristic. A man who loved another man was in no way tainted by effeminacy. Blüher clearly had a preference for the "men's hero," but he did not disparage effeminate homosexuals. Actually, he found them "fascinating," in part because they remind us of our universal bisexual nature. What's more, none of the types was sick. In contrast to Freud and the other practitioners of psychoanalysis of the time, he did not believe that inversion was something that could or should be healed through therapy.[139]

Blüher's next and arguably most important work, *The Role of Eroticism in Male Society* (*Die Rolle der Erotik in der männlichen Gesellschaft*), represented an effort to extend his earlier ideas into the areas of social and political theory. Published in two volumes in 1917 and 1919, it argued that the state was not simply rooted in economic activity, as liberals and Marxists alike believed; nor was it merely a cultural phenomenon, a by-product of what the philosopher G. W. F. Hegel called the "national spirit" (*Volksgeist*). Instead, Blüher believed, the state is fundamentally rooted in man's erotic drive. He acknowledged Freudian psychoanalysis as offering a fundamental reconceptualization of our psyche and the role that sexuality played within it. He went far beyond Freud, however, in suggesting that Eros is much more than simply an instinctual drive. In fact, he believed that Plato had been much closer to the truth when he had suggested that Eros is a kind of metaphysical force. "Eros," Blüher wrote, "is not sexuality; instead, it is that which gives sexuality its meaning."[140]

Besides Eros, the other major metaphysical principle is Logos—logic and rationality. Both forces are engaged in a "blood feud" with one another. Logos propels man to search for universals in his quest for knowledge. Eros, on the other hand, causes man to fall in love with the particular. Logos unites, while Eros divides. Logos yearns for the eternal, while Eros appreciates that which passes away.[141] Nevertheless, both are necessary for civilization. Art, in particular, requires both principles to work together. In poetry, for example, "Eros represents the sound, Logos the meaning."[142] Women, he believed, are indeed slaves to Eros. In the family, women play out their only real social role of ensuring the reproduction of the human species.[143] Men, on the other hand, have the ability to bring Eros and Logos into a creative synthesis. Through the social bonds that men create between each other, the human race vaults above the purely natural into a higher spiritual level. Tapping into the erotic energies buried deep in the human psyche, artists give us works of profound beauty. Soldiers demonstrate the highest acts of bravery and self-sacrifice. And, ultimately, men fall in love with the charismatic "men's hero." This sublimated form of erotic attraction, he suggested, is the main social bond that allows the state to adhere together. It enables men to perform those selfless acts that keep society functioning.[144]

Blüher's works were enormously controversial for suggesting that eroticism lay at the root of male relationships. Even if this eroticism was sublimated, it was not an aspect of masculine society that most middle-class men, raised in a Victorian world in which sexual topics were dealt with carefully and in hushed tones, were willing to acknowledge, let alone accept. Men were supposed to be rational and controlled. At least as long as they had the proper education and upbringing, they were not supposed to lose control to irrational or so-called womanly urges. His writings were accused of being a sign of the degenerate times, the product of a mind that had fallen prey to the "Jewish" ideas of Freud and his followers.[145] Nevertheless, they hit a nerve and attracted the attention of many important intellectuals and other prominent figures. For some young readers, as the historian Claudia Bruns argues, Blüher's ideas "liberated them from the chains of pure intellect, of teleology and subordination to economic rationalism."[146] And after World War I, his books would popularize the masculinist idea of the male-bonding community (*Männerbund*), a concept that would appeal to many looking for a way to unlock the hidden energies of the psyche and the dormant strength of the German nation. Such energies would be badly needed, Blüher's fans thought, if Germany was to be resurrected from military collapse and economic ruin.

The many scandals of the early twentieth century had not helped the homosexual movement at all. The Eulenburg affair left a strong impression with the public that homosexuals were a serious problem for national strength and state security. It contributed to establishing a stereotype of the homosexual enemy of the state (*Staatsfeind*) that Hitler would later exploit to help rid the Nazi movement of an important rival, Ernst Röhm. The Jansen affair had reinforced long-standing suspicions that homosexuals were a real danger for young people, perhaps hidden away in secret locations. There had been a few victories. An important alliance had been made with a key organization in the women's movement; together, they had helped stop the government from passing a stricter version of Paragraph 175. The campaign, however, had diverted the WhK from its main goal, namely, full repeal of the law. The victory of the socialist SPD in 1912 offered some hope for the future, but in general many of the last meetings of the WhK before the coming of war labored under a mood of discouragement.[147]

As news came into the country of the assassination of the Austrian Archduke Franz Ferdinand in late June 1914, and then the saber rattling began in July, the minds of most of the members of the WhK were no doubt elsewhere. Like many other Germans, homosexuals were generally caught up by the patriotic mood of August 1914 and rushed to volunteer for the army. A few, in fact, returned from immigration abroad using forged passports to have the opportunity to serve, thereby proving their patriotism and social worth. In a later book, *The Sexual History of the World War* (*Sittengeschichte des Ersten Weltkrieg*), Hirschfeld even told the story of a few women whose masculine appearance and behavior allowed them to be enrolled by deceiving volunteer agents.[148] By April 1915 the WhK's newsletter announced that hundreds of members, representing over half of the group's membership, were serving in the military. At least a few gay men felt that they had found a degree of acceptance among their fellow soldiers. The emphasis on "comradeship" might even have offered cover for a few homosexual relationships to develop.[149]

With the high casualties of the war, the authorities were not that eager to patrol for homosexuals in the military's ranks. It is also possible, as Jason Crouthamel suggests in *An Intimate History of the Front*, that they were concerned that investigations would damage the image of the military and the soldiers who served. There were some cases of Paragraph 175 involving soldiers, but prosecutors seem to have focused on instances of sexual assault or coercion, as well as on cases that created civil disturbances on the home front.[150] For soldiers with strong military records, judges and prosecutors were "willing to sweep the crimes under the rug once that disruption had been contained."[151] Cases involving consenting adults that did not involve a suicide or some other event that would draw public scrutiny were relatively rare.

After suffering through years of disastrous offensives on the Western Front and economic strangulation at the hands of a highly effective British naval blockade, Germany finally witnessed military collapse in 1918. A revolution broke out in November, producing a new democratic constitution by the following year. For the homosexual movement, new opportunities quickly appeared, taking advantage of newfound freedoms but also very much building on social and cultural advances that had been made in earlier decades. The historian Peter Gay once described the Weimar era as a period in which "outsiders" were "propelled by history into the inside, for a short, dizzying, fragile moment."[152] Perhaps this explains the fascination that it still holds for many gay men and lesbians. Certainly it was an exciting time in many ways. Gay and lesbian bars flourished in Berlin and many other cities. Homosexual periodicals, for a time at least, were openly sold in public kiosks. Gay men, lesbians, and men and women whom we would identify today as transgender formed clubs on a scale that was unheard of anywhere else around the world. But why did these things happen? Was it because of the revolution? Were the police more tolerant than they had been before? Had Germany become more tolerant as a nation in the 1920s? All of these are compelling questions that will need to be examined in the following chapters.

CHAPTER 3

The Growth of Urban Gay Scenes

CHAPTER SUMMARY

This chapter describes the growth of Germany's gay scenes in Berlin, Hamburg, Cologne, and elsewhere, which had started in the nineteenth century but reached full bloom in the 1920s. By the Weimar era, these scenes included not only a variety of bars, restaurants, and other meeting places for gay men and lesbians, but also a growing network of social clubs and even a surprisingly successful publishing industry.

OVERVIEW

The Weimar Republic—the name of the democratic government that was born in Germany after the disastrous First World War and the fall of the Kaiser's regime in late 1918—became famous for its experimental modernism and its relative openness with regard to sexuality. The gay scenes of Berlin, Hamburg, Cologne, and elsewhere contributed considerably to the country's reputation for permissiveness. These scenes included not only a variety of bars, restaurants, and other meeting places for gay men and lesbians, but also a growing network of social clubs and even a surprisingly successful publishing industry. These scenes were not born in 1919, however; in fact, they have a history stretching back into the nineteenth century. This chapter examines not only the various dimensions of Germany's gay scenes, but also the numerous social, economic, and cultural factors that contributed to their growth. Despite police efforts to watch and limit the areas that gay men and lesbians gradually made their own, Germany's gay scenes expanded steadily, offering opportunities to establish relationships, fashion identities, and pursue political projects. By the middle of the 1920s, many of the social clubs that had arisen from the social networks of the gay scenes were united in a new national organization, the Federation for Human Rights (BfM), under the leadership of the publisher Friedrich Radszuweit.

KEY TERMS
Claire Waldoff; Weimar Republic; Friedrich Radszuweit; German homosexual magazines; homosexuality in Weimar Germany

Whisnant, Clayton J.
Queer Identities and Politics in Germany: A History 1880–1945
dx.doi.org/10.17312/harringtonparkpress/2016.08.qipg.003
© Harrington Park Press, LLC, New York, NY 10011

FIGURE 7 **CLAIRE WALDOFF**

Waldoff was a prominent cabaret singer in Weimar-era Berlin. She was also a regular at many of Berlin's lesbian cafés and nightclubs. This chapter describes the growth of Germany's gay scenes in Berlin, Hamburg, Cologne, and elsewhere, which had started in the middle of the nineteenth century but reached full bloom in the 1920s. Source: Bundesarchiv, Bild 183-R07978. Photographer unknown

In the cabarets of 1920s Berlin, the singer Claire Waldoff (Figure 7) was one of the biggest hits. Having gotten her start back in 1908 at the Roland von Berlin, one of the most popular cabarets of the day, she stood out among the normally glamorous-looking performers who graced this establishment's stage.[1] To look at, she was rather plain: short and stocky, with thick red hair, and often unpretentiously dressed. Her performances were also quite simple, although the stanzas might be punctuated with a comic dance. Her voice, though, was unmistakable—a little raspy, perhaps, with its harshly rolled r's, but quite expressive nevertheless. From her first step on Berlin's stages, the audience loved her.[2] By the 1920s she had established quite a reputation, performing sometimes at multiple cabarets in a single night. She sang much-loved German folksongs and also originals, often distinguished by their satirical or comical content. Although born in the western Ruhr region of the country, she had picked up the Berlin dialect very easily. She "personified the image of the sassy kid from Berlin," observes the historian Claudia Schoppmann.[3] Indeed, she loved that city, with "its special atmosphere, its vivacity and curt character," as Waldoff put it.[4] Her songs, full of Berlin slang, spoke to the city's common person. They dealt with everyday worries but also were full of optimism and passion. Like the typical Berliner, Waldoff was dry, telling jokes in a deadpan manner.

When not onstage, she became a regular visitor at Berlin's lesbian cafés and nightclubs. She had met her lifelong love, Olga von Roeder, a baroness from the southwestern region of Swabia, during the First World War. They were both members of the Pyramid Ladies' Club, which met regularly in one of the lesbian bars. As horn players performed "the forbidden club songs," famous artists and models sat about, along with "beautiful, elegant women who wanted to get to know the other side of Berlin, the shady side." In the crowd there were even "simple, love-struck office workers."[5] One of Waldoff's friends was Marlene Dietrich, whom she had gotten to know long before Dietrich became famous. Among such a tolerant crowd, she was quite comfortable talking about her love for her "Olly."[6] Onstage, she was more reticent about her identity. As one scholar of cabaret notes, Waldoff mostly "sang heterosexual songs, about her boyfriend or her husband, but often mocking him or ironically lamenting her dependence on him."[7] At times, though, her true sexuality might be hinted at. In "Hannalore" she sang of the "most beautiful child from Hallesches Tor, that sweet, lovely thing with the prettiest bobbed head." Hannalore "wears a tuxedo and a necktie, and always a monocle hanging by a silk cord. She boxes and foxes, golfs and taps. And just between you and me, she cheats! Especially in May. And someone even told me she has a fiancé and a bride?!? But I do digress."[8] In other songs she told stories written from a male point of view. Many of her pieces were known for their sexual innuendo—admittedly standard for 1920s-era cabaret. She was a little more direct than most singers, though, and when something was too risqué to say out loud, she would substitute nonsense syllables, said in such a way that everyone in the audience knew exactly what was meant.[9]

Metropolitan, sexually aware and free, and ready to take advantage of all the excitement that modernity had to offer, Waldoff very much represented a Berlin that came into its own after the First World War.[10] The war had, of course, been a traumatic event for Germany. Before the war, the country had been widely perceived as a rising power—a nation whose military was almost universally recognized as the most formidable on the Continent, whose industrial economy was keeping pace with the United States' and rapidly catching up with England's, and whose reputation for learning and scientific achievement was admired around the world. The Germans had prided themselves on being both the defenders of traditional German *Kultur* and, simultaneously, at the forefront of historical progress.[11] Then, almost inconceivably, Germany lost the war. As an armistice was called in late 1918, years of deprivation and misery among soldiers and citizens alike led to revolution. The SPD took control of the situation, declaring Germany to be a republic and quickly writing a new, truly democratic constitution.

The young Weimar Republic faced serious difficulties in the first few years of its existence. Land was lost to France and Poland; the military was cut down to a small fraction of its previous size. The economy was crippled by unemployment, massive strike waves, and inflation that by late 1923 made the currency nearly worthless. Politically, the young democracy faced challenges from both communists on the left and authoritarian nationalists on the right. Amazingly, the Weimar Republic survived this turbulent period, and during the mid-1920s the government temporarily stabilized the situation. Even in the midst of the difficult postwar period, however, there were many people swept up by the revolutionary mood. With the SPD in charge, socialism, with its emphasis on equality and social experimentation, seems to have triumphed. Democratic freedoms were quickly expanding, as women received the right to vote for the first time and workers flexed their political muscle as never before. Although many of the cultural changes that took place in this period had their roots in prewar developments, they acquired much greater attention and a newfound standing in a world visibly shaken by war. Social observers and politicians across the political spectrum were united in the belief that the First World War had ushered in a "new era" when it came to morality.[12] Older values had lost their hold on society, and many went in search of new ideas, new forms, new language, and even a new foundation on which to build the modern world.[13]

For many observers, radical and conservative alike, Berlin's gay scene epitomized a world in transition. Clubs full of men wearing powder and rouge as well as short-haired women dressed in tuxedoes offered images of a world seemingly turned upside down. For the general public, this world was bewildering—and quite possibly terrifying. For Germany's gay men and lesbians, though, Berlin represented promise. Its gay scenes offered exciting places to hunt for love and happiness. Christopher Isherwood, a British writer who moved to Berlin in 1930 to spend a couple of years teaching English and exploring the city's bohemian underworld, put it simply enough: "Berlin meant boys."[14]

Isherwood—whose short stories based on his stay in Berlin eventually became the basis for the 1972 film *Cabaret,* with Liza Minnelli—might be the best-remembered champion of this side of the city, but in the early twentieth century he was not alone in believing that Germany's capital city offered homosexual men some of the best opportunities available for friendships, romance, and sex. In fact, as early as the turn of the century, Berlin's gay scene was attracting such notoriety that it frequently was mentioned in tourist literature and other published portraits of the city. Most of these works were written with an eye for sensation. Even before the First World War, these works were lifting up the city's gay scene as proof of the evils of urban life and the dangers of modernity; in them, Berlin became the country's Sodom and Gomorrah put together, a sure sign of the land's degeneracy. But such descriptions did not cause people to avoid the locations of the gay scene. In fact, visitors who wanted to see something unusual might be taken to see the city's gay balls, which Hirschfeld observed were "a Berlin specialty in their kind and duration."[15]

Berlin's gay scene was the most famous, but many other cities developed their own scenes. Like so many of the examples of "modernity" that we tend to associate with Weimar Germany, they were the products of a long historical development that can be traced well into the previous century. They had crystallized in the midst of a country being unified by Bismarck and Kaiser Wilhelm I, finding a space for themselves among the other commercial entertainments of late nineteenth-century cities. Their growth was also promoted, though, by the newspapers, magazines, tourist guides, and other print material of the era, which attracted attention to the scenes. Despite efforts by the police to watch and limit the areas that gay men and lesbians gradually made their own, the gay scenes of Germany expanded steadily, offering opportunities to establish relationships, fashion identities, and pursue political projects.

THE ORIGIN OF GERMANY'S GAY SCENES

Berlin's gay scene is not Europe's oldest by any stretch. London's most probably deserves that title, since by the early eighteenth century one could already find there taverns known as "Molly Houses," where effeminate young men, dressed up as women, were sought out as sexual partners. Still, in Berlin there are hints of informal circles of homosexual aristocrats and other so-called *Warme* (as gay men in Germany were called through much of the nineteenth century) dating to the late 1700s. In the 1830s, a young Bismarck, studying to be a lawyer at the University of Berlin, investigated a network of associations centered in Berlin that brought together men interested in "unnatural vice." As he recalled in his autobiography, the group had a complex organization that brought together members from all classes and even "reached into the highest circles." His efforts to prosecute the group came to nothing, though, which led him to suspect that there was a powerful noble with some influence in the Ministry of Justice who helped protect its members from criminal persecution.[16] Male prostitution could also be found in the city. By the 1840s a report on prostitution written by the police inspector mentioned the chestnut grove next to the choral academy building in the city's largest park, the Tiergarten, as a popular location for male prostitutes to meet their clients.[17]

Berlin was still a rather small city at the time, its population around only 400,000, whereas Paris's population had already reached one million and London's was fast approaching two million. Nevertheless, by the 1840s Berlin was emerging as the center of a Germany that was rapidly modernizing and industrializing. As the capital of the state of Prussia, the city had established itself at the forefront of international developments during the years of the Napoleonic wars with the foundation of the University of Berlin, the first modern, research-intensive university, which soon was home to some of Europe's most important names in mathematics, medicine, theology, philosophy, and history.[18] Then, in the 1820s and 1830s, Prussia organized a customs union with most of the other German states that had helped promote trade and manufacturing. At the same time, Prussia's ambitious and energetic Ministry of Commerce worked to expand Berlin's economic role by importing technology, organizing trade fairs, and financing city improvements.[19] Soon the region's first railroad lines were being laid, while the iron and coal industries expanded their production at a healthy rate.[20]

After the Revolution of 1848, which failed to overthrow the Prussian monarchy but nonetheless produced the state's first constitution, the economy of Germany finally achieved takeoff, as economists might describe it. The western region of the Ruhr became one of Europe's top producers of coal and steel, the latter industry dominated by the famous Krupp family that would eventually produce many of the weapons for two world wars. Railroads, with the help of such companies as Berlin's Borsig works, soon snaked across the region, connecting major cities with many smaller towns and even much of the rural hinterland. The eastern region of Saxony emerged as a top textile producer. Hamburg became one of Europe's biggest ports. And by the time that Germany was politically united in 1871, Berlin's population had shot up to roughly 800,000. By 1905 it had exploded to two million—not yet the size of London, which had grown to have well over six million people by this stage, but getting close to Paris's. The city was officially what the Germans call a *Weltstadt*—a center for international commerce and finance, the capital of a growing empire with colonies in Africa and the south Pacific, and a cosmopolitan city of truly historic stature.

Along with wealth came new forms of commercial development and urban entertainment. The city did remain strongly marked by Prussian militarism and the German monarchy in ways that might draw unfortunate comparisons with the freedoms of Paris, London, or Amsterdam. For those who preferred the history and aristocratic grandeur of Vienna, Berlin seemed a "parvenu capital . . . loud, pushy, and ostentatious."[21] Still, anyone who appreciated the hustle and bustle of modern life found much to appreciate. Enormous department stores such as Wertheim's, Tietz, and KaDeWe brought in goods from around the world. In the skies above the city, one could by 1909 occasionally get a glimpse of the earliest zeppelins flying overhead.[22] The grand, central boulevard, Unter den Linden, lined with its famous linden trees, became known not only for the opera house and imperial monuments but also for its busy grand hotel and restaurants. To the south of Unter den Linden is Leipziger Strasse, one of the chief shopping districts of the city. Bisecting the city north and south is Friedrichstrasse, known also for its shopping, but especially for entertainment (Figure 8).[23] To the west Bismarck helped construct a new boulevard to rival Paris's Champs-Élysées: the Kurfürstendamm, or "Kudamm," as most Berliners know it. Beginning roughly at Berlin's great zoo, today at the very heart of the city, the Kudamm runs southwestwardly, connecting the city with the prosperous suburbs of Charlottenburg, Wilmersdorf, and Grunewald. With a trolley that made it easy to move up and down the street, the Kudamm soon became famous for its shops, coffeehouses, hotels, restaurants, elegant apartment buildings, art galleries, and, after 1909, Europe's largest amusement park, the Lunapark.

For nighttime entertainment, Berlin offered world-renowned opera and a philharmonic orchestra, bars and dance halls for all types, and theaters of many flavors and sizes. The French journalist Jules Huret observed that the

FIGURE 8 **THE CORNER OF BERLIN'S FRIEDRICHSTRASSE
AND LEIPZIGER STRASSE, 1899**

Friedrichstrasse in particular was known for its prostitution, both male and female. Source: Bundesarchiv,
Bild 146-2008-0284. Photographer unknown

"nightlife of Berlin is surprisingly lively. Will it surpass even Paris in this respect? Will we have to find a new location for the contemporary Babylon and Nineveh? The carousing continues all night long on Unter den Linden, on the Friedrichstrasse, and around Potsdamer and Leipziger Platz. Many nightspots don't close at all. After the last guests have left, the clubs are quickly cleaned up and then it's time to start all over again." [24] Prostitution flourished along the busy area of Friedrichstrasse, where women could mill about the shopping arcades and amusement galleries unquestioned for long periods. [25] They were especially thick near the Panopticum, a well-known wax-figure exhibition of that time, since nearby there were stores that specialized in erotic postcards and books. [26] Moreover, what we tend to remember as "Weimar cabaret," with its mixture of song, satire, and short skits, actually got its start in the 1870s, when theaters such as the Bellevue and the Reichshallen switched to variety shows, followed by much larger commercial halls such as the Wintergarten and the Metropol. [27] And while Munich remained the center of the German art world at the turn of the century, Berlin nevertheless began to attract a growing number of avant-garde writers, theater producers, and painters. [28]

In the midst of this nightlife, a gay scene gradually took shape. Even during the economic explosion of the 1860s and early 1870s, the police were aware that certain bars and clubs were attracting groups of homosexuals, though not yet exclusively. Also from this era we have the first reports of homosexual masquerade balls, initially organized informally among circles of interconnected friends, but formalized into regular events by the end of the century. [29] Around 1880 the first bar to cater entirely to homosexuals opened. [30] It was joined by many others over the next three decades, and there were nearly forty by the beginning of World War I. [31] One journalist complained at this time that the "evils" of this city had grown to such an extent that foreigners were now referring to homosexuality as the "German sickness." [32]

Berlin especially earned a reputation for male prostitution. In 1914 the Berlin police department estimated that there were as many as two thousand male prostitutes working in the city. [33] Rent boys (*Strichjungen* in German) could generally be found hanging around the city's major train stations, or along the same streets female prostitutes frequented, such as the Friedrichstrasse. They could also be seen lingering near soldiers' barracks, since not a few of these prostitutes were themselves German soldiers looking for companionship and a little extra income. The most famous cruising spot, though, was the so-called gay path (*Schwuler Weg*), a particular trail through the city's largest park, the Tiergarten, that was well known by the end of the century for attracting male prostitutes and their clients. According to Hirschfeld, there was at that time a homeless homosexual man, often referred to as the "Tiergarten Park Butler," who sat on a bench near the entrance to the gay path. If one approached him and asked to buy a "ticket," he would ask for ten cents and then relate which areas were safe from police observation and other kinds of useful information.[34]

The rapid growth of the city and its economy was a major contributing factor to the development of a gay scene in Berlin. As a host of sociologists and social historians have argued, the appearance of massive urban environments unsettled traditional patterns of social life, creating the possibility for new social relationships and identities to form. As people moved into the cities, they escaped the narrow confines and family pressures that so often dominated the environment of villages and even small towns. In large metropolises like Berlin, gay men and women found a degree of anonymity among the crowds of people, which made it easier to risk making dangerous contacts. Perhaps most important, the sheer numbers made it more likely to find other gay men and women and to develop social networks of friendship that were based on same-sex desire.[35] The very complexity of large cities was also a contributing factor. The random interactions, the opportunities for physical movement, and the excessiveness of sights, sounds, and smells turned the city into a kind of text, so to speak, that was difficult to make sense of. Multiple interpretations abounded, and opportunities for pleasure that slipped beyond normative control (what the semiologist Roland Barthes called *jouissance*) were abundant.[36] "Queer Space," suggests Jean-Ulrick Désert, "is in large part the function of wishful thinking or desires that become solidified: a seduction of the reading of space where queerness, at a few brief points and for some fleeting moments, dominates the (heterocentric) norm, the dominant social narrative of the landscape."[37] True, the "concentration of these movements and subcultures in urban space has made it easier to both demonize and control them."[38] Nevertheless, the reality is that in most modern cities the police, lacking the physical or legal resources to fully destroy these scenes, found themselves more in a position of trying to contain them.

Economic development was perhaps important in other ways as well. With the rise of modern, market-oriented economies, there came an emphasis on self-control, at least in the middle and upper classes, that seems to have had a heavy sexual component. As the emphasis on self-restraint grew, many furtive forms of sexuality—chief among them masturbation and sexual acts between men, both of which had previously been frowned on but more often than not ignored when they did happen—came under suspicion. The "homosexual panic" discussed at the opening of the last chapter gradually began to set in. Some men reacted to this panic by eliminating physical warmth and affectionate language from their relationships with men. Other men who could not so easily stifle their desire for the love of other men found themselves pulled into the gay scenes, which became forges of a modern gay identity.

Other nineteenth-century transformations were also important in fueling the development of Germany's gay scenes. Since the 1980s, historians have increasingly put an emphasis on cultural transformations instead of simply focusing on social and economic changes. In this light, we might mention the importance of the increasing amount of printed material on homosexuality available in the last three decades of the nineteenth century. Taking advantage not only of advances in publishing but also of a growing audience for printed material in an increasingly literate and prosperous population, hundreds of new newspapers and journals appeared. Libraries and reading societies were established, even for the working classes. Penny romances and adventures stories appeared on the shelves; family magazines and large metropolitan newspapers written in an entertaining style targeted a wide-ranging audience.[39] Within this mass reading public, there also emerged a specific audience interested in information on same-sex desire. Karl Heinrich Ulrichs won an early censorship case in a Leipzig district court in 1864, which laid the groundwork for the publication of material dealing with homosexuality as long as it had "scientific" value.[40] Max Spohr's press in Leipzig was an early company to focus on sexological topics, publishing Hirschfeld's *Sappho and Socrates* in 1896, as we have mentioned. Between 1898 and 1914 it published over a hundred books and brochures on homosexuality as well as the WhK's *Yearbook for Intermediate Sexual Types*.[41] Adolf Brand had more difficulty with the German censors, but for those readers his magazine *The Special One* was able to reach, it also was important for giving homosexual men a vision of a "manly culture."

The gay scenes that developed at the end of the nineteenth century seemed right at home in the world of 1920s Germany. Weimar is still remembered as the high point of modernism. Artists such as Hannah Höch and John Heartfield embraced the "anti-art" movement of Dada born in Zurich during the war, creating frenzied and jarring visual works by cutting up pieces of newspapers, magazines, advertisements, and other kinds of popular media and pasting them together.[42] George Grosz and Otto Dix gave us some of the most influential visions of postwar Germany, interpreted as a bleak, urban landscape littered with cripples, prostitutes, and serial killers.[43] Alfred Döblin's masterwork *Berlin Alexanderplatz* experimented with a new style of language that he hoped would better capture the sensations encountered in the modern metropolis.[44] And architects such as Bruno Taut, Erich Mendelsohn, and Walter Gropius designed buildings that they hoped would "herald a new modern era, a world that would be creative, joyous, and dynamic."[45] In the realm of popular culture, changes were also under way. New kinds of entertainment came in the form of movie palaces and dance halls, radio, and phonograph records. Jazz music, having been brought over by American soldiers during the war, acquired enthusiastic new fans, and with it came fresh styles of dancing, such as the foxtrot and the Charleston.[46] Directors such as Robert Wiene, Fritz Lang, and F. W. Murnau took film in new directions, pioneering innovative techniques and exploring themes such as individual consciousness, the modern city, and death.[47]

Perhaps more than anywhere else, Weimar Germany became associated with experimentation in sexuality. Taking advantage of the dismantling of much of Germany's censorship apparatus during the revolution, sex reformers of many sorts jumped into the limelight. They warned of a "specter" of sexual misery that haunted the country.[48] Social problems such as syphilis, unwanted pregnancies, and marital unhappiness acquired new significance in a nation that had suffered the deaths of so many young men during the war. How could a country hope to raise birth rates if such issues were not dealt with effectively? And not all reformers were driven only (or even primarily) by population anxieties. Actually, the common denominator among the sex reformers was a "vision of a 'healthy' modern society," as Atina Grossmann has observed. Opening up access to legal abortion, contraception, and sex education would "assure a new 'rational' social order that was both stable and humane and that would promote both collective welfare and individual happiness."[49] Leftist physicians helped establish and run hundreds of counseling clinics across the country that provided a range of advice and services, especially to the poor.[50] Freudian psychoanalysis acquired an institutional foundation, particularly in Berlin, where Karl Abraham and Karl Ettington in 1920 established the Psychoanalytic Polyclinic (which would later grow into the Psychoanalytic Institute).[51] More conventional figures such as the Dutch physician Theodoor Hendrik van de Velde, whose marital advice literature promised to create happy marriages through enduring sexual bliss, attracted huge audiences for their books and speaking engagements.[52]

For those looking for sexual adventure, the cities of Germany were "enticing, promising, fascinating"—a conglomeration of "endless possibilities."[53] On the stages of Berlin, the Tiller Girls showed off their legs, dancing a Rockettes-style performance that amazed and titillated spectators.[54] In crowded cabarets, audiences admired "tableaux" of women posing naked or watched actors telling risqué jokes and singing lewd songs.[55] A few of the best-known cabaret performers, especially the comedian Wilhelm Bendow, developed openly gay personae on stage, although Claire Waldoff and the singer Paul O'Montis were more typical in the way that their sexuality was playfully and more subtly alluded to.[56] Pornography, sometimes of a shockingly sadistic or fetishistic character, moved out of the shadows. Nudism also evolved from being a fringe movement to garnering serious public attention. And although the proponents of nudism denied that this pastime had anything to do with sexuality, their interest in healthy, beautiful bodies and their devotion to all things natural meant that they very often had much in common with the sex reformers of the era.[57]

BERLIN'S GAY AND LESBIAN BARS

For gay men, lesbians, and individuals whom we would call transgender, Berlin in particular had a lure that was difficult to resist. By the 1920s this metropolis had acquired not only a preeminent position in the imagination of homosexual Germans but also a spot in "a global network of queer cities," which also included Vienna, Paris, Rome, London, and New York.[58] Christopher Isherwood was not the only prominent foreigner to make the journey to Berlin specifically to explore its sexual underworld. The British poet W. H. Auden had arrived somewhat earlier, in fact, and was responsible for talking his friend Isherwood into making the trip. Many other friends in their literary circle became "sex tourists" in the city, as did a range of other British and American authors and writers.[59] And there were internationally famous performers who made sure to visit Berlin on their rounds through Europe, such as the Norwegian Rocky Twins (shown on the cover of this book), who became famous in Paris in 1928 but made stops in Berlin in the early 1930s.

Those who went to Berlin found much to be impressed by. Hirschfeld estimated that between ninety and one hundred gay bars could be found in the city by 1923, a number confirmed by other sources.[60] The gay scene was remarkably spread out across the city, in part because the city's policies toward female prostitution kept a single red-light district from forming.[61] Some of the oldest bars had appeared near Unter den Linden, though most of these had shut down by 1900.[62] Friedrichstrasse remained a focus for gay men after World War I, especially for those interested in male prostitution. Nearby one could find homosexual bars like the Marienkasino, the Scheunenviertel, the Café Nordstern, and the Adonis-Diele. The most upscale spots were generally in the western part of the city, from Bülowstrasse roughly to the Kudamm.[63] In the area around Nollendorfplatz, in particular, one could find a cluster of gay clubs, including the Nationalhof, the Continental Club, the Bülow-Kasino, and the Dorian Gray. Not far from here was the most famous of the Weimar gay establishments—the Eldorado. There were also homosexual bars scattered out in other neighborhoods, however: along Potsdamer Strasse to the southwest, and in the working-class suburbs to the north and east of the city.[64]

By the turn of the century, a fair amount of diversity had developed among the bars. Magnus Hirschfeld, who was well acquainted with Berlin's scene, observed in his 1912 study that each bar "has its special mark of distinction; this one is frequented by older people, that one only by younger ones, and yet another one by older and younger people." There were larger clubs that offered singing, cabaret, and theater, whereas smaller ones focused more on giving men a chance to mingle among themselves, perhaps providing a piano player to offer entertainment. The establishments were divided by the social background of their clientele. "There are bars for every social level," Hirschfeld pointed out, "elegantly outfitted bars in which the cheapest drink is one mark, down to the middle class taverns, where a glass of beer costs 10 pennies."[65]

At the bottom were the hangouts for working-class men, many of them male prostitutes. Some of this lower level were frequented almost entirely by soldiers looking to make some easy cash.[66] One of these soldiers' bars, The Mother Cat (*Zur Katzenmutter*), was visited by the criminologist and psychiatrist Paul Näcke in 1904. Consisting of two small rooms on the ground floor of a larger building, one of which was decorated with small pictures of cats, the bar was packed the night that Näcke visited. "Almost half of the visitors were soldiers of different sorts, although they all sat apart from one another and often with a civilian instead." He watched as the hostess brought beer to the patrons, who talked with one another and occasionally left together. Outside the bar was a street where soldiers hung about, waiting to leave with "anyone who would take [them]."[67] Not surprisingly, most of these bars were in the vicinity of the soldiers' barracks. They very often were short-lived, since the military quickly moved to shut them down once the authorities learned about the activity going on there.[68]

Besides the Mother Cat, Näcke visited several other bars that were gathering places for gay men from the working classes and lower middle class. They also tended to be small—again, normally with only two rooms—but the atmosphere might be slightly more festive. In one of the establishments, he had the pleasure of hearing the local bartender sing a song about "the third sex" that one of the members had composed. As the bartender sang, he threw off his apron, pulled on a braided wig and woman's hat, and "made all kinds of feminine movements and facial expressions that a professional female impersonator could hardly improve on."[69] Another of the bars was full of feminine-acting men, many of whom were dancing together in pairs in the main room. Everyone behaved well, and in fact Näcke commented on how clean and orderly the bars were. He saw no evidence of drunkenness;

he saw nothing lewd and did not even hear a dirty joke. The most shocking thing he saw all night was a couple who were kissing quite passionately in one of the corners of the room—and even this he did not find particularly "disgusting."[70]

Years later, Christopher Isherwood would make a similar observation about the first Berlin bar that he visited with his friend W. H. Auden in 1928—a place he called the "Cosy Corner" in his autobiography, but which in fact was Noster's Cottage (*Noster's Restaurant zur Hütte*). First established in 1909, Noster's Cottage was a pub near the working-class district of Hallesches Tor, one that was normally avoided by tourists. Despite the rough neighborhood, though, "nothing could have looked less decadent than the Cosy Corner. It was plain and homely and unpretentious." On the walls hung photographs of boxers and racing cyclists. In fact, the only real attraction was the boys. With their sweaters and jackets taken off, "their shirts unbuttoned to the navel, and their sleeves rolled up to the armpits," they waited around patiently for locals to come and pick them up.[71]

Hirschfeld also emphasized the orderliness of most of the bars. A few of the "plainer" establishments did have connecting private rooms where couples could slip away for sex. Offering such facilities normally led to the bars being closed and the owners being arrested for pandering, however, and so this practice was rare.[72] Generally, the bartenders worked to maintain a clean atmosphere. This did not mean that the crowd did not have fun, though. On Saturdays and Sundays the bars were often packed beyond capacity. Music was common: "Piano player and singers, who are often called by feminine names, are generally popular and, like the waiters, who are often the partners of the owners, are smothered with compliments and friendly words by the guests." In many of the restaurants, effeminate homosexuals felt relaxed enough to "give free rein to their feminine nature." And men felt comfortable enough to dance close to one another, as one partner "languish[ed] in the arms of his leading partner."[73]

The chief Berlin attractions were the transvestite venues. By far the most famous was the Eldorado (Figure 9), a nightclub whose festive atmosphere attracted not only homosexuals but also artists, authors, celebrities, and tourists wanting to admire a piece of "decadent" Berlin or catch a glimpse of someone famous.[74] Another cabaret, less well remembered today but nearly as well known at the time, was the Mikado, opened in 1907 and closed only in the last days of the Weimar era. One writer remembers visiting the club not long after it had opened and seeing Adolf Brand and other well-known figures in the audience. At the piano sat "the Baroness," playing songs written by Philipp Eulenburg himself.[75]

FIGURE 9 **THE ELDORADO IN 1932**

This was Berlin's best-known transvestite revue. Its reputation made it a regular stop for tourists or others wanting a taste of Berlin's decadence. For this reason, though, it was perhaps not the best representative of Berlin's gay scene. Source: Bundesarchiv, Bild 183-1983-0121-500. Photographer unknown

Lesbians could also be found in some of the bars that were devoted mostly to gay men. Hirschfeld remembered seeing lesbian couples frequently in the Bülowkasino on Bülowstrasse.[76] They also were often seen in the larger clubs of the 1920s, such as the Topp and the Eldorado. The Dorian Gray, one of the oldest and best-known gay clubs by the Weimar era, had a special night set aside for women. Entertainment included dancing, a stage show, and special theme nights such as a Bavarian alpine festival and a Rhenish grape harvest celebration.[77] By the turn of the century, there were also a handful of exclusively lesbian bars in the city. Hirschfeld noted that they were fewer at this time because, he thought, lesbians were very often happy to spend time alone with their girlfriends when they had one. Those who did frequent the bars were often rather masculine, he observed. "The owners and waiters of homosexual women's bars tend to be virile Urninds; most of them serve in men's clothing."[78] Hirschfeld seems to have been wrong, though, that women simply preferred quiet quarters: after the First World War, the number of lesbian clubs and cafés exploded, and by the mid-1920s there were over fifty of them in the city, which were as diverse as the male establishments in terms of size, class served, and entertainment offered.

Ruth Margarete Röllig, who wrote a famous city guide to the Berlin lesbian scene in 1928, remarked, "Here each one can find their own happiness, for they make a point of satisfying every taste."[79] According to Hirschfeld, some of these lesbian bars could be a little rowdy: he knew of one lesbian cabaret where a performer had been arrested when her act became too bawdy.[80] In general, though, most were as tame as their male counterparts. The atmosphere was generally refined; the lighting was soft and sentimental music played in the background.[81] One of the most famous was Chez Ma Belle Sœur on Marburger Strasse, decorated in Greek-style frescoes and furnished with private booths, where couples could take refuge behind curtains. Things could get wild here, but many of the locals thought that this club was mostly a showplace for tourists. They preferred more private and subdued clubs, such as The Maly and Jugel on Lutherstrasse, where a thick, black curtain blocked the view of the interior from the street. Inside, the decor was a tasteful mixture of gray and garnet red, and there were comfortable armchairs to sit in and a piano for entertainment.[82]

Like the gay bars, many of the lesbian bars were segregated somewhat by class. There was the exclusive Club Monbijou West, open only by invitation, and the elegant Pyramid, full of artists and celebrities. There were bars for older patrons, cafés for prostitutes and their customers, and the working-class Taverne, "known for its open displays of sexuality, beery rough atmosphere, and frequent outbreaks of physical violence."[83] As Marti Lybeck has demonstrated in her book *Desiring Emancipation,* many middle-class women were still quite worried about respectability in the 1920s, and advertisements for lesbian bars often went to great lengths to reassure readers that their events were "restrained and dignified."[84] Nevertheless, part of the excitement of Weimar's lesbian scene was the way that it made contact between previously isolated social groups possible. Before the war, artists, prostitutes, professional women, and single working-class women had frequently lived in small, same-sex circles that occasionally permitted lesbian relationships to develop within them. In the 1920s a mixing took place between these circles that allowed new opportunities for articulating a sexual identity, one that "suggested linkage across class, gender, and culture."[85]

Berlin's various homosexual establishments became famous for the elaborate gay balls that they would throw on regular occasions. One French observer of the city around the turn of the century noted that gay balls were held often several times a week in different clubs during the festive season between October and Easter. On some nights, one could even find more than one ball being held somewhere in the city.[86] Although admittance tickets could be expensive, the events were still very well attended. At one New Year's ball that Hirschfeld went to, more than eight hundred people were counted. The rooms began to fill as the evening approached midnight; some people were in suits or "fancy dress," but many were in costume. "A few appeared in masks that completely hid their faces; they came and went without anyone having had any idea who they were; others left their cocoons approximately at midnight." Not a few of the men were dressed in women's clothing. One visitor from South America had on a Parisian dress that cost him a small fortune. Wealthy gentlemen would take the occasion to show off a bit, arriving in elaborate dresses and being greeted with much fanfare. Very often, they would show up and act like a woman the entire night, despite sporting a dashing moustache or even a full beard. Sometimes, though, the costumed men could be more convincing. On the particular evening that Hirschfeld was there, one of the men in the crowd put on such a successful performance at being a woman that he fooled a police officer who had attended to make sure things did not get out of hand. After two hours of dancing and parading, the time for coffee came. Long tables were pulled out, and everyone took a seat. Female impersonators danced and sang some humorous songs. And then the evening resumed as before, and everyone stayed well into the morning.[87]

Lesbians sometimes could be found at the male gay balls, and lesbian bars held their own balls. These occasions were different from those of their male counterparts not only in terms of costume, but also generally in their excluding men entirely. The most exclusive ball in the prewar period was a private party, open only to those with an invitation, arranged by a prominent Berlin lady. Normally it took place in the ballroom of one of the city's grand hotels. Couples would arrive beginning at eight in the evening, costumed as monks, sailors, clowns, Boers, Japanese geishas, bakers, and farmhands. They would sit down to eat at tables lined with flowers; the director, dressed in a "gay velvet jacket," would greet the guests and give a short speech. After dinner, the tables would be put away, and the orchestra would begin playing waltzes and other lively dancing music while the couples would dance through the night. In a nearby room, others would drink, make toasts, and listen to singing. "No bad moods cloud the universal joy," remarked one female participant, "including those of the last woman participants who leave the place at the dawn's early light into the cold, February morning. It is a place where among people who feel the same way they could dream for a few hours about being who they are inside." [88]

CRUISING IN PUBLIC

Gay men in Berlin took advantage of many of the public spaces available to them to meet sexual partners. As the presence of soldiers and working-class rent boys suggests, cruising was an activity that blurred the lines between homosexual and heterosexual. The overlap between areas frequented by male and female prostitutes is a reminder that many young men at this time, not yet married and living and working largely in all-male environments, were not always so picky about whom they had sex with. Although not as much work has been done on this topic as has been done in other national contexts, there is certainly evidence enough that soldiers, sailors, migrant workers, or simply young men in search of whatever opportunities might arise in the city (legal or otherwise) might make themselves sexually available to other men. [89]

Public toilets were a popular option for those who liked to have sex in public, as they were in other major cities in Europe and North America. [90] Constructed in Berlin beginning in the 1860s in an effort to deal with the growing sanitation problems, the green-painted, steel-framed, octagonal urinals became an easily sighted feature of the city's modern landscape. By the turn of the twentieth century, they could be found around major plazas, at the intersections of busy streets, near Berlin's major train stations, and in the vicinity of the city's public parks. Under the pretext of using the facilities, a man seeking a sexual encounter with another man could easily enter and begin to give signals of his intentions—a lingering glance, for example, or the exposure of an erect penis. Some men, playing it safe, might be satisfied with voyeuristically watching other men urinate. Others might make more aggressive advances and hope that they were not dealing with a blackmailer or an undercover policeman. Certain urinals were well known in the gay scenes for attracting gay men and male prostitutes. One might be able to identify them by the graffiti, Hirschfeld pointed out: "The graffiti and drawings you encountered in the toilets often make reference to homosexuality; they can be solely same-sex obscenities treated in word and picture, or certain offers, requests or meetings."[91] In the bathrooms of major train stations, peepholes fashioned for communication and voyeurism might also give them away. For men with a taste for working-class "trade" or who simply enjoyed a little risk, such public toilets could be a good option for quick, anonymous sex.

The most popular toilets were very often part of a larger strip used for cruising. In Berlin the most famous of these strips was the "gay path" in the Tiergarten, but there were others. Friedrichstrasse was one of the most popular. Another was along the Kudamm, running from a toilet in the western neighborhood of Charlottenburg to a toilet in nearby Wilmersdorf.[92] Certain busy intersections or public squares, especially Alexanderplatz, offered opportunities for milling about aimlessly for hours without being too noticeable. And then there were the sidewalks in front of places known to be frequented by homosexuals or other men open to same-sex encounters—local gay bars, but also certain theaters, harbors, wharfs, soldiers' garrisons, and even post offices (whose dispatchers, apparently, were a preferred sexual target for some men). Occasionally, public places might offer dark or hidden locations ideal for quick sex. Very often, though, men would only meet in such a place and then retreat to a private room or a hotel. In Berlin there were plenty of cheap hotels and pensions that were used by both male and female prostitutes for quick encounters. Even some nicer hotels were available, owned by sympathetic souls who operated them exclusively for homosexual men and women from out of town who needed a place to stay for a while, sometimes as long as a month. "In Berlin," noted Hirschfeld, "I know about approximately twelve guest-houses that belong in this category, which are maintained by homosexual men and women for their own kind; a few of them are maintained in grand style."[93]

In many major cities such as Vienna, Paris, and New York, public baths and saunas were another popular place for gay men to meet. In Germany baths frequented by gay men were not as common because the country's criminal law made it possible for an owner to be prosecuted for procuring if it could be proven that his establishment was being regularly used by men for sex. Still, the occasional trial of a bath owner is good evidence that such activities did occasionally take place.[94] One private bath in the city open only to members became infamous after the owner was arrested; in the trial it came out that he had offered not only private cabins for men to have sex in, but also "masseurs" who were in fact male prostitutes hiring out their services. Such incidents were rare, though. Most owners actively tried to discourage unwanted advances from taking place in the baths. Some were realistic, though. A few hung signs at the entrance explicitly asking homosexuals to be discreet.[95] Occasionally, an incident would be reported in the paper, giving some small hint about what might be happening while others were not around. Such reports are also an indication, though, of how dangerous such activity could be. More commonly, the baths or other swimming establishments were used by gay men merely as meeting places, or simply for "feasting one's eyes on nice bodies."[96]

THE GAY SCENES OF OTHER CITIES

Berlin may have acquired an international reputation by the 1920s for its gay scene, but it was not the only German city where gay men and lesbians were seeking out places to meet. Not surprisingly, the port city of Hamburg, with its large migrant worker population, its many sailors coming in from the sea, and its infamous red-light district of St. Pauli, had a lively scene. Like Berlin's, its population had also exploded with Germany's economic takeoff and by World War I was fast approaching one million people. One author described Hamburg in 1897 as "the German city most troubled by Uranians," estimating that every fourth man who walked along the main shopping street of the city, the Jungfernstieg, was gay and another sixth was bisexual.[97] Though this observer's estimate was no doubt exaggerated, other people also remarked about the city's reputation. Abraham Flexner, an American social observer of prostitution in Europe who worked with the antivice society known as the Committee of Fourteen in New York, described Hamburg in 1914 as being outdone only by Berlin and Paris in the number of "notorious resorts" that it offered to those "addicted to homosexuality."[98]

Most of the Hamburg's gay bars in the early twentieth century were located right in the downtown area, especially in the entertainment district that developed in St. Georg, near the city's main train station, but also in the "old city" (*Altstadt*) and "new city" (*Neustadt*) districts directly south of the Alster lake. These locations were convenient for transportation and picking up male prostitutes near the train station, and they were also near the lake and the park area around the Bismarck monument, both of which offered well-trafficked walkways for cruising. One of the first gay bars of the city was called—in a winking reference to Frederick the Great, who was widely believed to have been gay—the King of Prussia (*Zum König von Preussen*). At the turn of the century, it was the only club in the city where men dared to dance openly with one another. By the 1920s it had closed down, but it was replaced by many others—perhaps as many as thirty. There was the Casino on Rosenstrasse and the Tusculan on Alsterdamm. The Rhine Gold Restaurant and Café on Lilienstrasse advertised itself as a "comfortable location for both male and female friends" that offered "musical entertainment and dancing." The Brennerburg on Brennerstrasse obviously was hoping to attract tourists by noting that "English is spoken" in its advertisements. [99]

The most popular of the Hamburg's gay bars, though, was the Three Stars (*Zu den Drei Sternen*), located on Hütten Strasse. The British author Stephen Spender visited the bar once in 1929 and gave a memorable description of it in his autobiographical novel *The Temple*. "But for some rough wooden chairs and tables," he wrote, "it was unfurnished. It had the air of a louche Parish Hall with a platform at one end on which a band of untalented musicians were playing jazz." Men danced on the main floor. Youths dressed in women's clothes went table to table, teasing the guests. At the tables sat not only single men but also heterosexual couples, who had apparently come in to enjoy the ambience. And against the wall stood "working boys wearing cloth caps, and a few sailors." All of them male prostitutes, they stood around the edges of room with serious looks on their faces, generally leaning against the wall and waiting to be invited over for a drink and company. [100]

Another major city in the north was Hannover. Even though it was smaller, with a population of only around 300,000 in 1910, homosexual men and women could still find places here to meet. Probably the earliest was the Ballhof on Burgstrasse. Beginning around 1919, the ballroom specialized in bringing Berlin-style gay balls to Hannover. One of the city's local gay celebrities, the female impersonator Friedel Schwarz, entertained audiences on the cabaret stage of the Ballhof. Another attraction was Wilja, another well-known (and very effeminate) gay man in the city. Besides dancing and watching performances, one could buy some of the gay magazines of the day in the Ballhof. The building was in bad shape, though, and by 1922 it had closed down. [101]

The Ballhof was quickly replaced by others, however. There was the Black Cat Café (*Café Schwarzer Kater*) on Windmühlenstrasse and the National Café (*Café National*) on Nordmannstrasse. [102] The German-Jewish philosopher Theodor Lessing, who was born and raised in Hannover, described a gay bar apparently known on the streets as the "Gay Appetite" (*Zur schwulen Guste*), located in the "oldest and most disreputable streets of the old part of the city" where lesbians and gay men gathered to dance. [103] For a brief period in the early 1930s Hannover had its own Eldorado, which apparently tried to attract lesbians, since it advertised in one of Weimar's lesbian magazines. It stayed open only about six months, though. More well liked was the Neustädter Guest House (*Neustädter Gesellschaftshaus*), which took over the job of hosting gay balls after the Ballhof closed down. But despite the availability of such bars that exclusively served gay men and lesbians, one of the most popular places continued to be an establishment with a mixed audience, the Continental Café. One writer who remembered the location observed, "Behaving thoroughly respectably, couples sharing yearning glances and light touches sit about. Sometimes a guest takes a turn with the much admired leader directing the band, or they would pick up a violin, or even sing a wistful song from where they sit. For like the gypsies, with whom they share many similarities, homosexuals are consumed by melancholy."[104]

In the western region of Germany, known as the Rhineland, both Cologne and Düsseldorf possessed active scenes. In Cologne, which had grown to around a half million people by 1910, there were several parks that became favorite cruising spots for gay men. The City Forest and the Beethoven Park were especially favored. For prostitutes, men would generally go to the area around the main train station. And then there were also several gay bars that opened after the war. The Dahlhaus Restaurant on Hahnenstrasse was one of the first. By 1920 it was the meeting place for a local friendship club that put on a regular cabaret night for members on Sundays. Nearby was the Nettesheim Casino, a favorite place to go to dance. Here one could also buy some of the homosexual publications that were available on the Weimar market. By the mid-1920s, though, the most popular gay nightclub in the city was the Sleeping Beauty, a transvestite cabaret with entertainment provided by Tilla and Resi. Tilla became well known for her "Salome number," whereas Resi did a flamenco-style "Carmen dance" that attracted visitors from miles around. And then there were the tables, each one featuring a private telephone (as the film *Cabaret* depicts) that could be used to call men sitting at neighboring tables to ask them to dance.[105]

In nearby Düsseldorf, restaurants such as the Tivoli and the Dammer began to attract a homosexual clientele after the First World War. Bergerstrasse, a street located near the old town district, with its many breweries and other nightlife, became an important focus of the scene in the early 1920s when the Restaurant Arcari and, on the other side of the street, Mombour's opened up. The latter was especially popular. Besides dancing and music, the bar became known early for its cabaret performances that featured transvestites such as Hubertine. By the early 1930s it was joined by other establishments scattered about the city. There was Lettmann's on Kölnerstrasse and the Little Corn Flower (*Kornblümchen*) on Mintropplatz. The Schmalbach Inn on Hohestrasse and the Rheinfahrt Restaurant (*Zur Rheinfahrt*) on Brückenstrasse became known as more intimate locations where it was easier to develop a relationship. Those who wanted a night out on the town headed over to the Tosca Palace (*Tosca-Palast*) on Rethelstrasse. Although this dance hall was also popular among heterosexual couples, one visitor who was later arrested by the Nazi Gestapo admitted that a large section of the audience was gay. The owner of the palace was himself the leader of Düsseldorf's local gay social club. Remarkably, it remained open for some time after the Nazis took power, and it became legendary in its day among the local gay population.[106]

In contrast, southern Germany was much less hospitable. Munich was a good-sized city of a half million people, and, given its reputation for being the artistic hub of Germany, one might assume that it would be a beacon for gay men in the region. The conservative atmosphere of Bavaria, however, with a culture heavily stamped by Catholicism, could still be felt in the city, despite the city's bohemian element. Munich's police showed little of the tolerance exhibited by their counterparts in Berlin. The result was that gay establishments were hard to find.[107] The journalist Wilhelm Craemer mentioned in 1904 that a "Café Alfred" and another restaurant called "The Polish Court" (*Zum polakischen Hof*) were known as meeting places for gay men. Several others appeared after the war, though generally only briefly, since the police were very active at the time in shutting down locations that became known to them. Only at the end of the 1920s did two more long-lasting gay gathering places appear: the pub Schwarzfischer on Dultstrasse, and the Arndthof in the Glockenbachviertel. In the meantime, gay men cruised the central train station and the main squares of the city, such as the Karlsplatz, the Lenbachplatz, and Odeonsplatz. As in other cities, they took advantage of public parks, especially the English Garden, with its lush scenery and many winding paths that offered lots of hidden spots for sex. They also met in private circles that congregated regularly at various homes.[108]

POLICING HOMOSEXUALITY

By the end of the nineteenth century, most large cities had established homosexual squads (*Homodezernate*) that began to watch Germany's gay scenes closely. These units generally had the job of investigating not only possible infractions of Paragraph 175 but also a range of other crimes connected with homosexuality, including male prostitution, blackmail, personal ads, exhibitionism, gay pornography, and the sale of goods intended to be used for sexual purposes by gay men.[109] The creation of such squads was not prompted solely by the emergence of these scenes. Actually, they were more directly caused by a whole series of transformations related to the professionalization of police work, including the enlargement of the police force and the reorganization of the department around distinct specialties of police operation.[110] Every city was different, but in many areas the homosexual squads either worked closely with or were a subdepartment of the vice squad (*Sittenpolizei*), which monitored female prostitution and sometimes other "moral crimes" such as gambling. In the government there were many who believed that homosexual squads could contribute to law and order in a considerable way by taking advantage of modern scientific fields such as criminology, psychology, sexology, and medicine.

From their inception, the homosexual squads were involved with a range of reforms designed to modernize police procedure, making it more efficient and effective. Since at least the mid-nineteenth century, many criminal police units had kept lists of known homosexuals. Today these lists are often colloquially known as the "pink lists" (*Rosa Listen*), but at the time they were called the pederast lists. Toward the end of the nineteenth century, these lists were formalized into extensive criminal files and rogues' galleries (*Verbrecheralben*) of known homosexuals, all organized on index cards that included basic personal information and to which were attached pictures and fingerprints.[111] In Berlin the homosexual squad from around the turn of the century also came to work closely with a specialized homosexual patrol, a unit of plainclothesmen who made regular patrols through bars, swimming pools, parks, bathrooms, and other areas of the gay scene. They also were sometimes charged with carrying out police raids.[112]

Not a lot is known yet about the pre–World War I homosexual squads, though Jens Dobler's research on Berlin's squad in his book *Between a Policy of Toleration and Crime Fighting* (*Zwischen Duldungspolitik und Verbrechensbekämpfung*) suggests that they could sometimes include progressive police officials who stayed abreast of the current scientific research on homosexuality. They could also be sympathetic with the homosexual movement's call for decriminalization. In fact, Robert Beachy has recently argued in his book *Gay Berlin* that the tolerant attitude of Berlin's homosexual squad, led by Commissioner Leopold von Meerscheidt-Hüllessem during the first fifteen years of its existence, was a prime factor in the high visibility of the scene. Hüllessem worked closely with Hirschfeld and other observers of the city's gay scene, even escorting them on tours of the bars and gay balls at times. His example was closely followed by his successor, Hans von Tresckow.[113] Hirschfeld, for his part, recognized that this police attitude was largely pragmatic. "Less because they want to allow Uranians the harmless pleasure of their entertainment," Hirschfeld pointed out, "than out of the correct assumption that these gathering spots essentially facilitate their supervision of the homosexuals and those elements that enrich themselves at their expense by blackmail and theft." Furthermore, the police preferred to keep an eye on the homosexuals in the limited confines of familiar bars and were afraid of driving their activities into more secluded locations if the bars were shut down.[114]

One might assume that the vitality of Weimar Germany's gay scenes is easily traceable to the revolution of 1918–19 and the freedoms that came with democracy. Recent research, however, has uncovered the surprising fact that policing in 1920s was actually more repressive than it had been before the war. The rise in the conviction rates in the course of the decade is still not entirely explained, but research done in Berlin at least suggests a partial answer. Dobler notes that the character of the city's homosexual squad changed considerably in the mid-1920s after a new leader, Bernhard Strewe, was appointed. Strewe was noticeably more politically conservative and temperamentally hostile to homosexuality than his predecessors. Under his leadership, the homosexual squad intensified its activities against homosexuality tremendously in the middle years of the decade, in concurrence with a large crackdown on prostitution and other aspects of the city's nightlife.[115]

Other cities or regions have not been studied as closely as Berlin, but what work has been done suggests that Berlin was not an isolated case. A historian of Düsseldorf's local gay scene notes that after the establishment of a new homosexual club (a chapter of the Federation for Human Rights, which we will examine in a moment), the local police tried to crack down on the organization by threatening to revoke the liquor license for any bar or restaurant that agreed to host a local chapter of the organization.[116] In Hannover the 1924 trial of an infamous serial killer, Fritz Haarmann, who murdered and butchered a number of young men and male prostitutes, led to a massive police assault on the city's gay scene in 1925, during which many of the popular bars were closed.

Tying together these various efforts to suppress local gay scenes may prove difficult since they are most easily traceable to local events rather than national trends. Nevertheless, a noticeable rise in national conviction rates in the mid-1920s does suggest that something was happening on a national scale. It is too early to say for certain which changes might have been responsible for the increase, but it deserves more attention from researchers. The historian Edward Ross Dickinson observes that the high criminality rates for homosexuality runs counter not only to Weimar's reputation but also to the general trend for the legal system as a whole to focus increasingly on coercive, rather than "victimless," sexual crimes in the early twentieth century. He speculates that "the special treatment of this crime suggests that the

Weimar state aimed at the 'normalization' of sexual behavior specifically as it related to reproduction."[117]

The fact that the development of the Weimar gay scenes and the organization of homosexuals occurred despite the escalating arrests and convictions under Paragraph 175 in the 1920s does not mean that there was *no* relationship between legal enforcement and the flourishing institutions of Weimar gay life. Despite some police efforts to close down gay bars, in general the police rarely made mass arrests in the bars.[118] Policing of the gay scenes remained restricted by the assumptions embodied in the German notion of a "legal state" (*Rechtsstaat*).[119] To ensure a conviction, the police were required to present evidence that specific sexual acts had taken place. While acquiring such evidence, the police had to respect a number of basic constitutional rights guaranteed to the individual. They were certainly permitted to keep information on suspected homosexuals, but suspicion was not enough to justify an arrest or an indictment. Finally, if a man was convicted of breaking Paragraph 175, he could count on being punished in no other way than what was spelled out by the law itself. How important these basic assumptions were to the operation of the gay scenes is demonstrated by what happened when they could no longer be counted on under the Nazis.

GAY AND LESBIAN SOCIAL NETWORKS AND FRIENDSHIP CLUBS

Gay scenes are composed not simply of locations for people to meet but also networks of men and women who maintain friendships and love affairs, despite the social stigma that they face if these relationships are ever discovered. In the early twentieth century, these networks of men and women generally took the form of informal circles. They might meet in gay bars, but just as often they would see each other at a neighborhood restaurant or in the home of a friend on prearranged days. Normally comprising ten to twenty people, but occasionally as many as sixty, these circles would gather for dinner or afternoon coffee or tea; they might hold socials and even dances in their homes, and even arrange for summertime picnics or other kinds of group outings. Although occasionally there were rumors of such circles hosting massive orgies, in fact Hirschfeld noted that almost always "urnish society is thoroughly decent." It was one of the unfortunate misconceptions of heterosexuals that "whenever homosexuals are friends with each other, sexual intercourse also occurs between them. Nothing is more erroneous."[120]

Homosexual circles were very often segregated by class, but they could be found even among working-class gay men and women. Hirschfeld remembered being invited to one of these gatherings in a local bar in one of Berlin's working-class suburbs, where a member was celebrating his birthday. The group, which that day also included the heterosexual brothers of the man having the birthday, ate sausages and potato salad while listening to the bar-keeper play the piano. Soon, one effeminate man nicknamed "Swanhilde" got up to give a performance that involved his doing various imitations, including one of the dancer Isadora Duncan, that soon had the group laughing hysterically. Another man, who worked professionally as a female impersonator, then got up to run through some of his numbers. This performance was followed by a very masculine-looking worker, a balding coal miner with muscular, tattooed arms, getting up to sing a number of bar songs. "With a popular Berlin accent," Hirschfeld recalled, "he sang a series of songs that were not exactly prudish, with many errors in grammar, without a trace of a singing voice, each line supported by grotesque gestures, though in his awkwardness everything integrated so well that he was not without effect."[121] These songs soon had the group on their feet. The tables were pushed away, and the crowd began dancing. Suddenly, an interruption: a policeman, hearing the commotion inside, had walked in and was looking over the group rather sternly. Silence hung in the air, but only for a moment. One brave man in the crowd, a musician by profession, grabbed the policeman around the waist and danced him out into the middle of the floor. Taken by surprise, the policeman could do nothing but dance along, and soon the party had resumed. "A situation comedy that could hardly be retold," remarked Hirschfeld.[122]

Hirschfeld described another birthday event in his book *Berlin's Third Sex* (*Berlins Drittes Geschlecht*), this one celebrated by a group that met in one of the gay bars regularly for coffee and pastries. Again, most of the members were working-class. As they arrived, each one presented the honored guest a gift—something he had made with his own hands or had baked, or maybe even a bouquet he had assembled. The friends greeted each other with "dainty bows" or curtsies and then kissed each other on the cheeks. Much of the night was marked by a mock formality. Several of the members were addressed as "the baroness" (*die Baronin*) or "the director" (*die Direktorin*). Soon the crowd grew loud, as the members rapidly consumed their coffee and cakes, all the while telling stories, laughing heartily at each other's jokes, and occasionally "screeching" with excitement. Songs were sung, toasts given. The celebration climaxed when one of the members was coaxed into sitting down at the piano, where he began to belt out the birthday boy's favorite song in a "melodious alto."[123]

Such informal circles of men and women were fairly common in the gay scenes of Berlin and other German cities. Occasionally, such circles would become formalized into clubs or associations. At the turn of the century, such clubs were still rather rare. There was of course Adolf Brand's Community of the Special (GdE), made up primarily of readers and contributors to his journal *The Special One*. Hirschfeld also mentioned another literary club, the Platen Society, that was made up of homosexual men. Some of these clubs were not all that different from a more informal circle: the Lohengrin Club, for example, was centered on a man in the wine business, nicknamed "The Queen," who organized musical performances and maybe a little theater for his friends. Others were on the face of it clubs devoted to a particular pastime or interest: hiking clubs, for examples, or patrons of music and the arts. Only insiders knew that the club members also happened to be entirely homosexual. Hirschfeld noted that bowling clubs were an especially popular form of entertainment among Germany's working-class lesbians.

In the wake of the Eulenburg scandal, a small Berlin newspaper, *The Great Bell* (*Die Grosse Glocke*), made it its business for a time to out several lesbian circles and clubs in the city. One of them was the New Women's Community (*Die neue Damengemeinschaft*), a group of elite and professional women who met Wednesdays at a local café. Led by a woman described as an "Amazon" who occasionally wore a tuxedo to events, the club even placed classified ads in local papers to try to reach other "like-minded" women. The ads informed newcomers to wear a red rose to identify themselves, and to use the passwords "Sappho" or "Aphrodite" when they arrived. Club members were clearly not happy with being identified publicly as homosexuals, and they brought a libel suit against the editor of *The Great Bell* in 1909. In the course of the court case, it became clear that not all the women in the club were lesbians, and several were clearly shocked at the sexual advances made by the club president. Some witnesses, however, acknowledged that they came to the club because they were homosexuals. Numerous members had paired up into long-lasting relationships. At least one woman's marriage had broken down when her sexual activities with other women came to light. Taking these circumstances into account, the judge decided in favor of the *The Great Bell*'s editor.[124]

The number of homosexual social clubs exploded after the conclusion of World War I. In the wake of the November revolution, which ended the German monarchy and ushered in full democracy in the form of the Weimar constitution, such groups mushroomed at the grassroots level in many towns and cities across Germany. They commonly took on names like the Club of Friends (*Club der Freunde, Club der Freunde und Freundinnen*) or the League of Friends (*Freundschaftsbund*). Unlike the WhK, which always had an overwhelmingly scientific bent to it and possessed only around a thousand members by 1914, friendship clubs were predominantly social societies that organized conversational meetings, dinners, parties, and celebrations and soon included thousands of participants nationally. They generally did not neglect educational and political work, but it was always understood that at the core was, as the historian Andreas Sternweiler has put it, the "feeling of community (*Gemeinschaftsgefühl*) . . . that enabled a gay sense of self." [125]

By the mid-1920s, every major German city had at least one gay social club. Hamburg, for example, had two groups: the League of Friends for Greater Hamburg (*Verband der Freunde und Freundinnen Groß-Hamburg*), which was interested primarily in organizing social opportunities; and the Hamburg Society for Sexual Research (*Hamburger Gesellschaft für Sexualforschung*), which held talks on scientific matters and attempted to promote the abolition of Paragraph 175. [126] The vast proliferation of these local groups seemed to call out for some sort of national umbrella organization, and so on August 30, 1920, the friendship clubs in Berlin, Hamburg, Frankfurt, and Stuttgart came together to form the German Friendship Alliance (DFV, *Deutsche Freundschafts-Verband*), headquartered in Berlin. Not surprisingly, the organization had many connections with the WhK. Hirschfeld himself participated in some of the alliance's activities. The DFV organized two national meetings to bring together members of the numerous friendship clubs, the first in Kassel in March 1921 and the second in Hamburg in April 1922. Through these meetings the organization was successfully able to extend its reach, adding many new local clubs to its membership roster.

As the DFV grew larger, conflict erupted in 1922 over the direction the group would take. In the course of this fight, an important figure emerged: Friedrich Radszuweit (Figure 10), a businessman from Berlin who had become an influential member of Berlin's local friendship club. He convinced that city's group in 1923 to rename itself the Federation for Human Rights (*Bund für Menschenrecht,* BfM). As the leadership of the club was largely the same as the leadership of the national DFV, Radszuweit took control of the umbrella organization and renamed it too. His leadership brought new energy to the organization. Radszuweit established a more disciplined and centralized structure for the national organization. [127] In the next years the BfM took on a more active role in spreading its reach beyond Berlin by helping form and promote chapters in new locations. The result was that the organization grew dramatically from having a little more than 2,000 members in 1922 to perhaps as many as 48,000 by the end of the decade. [128] Its membership included mostly a broad range of middle-class Germans—especially independent businessmen, employees, and government workers—but also some craftsmen and laborers. Most were rather young: men in their twenties and thirties.

FIGURE 10 **FRIEDRICH RADSZUWEIT**

From 1923 until his death in 1932, the businessman and prominent gay activist Friedrich Radszu-weit led the Federation for Human Rights (BfM). He built up a remarkable number of gay and lesbian magazines from scratch, and by the end of the 1920s he played a critical role in the fight against Paragraph 175. Source: Schwules Museum, Berlin

Friedrich Radszuweit quickly became one of the most prominent gay activists in Weimar Germany, taking a place alongside Magnus Hirschfeld and Adolf Brand. He was not universally appreciated, however. He did not shy away from a fight, and in the course of the decade he became embroiled in a number of very public arguments with Hirschfeld and others. Many also thought him domineering in his efforts to expand his organization. Toward the end of the decade, he even seems to have been actively trying to promote a leadership cult around himself.[129] Along the way, he made quite a few enemies, including many early leaders within his own organization. The result was that in March 1925 a group of disaffected members left the BfM and reestablished the DFV. Although the splinter group was made up initially only of Berliners, it picked up supporters in several eastern German cities—such as Leipzig, Dresden, Chemnitz—and even in Vienna by 1928.[130] The organization never got as big as the BfM, but for a time at the end of the decade its rivalry with Radszuweit's federation contributed to the diversity of reading material available to a gay audience.

There were few women in the friendship clubs, but there was nevertheless a separate women's division (*Damenabteilung*) of the BfM that formed in 1927. The division was led by Lotte Hahm, probably the most important lesbian leader during the 1920s. Her image appeared frequently in the lesbian magazines of the decade, on covers and in advertisements. Generally shown in a short haircut and wearing masculine clothing, she offered other lesbian women one "figure of identification and emulation," as Marti Lybeck notes.[131] Hahm was the owner of several lesbian bars in Weimar Germany, and she also established a lesbian social club called Violetta that had four hundred members in 1926.[132] Violetta sponsored regular balls where women danced together to jazz music, stopping only to listen to singers or laugh with comedians. For a time, Hahm was affiliated with the DFV, but in 1928 she made a very public split with this organization and joined Radszuweit's BfM instead.[133] After taking charge of the BfM's women's division, she hoped for a time that it would evolve into the autonomous Federation for Ideal Female Friendship *(Bund für ideale Frauenfreundschaft)*, which would simultaneously take on more feminist issues.[134] This enterprise failed, but she remained active in the BfM. She saw herself as not simply a lesbian but also a transvestite, and in 1929 she helped establish a transvestite group for both men and women called d'Eon.[135]

The rapid expansion of gay and lesbian clubs across Germany took place at the same time that gay publishing exploded in Berlin. Figures such as Max Spohr, Adolf Brand, and Magnus Hirschfeld had already taken some steps in this direction around the turn of the century, as we have seen. All of the material that these individuals published, however, had been restricted by the need for this material at least to appear scientific if it did not want to fall afoul of the imperial censors. In the Weimar era, several men and women saw an opportunity to build a publishing industry that might address a much wider swath of the population. The Weimar constitution banned censorship (with certain exceptions, as we shall see), and the new democratic government quickly dismantled the bureaucratic and police apparatus that had developed after the *Lex Heinze* of 1900 to watch for obscene and other troubling material.[136] The pioneer was Karl Schultz, who established a new press in Berlin and published the first issue of *Friendship* (*Die Freundschaft*) in August 1919 (Figure 11). It consciously addressed both gay men and lesbians from all social classes, and it worked to extend its readership to new corners of the country. It appeared weekly, starting with a print run of 20,000—far more than the roughly 1,500 copies ever managed by Brand's *The Special One*. More important, thanks to the lifting of censorship, the magazine was openly hung in the windows of newspaper stands and kiosks all around Berlin.

The historian Stefan Micheler, who has done the most intensive research on the Weimar-era magazines, has characterized *Friendship* in this early period as an "agent" for "friends of both sexes" (*Freundinnen und Freunde*) that offered education, advice, and entertainment. The editors of the magazine during these early years—Karl Schultz, A. Lange, and Max Danielson—helped establish its look and tone. On the pages of *Friendship* readers could find short stories, essays, and poems. They were invited to write letters, engage in debates, and contribute pieces themselves. They also found hints for how to meet other "like-minded" friends. From the very first issue, *Friendship* published personal ads to help men and women develop relationships. By the second week, it was running advertisements for local gay and lesbian bars.[137] The success of *Friendship* in the first few years encouraged Karl Schultz to try out a second title in April 1921: *Uranus* (*Uranos*)—a name inspired by Karl Heinrich Ulrichs's aborted attempt to found a magazine with the same name back in 1870. This periodical had a more literary character than *Friendship,* and Schultz clearly hoped to attract many of the same educated readers who might have bought Brand's *The Special One* or Hirschfeld's *Yearbook for Sexual Intermediaries*. Almost immediately, *Uranus* ran into financial difficulties. The

FIGURE 11 *FRIENDSHIP*

One of the earliest Weimar-era gay magazines with a mass readership, *Friendship* was successful enough early on to encourage many others to follow after it. Although it went through a rough patch in 1923, it revived afterward and stayed on the market until 1933. This particular issue, from early 1933, announces and article by Ferdinand Karsch-Haack, "The Liaisons of Prince Heinrich, the Brother of Frederick the Great." Source: Schwules Museum, Berlin magazine failed to pick up many subscribers, and soon its editors had to give up hope that it might be published every week. By early 1923 it was gone from the shelves.[138]

Friendship, however, still continued to do relatively well in 1922. Its print run expanded, perhaps reaching 40,000 to 50,000 in the course of the year. The length of the magazine also increased. Whereas at the beginning it had included a mere four pages, *Friendship* reached twelve pages at the height of its influence in 1922.[139] Its success inspired two short-lived imitators: *The Sun* (*Die Sonne*), based in Hamburg, and *The Hellenic Messenger* (*Hellasbote*), which, like *Uranus,* had a slightly more literary and academic focus. By 1923 fate seemed to be turning the first wave of homosexual magazines. Although the Weimar constitution had in general forbidden censorship, it did allow legal measures to suppress obscenity and to protect youth from potentially dangerous printed material. The result was that prosecutors could still rely on the obscenity law (Paragraph 184) to bring those people who produced material deemed pornographic to court.[140] Two court cases led to the conviction of two of *Friendship*'s editors.[141] By 1923 several readers were complaining that it was hard to find an issue of *Friendship* if you did not grab it off the stand when it first appeared. Apparently, the police were diligently carrying out their ordered confiscations. What is more, at least one company that owned a string of newspaper stands decided to boycott the magazine entirely.[142] The combined weight of the legal attacks, financial difficulties, and the hyper-inflation of 1923 was enough to force *Friendship* to stop publication during the second half of the year.

Nevertheless, the magazine had proven that there was a market for material written for homosexuals. It did not take long for new magazines to appear to fill the gap. A second wave of publications began shortly after Friedrich Radszuweit established the BfM in 1922. A good businessman, he hoped to use the organization as a platform for building a new press under his control. In early 1923 he started his own magazine, *The Pages for Human Rights* (*Die Blätter für Menschenrechte*), which soon took over the role of official organ for the BfM from the stumbling *Friendship*. In 1924 he started new titles to target specific audiences.[143] In September he established *The Girlfriend* (*Die Freundin*), the first magazine to aim itself specifically at lesbians (Figure 12). It was followed in 1925 by *The Friendship Paper* (*Das Freundschaftsblatt*), aimed specifically at a male audience. Its look and content were very similar to those of the earlier *Friendship* and were clearly designed as a replacement for this much-loved periodical. It took over as the chief weekly of Radszuweit's press (*The Pages for Human Rights* being demoted at this point to a monthly news-letter for his organization).

Erscheint jeden Mittwoch

5. Jahrgang – Nummer 11
11. September 1929

20 Pf.

Die Freundin

Wochenschrift für ideale Frauenfreundschaft. – Offizielles
Publikationsorgan des „Bund für Menschenrecht, e. V.", Berlin.

Bezugspreis im geschlossenen Brief monatlich Berlin 1,40 Mark, außerh. 1,80 Mark. Drucksache
Berlin 0,80 Mark, außerh. 1,— Mark. Ausland 2,30 Mark, Drucksache 1,30 Mark
Redaktionsschluß: Montag mittag 1 Uhr, für die kommende Woche. — Geschäftszeit: 8 – 6 Uhr
Geschäftsstelle: Berlin S 14, Neue Jakobstraße 9 (Untergrundbahn Inselbrücke und Neanderstraße)
Tel.: F. 7. Jannowitz 4545. — Postscheckkonto: Anschrift Friedrich Radszuweit, Berlin Nr. 151122

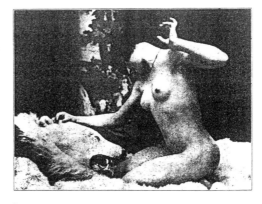

Damenklub
Monbijou

Tanzleitung Kati

Nach wie vor

Jeden Mittwoch

Sonnabend

Sonntag

Nur im

Amerikanischen

Tanzpalast

Kommandantenstraße 72

(Spittelmarkt)

Herren haben keinen Zutritt!

Damenklub „Violetta"

Nicht mehr Nationalhof,

sondern **nur jeden Mittwoch**
Sonnabend
Sonntag

Amerikanischen Tanzpalast (Zauberflöte)

Kommandantenstraße 72 (Spittelmarkt)

Klubleitung Lotte Hahm

FIGURE 12 *THE GIRLFRIEND*

One of Friedrich Radszuweit's successful titles, *The Girlfriend* was the world's first magazine to target a
specifically lesbian audience. It was also one of the first homosexual magazines to be affected by the 1926
Law to Protect Youth against Trash and Smut. The cover of this 1929 issue includes advertisements for two
lesbian friendship clubs (Damenklub Monbijou and Damenklub Violetta) as well as a mention of the important lesbian organizer and self-identified transvestite Lotte Hahm. Source: Schwules Museum, Berlin

Radszuweit's press also printed a gay literary and entertainment magazine, *The Island* (*Die Insel*), which, according to one historian, had a press run of 140,000 by 1930![144] He even tried to establish a magazine for transvestites called *The Third Sex* (*Das dritte Geschlecht*) in the early 1930s, although only four issues of this magazine appeared.[145] In addition, Radszuweit's press published pamphlets and books, and in 1923 he took the step of opening a bookstore. First located on Prinzenstrasse, and later on the ground floor of the press's office building at 9 Neue Jakobstrasse, the bookstore sold a range of material, including homosexual literature, scientific studies of an academic nature, and educational material written with a popular audience in mind. Naturally, one could also find the press's magazines on display in the window.[146]

By the middle of the decade, though, Radszuweit's press was facing some competition. Around the same time that Radszuweit began to print *The Girlfriend,* there was also an attempt to establish an independent lesbian magazine, *The Pages of Ideal Female Friendship* (*Blätter Idealer Frauenfreundschaft*). The magazine's founder, Selli Engler, hoped that it would kick-start a new organization for women, the Ladies Club of Readers of the Pages of Ideal Female Friendship (*Damen BIF Klub*). Both the magazine and the club proved short-lived, but Engler went on to write many pieces for the other lesbian magazines during the rest of the decade.[147] Another magazine was *Fanfare* (*Die Fanfare*), established by Ernst Neuberger in early 1924. It had a strongly literary character and was probably closely linked with a gay theater association in Berlin. For a short time, it also served as the official organ of the refounded DFV. Many of the authors for *Fanfare* took a strongly masculinist position when it came to cultural and political debates. However, the viewpoints were more mixed than you would find in *The Special One,* and there also were some female readers of *Fanfare.*

Friendship managed to make a comeback in the period after 1924. The owners of the old magazine had not given up on their project, and a few issues appeared on the stands in late 1923 and early 1924. Finally, in April 1924 it came back into publication on a regular basis—though monthly this time instead of weekly. Its character had changed pretty radically. Robbed of its connection with the nation's friendship clubs by Radszuweit's growing press empire, the new version of *Friendship* switched its target audience to more-educated readers. It included literary contributions, book reviews, discussions of current films and theater productions, and occasionally short political essays. The new editor, Georg Plock, avoided the personal ads that had caused the magazine so many legal problems earlier, though they were printed in an insert that was sent with subscription issues.

One of the previous editors of *Friendship*, Max Danielson, had had a falling-out with Radszuweit in 1925 and tried to establish his own magazine in 1928 along the lines of the old editions in conjunction with a new publisher in Berlin. *The New Friendship* aligned itself with the clubs in the refounded DFV, which were left without an official organ after *Fanfare* folded in 1925. It was joined by a new magazine that addressed lesbians, called *The Love of Women* (*Frauenliebe*) at first and *The Bachelor Girl* (*Garçonne*) a little later. Because they were printed by the same press, *The New Friendship* and *The Love of Women* reproduced a lot of the same articles and used many of the same authors. *The Love of Women*'s print run was rather limited, most probably never exceeding 10,000 copies.

The new wave of magazines that appeared after 1923 was not spared the legal attacks that had led to the demise of the original *Friendship*. Although, for reasons that are unclear, public prosecutors brought no pornography charges against the magazines in 1923 or 1924, afterward they resumed their offensive. The full scope is not known, as we mostly have to piece together the story with what was reported by the magazines themselves. It is likely that both *Fanfare* and *The Hellenic Messenger* were shut down by pornography charges.[148] The editors of Radszuweit's various magazines were also indicted on several occasions for producing obscene material and for procuring sex for others by printing personal ads. Whether they were convicted is not known but seems likely given how other cases generally went in the decade.

By 1928 the gay press was also subject to a new law, the Law to Protect Youth against Trash and Smut. This law has a long history going back to the 1890s, when a flood of cheap paperbacks had provoked moral purity activists, church leaders, and educators to form a broad coalition against "trashy" reading material. Although the war and revolution had proved a setback for the movement, the Weimar constitution specifically stated that its ban on censorship did not mean that "special measures" could not be taken to protect youth when necessary. The result was that the anti–trash and smut movement got going again in the early 1920s, culminating in 1925 with the drafting of a law by the conservative German National People's Party that proposed the establishment of a series of federal and state review boards to examine all available printed material. If these review boards decided that a book or periodical was dangerous to youth in some way, its title would be placed on a list that was circulated regularly to the local police and other government agencies. A pornography conviction would also cause the relevant publication to be automatically listed. Although registered publications were not technically censored, they could not be put in windows or placed on racks where children and adolescents could easily get hold of them. Anyone convicted of selling them to a child under the age of eighteen could be fined or even sent to prison. In the case of a periodical, if two issues within a year were placed on the list, the entire title could be affected for a whole year. Although the law was enormously controversial, a coalition of conservatives and liberals supported by representatives of the Protestant and Catholic churches managed to get the law through the Reichstag in 1926. Implementation of the law proved slow; the review boards issued their first decisions in December 1927 and afterward gradually began to add new titles to the list.[149]

One after another, the friendship magazines found their names registered with the review boards. The lesbian magazine *Girlfriend* was the first affected (in June 1928), followed soon afterward by Radszuweit's *Friendship Paper* and many other titles. When their titles were judged "smutty" enough to be included on the register for a full year, the editors were faced with a tough decision. Should they continue to print, even when advertisements would dry up once they could no longer have their magazine openly displayed for a year? Should the editors change the magazine's name, even though readers might not recognize the new title as something they want to read? Or should the editors simply stop publication for a year and wait it out, hoping that readers would return once the year was over? In the last years of the Weimar Republic, the editors of the friendship magazines tried all these strategies. Radszuweit's press temporarily stopped publication of *Girlfriend,* replacing it temporarily with *Single Women* (*Ledige Frauen*), which ran from mid-1928 until mid-1929. In one of the earliest issues, the magazine said that its goal was to give single women (and also divorcées and married women who felt no particular attachment to their husbands) a chance to express their "needs, worries, joys, and problems."[150] It promised to print letters from unmarried women and to offer tips to help solve daily problems. In fact, though, much of the content of later issues was devoted to short stories and serialized novels with homosexual characters, content that was very similar to *Girlfriend*'s. One serialized novel, *The Club of Girlfriends* by Marie Luise von Bern, started its story in *Girlfriend* but then concluded in the pages of *Single Women* under a slightly different title (*The Gala of Girlfriends*). Many of the issues included a picture of a topless model on the cover, which also leaves the declared intention to reach a female heterosexual audience in doubt.[151]

The publishers of the rival lesbian magazine, *The Love of Women,* also tried a new title to get around the law. During the public ban of 1928, they continued to print *The Love of Women* but also produced a new magazine with the title *Women's Love and Life* (*Frauen Liebe und Leben*) for a short period. This magazine had the same editor but otherwise had a substantially different appearance and content. Its intended audience was much wider, since it hoped to address both homosexual and heterosexual women. It addressed everything from modern science, fashion, and art to exercise and personal issues. Many more of its articles were written by men. This magazine did not last long, and by 1929 *The Love of Women* was allowed once again to be publicly displayed. But then in October 1930 an issue of the magazine was declared by the courts to be pornographic, and once again it could not be displayed. This time the publishers decided to change its name to *The Bachelor Girl* (*Garçonne*), although for a brief time in 1930 both titles were printed in order to give previous readers a chance to be told of the change. The content of the new magazine did not differ drastically from its predecessor's. Indeed, to make the connection with the earlier magazine clear, a special supplement called "The Love of Women" was included with *The Bachelor Girl.*[152]

Changing titles was rife with complications, so in most cases the publishers did their best to push through the ban. Radszuweit's *Friendship Paper* was published continuously until 1933, despite landing on the review board's list several times. The rival *Friendship* also managed to last until 1933, despite also being affected by the ban. Of all the gay magazines, only Radszuweit's *Pages for Human Rights* and the newsletter for the Hirschfeld's WhK were spared the arm of the law. Why exactly is unclear, though Micheler speculates that their content appeared scientific or serious enough to avoid legal action.[153]

Taken all together, magazines such as *Friendship, The Friendship Paper, Girlfriend,* and *The Bachelor Girl* served as important media for gradually linking homosexuals all across the nation into a common network of readers. They became the backbone for what Michael Warner has called a "counterpublic."[154] A symbiotic relationship formed between this counterpublic and the urban gay scenes. Much of the information readers found in the emerging gay publishing industry as well as in the wider public sphere would have directed them toward the urban gay scenes, especially Berlin's. In this way, the growing amount of printed material functioned as a crucial communications network, linking scattered individuals into new social formations and yielding an "imagined geography" of Germany's gay world that increasingly promoted Berlin as its metropole.[155] The position was then confirmed by the presence of Hirschfeld's WhK, Brand's GdE, the central headquarters of the BfM, and most of the gay and lesbian presses. By the 1920s Berlin was easily imagined by homosexuals throughout central Europe and beyond as an exciting place, full of opportunities for them to find sex and new relationships. What is more, it was a place where their basic sense of self could be affirmed.[156] As Hirschfeld observed as early as 1904, "Homosexuals from the countryside who visit such bars for the first time have been seen crying from being so deeply moved." [157]

If gay and lesbian publishing helped focus attention on Berlin, in smaller cities and even rural areas gay magazines served as seed crystals around which a web of new relationships could form. These texts allowed gay men and lesbians all over the country to imagine themselves as part of a larger community. [158] This "imagined community," to use the influential term of the political scientist Benedict Anderson, was never exactly identical with the urban gay scenes of Germany. [159] It was always conceived as an indefinite group of men, potentially quite large, who were spread out over the entire world but who were very often hidden in plain sight. In provincial cities, friendship clubs emerged from networks of readers, and magazines could promote these clubs by advertising events. They helped raise the political and social awareness of homosexuals, which the editors hoped would make an important contribution to the repeal of Paragraph 175. [160]

The overall picture of gay life in Weimar is perhaps not quite as rosy as we tend to remember. Policing continued, and perhaps even intensified mid-decade. Many of the gay magazines that appeared lasted only a year or two, and those that survived faced obscenity charges and by 1927 review boards that judged most of them to be "trash and smut." Nevertheless, what achievements were made were remarkable in comparison to what came beforehand and certainly what came afterward. The gay and lesbian bars, the cruising scenes of Berlin and elsewhere, and the homosexual magazines created networks of relationships and cultural space for experimentation with new forms of expression and self-awareness.

Especially through the texts of the homosexual counterpublic, gay and lesbian readers came to a new understanding of who they were and the role of same-sex desire within their lives. As Laurie Marhoefer writes in her recent book, *Sex and the Weimar Republic,* they "made it possible for readers to imagine queer lives for themselves." [161] Readers who were at some level conscious of experiencing sexual attraction toward members of the same sex read sympathetic descriptions of homosexuality with enthusiasm, of course, but they also were interested in material that we would read as heavily prejudiced: much of the scientific literature, for example, as well as sensationalist reportage on the "decadent" city. Homosexual readers were accustomed to taking on the role of the "gay detective," as the historian Martin Meeker calls it—being constantly on the watch for "signs, symbols, and information passed surreptitiously," searching through vast amounts of material for hints of same-sex desire, reading against the grain to yield voices that affirmed their sexual yearnings.[162]

Consequently, to understand the range of identities that gay men and lesbians constructed in Germany in the late nineteenth and early twentieth centuries, it is important to consider the whole range of representations of same-sex desire that were available to them. This topic will be the task of the next chapter. Beginning with a short survey of the traditional prejudices about sex between men and between women, it will then examine the literature, artistic representations, and early films that represented same-sex erotic desire. The guiding question will be simply: How did men and women who experienced such desires as significant aspects of their lives come to understand these sexual feelings, their selves, and their relationships?

CHAPTER 4

Representations and Identities

CHAPTER SUMMARY

This chapter investigates the features of German culture that informed people's understanding of same-sex desire, especially the country's strong classical and Romantic traditions in literature and the arts, but also more modern influences. It considers as well the role played by the homosexual press by the 1920s in offering a space to express some of these understandings and identities.

OVERVIEW

Since the publication of the philosopher Michel Foucault's work on sexuality, in the 1970s, historians, sociologists, and queer theorists have considered the emergence of sexual identities. Sociologists and many social historians have tended to emphasize the importance of urbanization and economic transformation in the formation of sexual identity. Others have taken their lead from Foucault by tracing the influence of scientific understanding and medical knowledge about sexuality. Still others have suggested the roles that the middle-class ideal of romantic love, changing gender norms, and even nationalism might play. Most fundamentally, perhaps, queer theory has made us attentive to the multiple ways of understanding and defining sexual identity. What seems clear is that multiple social and cultural forces were at work, forces that both created constraints on how people could behave and generated new opportunities for self-understanding.

As men and women began to develop identities in which deep physical or erotic attachments to members of the same sex played an important role, they found they had much available in their society and culture to work with. This chapter focuses mostly on the efforts of recent historians to broaden our understanding of science's effects and in other ways expand the conversation to include additional factors. It considers the importance of the classical heritage in some detail, but it also examines the significance of the Romantic tradition, ideas about "modernity," and the homosexual press for the articulation of homosexual identity. Special attention is given to the poems of Stefan George, the photographs of Wilhelm von Gloeden, the film *Girls in Uniform,* and novels written by Klaus Mann, John Henry Mackay, and Anna Elisabet Weirauch.

KEY TERMS

Germany; gay and lesbian identity; Stefan George; Wilhelm von Gloeden; Klaus Mann; *Girls in Uniform* (film)

Whisnant, Clayton J.
Queer Identities and Politics in Germany: A History 1880–1945
dx.doi.org/10.17312/harringtonparkpress/2016.08.qipg.004
© Harrington Park Press, LLC, New York, NY 10011

FIGURE 13 **THOMAS MANN IN 1929**

Thomas Mann is one of the best-known German authors, famous for works such as *Buddenbrooks* and *Death in Venice*. Two of his six children, Klaus and Erika, became well known in 1920s Berlin for their artistic accomplishments and their relatively open sexuality. Taken together, they represent just a sample of the variety of sexual identities that could be found in Germany during the late nineteenth and early twentieth centuries. This chapter investigates the features of German culture that informed people's understanding of same-sex desire, including the country's strong classical and Romantic traditions in literature and the arts, as well as more modern influences. It also considers the role played by the homosexual press by the 1920s in offering a space to express some of these understandings and identities. Source: Bundesarchiv, Bild 183-H2554. Photographer unknown

As a boy growing up in the 1880s and early 1890s, the author Thomas Mann (Figure 13) turned to German literature and to the Greco-Roman past to make sense of his erotic feelings for other boys his own age. He especially loved the works of Friedrich Schiller and Count August von Platen—neither of them necessarily unusual choices for a future writer, since both were (and still are) canonical figures of early nineteenth-century literature. What he saw in these works is revealing, however. He admired Schiller for his passionate friendship with Johann Wolfgang von Goethe, another German author of tremendous significance for the nation's literature. In a school essay he described Schiller's feeling for Goethe as "the greatest romance of the early nineteenth century."[1] Mann admired the poet Platen, on the other hand, for his "mournfully sensuous syntax, filled with languorous echoes and delayed gratification," as Mann's biographer Anthony Heilbut describes it.[2] Much of the literature from the early nineteenth century was saturated with a passion for classical Greece and Rome, and such imagery would emerge as a recurring theme in the books that Mann would write later. Like many of the ancients, Mann appreciated male beauty, especially of a youthful variety. This passion did not disappear as Mann grew up, and many of his works include main characters struggling with homoerotic feelings—for example, Tonio Kröger in the novella of the same name (1903) and Hans Castorp in *The Magic Mountain* (*Der Zauberberg*, 1924).[3]

Mann's most famous depiction of this struggle comes in the novella *Death in Venice* (*Der Tod in Venedig*, 1912), the story of the writer Gustav von Aschenbach, who finds himself haunted day and night by thoughts of young Tadzio, a Polish boy whom he meets while vacationing in Venice. Although possible to rationalize as an allegorical meditation on the creative process or even as an updated retelling of Greek mythology, such interpretations require overlooking some fairly obvious description of homosexual passion.[4] Heilbut goes so far as to say, "From one perspective, the homosexual element in German poetry reaches its culmination in [Mann's] Venice, the site of Goethe and Platen's most impassioned lyrics."[5]

Despite his sexual preferences, Mann married and eventually had six children, two of whom grew up to be homosexual, much more openly than their father ever was. The oldest daughter, Erika, became a recognized theater actress on the stages of Berlin. The oldest son, Klaus, followed in his father's footsteps, becoming an author of several well-known books, the most famous of which is *Mephisto* (1936). The two children had grown up close, sharing a bedroom and playing together frequently.[6] When they went off to Berlin as young adults, they remained tied together, sharing two rooms and exploring the cabarets, jazz venues, and cocaine dens of the city. Klaus struggled to develop a voice of his own, often taking risqué topics such as incest and homosexuality as themes for his works. The historian Harry Oosterhuis has noted that Klaus's life "can easily be interpreted as an act of defiance against his father's conservative, detached stance." He was "more or less open about his own homosexual preference, seeking actively to make it an integral part of his private and public life."[7] Erika's relationship with her father was less strained, but she also was interested in establishing her own image. She became "a symbol of the daring new woman of the Weimar Republic," as the biographer Andrea Weiss puts it, with her short hair and numerous love affairs with both men and women.[8] Even while pursuing their own lives, they remained close. In fact, for a time their love lives were intertwined in ways that probably seem bizarre to us. Klaus was engaged for a few years to Pamela Wedekind, who was actually Erika's lover. Erika, for her part, married in 1924 the actor Gustaf Gründgens, who also had a brief but passionate affair with Klaus. The siblings never entirely escaped the shadow of their father's reputation, but they were clearly very different from him: fun, vivacious, and eager to embrace the modern world with all the excitement that it had to offer.

Although Thomas Mann and his children Erika and Klaus ultimately lived out their sexual lives in very different ways, each was engaged with a central problem that historians have suggested was important for people who lived in this era, namely, the reevaluation of the importance of sexuality for life, happiness, and self-understanding. How and why exactly this problem emerged at this time have proved to be complicated questions. Sociologists and many social historians have tended to emphasize the process of urbanization and economic transformation in the formation of sexual identity. Both, as we saw in the last chapter, created new social spaces and new ways for people to relate to one another. In the 1980s and 1990s many social historians fused this argument together with a second offered by Michel Foucault, who argued that the spread of a scientific understanding and medical knowledge about sexuality that we examined in the first chapter of this book was absolutely fundamental to the modern homosexual identity.

Recently, there has been some reaction against the almost canonical status that Foucault's explanation achieved for a time among historians of sexuality. Oosterhuis's research on Krafft-Ebing suggests that we scholars need to contextualize scientific discourse a little more carefully than we have often done. He argues that medical texts need to be understood in relation to the social conditions in which they emerged and were read. Similarly, Linda Doan's work on the effect that sexology had on British culture and on lesbians in particular during the 1920s is a reminder that who was reading these texts, and what goals these readers had in mind as they did so, could radically influence their interpretation. She observes how selectively lawyers and legislators used sexology in public and court debates, borrowing its authority for their own purposes while also grafting it onto language and arguments that were very unscientific in nature.[9] But lesbians could be equally selective in their own way. They took ideas that were sometimes interwoven with language that was at best unsympathetic toward women and then reworked them for their own purposes.[10]

Both Oosterhuis's and Doan's research suggests the ideological power of the sexual sciences should not be overstated. There were other social changes that were equally important for the evolution of nineteenth- and twentieth-century sexuality. Oosterhuis highlights the importance of the middle-class ideal of romantic love and the spread of autobiographical self-analysis among the educated classes.[11] We also cannot forget about the ramifications of changes in gender norms and the relationships between men and women. When it comes specifically to the development of a lesbian identity, historians have noted the significance of the women's movement and the appearance of the so-called New Woman at the end of the nineteenth century. Not all feminists or New Women were lesbians, of course, but women who did feel an emotional or sexual pull toward other women could feel sufficiently emboldened by these social changes to dare to lead a life independent of husband and family. "Love between women," Lillian Faderman observed in her seminal study, *Surpassing the Love of Men,* "could take on a new shape" as women gained both financial independence and "a support group so that they would not feel isolated and outcast when they claimed their independence."[12]

Another group of scholars has pointed to the rise of nationalism in the nineteenth century, which functioned as a "normalizing process that imagined modern collectivities as ethnically homogeneous and inherently masculinist entities."[13] As George Mosse argued in his pioneering work *Nationalism and Sexuality,* an ethic of respectability rooted in middle-class sensibilities was transformed into a vehicle for forging and strengthening the nation-state in the midst of massive social and economic change. Sexual passions became a source of intense anxiety and were isolated as a potential source of sickness and national weakness. Manliness came to be imagined as meaning "freedom from sexual passion, the sublimation of sensuality into leadership of society and the nation."[14] The male homosexual, in contrast, was defined as a dangerous outsider whose lack of restraint threatened the family, the social order, and the nation at large.

We also need to give other kinds of texts besides scientific articles and medical books their due. Newspapers, magazines, pamphlets, broadsides, cinema, and novels all played some role in defining what people thought about same-sex desire. The move to widen the range of texts has opened up opportunities for scholars to borrow insights from queer theory and cultural studies. Judith Butler's groundbreaking book *Gender Trouble* can easily be read as a call for scholars to venture beyond written texts to get at styles of dress, body language, manners of speech, and other aspects of what she calls a "performance of self."[15] This work resonated in certain ways with the efforts of social historians who were trying to capture a "History of Everyday Life" (*Alltagsgeschichte*) by borrowing insights from anthropology and ethnography.[16] Although more work needs to be done here, there have been a few who have followed such examples to uncover new dimensions of identity construction.[17]

Most fundamentally, perhaps, queer theory has made us attentive to the multiple ways of understanding and defining sexual identity. Even after the mental habit of dividing people into homosexual and heterosexual categories became established in the early twentieth century (discussed in chapter 2), efforts to "fix or name sexual identities" continued to be "overdetermined by other conflicts," as Michael Warner once put it in a seminal essay.[18] Class, gender, race, ethnicity, and other bearers of identity and status almost always left their mark. Furthermore, multiple understandings of sexual orientation, its relationship to the human psyche, and its implications for gender circulated in the nineteenth and early twentieth centuries. What seems clear at the moment is that there were multiple social and cultural forces at work, forces that both created constraints on how people could behave and generated new opportunities for self-understanding.

As men and women began to develop identities in which deep physical or erotic attachments for members of the same sex played an important role, they found they had much available in their society and culture to work with. Their new identities were composed by *bricolage,* to use a term introduced by the sociologist Claude Lévi-Strauss in the 1960s. In other words, they involved a reworking of the available cultural material, putting it to use in novel ways to solve new problems or accomplish new goals.[19] The result was an extremely diverse set of sexual identities. Modern medical science did have some influence on these identities, but other social and cultural factors, such as class, age, and occupation, all played a role. In fact, Marti Lybeck's study *Desiring Emancipation* suggests that Berlin's gay scene brought together working-class women whose jobs allowed them to live without marrying, female prostitutes who had found companionship with each other, wealthy socialites who could explore the consumer opportunities offered by the city, and professional women whose work required them to be more careful of their reputations.[20] It may prove impossible in the end to catalog all the possibilities (and anyway it is certainly too early to begin this project now), so instead we might simply examine some of the sources that commonly informed these identities as they emerged.

The differences between the way that Thomas Mann and his children lived their lives suggest that cultural shifts were taking place, which this chapter will explore. Since the role of sexology in shaping identities is considered in earlier chapters, this one will focus mostly on the effort of recent historians to complicate our understanding of science's effect and in other ways broaden the conversation to include additional factors. It will naturally consider the importance of the classical heritage in some detail, but it will also examine the significance of the Romantic tradition, ideas about "modernity," and the role that the homosexual press played in an articulation of homosexual identity.

PREJUDICES ABOUT GAY AND LESBIAN SEX

Germany inherited many prejudices against same-sex desire from the past. According to medieval Christianity, sodomy was a sin and an unnatural act. It was perverted (*pervers*) and deviant (*abartig*). The law defined it as a criminal indecency (*Unzucht*), a word that in German carries connotations of a lack of discipline (*Zucht*). Thus, it was seen as disorderly or out-of-control desire. It was a filthy act—*Schmutzerei* or *Schweinerei*. The latter term in particular brings to mind a pig (*Schwein*) rolling around in the mud. In the eighteenth and nineteenth centuries, men who had sex with other men were sometimes called pederasts by the better-educated classes. Among the rural and working class, they were known as *Spinatstecher*, or "spinach prickers," a crude allusion to anal intercourse.

Although same-sex acts had long been a crime in much of the German-speaking world, the association between these acts and criminality grew only as the number of newspapers and other print sources expanded.[21] Especially during the media explosion that took place at the end of the nineteenth century, Germans had plenty of chances to read about arrests and court cases involving homosexuals.[22] In the sensationalist boulevard press, reports normally implied that homosexuals were denizens of a criminal underworld. By this time men who preferred to have sex with men were most commonly called "warm brothers" (*warme Bruder*). This term's origin is less clear than that of some of the other language, but "warm" is probably an allusion either to affected and emotional behavior or to sexual heat.[23] Even more debated is the origin of *schwul*. It might have come from the cant of the criminal milieu, or possibly from students, who in the eighteenth century described someone in trouble as *in schwulibus*. Or it may be simply an extension of "warm," since *schwül* means hot and humid. At any rate, Berliners used this term in the nineteenth century, though no one is sure if it originated there.[24] By the 1920s it was used widely in many other dialects. Today, we often translate the term as "gay," since it has been widely adopted by gay men in Germany as a self-description. Before the 1970s, though, the term almost always had a pejorative connotation. The American slang *fag* probably gives a better sense of what was implied.

Modern medical science produced some opportunities for creating more positive representations of same-sex desire, as we have seen, but it also unfortunately created a host of new prejudices. Forensic doctors and psychiatrists began to talk about this desire as a mental illness. Many saw it as a neurosis and, for Krafft-Ebing and the many psychiatrists who followed him, a perversion. For some it was simply an accumulation of bad habits; for others it was a mark of hereditary degeneracy. And because many psychiatrists believed that homosexuality was a kind of gender inversion, they helped spread the assumption that all homosexuals were effeminate. Historians are actually deeply divided about whether forensic doctors and psychiatrists created this "third sex" model of homosexuality or only popularized a conception generated in the gay scenes of London, Paris, and Amsterdam during the eighteenth century.[25] Whatever the origin, what is certain is that by the end of the nineteenth century in Germany, the association between homosexuality and gender inversion was shaping both popular prejudice and homosexual identities. At the same time that homosexual activists were using the concept of the "third sex" to argue for legal reform, church leaders, moral purity activists, and many other public figures were using the stereotype to warn about German national weakness, to plead for moral reform programs, and to question the competence of Germany's leaders.[26] In the gay scenes, an effeminate homosexual was referred to sometimes as a *Tante* or a *Tunte*—literally "aunt," though "fairy," "pansy," "sissy," or possibly "queen" might give a better sense of the word for English speakers. Gradually, the use of *Tante* or *Tunte* in this way became familiar to a wider public in the early twentieth century.

There were fewer words to describe women who had sex with other women, perhaps some indication that Germany was less anxious in general about this kind of sexuality. When such women were discussed, educated Germans might make some reference to the Greek poet Sappho. Alternatively, they might borrow the French word *tribade,* which suggests the importance of French pornography in shaping what people thought about this kind of sex from the sixteenth through the eighteenth centuries. Since this literature was aimed at titillating primarily a male, heterosexual audience, sex between women was given a more positive spin than male homosexual sex was. It was imagined as sexually exciting for women but ultimately not fulfilling. It was foreplay, awakening women's passion so that they could eventually turn to men. As Lillian Faderman wrote, "In men's phallocentric world it was inconceivable that a woman's sexual pleasure could be significant if the male were absent."[27] As Faderman also observed, however, even this pornography was often haunted by a fear of female independence. Frequently, the aggressive sexuality of the chief character in such works is a sign of her desire for masculine power and sometimes even for male genitalia. Long before the gender inversion model was spread by medicine in the second half of the nineteenth century, there was a tendency to equate lesbianism with gender transgression, as illustrated in the novel *The Nun* by the famous French philosophe Denis Diderot.[28] The female desire that drove women to such acts was described as a kind of madness, and it was very often textually linked to sadomasochistic practices such as flagellation.

As this short summary of prejudices against homosexuality suggests, Germans had plenty of terms to describe men and women who had sex with members of the same sex. Forging something positive out this morass of misconceptions and antipathies was going to be difficult, however. Sodomites, pederasts, spinach prickers, sissies, tribades—all these descriptions portrayed homosexuals as social outsiders, or "Others," to use more academic language. None was going to be easily adopted as a self-description.

FIN-DE-SIÈCLE TRANSFORMATIONS

Nevertheless, European culture was going through some significant changes at the end of the nineteenth century that would ultimately create opportunities for a reevaluation of homosexual desire. As we saw in chapter 1, both the legacy of Enlightenment philosophy and science-based medical knowledge offered alternative perspectives on homosexuality. Given this context, it is understandable that much of the literature addressing homosexuality cited various medical or legal arguments for tolerance and legal freedom, as the literary critic James Jones has shown. Unfortunately, few examples of this type of work are as imaginative or timeless as the books of Thomas Mann. Ludwig Dilsner's play *Jasmine Blossoms* (*Jasminblüthe,* 1898) is, sadly, quite typical in the rather forced way that it moves from didactic speeches to tragic endings.[29] Only slightly better is Aimée Duc's *Are They Women?* (*Sind Es Frauen?* 1901), set in Geneva among a group of female university students. These virile-looking women spend a lot of time talking about Krafft-Ebing, modern research into homosexuality, and the challenges facing women trying to pursue a medical degree. The main characters fall in love, separate, and are reunited in the end.[30] The story is sentimental but at least does not end in suicide. James Jones notes, in fact, that the novel was important for suggesting that homosexual characters could "achieve love relationships which promise fulfillment, not failure."[31]

Medical works and scientific theorizing about homosexuality offered new language and perspective on same-sex desire, but they cannot account for all the new interest in this form of love. Equally important was the way that sex in general was made a central theme of their work by artists and authors all across Europe beginning in the 1890s. In the English-speaking world, we cannot think of the fin de siècle without Oscar Wilde or Aubrey Beardsley coming to mind. For those readers who favor French literature, Marcel Proust, Paul Verlaine, and André Gide are ready examples. Not coincidentally, this new emphasis on sex happened at the same time that intellectuals such as Sigmund Freud and Henri Bergson were theorizing about the importance of the unconscious and irrational impulses for mankind.[32] As a major theme, sex proved useful for those people wanting to express their disgust toward the hypocrisy and double standard that they felt permeated the bourgeois culture around them. In Vienna authors such as Arthur Schnitzler and Hugo von Hofmannsthal, as well as artists such as Gustav Klimt and Egon Schiele, used sexual representations to "unveil bourgeois society's sense of security as a façade, full of empty conventions."[33] From this perspective, sexuality became symbolic for the hidden life of humans—their real nature, which had been stifled by centuries of Christianity and hidden by Victorian prudery. It was energy, spirit, vitality, instinct. And thanks to the nineteenth-century preoccupation with autobiography, it became the truth within us that had to be found and eventually revealed. This kind of attitude toward sexuality borrowed much from early nineteenth-century Romanticism, with its love of nature and suspicion of civilization. It allowed many Romantic perspectives and symbols to become revived in the art and literature of the turn of the twentieth century.

Several artists and writers connected homosexuality in an explicit way with some figures that had long fascinated the European creative class, namely the ephebe and the androgyne. For centuries, the ephebe had served as a symbol of youth and vitality, and at the end of the nineteenth century it acquired new significance as European society became obsessed with—and at the same time anxious about—adolescence.[34] The androgyne, on the other hand, combined masculine and feminine qualities into one being, thereby expressing a yearning for a healed world, one in which people still exist in "that primal state of perfect interior balance."[35] Both the Romantics and gothic novelists of the early nineteenth century had occasionally used androgynous characters or images in their works in this way, and at the end of the century the androgyne would reappear with a similar meaning in numerous poems, stories, and paintings.

Frank Wedekind's *Spring Awakening* (*Frühlings Erwachen*, 1891) is one of the most famous German works that fuses neo-Romantic themes with a more modern theatrical presentation. A "mosaic of monologues and short scenes" tied together only loosely into a plot, the drama explores the difficulties of language in capturing everything real and important in life.[36] It centers on a group of fourteen-year-old youths entering puberty, each one struggling with his or her sexual desires and more often than not coming to a tragic end. One girl, unable to get the facts of life explained to her by her mother, ends up getting pregnant. Her mother arranges an abortion, but the doctor botches it and she dies. The boy who has fathered the child is expelled from his school. One of his schoolmates, unable to focus academically because of his confusing sexual preoccupations, flunks out and shoots himself. A minor character, Hänschen, has his homosexual impulses awakened by his readings of Shakespeare and his glimpses of nude paintings in the school's curriculum. In one of the last scenes of the play, he and another male classmate confess their love for one another. The scenes in which Hänschen is featured, observes the historian Peter Jelavich, "illustrate in outrageous fashion Wedekind's carnivalesque contention that the erotic components of genuine classicism can explode the cerebral schooling of the 'classical' Gymnasium."[37]

More run-of-the-mill Romanticism suffused much of the art and literature that appeared in the homosexual magazines. And in the photographs and short stories published in the friendship press of the 1920s, many authors saw the countryside as a space for refuge, relaxation, and sexual discovery. A large number of the stories in the lesbian press used natural settings such as the mountains or the seashore. One can easily interpret these stories as a firm rejection of the identification between homosexuality and modernity made by so many moralizing figures at the time. Most commonly, the characters are presented as fleeing the city, especially "murderous" (*tötende*) Berlin, with its noise and monotonous daily routine. In more natural settings, the "protagonists feel themselves to be understood and accepted," observes Heike Schader in her study of German lesbian magazines, *Virile Women, Vamps, and Wild Violets* (*Virile, Vamps und wilde Veilchen*). In one typical story, the character falls asleep sunbathing nude on a beach and has an erotic dream that "opens a new passion within her, a sexual excitement never yet known, and she worries that her everyday life in Berlin will now be unbearable."[38] Escape from the routine and social conventions of civilization allows new pleasures to be discovered, new forms of self to be explored, and new kinds of relationships to be established. Sometimes the escape into nature might also be presented as a passage through time into a long-lost past. Or, more simply, it might be an entry into a richer, fuller world of meaning in which nature becomes almost a divine presence.

At least implicit in much Romantic art and literature was a critique of the controlling and stifling tendencies of society. Such a critique was central to the most famous lesbian film of the Weimar era, *Girls in Uniform* (*Mädchen in Uniform,* 1931). The film tells the story of a sensitive young girl named Manuela von Meinhardis, who is sent off to a boarding school for the daughters of poor aristocrats in Potsdam. The atmosphere is oppressive. The headmistress sees herself as an embodiment of Prussian discipline, carrying a cane with her wherever she goes. Much of the film, however, focuses on the relationship that develops between Manuela and an attractive, sympathetic teacher, Fräulein von Bernburg. After the successful performance of a school play and a "day of harmless saturnalia and light spirits," Manuela's "pent-up passions explode."[39] She has a little too much alcohol-spiked punch and declares her love for her teacher in front of the entire school. The headmistress cracks down on Manuela, forbidding anyone else in the school to talk to her. In the original version—a play called *Yesterday and Today* (*Gestern und Heute*) performed in Berlin in 1931, and written by the German-Hungarian writer Christa Winsloe, who was in the process of coming out as a lesbian— Manuela throws herself down a staircase at the end of the production, killing herself.[40] In the film version, she is narrowly saved by her schoolmates' arriving just in time—but not before the effect of the near suicide can be felt. "An old stooped woman," the headmistress "retreats under the accusing stares of the girls and silently disappears in the dark corridor."[41]

The film is indeed a critique of Prussian authoritarianism and a "plea for its humanization," as Siegfried Kracauer observed, but it is also very much a lesbian film, as the film critic Richard Dyer points out. True, the film production was not as obviously lesbian as the play put on in Berlin earlier in the year; in the latter, Bernburg was played by Margarete Melzer, described as a "real butch type" by the actress who played Manuela in the film version.[42] Still, in the film there are shots of girls "lying together in bed, bathed in the dappled light that suggests romance."[43] Another scene lingers on the kisses that Bernburg gives to all the girls as she wishes them a good night's sleep.[44] And if the viewer missed such moments, it would be difficult to ignore the pronouncement made by the teacher shortly before the suicide attempt: "What you call sins I call the great spirit of love, which has a thousand forms."[45] One writer for the lesbian magazine *The Girlfriend* found this speech quite moving. In her words, Dorothea Wieck, who played Bernburg in the film version, "knew how to express the struggle between her self-control and her disposition both in terms of her performance and in terms of her spoken lines. In this way she proved herself to be an artist with a real claim to being considered one of the foremost interpreters of female characters who are psychologically difficult and yet faithful to their humanity."[46]

The suicide that concluded the stage version of *Girls in Uniform* was actually much more typical of most literature dealing with homosexuality. Tragic endings are common in Romantic literature, and they tended to haunt a large amount of the fiction dealing with homosexuality from this period. Death and suicide were useful, after all, in driving home the social criticism intended by the author. But they could simultaneously have other functions. If asked, Freud might have suggested that the main character's downfall served to work through the author's own troubled feelings about such sexual impulses. In at least a few instances, such a diagnosis would strike us as fitting. For example, Maria Eichhorn's *Diary of a Teacher* (*Tagebuch einer Erzieherin,* 1904) is the story of a sadomasochistic relationship that develops between a teacher and her pupil, the latter's awakened sexual appetite causing her to turn to prostitution. Eventually, she becomes a dominatrix. She does marry, but a return to heterosexuality does not spare her from death at the end of the novel.

Tragic conclusions also generate pathos. In many of these works, death highlights the human dimension of simply living with emotions that are not widely shared. Probably the most famous example is the Austrian writer Stefan Zweig's *Confusion of Feeling* (*Verwirrung der Gefühle,* 1927), a masterful portrait of a troubled relationship between a homosexual professor, his wife, and a student who has come to live with him and study under him. Lesser-known works that fit this description would include Adolf Brand's short story "Pitiful Young Lad" ("*Armer Junge,*" 1898), in which the author portrays the sad relationship between a homosexual soldier and the heterosexual friend whom he has fallen in love with. In the end, faced with the loneliness of loving another who cannot return his feelings, the soldier shoots himself.[47]

Hanns Fuchs, one of the authors associated with Brand's circle of masculinist friends, also wrote a romance novel focusing on a young homosexual soldier. *Eros between You and Us* (*Eros zwischen Euch und Uns,* 1909) tells the story of an officer named George struggling to come to terms with his own sexuality at the same time that he seeks acceptance among family and friends. For a time, a fellow officer takes him under his wing, escorting him to a party full of homosexual men. George's brother and sister also give George their love, approving of a friend named Hans Wandersloh, with whom George falls in love. Their mother, however, proves more difficult, as does the voice of his inner conscience. George cannot dodge the feeling that there is something wrong with him, and he visits doctors several times seeking a way to overcome his affliction. Eventually, he follows one doctor's advice to marry, and he chooses Wandersloh's sister as a spouse. The emotional struggle proves too much; he dies from a nervous breakdown. In this instance, it is not society itself that kills George exactly, but his failure to achieve some level of self-acceptance.[48]

GREEK LOVE

Underlying much of the neo-Romantic fascination with homosexuality and homoeroticism was a much older body of ideas and images that offered positive associations connected with same-sex desire, namely, those related to ancient Greek and Roman culture. The Germans had always been remarkably successful in fusing Romanticism and classicism despite the tensions that theoretically exist between the two styles, and so it is unsurprising to see the love of nature appear as a major theme in essays, stories, and photographs dedicated to Greek love. Stories of Sparta and the Sacred Band of Thebes; myths involving Zeus and Ganymede, Apollo and Hyacinth; Socrates' love for Alcibiades, Achilles' for Patroclus; Sappho's poetry and Plato's *Symposium*—all these and more offered a rich store of ideas for anyone seeking an understanding of sexual feelings for members of the same sex. As the historian Peter Gay writes, "To assimilate modern homosexual affairs to the exalted classical heritage was to borrow from its dignity, to claim a kind of historic rightness. The device was transparent, but no less popular for all that."[49]

The masculinists associated with Benedict Friedlaender and Adolf Brand were the most forceful champions of a male homosexual identity based on memories of ancient Greece and Rome. Because of the continuing importance of a classical education in the nineteenth and early twentieth centuries, however, such an identification was available to a much wider group of people than the relatively small number of men in Brand's circle. An admiration for ancient Greece was a European-wide phenomenon, of course, but one might easily argue that the love of Greek classicism expressed in a whole era of German literature, from Johann Joachim Winckelmann in the 1760s to Heinrich Heine in the 1840s, turned it into a fundamental feature of Germany's educated elite. Not a few of these authors, especially Winckelmann, Johann Wolfgang von Goethe, and Count August von Platen, expressed a love for male beauty and intimate friendships with other men in their works that have raised questions about their sexuality.[50] Although such clues were either studiously ignored or carefully interpreted as "mere symbolism" by German educators through most of the nineteenth century, they were not missed by readers inclined to go looking for them.

The fascination with antiquity persisted, especially among those homosexual writers born in the 1860s and 1870s. For this generation, medical writings and pamphlets arguing for homosexual emancipation were too rare to have made much of an imprint during their crucial adolescent years, so Greek texts and classical German authors were generally the most decisive influences as they worked through their sexual impulses. Besides Thomas Mann and the equally well-known French author André Gide, another good example is the poet Stefan George. Although not as well known today in the English-speaking world as either Mann or Gide, at the turn the twentieth century he was the face of "art for art's sake" in Germany, the national equivalent of Oscar Wilde in Great Britain, or Stéphane Mallarmé in France. Inspired by the French poetry of Mallarmé, Charles Baudelaire, and Paul Verlaine, which he discovered during a vacation to Paris in 1889, he began to write and publish symbolist poetry of his own during the early 1890s. He believed that poetry had the ability to change the world. For Stefan George, "poetry struck at the heart of the matter," wrote the historian George Mosse, "and was, at the same time, impartial and uncommitted to any particular political solution." The poet "was in direct touch with the pulse of the nation."[51]

Stefan George settled in Munich, finding allies and admirers among the many university students and artists settled in the Schwabing neighborhood of the city. By the mid-1890s a circle of George disciples had coalesced. They were bound together by their hatred of everything rational, materialistic, bourgeois, and modern—what they denounced as the "spiritlessness of the times." Traditional values such as dignity and individuality, they believed, "had succumbed to the necessity of disguising the self behind so many roles, personae, or assumed identities."[52] Perhaps more important, though, was their absolute devotion to George, whom they came to see as a spokesman for the "Secret Germany" that stirs "underneath the desolate superficial scab," as one of George's most enthusiastic followers wrote.[53] By the end of the 1920s his admirers had spread far beyond this inner circle to include a much wider public of Germans searching for hope and meanings in the turbulent era that followed the First World War. For them he was the prophet of a "New Reich" (the title of his 1928 books of poems) who "represented to many of his countrymen the quintessence of a new German culture," and who offered "a model of acting and being."[54]

Even for the readers at the time, the homoeroticism of his poems was difficult to miss. His *Algabal* (1892) imagines the mythic world of the Roman emperor Elagabalus, one of the most decadent of the Roman monarchs. Living in a palace of gold and gems, surrounded by submissive slave boys and officials waiting to fulfill his every need, Elagabalus has built for himself a temple to a hermaphroditic god, whose dual sexual nature mirrors the emperor's own wish to give birth.[55] *The Year of the Soul* (*Das Jahr der Seele,* 1897) tells the story of a poet who renounces the love of a woman, that "pale flower with the diseased heart," in favor of a newfound happiness in the companionship of male friends. Most famous is his book *The Seventh Ring* (*Der Siebente Ring,* 1907). After taking the reader through meditations on the ruin and corruption of the world around him, this work moves on to two sections of love poems dedicated to close friends. Especially in the "Maximin" poems at the very center of the book, Stefan George's yearning for his recently deceased friend, Maximilian Kronberger, takes on a sexual dimension, as his friend is transformed in the poems into a god. In these poems, the poet expresses his desire "not just to fuse with but actually to engulf and absorb his idealized lover." Maximin is presented as a miraculous being, a Christlike figure offering resurrection and eternal life. His kiss calls one to worship him. His presence dissolves one. His love extinguishes sufferings "in deeper fires."[56]

George's poetry was widely admired in gay circles. Brand's *The Special One* included many of his works on its recommended reading list. Hirschfeld's *Yearbook for Sexual Intermediaries* published an essay in 1914 by Peter Hamecher titled "Male Eros in the Work of Stefan George."[57] In public George's followers were fairly defensive about the rumors about his sexuality, especially in the wake of the Eulenburg scandal. In a 1912 essay published in the George circle's chief political forum, *The Yearbook for the Spiritual Movement* (*Jahrbuch für die geistige Bewegung*), two of his close friends denied that the cult of friendship between men as honored in George's poetry had anything to do with Paragraph 175 or the perversions studied by sexologists.[58] In private, however, members understood perfectly well George's wish to have a constant stream of attractive young men passing through his circle.[59] Although theoretically looked after as potential young poets, very few of these hopeful pupils turned out to have much talent to speak of.

To what extent there was a physical aspect that developed alongside the strong bonds of affection and loyalty that existed between George and any of his followers is hard to say. Stefan George was purposely circumspect in his letters, and he demanded a similarly cautious attitude from his close friends in their correspondence. In general, George asked them to burn letters from him, especially if they contained anything sensitive. Only one surviving letter from his devotee Ernst Glöckner hints at sexual contact between the two. Shortly afterward, Glöckner wrote a second apologizing for his indiscretion: "From now on I will never speak about it again."[60]

Naturally, George never spoke candidly about his sexual feelings in any public forum or setting. His thoughts, however, might be guessed from a preface that he wrote to his translated version of Shakespeare's sonnets, a large number of which are notable for their homoeroticism. Stefan George approved of the passionate devotion (*leidenschaftliche Hingabe*) that Shakespeare expressed toward the "Fair Youth" in that group of poems, and he regretted the inability of his age to appreciate the "supersexual love" (*übergeschlechtliche Liebe*) embodied in them. What exactly he meant by "supersexual love," of course, is open to interpretation, as Marita Keilson-Lauritz points out. Does he mean "sex-transcending?" "Gender-transcending?" Or, most likely, the kind of "spiritual love" that Plato opposed to "earthly love" in his *Symposium*, a love that aims at a man's nobility of soul. This would be a "Sexual-but-also-something-more-than-sexual love."[61]

Such a reading of Stefan George's words would be in line with the antics that took place at times among his circle of friends. In the 1890s one of the most important figures in George's circle was Alfred Schuler, a lover of ancient Rome who championed neopaganism, occult worship, and anti-Semitism in the bohemian cafés of Munich. He was also fascinated by all things sexual. Those who knew him well understood that his hatred for the modern world was fueled by his "homoeroticism, which was feminine and primitive," as one person commented. Schuler was "fascinated only by male strength, by young soldiers and sailors, boxers and wrestlers, by muscle-bound workers in overalls and by strapping farm boys in lederhosen."[62] Many around him were undecided whether he was a harmless buffoon or disturbingly crazy.[63] George was not particularly anti-Semitic, and his circle always contained a number of Jewish Germans. George, however, did share Schuler's love of the ancient world and his hatred for all things modern. Around 1900 he began to attend Greek- and Roman-themed costume balls put on by Schuler and several other members of his circle. A great deal of money and effort was spent on designing costumes and scenery. Admittedly, many who attended simply saw it as great fun, a chance to mingle and drink wine. But those in the "Cosmic Circle," including George and his devotees, saw it as a mythic event, a "world-creating" atmosphere that had the potential to transform life and the human psyche.[64]

This is not to say that George had entirely bought into all Schuler's excesses. Several comments that he made to friends make it clear that George also recognized that Schuler was, actually, a little crazy. But insanity, too, could have it purpose, George thought. And he certainly appreciated the power of ritual, as demonstrated by George's longtime residence in Munich, known by many as the "Globe Room." Here, dressed in a long white robe, surrounded by friends dressed in yellow, purple, and dark blue garments, George would receive visitors. The room was mostly bare. There was a simple, unstained shelf that ran around the walls of the room, and a table in the middle covered with a plain white tablecloth. Over it hung a "simple sun-like lamp," its diffuse light giving a glow to the room. On one wall, over a pile of manuscripts, was a photograph of a nude young boy, the "Maximin" of the poems, with buttocks and back to the camera. It was a space designed to set a mystical ambience. It cast a spell that quite a number of people fell under while visiting.[65]

CLASSICAL ART

Just as important as the writings of Plato or the poems of Goethe for the generation of homosexuals who came of age around the turn of the century was classical art. Greek art, but also nude images and statues from the Roman period and the Italian Renaissance, seems to have represented a vision of a time when love and beauty of all kinds were appreciated and accepted. Admittedly, Europeans had done what they could to strip this art of its eroticism. Since the Renaissance, classical educators had interpreted the nude form as a symbol of purity and idealized human beauty. This reading was the compromise that had to be made to allow this artistic tradition to reemerge in the fifteenth and sixteenth centuries in a Christian culture that was still suspicious of the erotic potential of the naked body. The upside was that the nude was embraced once again by Renaissance and Baroque artists. In the nineteenth century, despite the proliferation of artistic styles, many artists continued to privilege the study of the nude figure as the highest aim of art. Jean-Hippolyte Flandrin's paintings and Auguste Rodin's sculptures are probably the best-known works of the type from this era. At the end of the century, Frederic Leighton, Thomas Eakins, and Henry Scott Tuke were also making names for themselves by painting nude young men.[66] In addition, classical nudes influenced several artists connected with the British aesthetes and French symbolists, such as Simeon Solomon, Gustave Moreau, and Aubrey Beardsley.[67]

The extent to which homoerotic motives consciously or unconsciously influenced this art is a matter of some debate. Some of the artists who specialized in male nudes are known to have been actively homosexual, but in most cases we can only speculate about their attraction to the male form. What is certain is that this art was widely admired by homosexual men. Male homosexuals of some means loved to surround themselves with bronzes of Icarus or Hermes, copies of any number of paintings of Saint Sebastian, or reproductions of *Boy with Thorn* and *The Praying Boy*. Reproductions of famous sculptures by Michelangelo, Benvenuto Cellini, and François Duquesnoy showed up in many homes. Paintings of attractive youths were also popular, especially Thomas Gainsborough's *Blue Boy* and portraits by Anthony van Dyke and Franz Defregger.[68] The extent to which lesbians appreciated the female nude is not as well studied. Because such images were usually created by men with a male audience in mind, the erotic potential of the nude female form has generally been understood to be heterosexual. The use of female nudes on the covers of lesbian magazines, however, suggests that future research might open up new ways of viewing such art.

Around the turn of the century, there were a number of German artists working who were thought by gay men to be homosexual themselves. Christian Wilhelm Allers was living and working on the Italian island of Capri when the Krupp scandal broke out, and the Italian press accused him of pederasty, for which he eventually was convicted in court. He fled before being sent to prison. Afterward, he disappeared to the Pacific islands, where he continued for some time producing remarkable images of local youths.[69] In homosexual circles, gay men also talked about the painter Sascha Schneider, who designed the book covers for the famous German author of Westerns, Karl May. Elisar von Kupffer, a prominent artist in Adolf Brand's circle, updated the classic nude by fusing it with a post-Impressionist style. Along with his companion and lover, Eduard von Mayer, he developed a mystically tinged, pantheistic philosophy called Clarity that acquired some influence in the 1920s.[70]

The German artist probably best remembered for producing classically influenced homoerotic images is Wilhelm von Gloeden. In his early twenties Gloeden moved to the Sicilian town of Taormina in 1878. By this time Taormina had long been a regular stop for European tourists. Warm waters, gorgeous beaches, picturesque landscapes with a view of Mount Etna, and traces of Greco-Roman ruins all made the area an ideal choice for anyone looking for escape. Germans in particular were not rare among the stream of tourists; Goethe had mentioned the location in his well-read travel journal, *Italian Journey,* at the beginning of the century.

Wilhelm von Gloeden's family was of aristocratic lineage, although his claim to being a baron born in Castle Volkshagen, near the small northern German town of Wismar, is probably fictitious. At school he had studied art history, and, for a short time, he attended the Weimar Saxon–Grand Ducal Art Academy. In 1876, however, he grew sick from a lung infection. His doctor recommended that he travel south for weather more conducive to good health. Leaving Germany, he moved to the warmer climate of Italy, staying for a short time in Naples before taking up permanent residence in Taormina. Soon after moving there, Gloeden met the landscape painter Otto Geleng, who had been in Taormina since the 1860s, producing views of the mountains and ruins in the area. Geleng had developed strong relationships with the local population and even had managed to become mayor of the town in the 1876. Geleng and Gloeden soon became good friends, and through him Gloeden got to know many of the local Sicilians.[71]

Like many educated northern Europeans, Gloeden brought with him a classical schooling and a Romantic hope of finding a land lost to time. Looking back on his early impressions of the area, he admitted, "The reading of Homer, of Theocritus's poetry in Sicily stirred up my imagination." Observing the "rocks and sea, mountains and valleys," he could not help thinking of "Arcadian shepherds" and the Homeric Cyclops Polyphemus, who was supposed to have resided on the island.[72] Gloeden had brought a camera along with him, and in Taormina he soon began to take pictures of local scenery as well as of young people whom he met in the area. What began as a hobby advanced quickly, thanks to the tutelage of two local Italian photographers. But whereas his mentors tended to specialize in portraits of the local population and postcard-style landscape scenes, Gloeden was clearly drawn to images of youthful bodies.

Although both males and females appeared in his photographs, his most common subjects were prepubescent boys, who frequently appeared draped with Greek-style garments or sometimes entirely nude except for an ornamental wreath of flowers or leaves on their heads. Gloeden was not the first to transfer many of the key features and ornamentations of classical art to photography. Actually, one of the first to make nude photographs in this style was a cousin of Gloeden's, Wilhelm von Plüschow, who moved to Rome during the 1870s and, under the Italianized version of his name (Guglielmo Plüschow), began to take photographs of local young men. Since Gloeden passed through Rome on his way to southern Italy, it can safely be assumed that Plüschow was the inspiration for Gloeden's taking up the hobby a few years later.

Gloeden left his own mark on the art form, though. He was a pioneer in taking the human figure out of the studio and into the open air to photograph (Figure 14). The bucolic Sicilian scenery cemented the impression that his subjects had been pulled out of some archaic past when humanity still lived in close contact with nature. Like classical statuary, his models were supposed to represent a kind of idealized vision of mankind—innocent, pure, simple, beautiful. His subjects were drawn from local working-class families, though—mostly the children of local farmers, herdsmen, and fishermen— and so Gloeden concocted a makeup from fresh milk, olive oil, and glycerin to disguise scars and other skin blemishes. He also spent a lot of time carefully picking out locations and poses, since he worked exclusively with a glass-plate

FIGURE 14 **WILHELM VON GLOEDEN,** *SIZILIANISCHER JÜNGLING,* **CA. 1900**

This photograph of Gloeden's is very typical of his style: a boy posed in a classical style, with a wreath around his head; sharp shadows define the contours of his body.

camera that had a long exposure time. He had to carry a lot of equipment with him, and his models had to learn to hold a pose. Still, he did his best to make posing fun for the kids so that they would be relaxed and happy. The results of all of this hard work were well worth it: crisp images, the bodies often cut by Caravaggesque shadows, the photographs suffused by the serenity that one would hope to find on an Italian coast.[73]

During the 1890s Gloeden's business took off. The androgynous young men whom he photographed fit well into the fin-de-siècle atmosphere of Europe, where both literature and art were promoting the youthful ephebe as the aesthetic ideal. In 1893 his photographs appeared in the first issue of *The Studio,* an influential magazine for the fine arts published in London; they were printed right next to Aubrey Beardsley's famous drawing for Oscar Wilde's *Salome.* In Germany his photographs were published in *Art for Everyone* (*Die Kunst für Alle*) in 1893 and 1894. They were sold in art galleries in Munich, Leipzig, Paris, and Naples. They were used in art academies as study material for those interested in the human form.[74] His work became so popular that by the turn of the century he was reproducing his most popular ones as postcards to be sold to tourists and to be exported up north for sale.

The classically influenced style of nude photography pioneered by Gloeden and his cousin Plüschow would become very popular over the next decades. Adolf Brand took similar photographs, many of which were printed in his journal *The Special One.* Similar-looking images would appear in friendship magazines and nudist publications of the Weimar era. And even during the 1950s, as many of the German homophile periodicals began to favor the more muscular men that American beefcake magazines were making popular among homosexual readers, one could still find traces of the classicism favored by Gloeden.

Even though to our eyes it is difficult *not* to see the erotic intention behind these photographs, comparing them with some of the pornographic images that circulated in the turn-of-the-century black market helps explain how their claim to artistic status might be accepted. As one scholar has noted, there are no erect penises in any of these pictures and no overt sexual contact. In addition, the facial expressions suggest a "lofty remoteness rather than sexual availability or provocativeness."[75] But why can't art have erotic intention, we might ask today? Since at least the 1960s, we have grown used to the idea that the line between art and pornography is a fuzzy one, to say the least. And, as a matter of fact, at the turn of the century decisions about what was art and what was pornography could seem quite arbitrary. Gloeden's photographs were clearly embraced as art, but Plüschow's work eventually brought suspicion on him. Arrested in 1902 for the seduction of minors, he was spared conviction, probably because several wealthy and influential patrons were among his customers. Still, he spent several months in an Italian jail as an investigation was undertaken.[76] Adolf Brand was also arrested several times in Germany for producing pornography, even though his photographs were remarkably similar to Gloeden's. His magazine was confiscated, and during the 1920s it was added to the list of obscene publications kept by the government.

Today it is the age of Gloeden's subjects that gives us more problems than anything else. If we can set aside these concerns, however, it is possible to see them as an articulation of a certain understanding of what it meant to be a man who loved male beauty. Homosexuality is not something criminal, or sinful, or dirty, his pictures suggest. It is as beautiful and natural as the world we see around us. It is something that is as wholesome as the ancient Greeks, who created the touchstone ideals for Western culture and who therefore cannot be easily ignored.

HOMOSEXUALITY AND MODERNITY

Though a large number of homosexuals were doing their best to reinforce the positive connections between same-sex love and the ancient world, it is clear that many more people were becoming convinced that homosexuality was a particularly modern phenomenon. As we have seen, scholars are still debating the role of various changes associated with modernization, from the rise of the city to the formation of the modern nation-state, the development of urban gay scenes, and the articulation of a homosexual identity. At the turn of the century social observers and critics were much more likely to state the connection between modernity and homosexuality in blatantly moralistic terms. Modern life had uprooted stable small towns and pastoral rural communities, such writers insited, undermined faith in traditional Christian values, and weakened the social controls that encouraged common decency and moral living. Large cities were targeted as the epitome of everything wrong with the world: cash transactions replaced humane relationships, glitz and glamour substituted for real value, and tremendous disparities of wealth caused crime to run amok. Urban spaces were increasingly depicted in overtly sexual terms by a diverse number of authors, from medical experts to social critics.[77] Homosexual scenes in particular seem to have coalesced a great number of these fears. Here one found crimes such as blackmail and prostitution, gay bars where both beer and bodies were for sale, and effeminate fairies and butched-up lesbians who seemed obsessed with flaunting their sexual proclivities. Looking at such sights, quite a number of Europeans could not help thinking of the fate of the Roman Empire, where immoderation and sexual excess had supposedly contributed to political collapse.

Such a conservative attitude toward homosexuality was common in sermons, newspaper articles, journalistic exposés, and titillating tourist literature. It also found expression in novels by conservative writers. Stefan Vacano's *I Lay in the Deep Night of Death* (*Ich lag in tiefer Todesnacht,* 1908) is fairly representative of this genre. The novel takes the form of a series of letters and diary fragments collected by the main character's sister. The young man's relationship with a Berlin music critic causes him to fall victim first to blackmail and then to prostitution. The story takes one through dark clubs in the Danish gay scene, and then to the island of Capri, where the protagonist finally has the revelation that only God can save him. He has a vision of Jesus in Egypt, where the divine figure tells him to return to his mother in Berlin. His soul is saved but, alas, not his life. In Berlin, unable to find friends or a job, and renounced even by his mother, who refuses to forgive him for his "crime against nature," he is hit over the head by a pimp. He dies of a concussion, but with a picture of Christ next to him.[78]

More surprising, perhaps, are the number of more progressive artists who also connected homosexuality with modern decadence in some fashion. In Erich Kästner's satire of Weimar society entitled *Fabian: The Story of a Moralist* (1931), lesbian cross-dressers become the embodiment of a turbulent modernity in which certainties are lost and relationships are made superficial. Alfred Döblin's *Two Girlfriends and Their Poison Murders* (1924), his novelistic account of a 1922 court case of two lesbians who conspired to kill the husband of one of them, also reproduces many of the associations among lesbianism, medical degeneracy, and urban perversion, despite his desire to create a modernist narrative style that gave multiple perspectives and undermined easy assumptions about guilt. Irmgard Keun's *The Artificial Silk Girl* (*Das kunstseidene Mädchen,* 1932) arguably does a better job at challenging prejudices about lesbian sexuality. Doris, the main character in the novel, comes to Berlin and, after viewing the film *Girls in Uniform* in the theater, develops a more sympathetic view toward homosexuality despite being heterosexual herself. Nevertheless, as Katie Sutton has argued in *The Masculine Woman in Weimar Germany,* the kind of homosexuality that Doris views as positive is clearly feminine. Masculine lesbians, on the other hand, with their "stiff collars and ties," who are "so frightfully proud of being perverse," were manifestations of the seedy underside of Germany's capital city.[79]

The rhetorical link between homosexuality and modernity could take on many different hues as it was used for different purposes. As early as the 1830s, a handful of French novelists, including Henri de Latouche, Théophile Gautier, and Honoré de Balzac, had started to include "hermaphroditic" characters exploring their bisexual tendencies in Paris's bohemian world of artists, writers, prostitutes, and criminals. In some of their books, homosexual or bisexual characters can appear as suspicious denizens of the urban underworld, criminals and seducers of the innocent who symbolize the dangers of the modern city.[80] At other times, though, the gender fluidity of the central characters expresses a bohemian desire for "a new social order based on love and harmony."[81] Both interpretations very often sit side by side in the same book, and such a dual vision of the temptations and opportunities of modern bohemia was picked up by many German artists at the turn of the next century.

For example, Frank Wedekind depicted a similar view of bohemia in his two plays *Earth Spirit* (*Erdgeist,* 1895) and *Pandora's Box* (*Die Büchse der Pandora,* 1904).[82] Both plays center on Lulu, a young girl from the streets who has been rescued by the less than virtuous Dr. Schön, who makes Lulu his mistress but then marries her off to the wealthy physician Dr. Goll. Goll's death from a heart attack after finding Lulu in the arms of another man sets off a series of events in which Lulu is passed around from husband to husband, lover to lover. For a time she serves as a model for a painter whose specialty is cheap, pornographic postcards. Later she winds up working as a cabaret dancer. At every step, the "perversion of art" because of its commercialization is developed into a major theme, as the historian Peter Jelavich shows.[83] Lulu's victimization at the hands of greedy and depraved men also suggests mankind's (or perhaps better, womankind's) debasement in the modern world. The second play follows Lulu as she attempts to evade the law, working for a time in a circus and eventually ending up in London working as a prostitute. At the end, she is murdered at the hands of Jack the Ripper.

Lesbianism appears in these two plays in the form of Countess Geschwitz, who falls madly in love with Lulu. She helps Lulu escape from prison at the end of the first play and, disguised as Lulu, takes her place for a time. When the Lulu plays were filmed in condensed form by the well-known Austrian director G. W. Pabst (*Der Büchse der Pandora*, 1929), the character of Countess Geschwitz was the first lesbian character to appear in film. As the two plays had to be shortened dramatically to get them to fit in a single film, her role was considerably restricted and her character flattened. Unfortunately, what was left was a bit of a stereotype: Geschwitz was depicted as a decadent aristocrat whose extravagant life of luxury had spoiled her for all but the most excessive of pleasures.[84] In the film she appears as one of a string of depraved characters whom Lulu encounters on her path toward ruin. The outlines of this character were certainly present in the original play, but Wedekind sug-

gested that Geschwitz was meant to be much more than this. In the foreword
to the play, Wedekind proposed seeing the countess as a tragic figure alongside
Lulu.[85] Lybeck's analysis of this play questions whether such a simple reading
is possible, given the many negative stereotypes ("unattractive spinster, masculine usurper, masochistic compulsive pervert, and idealist intellectual") that
she represents.[86] Certainly, her willingness to sacrifice everything to save Lulu
does indeed make her a rather sympathetic character: she is the only person
in a long string of acquaintances who is willing to suppress her self-interest
to save another. Still, the Countess Geschwitz is best seen as reflective of
Wedekind's own complicated, modernist imagination. "Like Lulu," Lybeck
writes, "she was a protean mixture of elements that took on meaning given
the patterns, associations, and juxtapositions in any given scene. Geschwitz
was not consistently loving or narcissistic, masochistic or heroic, masculine
or hysterical."[87]

The artists of the 1920s left us many memorable images of Weimar Berlin's bohemia. In their paintings and drawings, the decadence that suffuses the
gay scene often serves not so much to condemn homosexuality as to turn it
into a sign of a traditional world in decay. From this perspective, the criminal
underworld and the bohemian quarters of major cities were spaces in which
a Nietzschean "revaluation of values" was possible. Their apocalyptic atmosphere could serve simultaneously as a condemnation of the contemporary
world and a call for regeneration.[88] In the paintings of Jeanne Mammen (Figure 15), or the pen-and-ink drawings of Christian Schad, gender ambivalence
and confusion might indeed be interpreted as expressions of anxiety, but they
could equally be seen as reveling in the possibilities opened up by modernity.
And even if many of these Weimar-era images are haunted by loneliness, sorrow, and poverty, the people portrayed in them seem to take some solace in
at least knowing what exactly is at stake. The paintings seem to suggest that
there is a kind of blunt honesty that shows through even when such a world
has its own kinds of masquerades. For those who find refuge here, it is much
preferable to the world of pretense lived on the outside.

Klaus Mann, whom we met at the beginning of this chapter, offered
one novelist's vision of such a world in his *Pious Dance* (*Der fromme Tanz*,
1926), with its depiction of Berlin as populated by cabaret singers, debauched
aristocrats, effete boys whose faces are caked with makeup, and wild young
men who are seemingly up for any kind of senseless fun. It is certainly not
Klaus Mann's best book, but for anyone hungry for images of decadent Weimar (like myself, who grew up listening to 1970s-era David Bowie and Iggy
Pop), it can nonetheless have a certain allure. The novel can easily be read as
Klaus Mann's coming-out story. It is "earnest, unapologetic, and extremely

FIGURE 15 **JEANNE MAMMEN (1890–1976),** *SIE REPRESENTIERT,* **CA. 1928. ORIGINAL WATERCOLOR AND PENCIL (REPRODUCED HERE IN BLACK AND WHITE). PRIVATE COLLECTION, BERLIN.**

The artist Jeanne Mammen did a number of drawings and paintings representing Berlin's nightlife in the 1920s and early 1930s. Born in Berlin, she also spent much time in Paris, Brussels, and Rome. Her artwork very often focused on women, especially the self-reliant "New Woman" of the Weimar Republic in different guises: eking out a living on rough city streets, enjoying one another's company at a café in the evening, or dancing with men at a late-night club. Quite a number of them, including this one, offered a glimpse into Berlin's lesbian scene. Source: Jeanne Mammen © 2015 Artists Rights Society (ARS), New York / VG Bild-Kunst, Bonn. Courtesy of the Jeanne Mammen Stiftung, Berlin. Photograph by Mathias Schormann, Berlin candid," observes one of Klaus Mann's biographers; it contains many obvious similarities to the author's own life.[89] The setting is dirty and sordid, and the characters are lonely and miserable. Moreover, the ending is not a happy one: the central character yearns to return home and yet is apparently compelled to continue his endless search for love. Nevertheless, he decides that since "the human body is alone for all eternity," it is love, even if that love must be renounced, that "is perhaps great enough to aid the beloved body in its loneliness."[90] And loneliness itself brings a kind of redemption as long as it is endured with a quiet piety.

Certainly not all homosexual writers were as taken with the decadent image of the city as Mann. In fact, if the short stories and serialized novels published in the friendship magazines of the 1920s are any indication, many more homosexuals saw the city not as depraved at all but instead as a space that offered freedoms. For them the city was a place to get away from the closed-minded countryside. Here there were daily chance encounters with strangers on the street, or perhaps in a park or a restaurant, where desires could be awakened. In many of the stories of the friendship press, the moment of recognition—of realizing through a smile or a glance that someone else felt the same way the main character did—was erotically charged.[91]

The masculinist and anarchist writer John Henry Mackay gave a memorable account of modern Berlin in his best work, *The Hustler* (*Der Puppenjunge*, 1926). This novel tells the story of Hermann Graff, a young man who has come to Berlin nominally to find work but, more important, to find love: "He had to win and have a human being that he loved. He also knew that this person could only be a boy . . . and he knew finally that he could not seek him out, but rather must find him as one finds good luck."[92] He did have luck. In fact, as he exits the train station, Graff catches sight of a fifteen-year-old boy who has come to Berlin in search of money and a good time. They get separated, but Graff's search for the teenager whom he had glimpsed in the train station quickly turns into an obsession that he cannot escape. In the meantime, the boy—whose name is Günther—heads out into the busy city of Berlin, hoping to meet up with a friend who has encouraged Günther to look for a future in the city. When Günther fails to find the friend, he quickly falls into a life of prostitution. This part of the story might seem at first to echo the moralizing tales of conservatives about the dangers of the corrupt city, but Mackay quickly undercuts this interpretation by pointing out that Günther's first sexual encounter had actually been with a priest back in his village, who gave him two apples for the favor. At least the men whom he goes with in the city pay him in cash. "Even if it had not been any great fun for him," Günther thinks afterward, "there had indeed been nothing special about it."[93]

Günther soon comes to like the lifestyle of the rent boy: the quick money, the occasional gifts that he gets from wealthy johns, and especially the boys whom he hangs around with on the Friedrichstrasse and in local gay bars, who could be great fun at times. The novel is perhaps most remarkable in its description of the city's gay scene, which is based on Mackay's own experiences. Hirschfeld himself praised this aspect of the novel, which in his words was "drawn by the brush of a genuine artist so true to life that many details come to light that ordinarily escape the superficial observer—and unfortunately even most professional observers are only superficial onlookers."[94] Mackay did meticulous research for the book, spending many hours in the city's gay bars, especially in the Marienkasino, on which the Adonis Lounge in the book is based. He watched the behavior of male prostitutes, listened to their stories and jokes, and used some of their odd tics and habits to enrich his characters.[95] The character of Günther has lots of adventures in the gay scene with various eccentric johns before he finally strikes up a relationship with Graff, who is excited to have the boy from the train station back in his life.

Perhaps one of the most tragic aspects of the book involves the problems that the two find in developing an intimate connection despite the ease of the physical relationship. They have very different social backgrounds, very different needs, and in the end very different expectations about what will come from being together. The story ends sadly, predictably, but long before the arrests that come at the conclusion of the story, the reader can sense that Graff's love for the boy was bound to be disappointed. At the very end, watching a group of hustlers go about their business in the Adonis Lounge, Graff himself begins to recognize the gulf that has existed between them: "He grasped much about Günther only now in detail. He, too, was young. He, too, wanted to enjoy his young life. With those his own age, when possible; with older men, if it could not be helped—in loud circles, pampered and desired, surrounded by flattery and gifts, from one hour to another, slipping or snatched from one arm to another."[96]

If many of the stories centered on men or women from the countryside who move to the city, urban modernity could also make contact with the rural and provincial surroundings, thanks to a traveler who might leave a copy of a gay magazine behind, as in one short story published in *The Bachelor Girl,* or one who more simply brings metropolitan styles and ways of thinking.[97] In Vicki Baum's *An Incident in Lohwinckel (Zwischenfall in Lohwinckel,* 1930), originally published in the popular weekly *BIZ (Berlin Illustrierte Zeitung),* an exotic film star named Lania finds herself stuck in a small German town after an unfortunate car accident. Her presence helps crystallize the emerging sexual identity of Fräulein von Raitzold, one of the aristocratic siblings who care for Lania as she recovers. Lania, aware of the young woman's attraction to her, flirts a bit, despite actually being heterosexual. She brags of knowing lesbians and of frequenting lesbian cafés. Unable to leave her poverty-stricken brother in the end, the masculine-behaving Raitzold does at least get a glimpse into a more tolerant world, and she feels less alone.[98]

At least one author questioned this easy equation between the modern city and homosexuality, though. Anna Elisabet Weirauch's *The Scorpion* also tells the story of a young woman from the provinces who goes to the city to find herself, only to flee back to the countryside in the end. *The Scorpion* is probably the most famous lesbian novel of the interwar period—besides Radclyffe Hall's *The Well of Loneliness* (1928), of course. This three-book cycle is remarkable in the way that, within the constraints of melodramatic fiction, it still manages to explore the complexities and challenges of self-discovery in a fascinating fashion.[99]

In contrast to so many of the stories from this era that uncritically accept the image of the masculinized lesbian, either because of its support in the sexological literature or because of its ubiquity in Weimar popular culture, *The Scorpion* explores the "multivalence of lesbian identity," as one scholar observes.[100] Although as an adolescent the main character, Mette, finds herself pulled into an intense relationship with an older woman named Olga, she eventually ends up rejecting a masculine identity for herself. During a meeting with a local doctor whom her parents send her to when they become suspicious about Mette's relationship with Olga, she comes across some medical descriptions of inverts, which only repulse her. And after Olga's suicide, she goes to Berlin, only to experience some deep ambivalence about the gay scene that she encounters there. As Katie Sutton notes, "Here she finds herself repeatedly caught between disgust at such openly displayed inversion and a strong desire to belong."[101] One evening, hyped-up on cocaine and flirting with a tall woman with the build of a "Greek boy," she has a nervous breakdown. She flees the city to take up a life of healthy gardening in the countryside. On the surface, this ending seems to represent a deeply conservative finale. We should not jump to conclusions, though. After all, in the next volume we learn that Mette does not give up her homosexual identity when she leaves for the countryside. Moreover, several of her new friends in the countryside prove to be remarkably open-minded about nonnormative forms of sexuality. One could easily argue that *The Scorpion* does not so much deny lesbian sexuality at the end as offer an alternative version of it. As Vibeke Petersen puts it, "The image of lesbianism is reconstituted as clean, natural, and restrained." Lesbians are portrayed as individuals who can safely live within a larger community.[102]

THE ARTICULATION OF SELF IN THE GAY AND LESBIAN PRESS

The amount of space that the homosexual magazines devoted to literature and art suggests how important these subjects were to their readers. In fact, as Robert Beachy has recently argued, the 1890s witnessed the birth of an early "gay" literary canon, thanks primarily to the efforts of German homosexual activists. The GdE, you will remember, was above all a reading circle for like-minded individuals. The WhK, for its part, organized a lending library and gave dramatic readings. The Spohr press published not only new works on the topic but also reissued valuable older works, including, importantly, Karl Heinrich Ulrichs's long-sold-out pamphlets. Moreover, *The Special One,* the various publications of the WhK, and the friendship magazines of the 1920s all published book reviews, discussed foreign literature that might not have been easily accessible to German speakers, and compiled lists of books (past and present) that might be of interest to homosexual readers. This literary canon, writes Beachy, "aided the construction of an identity, transcending time and place, as well as the formation of a cultural community, which allowed at least some to identify with a collective 'we.'"[103]

In building this literary canon, several writers began to construct a kind of "ancestral gallery" of honorary homosexuals that included ancient figures along with more modern nobles and artists. They presented homosexual biographies of King Edward II of England, King Frederick the Great of Prussia, King Magnus Eriksson and Queen Christina of Sweden, and the Duchess Luise Dorothea of Saxony and Gotha. They published discussions of the life and works of Leonardo da Vinci, Michelangelo, Pyotr Tchaikovsky, Oscar Wilde, and Hans Christian Andersen. The writer Ferdinand Karsch-Haack also spent much time in the early 1920s studying the history and cultures of other countries and writing up short portraits for *Friendship, The New Friendship,* and *Uranus.*[104]

Interestingly, what exact language should be used to describe this community was still some matter of debate. Although the word *homosexual* was widely used by gay men and lesbians by the 1920s, it was clearly not loved by everyone. In the friendship magazines, some men complained that the term's emphasis on sexuality led it to be associated with something "dirty." They hoped that a new terminology could be found that emphasized love and relationships and consequently might make it easier to accept publicly. Quite a few used *homoerotic* as an alternative. Others preferred *gleichgeschlechtlich*—a German term that does not translate very well, since it literally means "same sex," but often is rendered simply as *homosexual* in English. They talked of "male-male Eros" (*mann-männlicher Eros*) or more obliquely of "favored love" (*Lieblingsminne*). The word *invert* was borrowed from the sexological literature of the day and used fairly often. And many of the magazines published by Friedrich Radszuweit's press tried to push the politicized concept of "comrades of a species" (*Artgenossen*).[105] *Comrade* was an especially resonant choice, since it might have reminded people not only of the "comradeship" of the World War I front soldiers but also of the revolutionary "comrades" of 1918–19.

A simpler possibility was suggested by a popular cabaret tune from 1920, "The Lavender Song":

> We are simply different from the rest [*anders als die anderen*] of those
> who are loved while marching in step with the morality of the age,
> who go about a world full of a thousand wonders
> and somehow find themselves excited only by the most commonplace.
> About such interests we know nothing whatsoever,
> for we are all children of another world.
> We love only the lavender night, that sultry [*schwül*] evening,
> because we are indeed different from the rest.[106]

The phrase "different from the rest" had been used by Richard Oswald as the title of his 1919 film, and it would pop up now and again in the magazines of the decade.[107]

The most common alternative to *homosexual* in the Weimar era was simply *friend*. This term was frequently used in the names of gay and lesbian clubs as well as by many of the magazines that were organized in the Weimar era. Instead of bringing the sexual aspect of relationships to the foreground as *homosexual* did, *friend* and *friendship* put the emphasis on the emotional and personal content of relationships. Friendship is appreciated by nearly everyone, so using this term served as a means of justifying homosexual relationships. It allowed gay readers to expand their imagined community to include not simply classical German writers such as Goethe, Platen, and Schiller but also more contemporary writers such as Friedrich Nietzsche and Walt Whitman, both of whom were much admired in the gay community for their passionate tributes to male friendship.[108] Finally, *friendship* could at times also obscure the sexual element of a relationship between two men or two women. Those people in the know could infer what kind of relationship was meant by the context in which it was discussed, whereas others ignorant of the double meaning could innocently assume that only an ordinary friendship was being mentioned.

Female homosexuals used the female form of *friend* (*Freundin*), as well as *lesbian* (*Lesbianer*), and occasionally *tribade* (*Tribade*), though this term was rare by the 1920s. Alternatively, they might refer to the Greek poet Sappho. Very common, as well, were terms that implied the gendered appearance and role of a woman. Both *lad* (*Bubi*, which also pointed to the bobbed hair-cut that was popular in the 1920s) and *garçonne* (the feminine version of the French word for bachelor) implied a masculine appearance and could be loosely translated today as *butch*. In the literature of the 1920s friendship magazines, masculine lesbians were also described as the "Ben Hur type" and "Don Juans." The femme role was less likely to be named, although sometimes the word *Mädi* or *Dame* was used. According to Heike Schader, the scholar who has done the most in-depth analysis of the lesbian magazines of the 1920s, feminine lesbians were most often described rather than explicitly denoted in the stories.[109] Very often the role was implied more than anything and was understood in the context of a relationship to a "lad."

Other options available to homosexuals were terms associated with sexological theories of intersexuality, namely *third sex* and *Urnanian* (*Urning* or its feminine version, *Urnind*). Both terms appeared with some frequency in the lesbian magazines of the 1920s, but only rarely in the male friendship press. The main exception was essays that explicitly referred to Karl Heinrich Ulrichs's or Magnus Hirschfeld's theories, but even here there was a preference for *invert,* which had also been widely disseminated by sexological literature. Clearly the language that Hirschfeld had promoted at the turn of the century had failed to take hold among men as strong points of identification. This failure is a little surprising since many of the writers were clearly familiar with Hirschfeld's ideas. In fact, the homosexual magazines of the 1920s were full of essays that popularized both Ulrichs's and Hirschfeld's theories. (In comparison, very few of the writers showed any familiarity with Freud's ideas, and the one who was dedicated to popularizing Freudian theories in *Uranus* acknowledged that it was an outsider position within the debate.)[110] Both writers and readers who wrote letters to the editors assumed that homosexuality was an "inborn disposition" (*angeborene Veranlagung*) that was perfectly "natural," an idea most connected at the time with Hirschfeld.[111] One regular author for *Friendship* insisted that the existence of "inversion" in all eras, among all peoples, and even among many animals proved that there was nothing particularly unnatural or abnormal about it. Another writer insisted that only someone completely ignorant of modern scientific knowledge could demand that homosexuals deny their own nature.[112]

Most of the male authors and readers of the friendship magazines, however, were bothered by the gendered implication of terms such as *third sex* and Hirschfeld's theory of intersexuality. Gay writers acknowledged that there were effeminate homosexuals—generally using the rather prejudicial terms *Tunte* or *Tante*. Few if any of the writers in the magazines, however, described themselves as effeminate. In fact, several writers insisted that, in contrast with homosexuality itself, effeminacy was a behavior that was adopted by some homosexuals and was not natural at all. It was "playing at being women" (*Weiberspielen*), in the words of one writer.[113]

What did effeminate gay men think about such an accusation? Unfortunately, this question is hard to answer, since very few of them seem to have written for the friendship magazines. There is good reason to believe that they were out there. Richard Krafft-Ebing's case histories included examples of such men from the end of the century. And if the evidence left by Weimar-era novelists and artists is to be believed, effeminate behavior was common in the gay clubs of the 1920s. We could also point to the widespread practice of adopting a woman's name or title ("Queen," "Aunt," "Princess," "Duchess") within the gay scene as suggesting some level of feminine identification. Why these men did not defend themselves more in the friendship magazines is a mystery yet to be solved. The closest we come is some men insisting that it was permissible to act womanly in private circles, in gay clubs, or on special occasions.[114] Others might have revealed something about themselves when they discussed a temptation to behave effeminately that needed to be fought. Perhaps for some men effeminacy was a "temporary role," as Stefan Micheler argues—a behavior that could be turned on, so to speak, in certain environments and avoided in others.[115] It is interesting, though, that members of the press never used the terms *Tunte* or *Tante* to describe themselves. These terms were always applied pejoratively to others. Nor did the writers in the press apparently adopt less negative language such as *third sex*.

Speaking up for effeminacy was no doubt difficult in the 1920s, since the gay magazines exhibited a fair amount of hostility toward it. There were a few authors who defended effeminate male homosexuals against the epidemic of "pansy baiting" (*Tantenhetze*) that broke out in the friendship magazines of the early 1920s. One doctor writing in *Friendship* observed that it was incorrect to confuse effeminacy with weakness. "Gentle, womanly men" are often much "tougher and energetic" than we are led to believe, he wrote. And, vice versa, those who are "overflowing with a beer-belly and coarse masculinity" are not necessarily going to be anyone's "hero."[116] Such voices were generally drowned out, though, by a growing chorus of complaints about the effeminate behavior often on display in the gay scene. Not a few people seem to have found it personally repulsive, and others thought it hurt homosexuals as a group by reinforcing negative stereotypes. One writer took it as a personal challenge: we all need to "work hard on ourselves to discard every tendency toward effeminacy," he insisted.[117] In the early 1920s the magazine *Friendship* laid the groundwork for a new political approach based on winning "respectability" for homosexuals.[118] What we tend to remember as the homophile strategy of the 1950s—namely, the belief that homosexuals could acquire public tolerance for their sexuality by acting in orderly, self-disciplined, and above all gender-appropriate ways—was actually pioneered by the editors of this magazine and eventually adopted in the mid-1920s by Friedrich Radszuweit's press and political organization.[119]

One might think that this preference for a more masculine homosexual identity implied some sympathy for Brand and his fellow masculinists, but this was not the case. Most of the editors and writers associated with the male friendship press—and this includes Friedrich Radszuweit, who himself was very critical of Hirschfeld—saw the masculinists as a quarrelsome lot who tended only to hurt the homosexual cause by sowing discord in the movement.[120] Many were turned off by the elitist and chauvinist attitudes displayed in Brand's *The Special One*. And although a number of them harbored the same gender biases toward women that the average German male did during the early twentieth century, they seem to have believed that Blüher went too far with his rabid antifeminism. Most important, the editors of the friendship magazines became worried that the rather open pedophile leanings of many of the masculinists would alienate a German public.[121] In the early 1920s masculinist authors were still given a fair number of opportunities to voice their ideas in the friendship magazines. Especially in *Uranus,* masculinists were allowed to square off against Hirschfeld's supporters in debate. This magazine folded in 1923, however, and by the middle of the decade there was a noticeable tendency to exclude masculinist positions entirely from all the magazines except for Brand's. When masculinists were mentioned, they were often treated as extremist outsiders. "Only rarely," writes Stefan Micheler, "were the different conceptions of same-sex identity explicitly confronted with one another in the friendship magazines."[122]

This is not to say that masculinist arguments were entirely ignored. On the contrary, in his fascinating study *Images of Self and Images of Others* (*Selbtsbilder und Fremdbilder*), Stefan Micheler has found an interesting tension in many of the gay magazines created by an effort to fuse together the masculinist emphasis on the cultural purpose of homosexuality and the biological theories of Hirschfeld. Even if the two camps were clearly rivals, with very different ideas about the origins of homosexuality, a great number (and perhaps a large majority) of gay men saw important insights on both sides. Most male writers believed that homosexuality was inborn, but they sometimes took the argument in a direction that differed from Hirschfeld's. They suggested that if homosexuality existed in nature, it must have some higher purpose.[123] Perhaps homosexuals had some greater cultural function: to make artistic and philosophical contributions to the nation, or even to devote themselves to the needs of the state. This line of argumentation offered an opening for homosexuals to draw on Benedict Friedlaender's and Hans Blüher's ideas.

Still, this does not mean they embraced the notion of bisexuality advocated by many masculinists. Indeed, they seem to have wanted to draw a fairly firm line between homosexuals and heterosexuals. Radszuweit's *Pages for Human Rights* even reported on a revealing incident at a 1923 WhK conference. At the meeting, the masculinist activist Ewald Tscheck gave a talk in which he insisted that the division normally made between homosexuality and heterosexuality was a false one. According to the story, many people stormed out of the room in the middle of the talk, and those few who remained gave him little applause afterward.[124]

The female friendship magazines were different from their male counterparts in many important ways, despite being produced by the same presses. Male authors were not uncommon in the lesbian periodicals, whereas in the male magazines female authors were virtually nonexistent. Friedrich Radszuweit and other representatives of the homosexual movement commonly wrote columns for the lesbian magazines, and sexologists, doctors, and other specialists also contributed essays regarding their specific fields.[125]

The lesbian magazines were also different in that they self-consciously addressed a second audience: male transvestites, who were not necessarily assumed to be homosexual. They printed essays on transvestite issues that discussed both male and female varieties. They included letters from male transvestite readers, who asked questions and contributed to ongoing discussions. The meaning of *transvestism* itself, which had been coined by Hirschfeld only in 1910, was debated by some. As Katie Sutton observes, "This term was understood in a Hirschfeldian sense as going beyond cross-dressing to encompass other aspects of gender identity that would today be understood under the banner of 'transgender' or 'transsexual.'"[126] For a time, in fact, *Girlfriend* included a special supplement on transvestism, which in 1930 was briefly (and unsuccessfully) expanded into its own magazine, called *The Third Sex*. Why exactly an audience of male transvestites would read (or be welcomed by) the Weimar lesbian magazines is a question that has not yet been answered. Sutton argues that it implies "high levels of cooperation and crossover between transvestite and homosexual subcultures at both an organization and community level."[127] Schader, on the other hand, suggests that it was because "the image of the virile homosexual woman merged seamlessly into the image of the transvestite."[128] The importance of cross-dressing for many female lesbians made the magazines a useful forum for also discussing male cross-dressing issues. Or there is a third possibility, which is that they were excluded from the male magazines as representing the effeminacy that many homosexual men were trying to suppress among themselves.

There is no doubt that dual gender roles were embraced by the lesbian community in a way that they were not by the male gay community. Perhaps this is not surprising, given the way that androgynous and masculinized styles for women took off internationally. The bobbed haircut was popularized by film stars, fashion models, and other trendsetters in the 1920s, becoming a symbol of modernity, youth, vitality, and empowerment. Although some might interpret the *Bubikopf,* as it is called in German, as a sign of the breakdown of social order, many more for a time saw it as "attractive, practical, youthful, and flattering."[129] When it came to dress, women's clothing was overtaken by sleek, straight-waisted dresses whose lines looked very modern but also concealed feminine curves. For a time in the mid-1920s, the tuxedo jacket and formal dinner suit even became fashionable for women. As Marlene Dietrich demonstrated in the film *Morocco* (1930), such masculine attire became essential elements in a playful performance of gender ambiguity, one that was embraced by some brave women as a "liberating experience that offered women the opportunity to achieve spectacular aesthetic and erotic contrasts."[130] Early twentieth-century film was full of other examples of female cross-dressing, building on the long theatrical tradition of the "breeches role" (*Hosenrolle*).[131] In conjunction with important social changes taking place after the First World War—the rapid expansion of women's sports, the growing attention paid to female factory workers, and media focus on the modern housewife, who commanded a kitchen loaded with the latest appliances—such fashion changes put a multitude of fresh faces on the "New Woman."[132]

Even before the First World War, some lesbians had taken on certain aspects of masculine appearance, and now in the 1920s many lesbians embraced the new fashions. Ruth Röllig, a famous observer of the 1920s lesbian scenes, commented: "Generally these slender, often very elegant figures dress in a suit of black cloth, consisting of a narrow, smooth skirt, and gentlemanly jacket, under which they wear a silk shirt with collar, cuffs and tie, which has lately been joined by the obligatory monocle, a small extravagance which has established itself even in distinguished bourgeois society."[133] They saw these styles as reflecting an independence from collective mores and family life that they desired socially. They also embodied a sexually assertive role that they felt personally. Moreover, if the short stories and serialized novels published in the friendship magazines are any indication, many lesbians also found the virile-feminine roles erotically stimulating.[134] Lesbian magazines were full of stories in which central characters sported monocles, trim haircuts, and fashionable tuxedos.

Not everyone was happy with the new look. "All in all," wrote one reader in a letter published in 1931, "I find the behavior of our masculine women rather grotesque. It frequently seems as if virile homoerotic women want to force masculinity on themselves, which nevertheless seems on the surface to be only part of their inner character." Another reader worried about the negative attention that such lesbian fashions were attracting: "Often it is the insignificant, easily avoidable external matters that have the most provocative effect and do more harm than one believes they should."[135] In contrast with the male gay community, where there seemed very few men willing to defend gender transgression, however, there were many lesbians who spoke up in defense of virile lesbians. "I do not consider it wrong when a woman accentuates the masculine in her being. In my opinion, one should also not repudiate this disposition when it comes to external appearance." Yet another reader stated her clear preference for masculine-looking women: "For me a sweet, soft baby-doll face was almost loathsome."[136]

The women's friendship magazines became an important forum for debating the implications of these gender roles. Were virile women also more intelligent than feminine lesbians? Were they more prone to being unfaithful? Were feminine lesbians "real" homosexuals or only "pseudohomosexuals"? All these questions yielded heated debates. Clearly a number of lesbians had transferred some of the gender prejudices of the day to the various roles played out by homosexual women. But this tendency did not go undisputed. One reader protested that it was not necessary that virile "lads" imitate the "worst masculine characteristics."[137] These debates "point to a community," writes Katie Sutton, "trying to negotiate what it meant to be a homosexual woman at this period, and to what extent this was determined by ideas about gender."[138] No readers, however, disputed the existence of these roles or their importance for the lesbian community.

Indeed, the stories printed in the friendship magazines suggest that roles were an important aspect of the erotic imagination of many lesbians. The virile "lad" naturally was a recurring character, often being compared not only with Ben-Hur and Don Juan but also with an upper-class gentleman, or—if the woman was on the prowl for financial assistance in addition to love—a gigolo.[139] Sometimes the features of virile lesbians overlapped with those of the artist or intellectual, which Katie Sutton has identified as two of the recurring characters in these stories. They appeared as "well-dressed, independent, and stoic, but also rather dark and introspective figures, often from an upper-class background, and with a tendency to pine for their feminine lovers."[140] Feminine lesbians might appear specifically as exotic figures—African jazz singers or Japanese geishas—but also sometimes as seductive femmes fatales.[141] Athletic "sporting" types, with their beautiful, fit bodies, were also stock characters in many of the stories. Very often the authors compared them with Amazons.[142] In the stories, these characters were almost always matched up according to a law of binary oppositions: virile with feminine, rich with poor, young with old, student with teacher.[143] Letters written to the magazines, however, hint at a reality that was more complicated than this. Clearly there were virile lesbians who could not stand the sight of feminine women.[144]

When we examine the lesbian debates about identity, it becomes clear that lesbians were much more likely to entertain the arguments about bisexuality than gay men were. In fact, bisexuality was an issue that provoked heated discussion within *The Girlfriend, A Woman's Love,* and other lesbian magazines. There were certainly some contributors who said that being married or even sleeping with a man once should be enough to exclude an individual from the lesbian community. In the midst of making their point, such women could express some profound "disgust, fury, and hate" toward men, as Heike Schader observes.[145] Many other contributors, though, defended women who carried on relationships with both sexes—either out of true desire, or more commonly because of pragmatic circumstances of social setting or economic need. In letters to the editors, many self-identified bisexual women took an opportunity to tell their own stories of life and love. In them one gets glimpses of how the twists and turns of a life's course can create relationships between numerous individuals in which feelings, desire, obligations, and identities are often difficult and confused issues not easily sorted out.[146]

As many scholars have argued, there is good reason to believe that something like a homosexual identity was becoming firmly articulated in the two decades on either side of the turn of the twentieth century. Germany was not alone here, but Robert Beachy makes a compelling argument in his *Gay Berlin* that the specific national context—with its law against male homosexuality, rapidly developing psychiatric profession, relatively free press, and engaged audience of interested and literate middle-class readers—was particularly conducive for this identity to acquire a personal, social, and political valence that we would find familiar. As this chapter has suggested, however, to talk about "an identity" should not hide the fact that there were many different understandings of same-sex eroticism that circulated in the country, influencing how individuals we would see as gay, lesbian, or transgender today described themselves and their sexual desires. Some certainly turned to modern science, as Foucault once argued, but many others looked back to ancient Greece and Rome. Quite a few were impressed by the Romantics, who dramatized the struggle between self and society or, alternatively, saw their sexuality as the key to unlocking the excitements and freedoms of modernity. And as the homosexual magazines of the 1920s suggest, individuals could often pick and choose from these possibilities, blending them together while also giving them a particular inflection that was based on gender, class, or other social factors. One result was that the language that homosexual men and women used to describe themselves and their sexuality was quite varied.

We can use the word *identity* only in the sense that many of these men and women were beginning to see themselves, despite their diversity, as a single group. In the magazines, literature, and political movements of the era, there was a will to reach across social barriers, around obstacles to understanding, and even back through time to establish a foundation for new communities and common action. In both the male and female friendship magazines, many writers talked about the need for solidarity as homosexuals faced common challenges and problems.[147] It was this will that motivated the swell of interest in homosexual politics during the Weimar era.

CHAPTER 5

The Politics of Homosexuality in Weimar Germany

CHAPTER SUMMARY

This chapter tells the story of the homosexual movement and the fight against Paragraph 175 during the Weimar era. It considers how the First World War and the German revolution of 1918 created both new opportunities and new challenges for the homosexual movement.

OVERVIEW

This chapter considers how the First World War and the German revolution of 1918 created both new opportunities and new challenges for the homosexual movement. In the context of the flourishing gay scenes of the Weimar era, the homosexual movement experienced an amazing upswing in interest and participation. Socialist and democratic ideas were in the air at the opening of the Weimar era, and homosexual activists across Europe watched with excitement as the victory of communism in the Soviet Union led to the repeal of that country's laws against homosexuality. For many gay men and women it was an exciting time—especially for those in the big cities, where they found opportunities they had never seen before. Like many other Germans, gay men and lesbians were energized by the war and the revolution, which inspired them to make claims toward citizenship more forcefully than they had in the past.

There has, however, been a tendency to exaggerate Weimar Germany's tolerance of homosexuality. This chapter offers an important corrective. Conservative voices warning against the dangers of modern life were plentiful. Politically, parties such as the Catholic Center Party and the nationalist German National People's Party quickly recovered, while fringe parties like the newly organized Nazi Party lurked ominously in the background. The WhK, consequently, had its work cut out for it. Magnus Hirschfeld carried on with his business of spreading public enlightenment about sexuality and fighting against Paragraph 175. He was joined by both old friends and new supporters, but he also encountered many new challenges: professional adversaries, rivals for control of the growing homosexual movement, and, most dangerously, nationalist opponents of his sex reform agenda who would have been happy to see him dead.

KEY TERMS

Magnus Hirschfeld; Kurt Hiller; *Der Eigene;* Scientific-Humanitarian Committee; Federation for Human Rights; Paragraph 175; Weimar era

Whisnant, Clayton J.
Queer Identities and Politics in Germany: A History 1880–1945
dx.doi.org/10.17312/harringtonparkpress/2016.08.qipg.005
© Harrington Park Press, LLC, New York, NY 10011

FIGURE 16 **KURT HILLER**

A poet, pacifist, and political activist (among other things), Kurt Hiller played an increasingly prominent role within the WhK during the 1920s. He led an alliance of progressive political associations in the fight against Paragraph 175 and other sections of the legal code targeting sexuality. In 1929 he and his friend Richard Linsert took over the leadership of the WhK after Magnus Hirschfeld's retirement. This chapter picks up the story of homosexual politics in Germany, considering how World War I and the German revolution of 1919 created both new opportunities and new challenges for the homosexual movement. Although a real chance to repeal the sodomy law seemed within reach by 1929, it came with a catch that many homosexual activists (including Hiller) were unwilling to accept. Source: Lotte Jacobi Collection, University of New Hampshire. Thanks also to the Kurt Hiller Gesellschaft, Neuss, Germany

An increasingly important figure for the homosexual movement of the 1920s was Kurt Hiller (Figure 16), a lawyer by training but known in the 1920s mostly as a political writer and champion of Expressionist art. His diverse interests emerged early on. Born in Berlin in 1885 to a Jewish-German necktie manufacturer, he had gone off to the university believing he would pursue medicine, only to be diverted in other directions by his persistent preoccupation with literature and philosophy. Like many German students of the time, he moved around from school to school, studying at the universities of Berlin and Freiburg before eventually getting his law degree from Heidelberg in 1907. For his dissertation he developed a lengthy criticism of the German criminal code's laws against suicide, abortion, and male homosexuality. In some ways this piece was very much at home among the many neo-Kantians at the University of Heidelberg. Like his teacher Gustav Radbruch, Hiller relied on a Kantian conception of law as having the primary purpose of protecting freedom. In particular, he drew on the ideas of the early nineteenth-century Kantian philosopher Jakob Friedrich Fries, who believed that moral judgments could not be rationally argued but instead sprang forth intuitively from the core of our being.[1] Much more than Radbruch, though, Hiller was influenced by both the sociology of Georg Simmel and the radical skepticism of Friedrich Nietzsche. With their ideas in mind, Hiller raised serious questions about any law that assumed the existence of an objective moral code.[2]

Heidelberg's faculty accepted only the portion on suicide from his dissertation because the faculty considered the sections on abortion and homosexuality too radical.[3] The entirety of the work was published in early 1908, however, under the title *The Right to Oneself* (*Das Recht über sich selbst*). With it Hiller quickly acquired a reputation among Germany's progressive intellectuals as a powerful champion for individual rights. Kurt Hiller soon made the acquaintance of both Helene Stöcker and Magnus Hirschfeld.[4] In July 1908 Hiller joined the Scientific-Humanitarian Committee (WhK). His role in the WhK was minimal before the war, though, as Hiller was preoccupied with figuring out what he wanted to do with his life. He had a law degree, but his heart was clearly not in the law. Instead, he found himself drawn in the direction of literature.

In Berlin in 1909 he reunited with some of his university friends who shared a passion for modern art and philosophy, and together they formed a group called the New Club (*Der Neue Club*). "We had no preconceived philosophy in mind," recalled Hiller. "Instead, only a preference for a certain style when it came to poetry—a cleanliness of thought and unromanticism— the style of Plato, the style of Nietzsche."[5] Friedrich Nietzsche was indeed seen by the various members as the key inspirational figure. His call for cultural criticism that would pave the way for a "revaluation of values" was taken up by these young intellectuals, all of them disillusioned with the cerebral rationalism of much contemporary science. What was needed was "pathos": a mixture of reason and passion in which the modern spirit would be awakened by vital instincts.[6] All the intellectuals in the New Club were strong individualists. More than some of his colleagues, though, Hiller from the beginning tried to temper this individualism with a sense of social mission.[7] He was "concerned about personal freedom," but he was also careful not to become a "doctrinaire" individualist—or worse, a solipsist. "We were absolutely for society, even if we understood society to be something very different from what the Free Germans, the Young Germans, the Nationalists thought it to be."[8]

The New Club made critical contributions to the emerging Expressionist movement at the turn of the century. For his part, Hiller wrote poems and essays for the important Expressionist journal *The Storm* (*Der Sturm*). In 1912 he helped edit *The Condor* (*Der Kondor*), one of the earliest collections of Expressionist poetry. Around the same time, he also worked closely with two anarchists, Franz Pfemfert and Anselm Ruest, who established a new journal called *Action* (*Die Aktion*), which published both leftist political criticism and Expressionist literature. His work with *Action* was a sign of his drift toward left-wing political activism. As Hiller remembered it, however, it was the onset of the First World War that proved to be the decisive moment. Faced with this "mass-murdering madness," Hiller dove into pacifism and a much wider terrain of politics.[9] In the early years of the war, he started an annual anthology called *The Goal: Yearbook for Cultural Politics* (*Das Ziel: Jahrbücher für geistige Politik*), which gathered together artists and intellectuals interested in transforming society. In his contributions to these anthologies, he promoted a vision of a future socialist society—one created, though, not by the logic of capitalism in a Marxist sense, but by the liberation of minds. In this society, the monarchy would be abolished and a new government of intellectual elites (comparable to Plato's philosopher-kings) would take charge. They would create a new society in which wealth would be distributed equally, education would be promoted, individual freedoms would be made sacrosanct, and all forms of love would finally be permitted.[10]

His attention to sexuality at this stage shows that even in the midst of the First World War, the reform of Germany's sexual laws had not strayed from his attention. And after the war was over, his participation in the WhK took on a renewed importance in his life. He joined the group's executive board (*Obmänner-Kollegium*) after the November revolution and suggested forming an Operations Committee (*Aktionausschuss*) to help unite the WhK with the network of friendship clubs that were popping up all over the country. On August 30, 1920, an agreement was worked out with the clubs that had recently united into the German Friendship Alliance (DFV). Donations were solicited to help fund a new round of publicity. For a short time, the Operations Committee even managed to secure the cooperation of the masculinists in the Community of the Special (GdE), which despite tensions with the WhK was also optimistic about ridding the country of Paragraph 175. The Operations Committee quickly got to work circulating a new version of the old WhK petition. As before, its members sought out the signatures of well-known personalities; in the 1920s they persuaded Sigmund Freud and the famous Austrian writer Hugo von Hofmannsthal to add their names to the list.[11] The Operations Committee also wrote new pamphlets to be sent en masse to the newly elected parliamentary deputies.[12] On his own, Hiller wrote many articles criticizing Paragraph 175 for the important leftist journal *The World Stage* (*Die Weltbühne*).[13] He even penned a new book: *Paragraph 175—The Disgrace of the Century*, published by the Steegemann press in Hannover, which forcefully laid out his legal arguments for reform.

Hiller and many other critics of the law had reason to be optimistic about the prospects of repeal. In the context of the flourishing gay scenes of the Weimar era, the homosexual movement experienced an amazing upswing in interest and participation. Socialist and democratic ideas were in the air in 1918 and 1919, and homosexual activists across Europe watched with some excitement as the victory of communism in the Soviet Union led to the repeal of that country's laws against homosexuality.[14] There is no doubt that for many gay men and women it was an amazingly exciting time—especially for those in the big cities, where there existed opportunities many had never seen before. Like many other Germans, gay men and lesbians were energized by the war and the revolution, which inspired them to make claims toward citizenship in more forceful ways than they had in the past. They had made sacrifices for the war, like everyone else; now they were ready to insist that they be recognized as "upright people" who were "equal with others."[15] Adolf Brand and other writers for *The Special One* naturally saw the war as confirming the virile nature of the homosexual "men's hero" discussed by Hans Blüher in his works. Even Hirschfeld, however, despite his pacifist sympathies, felt that homosexual men had proven themselves "particularly suited to enduring the strain of modern war," as Jason Crouthamel notes. Because they were used to suppressing their love for other men, they were supposedly prepared emotionally to work through the trauma of loss.[16]

As the historian Stefan Micheler notes, however, "The 1920s were not as golden, liberal, or tolerant as has often been assumed."[17] Conservative voices warning against the dangers of modern life were plentiful. Politically, parties such as the Catholic Center Party and the nationalist German National People's Party quickly recovered, while fringe parties like the newly organized Nazi Party lurked ominously in the background. The WhK, consequently, had its work cut out for it. Magnus Hirschfeld carried on with his business of spreading public enlightenment about sexuality and fighting against Paragraph 175. He was joined by both old friends and new supporters, but he also encountered many new challenges: professional adversaries, rivals for control of the growing homosexual movement, and, most dangerously, nationalist opponents of his sex reform agenda who would have been happy to see him dead.

REVOLUTION AND CONSERVATIVE REVIVAL

When the war was finally over, Hirschfeld not surprisingly threw his support behind the socialist SPD and the new democratic government. In a speech to the League for the New Fatherland (*Bund Neues Vaterland*) in front of the Reichstag building on November 10, 1918, just a day after the monarchy had been abolished by the revolutionary government, Hirschfeld described the revolution as a historic rejection of militarism. "The union of all citizens of Germany," he proclaimed, "mutual care for one another, the evolution of society into one organism, equality for all, everybody for all and all for everybody. And what we want even more: the unity of all nations on earth; we must fight against hatred of other nations."[18] His long connections with Germany's SPD served him well in 1919 and 1920, when this party still held sway over politics. Along with two liberal physicians, he drew up a petition for the nationalization of health services. He managed to convince the German Ministry of the Interior to support the establishment of the Foundation for Scientific Sexual Research (*Stiftung für wissenschaftliche Sexualforschung*). Most important, he used his contacts to urge a reform of Germany's laws governing sexuality, especially Paragraph 175.

The SPD did not maintain control of the revolutionary situation for long. After the setback of 1918–19, conservatives of all stripes quickly rallied. In March 1920 right-wing paramilitary units known as the Free Corps (*Freikorps*), populated with World War I veterans and anticommunist officers, tried to seize power during the Kapp Putsch. This coup failed, but it did not stop antidemocratic forces from establishing a stronghold in Bavaria (and especially Munich, where Hitler would take his first steps into politics).[19] The perceived threat of revolution and socialism drove conservatives of many different kinds into a new party: the German National People's Party. Conservative Catholics remained independent, however, since their Center Party quickly proved itself to be an effective tool for representing Catholic interests. In 1920 the two parties together controlled only slightly less than 30 percent of the popular vote, but alliances could be built with the German People's Party, a right-liberal party that committed itself more firmly to democratic politics than the German nationalists did but that opposed the welfare state and the gains made by workers during the revolution.[20] There were also a small number of local parties with representation at the national level—especially the Bavarian People's Party and the German-Hanoverian Party—that could be counted on to cast conservative votes.

Losing battles on the social and welfare fronts in the early 1920s, conservatives quickly rallied around the fight against so-called immorality. Morality leagues dating back to the previous century, Christian women's organizations, and other church-affiliated pressure groups proved very effective in mobilizing their constituencies to support legislation and to participate in rallies, demonstrations, letter-writing campaigns, and boycotts.[21] Church welfare organizations such as the Protestant Inner Mission and the Catholic Caritas were also important, and each had working groups dedicated to population policy and sexual morality issues.[22] Anxieties about German birth rates, defense of the traditional family, policing of sexual morality and public decency, and the maintenance of laws against abortion and contraception were constant themes in the work done by these different groups. Clergy and politicians played an important role, but so did doctors and other professionals. For example, Dr. Hans Harmsen, a eugenics expert who had studied under the social hygienist Alfred Grotjahn, worked closely with the Inner Mission after he graduated in 1924, publishing numerous studies on demographic issues and moral questions.[23]

As early as April 1920, the morality campaign was able to win a victory in the Reichstag when its proponents used a wave of sexually themed "education films" (*Aufklärungsfilm*) to justify the reintroduction of state censorship over film production. Although the initial wave of these films dealt with serious topics such as venereal disease, alcoholism, and prostitution, they were quickly followed by a flood of imitations that took their stated goal of public enlightenment less than seriously. Many of these education films "elaborated upon matters of sex life with an undeniable penchant for pornographic excursions," noted Siegfried Kracauer.[24] Even the best of them dealt with taboo topics, though, and so they were quickly targeted by conservative organizations as a very public sign of Weimar degeneracy. Moral purity organizations held demonstrations against cinemas that showed the films; other protesters tore screens or otherwise tried to create havoc during viewings. Public prosecutors tried to press pornography charges against the producers, but they were told one after another that the obscenity law (Paragraph 184) did not apply.[25] The Weimar constitution had in general forbidden censorship, but it had made two important exceptions, one of them being the regulation of film. Stirred by the public uproar, conservatives in the Reichstag got busy drafting and eventually passing the Cinema Law (*Lichtspielgesetz*) in May 1920.[26] This law created a review board that checked all films before their distribution and evaluated all films released after the end of the war. It had the authority to ban any film it deemed a threat to state security or public order broadly defined.[27]

The passage of the Cinema Law was applauded by conservatives everywhere. In the elections of 1920 and 1924, conservative parties gained ground steadily, culminating by 1925 in a government dominated by Catholics, German nationalists, conservative Bavarians, and right-liberals. Conservative electoral victories laid the groundwork for the Law to Protect Youth against Trash and Smut, which, as we saw in chapter 3, created great problems for the homosexual press after it was passed, in 1926. We also examined the influence of conservative figures in local police departments, which seems to have produced a stricter attitude toward patrolling the gay scenes and the enforcement of Paragraph 175. Certainly, right-wing public figures were never satisfied with these victories, since they had not been successful in entirely eliminating the sale of homosexual magazines, even in conservative locations such as Munich.[28] Over time, however, there was a noticeable rightward trend in the political atmosphere of Weimar, indeed well before the devastating effects of the Great Depression.

For conservatives the prominence of the gay scene and the growing strength of the sex reform movement was just one glaring sign of the decadence and degenerate behavior that democracy, military defeat, and revolution had allowed to run rampant. The metropolis (*Großstadt*) of Berlin in particular seems to have represented the condition of the country, if not Western civilization at large. For everyone who saw the city as glamorous and alluring, there were many others who complained of the "whoring of Berlin."[29] Drawing on a long tradition of describing the city as a seat of sin and vice, religious authorities, nationalist politicians, and moral guardians of various sorts portrayed Berlin as a site of decay, where "everything is topsy-turvy."[30] One newspaper in the Ruhr town of Essen portrayed Berlin in 1927 as a city full of "bohemian cafés" and other dens of vice: "cocaine markets, homosexual paradises . . . 'Eldorados' of lesbian women" populated by deep-voiced "manly women" and "soprano-voiced, bosomy, and curvaceous men."[31] Such conservatives perceived a world in which numerous forces—democracy, Marxism, the working class, modernism, the women's movement, sexual "perverts," and, more and more, the Jewish race—were all in league to bring down the German nation, the German race, and quite possibly, if one believed Oswald Spengler's predictions in his popular work *The Decline of the West,* all of occidental civilization. But it was not only conservatives who were shocked by what they saw in the country's capital. Even a figure as cosmopolitan and liberal as the author Stefan Zweig could remark that "Berlin was transformed into the Babylon of the world. Along the entire Kurfürstendamm powdered and rouged young men sauntered, and they were not all professionals."[32]

Revelations about the Austrian Redl affair reawakened suspicions created by the Eulenburg scandal that homosexuals were a possible danger to the state. The story of Colonel Redl takes us back to the pre–World War I era. He had been an officer in the Austrian army who, despite coming from a poor family, managed to rise up remarkably high in the military hierarchy. In 1900 he became the chief of the army's counterintelligence agency, but two years later he began to slip secrets to Russian intelligence agents who threatened to ruin his career with the information that he was homosexual. Although initially the victim of blackmail, he soon began to take enormous sums of money in exchange for deliveries of Austrian codes, maps, mobilization plans, and fortification building specs. With the money that he made, he spent lavishly on a young cadet from one of the Austro-Hungarian Empire's elite units. In 1913 Redl was finally caught receiving two envelopes full of cash. He quickly confessed to treason. After further questioning, the investigators left him alone in a room with a Browning pistol sitting on the table. Redl took the hint and shot himself in the head.[33] The Redl affair was hushed up by the Austrians and kept quiet for nearly a decade. In 1924, however, the journalist Egon Kisch dug up information on it and published an exposé. Given the public mood of a country still looking for scapegoats for its humiliating defeat in the First World War, it is not surprising that the book attracted attention. Admittedly, an early silent film about the affair, Hans Otto Löwenstein's 1924 *Colonel Redl—Grave Digger of the Monarchy* (*Oberst Redl—der Totengräber der Monarchie*), ignored Redl's homosexuality, blaming his treachery instead on pure greed. In a second film treatment of the story, Karl Anton's 1931 *The Case of Colonel Redl* (*Der Fall des Generalstabs-Oberst Redl*), however, Redl's attraction to young men was alluded to more clearly.[34]

The danger to state security was certainly not yet a major obsession for conservative leaders. Much more worrisome in their minds was the threat to young people, especially young men. Modern times combined with the loss of the war, economic crisis, and the influence of feminism to create a confusing time for young people, they warned. Numerous books with titles such as *Youth in Sexual Distress, Sexual Dangers Confronting Our Youth,* and

The Depravity of Youth and How to Fight It appeared on the market.[35] In *A Pure Puberty* (*Reine Jugendreife*), the Catholic priest Tihamér Tóth called on young people to "fight the dragon" of modern civilization.[36] Dr. Erich Zacharias, a gynecologist from Dresden, decried the influence that the homosexual movement could have: "The doctrines of the so-called inversion are nothing less than a very dangerous and premeditated contamination of our youth, which is particularly receptive to such influences at the age of puberty. It bears within it the danger of homosexual poisoning, i.e. of a premeditated perversion of our youth."[37]

The image of the predatory homosexual was given a specific face in 1924, when the notorious serial killer Fritz Haarmann, the so-called Butcher of Hannover, made international headlines. Haarmann killed at least twenty-four (and probably more) adolescent boys between 1918 and his eventual capture, six years later. Most of his victims were runaways or male prostitutes whom Haarmann met roaming the main train station of the city. The Hannover police had been aware for some time that young men were disappearing from their city. Then, in 1924, bones began to wash up along the banks of the local Leine River. Dragging the river eventually produced many more—enough to account for twenty-two victims. A full-scale police operation was soon under way.

Haarmann became the focus of the police investigation only by chance—after a mother who had gone to the local police station recognized Haarmann's jacket lying on the floor as one that belonged to her son. Haarmann, it turned out, had been working for some time as a police informant. He was known to them as a local burglar and con artist who occasionally was useful for helping catch other thieves. He did have a previous arrest for molesting a seventeen-year-old. He also had been declared mentally ill several times and had even spent some time in an asylum. Deciding to watch his movements, the police caught him trying to lure yet another victim back to his apartment. A search of his room yielded evidence of blood as well as possessions known to have belonged to some of his victims. After a long interrogation, during which Haarmann was probably beaten badly by the police, he confessed to raping and killing a series of boys. At least a few of them he murdered by biting their throats while they slept. After killing them, Haarmann usually dismembered their bodies and threw their remains in the river. Haarmann's lover Hans Grans was also implicated and eventually convicted, though Grans's exact level of involvement remains unknown. Haarmann was tried and convicted in December 1924. He was beheaded by guillotine the following April.[38]

Haarmann's was the most famous of a string of serial murder cases that came to light during the 1920s. It became internationally known; 168 different newspapers reported on it during the trial.[39] It also fed an increasingly morbid public fascination with violence, murder, and sexual crime during the decade.[40] Soon afterward, the philosopher Theodor Lessing wrote a renowned book on the event that used it to raise troubling questions about the death penalty and the treatment of mentally ill defendants by the courts.[41]

For homosexual activists, the case was a real blow. It helped cement a growing association between homosexuals and child predators that was noticeable on an international scale during the 1920s. Local tabloids had a field day blaming all homosexuals for the bloody crimes. In Hannover the police quickly cracked down on homosexual activity in the city. Homosexual bars were raided; other known cruising locations were carefully watched. Gay men encountered suspicions and prejudice on a daily basis.[42]

Of course, long before Haarmann made headlines, Hirschfeld had already started to embody these fears for many Germans. For cultural conservatives and right-wing nationalists, he was not only the purveyor of toxic ideas about homosexual emancipation but also a socialist and a Jew. Before a speaking engagement in Hamburg in 1920, German nationalists planted fire and stink bombs near the stage that were designed to go off during the talk. Luckily, a warning was sent, and the police removed the explosives before anyone was hurt. Soon afterward, though, during a lecture in Munich, thugs sent by one of Germany's largest anti-Semitic leagues tried to break up the proceedings. Security intervened but could not entirely stop the catcalls or the violence that erupted outside the hall.[43] Hirschfeld managed to escape this time, but he was not so lucky the following year. Having returned to Munich to give a lecture on recent embryological research, he was attacked by a nationalist gang that spat in his face, beat him up, threw rocks at him, and left him bleeding and unconscious in the street. Hirschfeld revived in the hospital. He had a fractured skull and a concussion but was alive. The next day he had the strange experience of reading his obituary in a local paper, which had falsely heard that he had died in the encounter.[44] And this was not Hirschfeld's last brush with death. In 1923, while he was visiting Vienna on a speaking tour, young Nazis shot at him from the floor while others in the gang threw stink bombs and assaulted members of the audience.[45]

The violence aimed at Hirschfeld was just one indication of the clashing political tendencies of Weimar and, in a more general way, the contradictory impulses that were at work in the early part of the twentieth century. As one well-known historian of German history, Detlef Peukert, once suggested, Weimar Germany was torn apart by a "crisis-racked, modernizing society in which teetering over the abyss was the norm and the resolution of conflict was the exception."[46] Social and political institutions rooted in a traditional world were coming up against a society that was increasingly diverse and complex. Value systems that assumed some natural order to the social hierarchy were confronting louder and louder demands for social equality and individual freedom.[47] Hopes fueled by political revolution, scientific and technological advances, and rapid social changes hit up against enormous anxieties about the survival of society, morality, and security in the modern world. Such conflict has been present in every modernizing society, of course, but much historical work argues that these conflicts were particularly intense in Germany during the 1920s and 1930s. Again in the words of Peukert, "The glamour of modernization exerted a special fascination on the Germans, but its dark side, too, had a profound effect on lives that were shadowed by war, military defeat, a loss of confidence in old values, the bewilderments of hyperinflation and the blight of world recession."[48] The intensity of emotion generated by such contradictory feelings left its mark on the controversies revolving around homosexuality in the 1920s.

HIRSCHFELD, THE INSTITUTE OF SEXUAL SCIENCE, AND THE WLSR

The attacks on Hirschfeld's life were ironically also some tribute to his success. He was repeatedly assaulted precisely because he had been so successful at taking his message to the public. Most important for his own future and reputation was the opening of his Institute for Sexual Science (*Institut für Sexualwissenschaft*) in February 1919. With financial assistance from the government and aid from the Foundation for Scientific Sexual Research, Hirschfeld bought a palatial mansion at the edge of Berlin's Tiergarten. Working with a colleague, the psychiatrist Arthur Kronfeld, Hirschfeld established a cutting-edge facility for sexual science and medical assistance that by July became fully operational.[49] As it had once belonged to a famous Berlin violinist, the palace was furnished in style. "Their furniture was classic, pillared, garlanded," remembered Christopher Isherwood, who had lunch at the institute during his stay in the city; "their marble massive, their curtains solemnly sculpted, their engravings grave."[50] Another visitor to the premises was surprised by the decor: "That—a scientific institute? No cold walls, no linoleum on the floors, no uncomfortable chairs and no smell of disinfectants. This is a private house: carpets, pictures on the walls, and nowhere a plate saying 'No entrance.'"[51] Next to the main building was a house that Hirschfeld purchased in 1921 and then remodeled so that it connected with the original site. To enter the institute, one normally went in through this small corner house. Over the main entrance, a sign stood with the inscription "Sacred to Love and Sorrow" (in Latin).

The building was spacious, but it was also full of people going about their business. Staffed by four physicians and their assistants, the institute became a pioneer in offering sex counseling services, including marriage counseling, VD testing and treatment, sex education programs, and psychiatric therapy. In the first year of operations alone, 1,800 consultations were given. Naturally, gay men, lesbians, and other so-called sexual variants visited the clinic. Over the years Hirschfeld had developed a method of therapy designed to guide such patients toward self-acceptance and happiness.[52] The doctors also saw patients suffering from various endocrine dysfunctions and even drug addicts and alcoholics. Women with fertility issues came seeking help, and in 1920 the clinic carried out its first experiment with artificial insemination. The doctors frequently took on legal cases, collecting evidence that would eventually be presented in court. They offered lectures on a variety of subjects, including psychoanalysis, sexual pathology, forensic sexology, and the physiology of sexual differences.[53] Arthur Kronfeld even began the first sex-reassignment surgery in 1920. Although not a practice that either Kronfeld or Hirschfeld generally recommended, in the case of this twenty-three-year-old officer they were afraid that he might commit suicide if something was not done. Kronfeld removed the young man's testicles in the institute's clinic facilities. During the following year, two more surgeries were completed on the patient by a sympathetic gynecologist in Dresden who implanted an ovary and reshaped the patient's penis and scrotum into something resembling a vagina.[54]

Rooms in the main building of the Institute for Sexual Science were set aside for the private use of Hirschfeld and his assistant, collaborator, and longtime lover, Karl Giese. Hirschfeld had a large consulting room with a desk and three enormous windows that overlooked the balcony. Nearby was a comfortable salon with a grand piano and a figurine of Icarus. Space was allocated for the headquarters of the WhK. Above all, though, the institute was dedicated to expanding knowledge about every aspect of sexuality—biological, sociological, ethnographic, and psychological. Laboratories were established to carry out scientific research, and other rooms were used for X-ray investigations and experimental treatment with artificial sunlight.[55] The institute's library and archive housed some 20,000 volumes and over 30,000 photographs that attracted scientists from all over the world. For tourists there was a museum dedicated to the history and variety of sexuality, full of curiosities, specimens, and exhibits.[56] Here one could find samples of pornography made around the world and sketches of fantasies imagined by some of Hirschfeld's psychiatric patients. And photographs—lots of photographs, largely of the kind taken by Hirschfeld to support his theory of the relationship between hermaphroditism and homosexuality.[57]

Housed in his Institute for Sexual Science, and an increasingly important figure in Weimar's emerging sex reform movement, Hirschfeld found himself offered new opportunities to leave his mark on the German public. Just one of these possibilities was suggested by the film director and producer Richard Oswald. An Austrian-Jewish director who had moved to Berlin shortly before the war, Oswald started up his own film company in the city and quickly made a name for himself by taking on morally or politically sensitive topics.[58] At the beginning of 1919, he approached Hirschfeld with an idea for yet another film, this one dealing with the issue of homosexuality. The Cinema Law was not yet on the agenda, and so *Different from the Rest* (*Anders als die Andern*) was filmed in the first months of the year and released on May 24, 1919. Premiered at one of Berlin's largest cinema houses, the Apollo-Theater on Friedrichstrasse, the film was produced in line with the dominant cinematic style of the era, namely, silent melodrama. It stared Conrad Veidt, an early film star who made many movies in Germany in the early 1920s but today is probably best remembered for his role as the Nazi officer Major Strasser in the 1942 Hollywood film *Casablanca*. In *Different from the Rest,* Veidt played the violinist Paul Körner, who falls in love with one of his music students, thereby exposing himself to blackmail and eventually committing suicide. The plot of the film offered Magnus Hirschfeld an opportunity to make an appearance in which he lectured the audience on the nature and unfortunate fate of the "third sex." In case the audience had missed the message, the film ended with an image of Paragraph 175 being penciled out.[59]

The film generated an enormous public debate on the topic. After its premiere in Berlin, it was distributed widely throughout the country and abroad. For the most part film critics complimented the film, although conservative and nationalist papers decried it as lewd and dangerous. There were incidents at several screenings. In Berlin, uniformed soldiers led a walkout from the cinema. Disturbances in theaters in Munich and Stuttgart led the local police to ban the film.[60] The resulting publicity was probably responsible for the first of the threats against Hirschfeld made during his Hamburg lecture. As early as September 1919, legislators in the Prussian state government tried to get the film banned, only to be informed by the national minister of the interior that the obscenity laws could not be applied to the film. Opponents of this work and other so-called education films were not to be dissuaded. After the 1920 Cinema Law was passed, the review board banned the film from distribution in August. The film could still be shown to an audience of scientists and other specialists, but it was no longer available to the general public.[61] By this point, though, it had already become an enormous box-office hit and had achieved the critical goal of getting people to talk about the issue.

In the sexological profession, Hirschfeld continued to be active in trying to mobilize scientific opinion in favor of legal reform. A landmark moment for his career came in September 1921, when he organized a major sexological conference in Berlin. Held in the Institute for Sexual Science as well as in Berlin's Langenbeck-Virschow-Haus (a medical center with a suitably large auditorium), the First International Congress for Sex Reform on the Basis of Sexual Science brought together prominent academics and doctors from France, Italy, Holland, Scandinavia, Hungary, Czechoslovakia, the United States, the Soviet Union, China, and Japan. Law, contraception, sex education, eugenics, and psychology were among the topics presented.[62] The bulk of the papers focused on endocrinology and its significance for sexuality, but there were also several important talks by sex reformers. Helene Stöcker gave a paper in which she attacked traditional moral attitudes about sexuality. The feminist Mathilde Vaerting called for a new understanding of gender psychology that took better account of the social roles that men and women played.

The congress would be repeated again in 1928 in Copenhagen, at which Hirschfeld would help establish the World League for Sexual Reform (*Weltliga für Sexualreform,* WLSR) and would share a position on the executive board with the Swiss sexologist Auguste Forel and the British sex reformer Havelock Ellis. The WLSR program advocated causes that we would identify as progressive: for example, the liberalization of marriage laws, free access to contraception, repeal of laws against homosexuality, and toleration of nonmarital sexual relationships. It also promoted some political changes, especially eugenic controls over birth, that would make progressives today very suspicious. Underlying all these programs was an attitude that gained widespread currency in the 1920s that sexuality should be transformed through the application of science, rationality, and standards of efficiency and effectiveness.[63] Rivalries and differences over strategy and priorities always troubled the organization. Perhaps because of this tension, the group's attempt at establishing a journal never got off the ground. Furthermore, the organization's claim to be a "world" organization was rather exaggerated since there were very few members who did not come from either Germany or England. Still, by the early 1930s the WLSR boasted some 190,000 members who would lay the groundwork for international cooperation among activists interested in sexual issues.[64]

Eugenics was a recurring theme in Hirschfeld's professional work during the 1920s. This topic deserves some attention since it stands out as the one idea that Hirschfeld advocated that we today would not see as particularly progressive. From our point of view, it is connected with the worst kinds of racism and cannot be discussed without thinking of Nazi-style breeding and forced sterilizations. For a generation of researchers working in the 1970s and 1980s, Hirschfeld's advocacy of eugenics could easily be read as unwittingly laying the "scientific and ethical" groundwork for Nazi brutality.[65] Paul Weindling views Hirschfeld and his coworkers as "enlightened progressives by the standards of the age," but also "captives within a eugenic and biologistic framework."[66] Weindling adds nuance to the argument somewhat by insisting that "eugenics did not necessarily point the way towards Nazi racism," but he still sees it as inherently "authoritarian in that it offered the state and profession unlimited power to eradicate disease and improve the health of future generations."[67] At least implicitly, such interpretations were often underpinned by the work of Michel Foucault, which for a time made many historians deeply suspicious about the pernicious tendencies of science.

Since the 1990s, however, historians have increasingly hesitated to draw too straight a line between Weimar-era eugenics and the "racial hygiene" policies of the Nazi state. In early twentieth-century Germany, there were many different people representing opposing political, religious, and social backgrounds who advocated eugenics, including socialists and, surprisingly, even Catholics.[68] Yes, all of them accepted the notion originally promoted by the founder of eugenics, Francis Galton, that humanity could take charge of its evolution through an application of science and medicine. The many groups that accepted this idea differed greatly when it came to deciding which physical or mental traits should be encouraged or discouraged and which methods ought to be employed in accomplishing the basic goal of strong, healthy individuals. Birth control advocates pushed the value of free access to contraception; doctors suggested the role that marriage counseling and genetic screenings could play. Socialists saw eugenics' hope of producing healthy families as complementary to their goal of improving the working and living conditions of the working class. Middle-class liberals, on the other hand, saw eugenics as a possible corrective to the dangerous tendencies toward collectivism in the modern world. And right-wing racists, the group that we tend to be most familiar with when it comes to eugenics, imagined methods that might strengthen the Germanic race and nurture noble characteristics within the social elite.[69]

Hirschfeld's interest in eugenics was very typical of middle-class doctors, sexologists, and participants in the broader sex reform movement. For their part, many sex reformers saw eugenics as intricately caught up in the reforms that they hoped to make: free access to birth control, legalized abortion, widely available sex education, and, when necessary, sterilization.[70] Hirschfeld was a firm believer in the power of modern scientific research and medical intervention to make life better, and eugenics seemed to make a lot of sense from this point of view. As a socialist, he hoped that eugenics might be able to solve some of the perennial problems of working-class life, such as alcoholism.[71] Unlike some sexologists, he did not believe that homosexuality was a sign of degeneracy, and so eugenic methods were not needed to weed out this natural variation of biology. In fact, he hoped that homosexuals might ultimately benefit from eugenic measures being applied to the welfare state. If the "criminal tendencies" found among the working class could be addressed, over time homosexuals could find themselves less troubled by blackmail, violence, and other risks associated with male prostitution.[72]

Hirschfeld's brand of eugenics had very little in common with the kind eventually practiced by the Nazis. He certainly was no racist. Geniuses and saints came from all races, he wrote in his five-volume magnum opus, *Sexual Science* (*Geschlechtskunde*).[73] Moreover, nations represented complex mixtures of different races. He resisted the calls of some physicians for state-operated marriage bureaus that would investigate the moral, social, and family backgrounds of individuals before they were wed. Such methods, he insisted, were far too intrusive.[74] As Laurie Marhoefer writes, "Historians have concluded, rightly, that ideas about degeneration and support for eugenics within the homosexual emancipation movement did not pave the way for Nazi programs."[75] Indeed, the destruction of everything Hirschfeld worked for after the Nazi takeover is good evidence that "sex reform and social medicine underwent a definitive and irrevocable break in 1933."[76]

PSYCHIATRIC AND SEXOLOGICAL CRITICS OF HIRSCHFELD

Hirschfeld believed that some recent genetic and hormonal research had given the case for the heritability of homosexuality undeniable corroboration. The pioneering geneticist Richard Goldschmidt at the University of Munich put a new twist on intersexuality when he reported on his successful experiments with breeding a new species of insect in 1914. This variety of the gypsy moth had female chromosomes, but otherwise exhibited both masculine appearance and behavior. Two years later, he extended his results to human sexuality, suggesting that homosexuality could be understood as a form of intersexuality.[77] Even more directly relevant was the work of the Viennese biologist Eugen Steinach, who was able to demonstrate the role that sex hormones play in sexual differentiation in guinea pigs. In 1910 he had even carried out experiments at transplanting testicles onto castrated guinea pigs, which he believed proved that homosexuality resulted from hermaphroditic sexual glands.[78] After the war he experimented with transplanting healthy testicles into homosexual men and even had a film made in 1923 to publicize his work. Hirschfeld heralded Steinach's results as proof of his own theories, and he went so far as to refer a patient who wanted to reverse his sexuality to Steinach for transplant surgery.[79] Not surprisingly, a rash of unfortunate castration and transplant surgeries followed in the early 1920s.

Despite all the attention that Steinach's research gained, not everyone was convinced. In fact, if anything, scientific opinion on the psychological roots of homosexuality diverged considerably after the First World War as the related fields of psychiatry and psychotherapy became more complex. Political and institutional divisions between sex reformers and more mainstream sexologists also hardened, a trend that Edward Ross Dickinson suggests was already evident by 1908 but which took on wider political implications in Weimar Germany.[80]

The biological school of psychiatry remained the dominant one; however, the basic assumption of this school that psychological disturbances generally had physiological causes did not necessarily determine whether one believed that homosexuality was inborn or acquired. Many psychiatrists followed Emil Kraepelin—who by the early twentieth century had emerged as the most prominent psychiatrist in the country—in believing that there was a physiological disposition toward homosexuality rooted in a weakness of the nervous system, but that this latent disposition still had to be "awakened somehow."[81] In 1915 Kraepelin began to emphasize the role of seduction, masturbation, and other environmental factors in the emergence of homosexuality. After the war he and his various students and colleagues turned against Hirschfeld and the sex reform movement, arguing that Paragraph 175 was absolutely necessary to protect the country against the spread of homosexuality.[82]

An even more determined opponent was Albert Moll. Even before the First World War, Moll had started to call Hirschfeld's writings "a poison." Suspicious of Hirschfeld's tendencies to mix politics with science, Moll joined his colleague Max Marcuse in founding his own professional organization— the International Society for Sexual Research (*Internationale Gesellschaft für Sexualforschung*)—to foster "pure" scientific research, as opposed to "sex reform." His opinion of Hirschfeld was clearly tainted by his hostility to homosexuality. Homosexuality might be natural, Moll conceded, but that did not make it healthy. Adult homosexuals, he argued, required psychological treatment, and he did not even rule out the possibility that homosexuality might be "converted" through proper therapy.[83] After the war Moll became increasingly concerned about the possibility that young boys might be "seduced" into a homosexual lifestyle, and that in this way homosexuals might be "bred." In 1919 he joined Kraepelin and one other psychiatrist in recommending to the Film Review Board that the film *Different from the Rest* be banned from public consumption.[84] During the 1920s his attacks against Hirschfeld became increasingly personal, as Moll began alluding in print to Hirschfeld's "character" and "its problematic nature."[85]

A friendlier critic was Ernst Kretschmer, one of the rising stars in German psychiatry. Kretschmer made a name for himself with his 1921 book *Physique and Character* (*Körperbau und Charakter*), in which he argued that there was a strong connection between body shape and personality. All humans, he suggested, could be categorized into three basic phenotypes. Pynic individuals were chubby and rounded, jolly and good-natured. Asthenic people were long and lanky and tended to be introverted and shy, often having an eccentric side. Finally, the athletic type, with their powerful muscles and broad shoulders, were generally aggressive and cold, even ruthless sometimes.[86] Kretschmer's argument in *Physique and Character* had some vague similarities to Hirschfeld's research, which also had assumed that there was a close connection between physique and the psyche. Kretschmer himself made this point in a paper that Hirschfeld invited him to give to the Medical Society for Sexual Science and Eugenics in 1923.[87] As *Physique and Character* acquired international attention, it was widely understood to lend support to the idea that homosexuality was largely inborn.[88] Kretschmer certainly did not deny that biology played some role. In the early 1920s he thought that Steinach's research was especially important in this regard.[89] Like Kraepelin (with whom he otherwise rarely agreed), however, he believed that environmental causes could not be ruled out. In the 1930 edition of his influential textbook, he suggested that some homosexuals picked up the practice by being seduced by other homosexuals, and even more were victims of "hypochondriacal auto-suggestion": "This last factor refers to those psychopaths who lack confidence in heterosexual intercourse and have renounced it in the belief that they are impotent."[90] He certainly was not a defender of Paragraph 175, but his suggestion in *Physique and Character* that homosexuality might have some connection with schizophrenia indicates that Kretschmer did in fact see it as a fundamentally pathological condition.[91]

The main challenger to the dominance of the biological school was Freudian psychoanalysis. In the United States Freud's ideas were met with much interest and welcomed among medically trained psychiatrists and neurologists around the turn of the century, but the European medical profession remained rather skeptical about Freud's ideas through the 1930s. Although some of the earliest psychoanalysts had trained alongside other psychiatrists and sexologists in the local asylums and hospitals, the influence of the biological school of thought (as well as anti-Semitic prejudices in the German medical profession) led the emerging sexological profession to grow in a different direction from Freudian "depth psychology" (*Tiefenpsychologie*), as it was often called.[92] With the foundation of the Berlin Psychoanalytic Institute in the early 1920s, Freudians finally had their own institutional center. There were some trained physicians who worked with the institute; however, there was a noticeable left-wing slant among most of them. As in Paris and London, there were also many interesting and fruitful connections with local authors and artists.

In terms of his upbringing, culture, and attitude toward politics, Hirschfeld shared much of the same background as many of the Freudians. Hirschfeld was not one to hold grudges, and in the 1920s the old feud was put aside. In his three-volume *Sexual Pathology,* a textbook completed in 1920 that Hirschfeld hoped would become a standard reference work for doctors and university students alike, he made it clear that he fundamentally disagreed with Freud about the constitutional nature of the libido. He did, however, suggest that Freud had important things to say about the role of sexuality in many neuroses, especially hysteria and obsessional ideas.[93] Two of Hirschfeld's colleagues at the Institute for Sexual Science, Hanns Sachs and Carl Müller-Braunschweig, were members of the Berlin Psychoanalytic Institute.[94] Helene Stöcker also belonged briefly. Through such affiliations and many others, the Berlin Freudians were very much integrated from the beginning into the wider Weimar sex reform movement.

Psychoanalysis was changing fast during the 1920s. In the United States, Harry Stack Sullivan was laying the groundwork for a new approach to psychoanalysis that emphasized humanity's reliance on communication and interpersonal relations.[95] Berlin also proved to be a breeding ground for dissent, and many figures eventually broke with more orthodox practitioners.[96] In a number of papers Karen Horney began to explore aspects of a specifically feminine psychology, from which emerged her more culturally based approach that would mature later during exile in the United States.[97] Melanie Klein presented her first work on child psychology, which led her toward an alternative vision of the psyche, one that was much more unstable and fluid than Freud's was.[98] And in 1930 Wilhelm Reich moved to Berlin with his hope of fusing sexual liberation with communist politics.[99]

Over time, these various approaches and others would develop very different views toward homosexuality. In the 1920s, however, Freud was still the towering figure in the world of psychoanalysis, and his views on homosexuality had not changed drastically. In his 1920 essay "The Psychogenesis of a Case of Homosexuality in a Woman," he detailed the case of a lesbian whom he had been treating whose sexual orientation he traced to a critical moment during puberty when she learned that her mother was going to have another baby. Her sexual desire having only recently and weakly attached itself to her father, she felt spurned. "Furiously resentful and embittered, she turned away from her father, and from men altogether."[100] Her sexuality refocused itself on her mother, and from there on women in general. And yet, interestingly, he thought, she found herself attracted to rather masculine-looking women—most recently to a woman who reminded her of her brother. Her love "combined gratification of the homosexual tendency with that of the heterosexual one."[101] The outcome of this trauma was perhaps overdetermined, Freud observed, since analysis had suggested an earlier mother fixation that had not entirely been worked through. It also revealed a pronounced penis envy and a well-developed "masculinity complex" that manifested itself in her willingness to fight.[102] To her parents he could offer little hope that analysis would do much good for her sexual orientation. In fact, he remarked, "The removal of genital inversion or homosexuality is in my experience never an easy matter."[103]

When it came to the law against male homosexuality, Freud left no doubt. Not only did he sign the WhK's petition against the law, but in 1928, on the occasion of Hirschfeld's sixtieth birthday, he gave his respects in a special edition of *The Yearbook for Sexual Intermediaries:* "I have always expressed the view that the life and work of Dr. Magnus Hirschfeld against the cruel and unjustifiable interference of the law in human sexual life deserves general recognition and support."[104]

Freudian psychoanalysis clearly had much appeal for those psychiatrists and physicians who were dissatisfied with the biological orientation of their field. Psychiatrists who resisted the biological field but who were simultaneously alienated by the leftist leanings of so many Freudians, however, were gradually drawn into a different orbit, that of the emerging field of phenomenological psychotherapy (or anthropological psychotherapy, as it is more commonly known in Germany). The phenomenological school usually traces its history to the psychologist and philosopher Karl Jaspers, who published his *General Psychopathology* in 1913. Jaspers's work, inspired by Wilhelm Dilthey's argument that only empathy and understanding (*Verstehen*) allow one access to the inner workings of another human's mind, rejected the empiricism and materialist basis of the biological school in favor of an analysis of the "meaningful connections" that an individual makes within his or her own consciousness.[105] There were some definite similarities to Freudian psychoanalysis, since Freud also emphasized the meanings that individuals made within their own minds as determinative in some sense; however, in the end, the phenomenological school rejected psychoanalysis because of its dependence on the unconscious, which they saw as a "*carte blanche* on which almost any explanation could be written."[106] They regretted the tendency to reduce everything to sexual instinct by reading in unverifiable processes such as sublimation or censorship. In the words of Ludwig Binswanger, the best-known representative of the school today, Freud's view of humanity "is a scientific construct that is only feasible if it is based on the destruction of man's experiential knowledge of himself—a destruction, in other words, of anthropological experience."[107]

In a series of articles published in the late 1920s and early 1930s, the psychiatrist Viktor Emil von Gebsattel first explored a phenomenological approach to sexual perversions and, by extension, to homosexuality. Gebsattel had studied with Emil Kraepelin at Munich's University Psychiatric Clinic right after World War I. Although he successfully got through all his medical training and clinical work, he was unimpressed by Kraepelin's focus on physiological symptoms. His dissertation tried to develop a psychiatric approach to feelings, a realm of experience inadequately theorized within the biological school. And after moving to Berlin and setting up his own private clinic in the mid-1920s, he began to develop ideas rooted in philosophy, especially in the works of Wilhelm Dilthey and Theodor Lipps, which he had been exposed to during his undergraduate days in Berlin.[108] In his research on sexual perversions, he was inspired especially by the young philosopher Max Scheler, with whom he had developed a friendship in Munich before the war. Values, according to Scheler, are not subjective phenomena, but instead have an objective existence and are sensible to people by means of feelings.[109]

Scheler's emphasis on values fit well with Gebsattel's Catholic upbringing. Beginning in a 1929 essay on fetishism, Gebsattel developed a theory of sexual perversion that posited the existence of a self-destructive mania in a person that opposes his or her drive toward self-realization. He interpreted various varieties of sexual perversion as modes of enjoyment derived from destructiveness, which then compensates for failures of self-realization.[110] In a later essay he clearly connected this mania to his belief in humanity's fallen nature. In sexual perversions, Gebsattel wrote, one cannot ignore the "drive and attraction of men toward evil or—if we wish to avoid such moralistic language in an anthropological essay—the basic nihilistic streak in human nature."[111]

KURT HILLER'S GROWING ROLE IN THE WHK

Hirschfeld was clearly a long way away from convincing the entire sexological and psychiatric profession of the need to repeal the laws against homosexuality. Politically, however, the situation appeared more promising. In fact, Chancellor Joseph Wirth appointed a progressive lawyer and member of the socialist SPD, Gustav Radbruch, as the new minister of justice in October 1921. Radbruch saw it as a priority to rewrite the entire German penal code according to "the spirit of modern criminological thinking."[112] Philosophically, Radbruch was a neo-Kantian who believed that law was distinct from morality. As a professor of law at Heidelberg University, he had argued that laws might create the conditions for someone to live a moral life by guaranteeing personal rights, but they could not impose morality through obligations and restrictions. Morality was anchored in humanity's free will; it could be chosen but not forced. And since moral codes were ultimately relative and based only on subjectively held values, the best that the law could do was try to mediate between them. It should aim at establishing the framework for cooperation of free individuals through guarantees of basic equality and personal freedom.[113] As luck would have it, Hirschfeld knew someone who had a personal connection with Radbruch, namely, his fellow WhK member Kurt Hiller. Hiller had been one of Radbruch's students at the University of Heidelberg. Given that he also had many connections with other left-wing writers and progressive political activists, he seemed a natural to head up the Action Committee. Hiller's connection proved fruitful. Radbruch signed the WhK's petition against Paragraph 175, and in late 1921, as Radbruch's draft of an entirely revised legal code was being worked out, he received a delegation sent by the WhK to discuss the reform.[114]

Unfortunately, Hirschfeld's and Hiller's hopes were quickly dashed. Pressing economic problems and the mounting political turbulence of 1922 led Chancellor Wirth to resign in November, and Gustav Radbruch lost his position in the cabinet. He did return to the Justice Ministry in the second half of 1923, under the chancellorship of Gustav Stresemann, but by this time more pressing problems—the difficulties of making war reparation payments, the French invasion of the coal-rich lands of the Ruhr, and currency hyperinflation—kept Radbruch's draft from coming back for consideration. Even worse, when the government finally did revisit the criminal code in 1924, the constantly shifting political terrain of the Weimar era had pushed the government in a more conservative direction. A new draft, known as E1925, was produced that, while including a number of progressive legal innovations aimed at preventing crime instead of simply punishing offenders, was overall a much more conservative document than its predecessor. The death penalty reappeared, as well as the old provisions criminalizing certain kinds of sexual behavior, among them male homosexuality and male prostitution.[115] Hiller's reaction was unsurprising: "One could scarcely comprehend the backwardness of the government's draft," he commented.[116] It represented "the super-idiotic high point (or low point, if you prefer) of bigoted hypocrisy."

Taken aback by the proposal, the WhK quickly got to work to generate a response. Hiller contacted other organizations that could be counted on to oppose the new bill. Stöcker's League for the Protection of Motherhood lent Hiller its support, as did the German League for Human Rights (*Deutsche Liga für Menschenrechte*), the Society for Sex Education, the Society for Sex Reform, and the Organization for the Reform of Marriage Law. The new Coalition for Reform of the Sexual Penal Code, as the group called itself, chose eight individuals—including Hirschfeld and Stöcker—to help Hiller design an alternative draft of the criminal code. "We consulted together for months quite regularly," Hiller remembered, "very systematically, in a friendly way despite the often sharp debates among us. The results were quite good." [117] A large portion of the draft was actually written by Hiller and eventually published in 1927 as a cheap booklet to make it widely available. The draft naturally addressed that portion of the code dealing with sexual crimes, such as abortion, rape, seduction, incest, and the sexual abuse of children. Some paragraphs were kept, many more altered to make them more progressive. The proposed law against homosexuality was simply eliminated in the coalition's version. It was "incompatible with the results of scientific research and a modern conception of sex life." [118] It went against the modern view of law as being designed primarily to prevent harm but not otherwise act as a moral guardian. Past versions of the law had proven themselves ineffective and, in fact, had fostered further injustices and crimes. The new version of the law solved none of the problems, but it actually "made them considerably worse." [119] Although the press largely ignored the alternative draft, it did cause the Ministry of Justice to take notice. A sign of the group's success was the ministry's decision to write a series of responses, which were published in a very well-respected professional journal dealing with legal issues. [120]

Hiller's growing importance within the WhK posed a potential problem that Hirschfeld was slow to recognize. Hiller clearly admired Hirschfeld, but he had some growing doubts about Hirschfeld's ability to lead the group. "His competence as a researcher was unparalleled," Hiller would later write, "and he was a bold campaigner for the most unpopular things in the world. A great organizer, though, he was not." [121] As early as 1918 Hiller had expressed skepticism about the ability of science to convince the general public of the need for legal reform. [122] His view of homosexuality was actually influenced more by his classical education than by modern sexology. His sexual awakening had taken place as a teenager during a visit to a therapeutic hot springs bath (*Luftbad*) where a number of youths were practicing Greek-style gymnastics. Throughout his life he would find himself attracted to young, muscular, sculpted bodies.

Interestingly, many scholars have observed that Hiller had much in common with the masculinists who congregated around Adolf Brand. His artistic streak, personal connections with anarchists, and well-developed sense of elitism might have allowed him to feel right at home in the GdE. Whether it was the anti-Semitism and antifeminism sometimes found among masculinists that made him keep his distance or simply Hiller's guess that they would prove politically ineffective is hard to say. His decision not to align himself with the growing number of friendship clubs and Radszuweit's Federation for Human Rights (BfM) is easier to understand. In his autobiography the disdain that he felt for the "excess of dilettantism, folksy cluelessness, turgid speeches, absolute nonsense, and well-meaning but otherwise ignorant participants" found in such clubs is difficult to miss.[123]

For most of the 1920s, Hiller kept quiet about his misgivings concerning Hirschfeld. Nevertheless, he worked to include individuals in the WhK's leadership who he felt might be more reliable for the task ahead of them. One of his closest friends in the WhK was Fritz Flato, a probationary judge from Berlin who by the early 1920s was taking on a growing role in the organization. Remembered by one man who knew him as "talkative" and "very helpful," Flato was sent as the WhK's delegate to the DFV conference held in Munich in 1922. By mid-decade he had established his own legal practice in the city, which allowed him to defend men against Paragraph 175 charges. Once a week he offered free consultation to WhK members who had landed in some legal trouble. He also lent his services to Friedrich Radszuweit, whose press needed constant legal aid to defend itself against the police and local prosecutors.[124]

His other close ally was Richard Linsert. As a twenty-two-year-old communist from Bavaria and a founding member of Munich's local friendship club, Linsert had met Flato in 1922 at the DFV conference.[125] Flato had been immediately impressed by Linsert as someone who stood out among the other delegates. He spoke up often in a "clear and winning" manner in favor of "radical but quite reasonable" proposals.[126] Hiller asked Flato to hunt Linsert down and arrange a meeting. Later that year, the three of them met. Linsert was polite but somewhat "cool" and "reserved," Hiller remembered. He was good-looking, though: "No young man was more beautiful than he was—with an intertwining of sportiness and charm, poise and ease, toughness and delicacy." Physically he was small, yet he somehow came across as larger than he was. Intellectually, he was mature beyond his years.[127]

Hiller was smitten. He took Linsert under his wing and, together with Flato, sought to bring him into the leadership of the WhK. Linsert, Hiller thought, would make a nice replacement for the current secretary of the organization, a man for whom Hiller had limited appreciation—an aging fellow who had little intelligence and even less ability to manage a sizable institution.[128] It took some time, but in the spring of 1923 Hiller persuaded Hirschfeld to hire Linsert, first as an aide to the secretary, and then in 1926 as the secretary itself. Hirschfeld thought Linsert a bit of a troublemaker.[129] Linsert, for his part, felt a little out of his element among all the doctors, lawyers, and wealthy individuals who tended to congregate in the Institute for Sexual Science. But with the political work heating up in 1925, Hiller was very happy to have him around. His instinct for politics made him invaluable when it came to forming the Coalition for Sexual Reform. His "judgment, industry, negotiation skills, and faithfulness" proved vital in the ensuing political struggle.[130] Linsert helped Hiller with the writing of the Coalition for Sexual Reform's alternative draft of a legal code. As a good communist who was sympathetic with the working class, he wrote a sociological survey of male prostitutes in Berlin.[131] His connections with the German Communist Party helped ensure that the abolition of the laws against male homosexuality was made a plank in the party's platform during the 1920s.[132] At the end of the decade, he also coauthored two books with Magnus Hirschfeld, one on birth control and a second on aphrodisiacs.[133]

Together, Linsert, Hiller, and Flato were able to manage the reform challenges of the second half of the 1920s and nearly achieve their goals. They were not, however, able to shut down the political infighting that broke out within the homosexual movement itself.

RIVALRIES IN THE MOVEMENT

During the First World War, Adolf Brand had spent two years in the army. His magazine *The Special One,* in any case, had been forced to stop publication for lack of funds shortly before the war. The GdE stopped meeting while Brand fulfilled his military service. In 1919, though, the informal circle of masculinist writers and artists began to get together again. Brand was married now—he had met a friendly nurse named Elise Behrendt during the war—but he had not given up his commitment to the cause, and luckily his wife was sympathetic. She even let one of Brand's young models and lovers live with them in their home for a time.[134] Brand sent a GdE newsletter around in May to the old mailing list, announcing weekly meetings beginning the following month at one of the bars near the center of the city. For entertainment, a reading by Dr. Friedrich Jordan, a biologist and retired teacher from a local prep school (*Gymnasium*) was planned. Jordan was active in both the GdE and the WhK and had recently agreed to become the vice chairman of Brand's organization. Together, they hoped to extend the group's influence and develop it into a truly "international union for friendship and freedom."[135]

Brand ran into many obstacles in realizing this plan, though. When in November 1919 he finally managed to resume publication of *The Special One,* he already had one serious competitor for winning over Germany's homosexual readers, namely, *Friendship*. Funding would be a real issue. Whereas the most successful friendship magazines of the 1920s were able to achieve print runs of tens of thousands, *The Special One* never managed to surpass three thousand.[136] Then there were also problems with the government. In February 1920 Brand had to stop publication temporarily when a local authority with control over paper rationing in the difficult postwar economy refused to give Brand any material to print on.[137] *The Special One* appeared again in October, thanks to a press in Amsterdam, although importing the magazine raised its price considerably. At the end of 1920 Brand was accused by the state prosecutor of peddling pornography and soliciting sex through his magazine's personal ads. Stopping publication at the end of 1920, he tried out the strategy of establishing a new magazine beginning in February 1921, this one called *Friendship and Freedom* (*Freundschaft und Freiheit*). Appearing weekly, this magazine published not only articles on homosexuality, but also political articles with a highly combative tone.

The language in both this publication and *The Special One* became much more martial after the war, Jason Crouthamel suggests: "Words like 'sacrifice,' 'the front,' and 'battle' would all permeate the movement's way of thinking about the relationship between homosexual men and the prevailing culture."[138] Politically, Brand's magazines took a position that was a little difficult to pinpoint. On the one hand, articles in *Friendship and Freedom* attacked the forces of political conservatism in the young republic, especially devotees of the old monarchy and the powerful political hand of Catholic and Protestant churches.[139] Various writers for his magazines also carefully distanced themselves from the young republic and the forces of mass politics that it represented. True to their nationalist and Romantic ideals, the masculinists were deeply saddened by the military defeat that had given birth to Weimar; furthermore, they declared themselves in opposition to the materialism championed by the SPD. Democracy and the emancipation of women were described as poisonous for German culture. Brand's declared program of "liberal socialism," as he called it, with its focus on individual freedom, still hinted at the anarchism that had attracted his younger self. There was also, however, obviously much that he and other masculinists shared with more right-wing parties.[140]

Friendship and Freedom was not a success. Only eleven issues in all were published before it disappeared for good in April.[141] Then, in January 1922, Brand stood trial and was convicted under obscenity charges (though acquitted in the case of solicitation). He was fined 5,999 marks, admittedly a small amount given the inflation of the postwar years.[142] Brand resumed publication of *The Special One,* but it never appeared with much consistency. To get around the Law to Protect Youth against Trash and Smut of 1926, he tried out a new title called *Eros* in 1927. It stayed on the market until 1931, though, like *The Special One,* it also was published only irregularly.

The readership of Brand's magazines apparently remained quite small. Brand trumpeted his desire to establish new branches of the GdE, but he had little luck. In one issue of 1919, he mentioned that there was a group of students in Leipzig who were setting up a new branch, as well as a cadre of readers stemming from Hamburg's Wandervogel youth organization. Neither group was talked about again, though. The magazine had found some readers in Switzerland, but here also efforts to build an institutional basis for the readers came to nothing. Apparently Dresden was the only city besides Berlin where a long-lasting circle of readers crystallized. They met regularly in a local bar and restaurant called Armin's Hall (*Armin-Diele*). Meetings were often accompanied by music and readings or lectures.[143] Back in Berlin, the GdE remained a small, private society of people dedicated to Brand.[144] The masculinists devoted to his publications came mostly from the educated upper middle class; many of them were artists, professionals, academics, or intellectuals. As before, the GdE "insisted on a broad cultural and aesthetic program of promoting classical Hellenism in the service of its model of erotic male comradeship."[145] In the course of the 1920s, it became closely tied to one of Berlin's friendship clubs, the Baldur Lodge, which met regularly at a local bar, Beim Emil, in the Berlin neighborhood of Kreuzberg.[146]

Immediately after the war, by far the most famous masculinist intellectual was Hans Blüher, whose publications on the Wandervogel youth movement and the role of Eros in society had brought him renown. Intellectuals from all walks of life had taken notice of his books, and even someone as prominent as the writer Thomas Mann made reference to Blüher's ideas as he was puzzling over the problem of building a new social foundation for Germany.[147] During the war, though, Blüher's writing had taken a notably conservative turn as he began to attack the women's movement. Although his attitude toward women and the feminist movement was difficult to miss in his earlier works on the Wandervogel, his arguments became more polemical in works such as *What Is Antifeminism?* (1915), *Bourgeois and Intellectual Antifeminism* (1916), and *Polygyny and Motherhood* (1919). Always the maverick, Blüher went through pains to differentiate his stance (which he called "intellectual antifeminism") from the more run-of-the-mill position taken by other conservative parties (so-called bourgeois antifeminism). Nevertheless, he came to a very similar position in the end: women should stay out of politics, they should be excluded from the masculine atmosphere of the male-bonding society, they should not be educated alongside men, and they should work only when they are unmarried.[148]

His writings also took on a pronounced anti-Semitic character. Blüher's early work had used some racial ideas, though nothing particularly anti-Semitic in tone or in other ways different from what many German writers were exploring at the time. During the war, however, especially in the context of the controversy that surrounded his two-volume *Role of Eroticism in Male Society*, he increasingly began to use anti-Semitic language. As the historian Claudia Bruns writes, "The more clearly Blüher defended himself against the accusations of 'decadence' and 'degeneration' in his theories, the more anti-Semitic his defense strategies became."[149] After 1918 Blüher was clearly caught up by the wave of anti-Semitism that washed over much of German society.[150] He quickly distanced himself from his previous friends and colleagues, many of whom were radical anarchists or progressive-minded Jewish intellectuals. Kurt Hiller, who had gotten to know Blüher previously as a fellow member of the WhK, later remembered how shocking this transformation was: "For reasons that might be interesting for the psychologist but which surely had nothing to do with politics, Blüher broke suddenly with his philosophical past and transformed his camaraderie with me and us all into a sharp enmity. He changed from being critical of Christianity, and even an agnostic, into an unquestioning 'believer' and follower of protestant orthodoxy; from a republican into a devoted adherent of Wilhelm II; from a proclaimer of rational freedom in matters of sexuality into a 'transcendent'-conservative reinterpreter of his own previous tendencies; from a natural despiser of anti-Semitism into a metaphysical pamphleteer for anti-Semitism."[151] In works such as *Judaism and Socialism* (1919), *The Aristeia of Jesus of Nazareth* (1921), and *Secessio Judaica* (1922), Blüher developed a vision of Jewish society as attached too strongly to family and not enough to male-bonding societies or the state.

As was the case with his antifeminism, he also tried to differentiate his position from more run-of-the-mill anti-Semitism by insisting on differences among assimilated, amalgamated, and Zionist Jews. Blüher nevertheless ended up reproducing many of the prejudices of his day. The failure of Jewish society, Blüher argued, left its men spiritually sterile, incapable of bringing together Eros and Logos. Consequently, these men embodied the "negative characteristics of modernity, such as instrumental logical, mechan-

ical thinking, increased bureaucracy, the tendency to mass culture, liberalization, and depersonalization." [152] Such characteristics pitted the German state
against Judaism. Indeed, in *Secessio Judaica* he went so far as to suggest that
anti-Semitism was Germany's destiny: "Without wanting to admit it, anti-
Semitism has become a fundamental occurrence for German men. If you are
German, you can no longer consider whether you are for or against it. It has
already left its mark on you, and there is no escape." [153]

Although Blüher never gave up his interest in sexuality, he clearly had
switched his political allegiance. He came into contact with the much more
conservative Male Club (*Herrenclub*), populated by Prussian aristocrats and
wealthy industrialists. Through it he increasingly aligned himself with the
so-called Conservative Revolutionaries, especially the cultural historian Arthur Moeller van den Bruck—famous for giving Germany the phrase "the
Third Reich." He gave up his previous hostility to Christianity and eventually
would rejoin the Protestant church. In 1928 he even had opportunities to
visit the former German Kaiser Wilhelm II, then living in exile in Holland.
Through such contacts, Blüher's ideas and especially his conception of the
male-bonding community (*Männerbund*) would acquire widespread currency in nationalist and conservative circles. Eventually, they would make a
contribution toward Nazi ideology. [154]

As Blüher moved into new circles, his place as the chief ideologue of the
masculinist wing of the homosexual movement was taken by Ewald Tscheck.
Born in Berlin in 1895, the son of a goldsmith and a seamstress, Tscheck
began to work closely with Brand's publications soon after the war was over,
usually writing under the pseudonym St. Ch. Waldecke. He was a tireless
activist in other ways. He founded a gay leisure club called the *Wanderschar,*
about which we know very little, unfortunately. He was a passionate anarchist, helping found an association called the Individuals' League (*Individu-
alistenbund*) and writing several articles and essays for anarchist journals of
the day. He gave talks and led classes on various aspects of anarchist economic
and political philosophy to groups around the city. In 1931 he made his own
contribution to anarchist theory, entitled *Thoughts about Anarchy* (*Gedanken
über Anarchie*). As this list of activities suggests, Tscheck was above all an
intellectual. His friends and colleagues remember him always carrying a pile
of books around with him in a backpack. For gay men interested in learning
more about homosexuality, he founded a group called the Academic Workshop. At weekly meetings held in a local vocational school (*Oberrealschule*),
the group got together to read and discuss texts by Sigmund Freud, Gustav
Jäger, Walt Whitman, Edward Carpenter, Hans Blüher, Friedrich Nietzsche,
and other, less prominent intellectuals and writers. Most often, Tscheck him-

self led the meetings. The group worked closely with the GdE, which agreed to publish news about the Academic Workshop in its newsletter. Several local authors frequented the Academic Workshop, and Klaus Mann was known to visit on occasion.[155]

Tscheck is probably best remembered for his numerous attacks on Hirschfeld's theories and the work of the WhK. Tscheck, who increasingly set the tone for *The Special One* in the mid-1920s, published a pamphlet in 1925 entitled "The Scientific-Humanitarian Committee: Why Must It Be Fought and Why Does It Have a Dangerous Effect on the German Nation?" which summarized the masculinist criticisms of Hirschfeld's theories of intersexuality and tried to connect it with the widespread anxieties about the future of the country.[156] His criticisms of Hirschfeld could also become personal. Tscheck made an important contribution to a special issue of *The Special One* entitled *The Fairy* (*Die Tante*). The magazine was billed as a kind of lampoon—an "Issue Dedicated to Ridicule and Struggle" (*Eine Spott- und Kampf-Nummer*)—but its tone was downright nasty. It included a crude caricature of Hirschfeld as the "Sex-King" drawn by a would-be cartoonist, Oskar Nerlinger. Tscheck himself included a short satirical piece that imagined a future in which doctors would become millionaires from the fees charged for diagnosing men as homosexual, and the "Knowingly Humorous Committee" (*Wissentlich-humoristisches Komitee*) would concoct reasons for its existence even after Paragraph 175 had been abolished.[157] Several other pieces in the magazine took issue with Hirschfeld's notion of the third sex. From our point of view today, though, most startling was the willingness of these authors to use anti-Semitic ideas increasingly prominent in the Weimar era to attack Hirschfeld personally.[158]

The hostility of the masculinists to Hirschfeld did not prevent them from temporarily setting aside their differences in 1922 when it looked as if Radbruch's suggestions for a reform of the criminal code might come up for consideration. Their cooperation with Hiller's Operations Committee proved short-lived, though. In 1923 Brand's GdE publicly broke with Hiller and the WhK, citing a disagreement over whether it was appropriate to petition the Reichstag during a time of "national crisis." By this time, he had already expressed some pessimism publicly about whether legal change would really deal with the root of the problem, namely, deep-seated prejudices. Increasingly he saw the real task as being the construction of a "free" and "moral" society.[159]

By this time, Friedrich Radszuweit, as the new leader of the BfM, was also having second thoughts about his organization's alliance with the WhK. In a move designed to establish his own position within the homosexual movement, Radszuweit distanced his organization from the Operations

Committee in 1923 and began to aggressively criticize Hirschfeld's theories of intersexuality. Cooperation between the friendship clubs and the WhK was still discussed in 1924, but afterward Radszuweit increasingly defined an independent political position and strategy for his organization.[160] Radszuweit was certainly not opposed to scientific work on homosexuality. In fact, he relied on the specialists connected with the WhK to provide summaries of some of the scientific research on homosexuality for his *Pages for Human Rights* and the lesbian magazine *Girlfriend*. He basically agreed with Hirschfeld that homosexuality was an inborn trait. As we saw in the last chapter, however, Radszuweit and most of the other writers associated with his magazines were fundamentally opposed to the gender implications of Hirschfeld's work. The notion of intersexuality, he argued, was based on a limited sample of "abnormal" men, not on the "respectable homosexual."[161] "When will Hirschfeld realize that by revealing his freak show [*Abnormitätenschau*] to the public he does not help the homosexual struggle but only hurts it? . . . Why does Dr. Hirschfeld represent only these abnormalities that exist in a few isolated cases and not any number of homosexual men and women as they look in reality?"[162] As this passage suggests, his criticism of Hirschfeld's method often blurred with his own tendency to censure "fairies" (*Tanten* or *Tunten*) for their "strange" and "degenerate" behavior.[163]

This tension with Hirschfeld did not mean that Radszuweit aligned himself with the masculinists. He felt that their antifeminist stance and misogynist language were fundamentally wrong-minded. Their so-called manly culture, he wrote in an article for his *Pages for Human Rights,* will "always remain a specter [*Schemen*], for one needs to create not simply a masculine culture but also a feminine culture as well."[164] Politically, their ideas were dangerous since they tended to associate homosexuality with pederasty. He also distrusted the masculinists' cultural snobbery. Although many of the men in Brand's circle were anarchists or otherwise vaguely leftist, they still betrayed an elitist attitude born of education and an immersion in the art world. Radszuweit made it clear that he represented the "everyday" homosexual—the gay men and women of the middle class who, given the legal rights that they deserved, could make an important contribution to an orderly society and a strong state. He hoped that his movement would raise the public visibility of the "'respectable,' law-abiding majority of homosexual citizens," demonstrating to the rest of German society that not all homosexuals were child predators, effeminate "fairies," and criminal prostitutes.[165]

Radszuweit emphasized political efficacy. The heated debates between the WhK and the masculinists went nowhere and, if anything, may have just turned off potential supporters within wider heterosexual society. On this point he seems to have had the backing of many other writers in the various friendship magazines. As early as 1920, well before Radszuweit arrived on the scene, some contributors to *Friendship* were complaining about how public the two sides were being with their dispute.[166] Moreover, which theory about the nature of homosexuality was right was not as important as the question of which theory was more likely to achieve social recognition. From this point of view, both sides had proven themselves wanting.[167] This should not be taken, though, as suggesting that Radszuweit was a peacemaker—quite the contrary, in fact. The tone of his essays was normally quite polemical, and he was not above making personal attacks on his opponents. A "convinced propagandist," as Stefan Micheler calls him, Radszuweit had a tendency to make exaggerated claims and even sometimes to make statements that were plainly false.[168] Above all, he was devoted to the goal of building a nationally recognized umbrella organization for homosexual politics. If this meant skirmishing with other groups in the broader movement, then so be it.[169]

Politically, Radszuweit always insisted that his BfM remain unaffiliated. His members came from all walks of life and supported political positions that ranged across the spectrum. He very much wanted his organization to be open to all. According to a survey of his publications' readers, most supported the socialists, the communists, or the two liberal parties. Nevertheless, a not inconsiderable number supported the more conservative Catholic Center Party and the right-wing German National People's Party.[170] During elections Radszuweit would use his position as chief editor of his press's friendship magazines to come out in favor of those parties that formally supported the reform of Paragraph 175. He made it clear that such alliances were only temporary, though, and any party that supported reform could potentially receive his endorsement. For a time in 1924, Radszuweit considered establishing a "Homoerotic Friendship Party" that would represent homosexual interests and even put up candidates for public office. From the reactions in the friendship press, however, it seems his suggestion was received with skepticism at best. He continued to toy with the idea for some years but never actually made a move to found this party. Most likely he was dissuaded by the observation that creating such a party might actually cause the movement to lose leverage among the remaining political parties.[171]

Instead, Radszuweit focused on publicity and education. According to his annual report to his organization, he printed 200,000 copies of various kinds of education material and 1,840 brochures in 1924 alone. His contacts with the mainstream press had led to some positive reporting on the activities of the BfM, and in a couple of cases they had even reprinted articles from the *Pages for Human Rights*.[172] In the mid-1920s the BfM helped sponsor educational lectures on sexuality and over Easter weekend of 1926 even organized a series of public meetings in thirty-four locations. The same year it conducted a survey of its readers to get an idea of just how prevalent homosexuality was in society. It also carried out a series of mass mailings to parliamentary representatives at various points throughout the decade to try to garner support for the reform or repeal of Paragraph 175.[173]

PROPOSED LEGAL REFORM AND THE WHK'S LEADERSHIP CRISIS

Divisions within the homosexual movement were frustrating. In 1927 Hirschfeld commented, "Aside from a few minor cliques, homosexuals are in reality almost totally lacking in feelings of solidarity; in fact, it would be difficult to find another class of mankind which has proved so incapable of organizing to secure its basic legal and human rights."[174] It was not a good time for squabbling, since the new government draft of the reform bill, which had slowly moved through the bureaucracy and other government bodies since 1924, was finally sent to the Reichstag for consideration by Oskar Hergt, minister of justice under the Catholic chancellor Wilhelm Marx but himself a member of the right-wing German National People's Party. The code had been modified slightly in the intervening years, but the new draft (E1927) was still fairly conservative and retained a law against male homosexuality. E1927 was moved into committee, where it was taken over for consideration by Wilhelm Kahl, an elderly law professor who served as the chairman of the Penal Code Reform Committee (*Strafrechtsausschuss*). His party, the German People's Party, was fairly liberal for Weimar politics, but it did not support homosexual emancipation.[175]

Kahl, however, had been involved for a long time in the effort to reform Germany's criminal code, having worked under Kaiser Wilhelm II at the turn of the century, and he was someone temperamentally inclined toward compromise. He fought hard in 1928 to make sure that the reform process was not derailed by the May elections, which led to major gains for the two leftist parties, the Social Democrats and the Communists.[176] Under a new left-center coalition led by Chancellor Hermann Müller, the Reichstag took a new look at the proposed criminal code. In the Penal Code Reform Committee, a major debate over the future of Paragraph 175 (which in the new draft was called Paragraph 296) took place. The committee included twenty-eight members, who were very much divided over the law. Fourteen members belonged to leftist parties (the Social Democrats, Communists, and German Democratic Party) that favored striking the law from the books. Eleven members came from conservative parties (the Catholic Center Party, the Bavarian People's

Party, and the German National People's Party) that could be counted on to vote for maintaining the criminalization of male homosexuality.

Everything came down to three members from the right-of-center German National People's Party. Although two stuck to the party line and voted to keep the law, Wilhelm Kahl believed that compromise was necessary to get the code passed by the Reichstag. He broke with the rest of his party and cast the decisive vote against the law.[177] Although insisting that he still did not see "homosexuality as a morally allowable or justifiable act," he had come to accept liberal criticisms of Paragraph 175. Adults should have "free use of their own bodies" so long as they did not injure a third party. Moreover, Paragraph 175 was a "failed law" because it was so difficult to enforce and only encouraged blackmail and homosexual "propaganda" (referring to the homosexual magazines), which, he believed, were bigger dangers to society.[178]

The committee vote on October 16, 1929, to cut consensual sex between two adult males from the draft of the criminal code was seen by many as a major victory for the homosexual movement. Indeed, both liberal and right-wing newspapers treated it as a done deal.[179] It came with a catch, however, that would be difficult for many in the homosexual movement to accept. The very next day, the Penal Law Reform Committee quickly voted in favor of a new law, Paragraph 297, that made homosexual sex between men illegal in three "aggravated" cases: for an adult male (over twenty-one years old) to have sex with a minor; for an employer, teacher, or other authority figure to use his position to coerce sexual favors from a subordinate; and, finally, for a man to sell sexual favors.[180] This new law passed in committee with almost no opposition. Only the German Communist Party voted against it.[181]

Among homosexual activists, the proposed Paragraph 297 proved quite controversial. Friedrich Radszuweit and several other people connected with the BfM had made it clear in September that they favored the idea (though they did believe the age of minority ought to be set a little lower, namely, at eighteen). Adding Paragraph 297 to the law code was a necessary compromise that would help make the abolition of Paragraph 175 more palatable among conservatives. Just as important, it could actually be seen a measure that could protect the "respectable homosexuals" from several real threats. Accepting a law that criminalized sex between adult men and minors would make it clear in the public mind that most male homosexuals were not pederasts preying on young boys. The stipulation against male prostitution would actually guard "true homosexuals" against these "pseudo-homosexuals" who at best took advantage of the loneliness of gay men to make some easy money, and at worst beat them, robbed them, and subjected them to blackmail. They were responsible for the association between homosexuality and criminal violence in the minds of many. Making male prostitution illegal would also help gay men rid themselves of this stigma.[182] In an issue of *The Pages for Human Rights* published soon after the critical votes, Radszuweit took credit for the victory. Kahl, he argued, would never have agreed to split with his party if he had not been convinced by Radszuweit's organization's lobbying effort that Paragraph 297 was a viable and effective replacement for the existing law.

The WhK generally saw things differently. Both Kurt Hiller and his friend Richard Linsert described the votes of the Penal Law Reform Committee as not eliminating Paragraph 175 but in fact "exacerbating" the problem. Creating a law that established a much higher age of consent for men than it did for women (which was set at sixteen by German law) was completely "laughable."[183] The law against male prostitution only criminalized male homosexuality in another form, since many gay men were driven to pay for sex by a lack of sexual opportunities. Furthermore, even if not all male prostitutes were homosexually inclined, their sexual choices were generally compelled by poverty and a lack of other choices. As a good communist, Linsert certainly would not support a law that so clearly targeted working-class men.[184] Blackmail was a real danger, as Hirschfeld and other members of the WhK certainly recognized, but one did not solve the problem by making male prostitution illegal. Only total decriminalization and public education to remove the stigma of homosexuality would solve this problem.

Once the votes were taken in the Penal Code Reform Committee, however, the leaders of the WhK were faced with a difficult decision. Should they support a proposed criminal code that gave them at least part of what they wanted or oppose the code on principle? The details about the debate that ensued are not known, but clearly it was a hefty and contentious one. Laurie Marhoefer, in fact, has argued that the controversy almost led to the organization's demise in 1929. It certainly unleashed a power struggle within the WhK. Before the vote in the Penal Law Reform Committee, there had been some differences between Hiller and Hirschfeld over how to handle the politicians involved and how closely to work with Radszuweit. The exact details of this disagreement over tactics are difficult to reconstruct, but Hiller clearly came to the conclusion that Hirschfeld's own vanity was getting in the way.[185] Hiller, who as we have seen had long harbored doubts about Hirschfeld's abilities as a leader, now demanded that Hirschfeld step down as chairman of the WhK. He was aided by his friend Richard Linsert, who took the lead in the smear campaign against Hirschfeld. In a pamphlet distributed during the struggle, Linsert accused Hirschfeld of disregarding decisions made by the WhK's executive board. In a move designed clearly to distance the WhK from the proposed legal reform, he blamed Hirschfeld for colluding with Kahl to produce a bill that was highly dangerous to homosexual rights. His willingness to go behind the back of the board was a sign of deeper problems, however. Linsert accused Hirschfeld of misusing WhK funds for his own benefit and of diminishing the WhK's reputation by taking money from a pharmaceutical company known mostly for producing a sham drug for impotency.[186]

Wounded by the accusations, Hirschfeld agreed to step down as chairman. He was replaced by his friend Otto Juliusburger. Hiller was promoted to vice chair. At a special meeting of the WhK on November 24, 1929, Hirschfeld thanked the organization for all its hard work over the years. A friend of his, Karl Besser, returned the thanks, publicly praising Hirschfeld for his research and his vision. Bad health and exhaustion, Besser argued, were the real reasons that Hirschfeld was leaving at this moment, not the recent attacks.[187] Clearly, Hirschfeld still had supporters in the organization. Indeed, at the annual meeting the following February Hirschfeld was reelected to the executive board. Letters that have turned up suggest that at least a few members were mystified by Linsert's attacks.[188]

His public remarks notwithstanding, Hirschfeld did not leave his position as leader of the WhK on entirely friendly terms. There were some fights between Hirschfeld and the new leadership over finances, which were partially underwritten by aid from his Institute for Sexual Science and, quite possibly, Hirschfeld's own pocket. The WhK was also forced to vacate its offices in the Institute for Sexual Science and find a home elsewhere. Fund-raising was badly needed, the WhK leadership noted.[189] Hiller and Linsert, for their part, quickly went to work defining a new line for the WhK. In a later newsletter, they suggested that the wrong turn had been linked to Hirschfeld's scientific work: "The constant connection of the homoerotic phenomenon with effeminate phenomena, with hermaphroditism, transvestism, and other more or less repellent freaks of nature [*Naturspielen*], has not helped the efforts at enlightening the public and liberating male-male love, but only hurt them. That which made Sparta strong, a work by Michelangelo brilliant, has nothing in common with bearded women, full-breasted men, or other monstrosities. The cult of heroes, the cult of youth, the love of man for man should not appear in the same atmosphere as a sexological panopticon."[190]

After the leadership struggle, there was a noticeable shift in the propaganda effort away from Hirschfeld's theory of intersexuality. New scientists were brought in to support the reform effort, most noticeably those, including the psychiatrist Robert Gaupp, who might have favored the repeal of Paragraph 175 but who still saw homosexuality as deeply pathological and having some real potential to infect young people.[191] The WhK was also

much more likely now to publish essays that made legal and political arguments for reform. It even published an article by Arthur Kronfeld suggesting
that the question of whether homosexuality was inborn was entirely irrele-
vant to the WhK's work.[192]

The new WhK leadership came out firmly in opposition to Paragraph 297. Linsert had already made his thoughts on the proposed law
against male prostitution known in a 1929 book on the subject. Based on a
sociological survey of male prostitutes living in Berlin, this book painted a
highly sympathetic view of these men trying to eke out a living in the city.[193]
His book also compiled the opinions of many eminent thinkers (including
Martin Buber, Albert Einstein, and Theodor Lessing), who all agreed that it
made no sense to make male prostitution illegal while female prostitution
was largely permitted.[194] Hiller, whose first sexual experience was with a male
prostitute and who for a time relied on rent boys for occasional companionship, argued that it would be equally ridiculous to make poetry illegal just
because there were a few dangerous poets in the bunch.[195] In the first newsletter written after the change in leadership, Linsert and Hiller described the
reform as "one step forward and two backward."[196] Concluding that "our
constant demand for the equality of the homosexual minority with the majority of the population has in no way been respected," they came out against
the proposed criminal code.

As it turned out, all consternation about whether to support the new
criminal code was for nothing. In 1930 the government turned the draft over
to a committee that was trying to create more unity between the Austrian and
German legal codes. Austria also had a law against male homosexuality, and in
another close vote this committee decided to put a similar law back into the
draft.[197] By this time, the effect of the stock market crash on Wall Street was
already beginning to ripple throughout the world. Soon the democracy of the
Weimar Republic would find itself undermined by the rightward swing of
the voters and the authoritarian tendencies of the central government.[198]
In 1930 the Nazi Party won a staggering victory in the federal elections:
overnight it grew from a small fringe party with only twelve seats in the
Reichstag to become the second most powerful political party in the land.
Homosexual activists recognized that they were in trouble. In his magazine
Friendship, Radszuweit admitted that "now our cause to eliminate Paragraph 175 has become almost useless."[199] With the growing power of the
Nazi Party and the staggering economic problems that Germany faced, the
proposed legal code was tabled indefinitely. Paragraph 175 would stay on the
books. It would be many, many years before repeal seemed possible again.

Did the assertiveness of Weimar's homosexual movement, or more simply the international reputation of Weimar's gay and lesbian scenes, contribute at all to the downfall of the democratic government? Scholars and nonscholars alike have often assumed that the Weimar Republic's reputation for "moral decadence" among many Germans was at least indirectly responsible for the demise of the fragile Weimar government and the emergence of the Nazi regime. From Friedrich Meinecke's sociological analysis of *The German Catastrophe* (1946) to Gerhard Ritter's much more conservative investigation of the roots of Nazism, many scholars have argued that the decline of Christianity, exacerbated by the "moral collapse" that followed Germany's defeat in the First World War, was to blame for the sexual experimentation of the 1920s and the turn to violence after 1933. Such an analysis was echoed in many popular representations of Weimar—ironically even in the 1972 film *Cabaret,* in which the MC, played by Joel Grey, transitions slowly from a devil-may-care character into the devil himself. Alternatively, historians have presented Nazi prudishness as an inevitable backlash against Weimar excesses, an expression of a traditional, bourgeois sensibility reasserting itself after being temporarily sidelined by the socialist revolution of 1918–19.[200]

In both versions, the sexual politics of the 1920s played heavily into a story about how Weimar was a "doomed republic." During the 1990s, however, a number of historians began to question whether the Weimar Republic really was doomed from the beginning. Doing research in a remarkably diverse number of areas—from national politics to economic change, welfare policy to military planning—they have offered a picture of the Weimar Republic as being more stable than previously imagined, at least until the Great Depression set in during 1929. Even if not widely loved, it was held together by a number of pragmatic alliances that allowed the political arena to function.[201] After all, it successfully weathered the Kapp Putsch of 1920, the French invasion of the Ruhr, and the hyperinflation of 1923. When Weimar politics did start to come undone in the early 1930s, there is good reason to insist that sexual politics had very little to do with it, as Laurie Marhoefer has recently argued.[202] Even if many of us currently might hesitate to go along with Marhoefer's claim that there was in fact a "Weimar settlement" on a broad range of issues involving sexuality in the 1920s, numerous historians would now agree that foreign policy, economic issues, and the perceived threat of communism weighed far more heavily in people's minds at the time. The sexual politics of the 1920s was certainly intertwined with the "ambiguities of modernity," as many historians are now thinking about it, and at times could become quite belligerent. But "the ambiguities of modernity did not stop at the gates of '1933' but continued well into the 1940s," notes one historian.[203] As we will see, this observation applies just as well to the politics of homosexuality as it does to other areas of sexual politics.

After the Great Depression set in, the pragmatic alliances that had been at the heart of the Weimar political system began to break down; governments were faced with very difficult political choices to make in a range of areas. Conservative forces, which had never been attached to Weimar's parliamentary institutions, to say the least, began to cast about for alternatives that might return authority to the state. The shift in mood was evident in the debates about Paragraph 175, as witnessed by the renewed vigor with which conservative religious and political figures dove into the "battlefield of ethics," as Andreas Pretzel puts it.[204] In the early 1930s, faced with an increasingly polarized electorate and a deeply fractured Reichstag, the government slipped toward authoritarian solutions.[205] By the summer of 1932, as the country descended into violence, the destruction of democracy was largely inevitable, especially after Chancellor Franz von Papen issued the emergency laws that enabled him to seize control of the regional government of Prussia. With his wide-ranging police powers, Papen went to work cracking down on what he considered some of the more "dangerous" aspects of Berlin's infamous nightlife. As part of this effort, Berlin's police force carried out a series of raids against lesbian and gay bars; the police also announced their intention not to issue dance permits to homosexual nightclubs. Business obviously was hurt, evidenced by the fact that some of the best-known establishments, including probably the Eldorado, had closed down by the beginning of 1933.[206]

But these efforts paled in comparison to what came after the emergence of the Nazi regime. In the course of 1932, the Nazi Party won large victories in the two parliamentary elections while simultaneously contributing to the breakdown of social order by clashing violently with communists in the country's major cities.[207] By early 1933 the repeated electoral successes of the Nazis convinced many mainstream nationalists and conservatives, as well as a number of well-placed wealthy individuals, that the party was the only hope for restoring political order to the country. The decision to hand the government over to Hitler, however, was ultimately up to the nation's president, Paul von Hindenburg, an ex–World War I general who was still widely perceived as one of the heroes of the war. Although President Hindenburg was no friend of democracy, he nevertheless hesitated to put the country into the hands of Hitler, whom he saw as a dangerous demagogue and rabble-rouser. In the end, though, he bowed to the pressure put on him by prominent men around the country. On January 30, 1933, he appointed Hitler as chancellor of the dying republic.[208]

That night, Berliners watched as Nazis paraded by torchlight through the center of the city. Many Germans, including no doubt some gay men who were either Nazi Party members themselves or sympathetic to Nazi calls for a rebirth of the nation, greeted the news that Hitler had finally taken the reins of government with excitement and hope. Others reacted differently, experiencing a wide spectrum of feelings that ranged from fear and alarm to skepticism and indifference.[209] Among them would have been not only most of the leaders of the WhK but also some masculinists such as Adolf Brand, who had never liked the Nazis and who in the last years of Weimar had publicly aligned himself with the left-wing parties.[210] Unfooled by rumors that there were numerous homosexuals in the ranks of the Nazi leadership, these men would not have been surprised to find the gay scene subjected to intense policing during the early months of the regime.

CHAPTER 6

Nazi Persecution

CHAPTER SUMMARY

This chapter discusses the effects of the Nazi regime on gay men and lesbians. It considers the motives behind Nazi policies toward homosexuality and also probes the thorny issue of whether scientific research into homosexuality opened the door for the Nazis to send homosexuals to the concentration camps.

OVERVIEW

When the Nazis took over Germany in 1933, they destroyed the constitutional framework of the short-lived Weimar Republic and thoroughly smothered much of the vibrant social and political culture that had developed in the country since the mid-nineteenth century. The urban gay scenes of Berlin and elsewhere, as well as the homosexual movement itself, were notable casualties. This chapter discusses the effects of the Nazi regime on gay men and lesbians. Although the Nazi Party had contained some homosexuals in its ranks during its rise to power—most notably Ernst Röhm, who headed up the party's stormtroopers—this fact did not stop the party from strengthening the country's laws against male homosexuality or from organizing a police crackdown. Hitler's government closed most gay and lesbian bars, shut down the homosexual publishing industry, and eventually interned thousands of gay men in Nazi prisons and concentration camps. The Nazi regime did not target lesbians with anywhere near the same intensity that it targeted gay men, but that does not mean that lesbians were unaffected by Nazi policies. Their bars, publications, and social clubs were closed down, and they were subjected to the immense pressure brought by the Nazi Party on all women to conform to traditional gender norms, to get married, and to have children.

This chapter considers the motives behind these Nazi policies toward homosexuality. Furthermore, it examines the fate of those scientific and psychiatric institutions that had devoted so much time to homosexuality since the mid-nineteenth century. In the process, this chapter also probes the thorny issue of whether scientific research into homosexuality opened the door for Nazi persecution. It concludes with some reflection on the sexual opportunities created by the Second World War.

KEY TERMS

homosexuality in the Nazi Party; Ernst Röhm; pink triangle; concentration camps; homosexuality and the Holocaust

Whisnant, Clayton J.

Queer Identities and Politics in Germany: A History 1880–1945

dx.doi.org/10.17312/harringtonparkpress/2016.08.qipg.006

© Harrington Park Press, LLC, New York, NY 10011

FIGURE 17 **ERNST RÖHM (CENTER) IN 1931**

As one of the founders of the SA stormtrooper unit, Röhm was one of the most important Nazi leaders. He weathered a scandal when his homosexuality became widely known in the early 1930s, only to be murdered during the 1934 Night of Long Knives. This chapter discusses the results of the brutal and heartless Nazi regime for gay men and lesbians. It considers the motives behind Nazi policies toward homosexuality and also probes the thorny issue of whether scientific research into homosexuality opened the door for the Nazis to send homosexuals to the concentration camps. Source: Bundesarchiv, Bild 102-14393. Photograph by Georg Pahl

In 1921 Ernst Röhm (Figure 17) was one of the top Nazi leaders—arguably the second-most important, next to Hitler himself. He had joined the party in August 1919 and had taken control of the party's tiny security squad, transforming it into the infamous SA, the paramilitary unit of stormtroopers who, it was hoped, would one day help the party overthrow the government. Much more than Hitler, who had been only a military runner during the war, Röhm had military experience that everyone respected. He had served as an officer in a Bavarian regiment since 1908, and during the First World War he had been stationed in the trenches, was seriously wounded twice during combat, and by the end of the war had been promoted to captain of the Kaiser's army. During the war he came to idealize the community of fighting men whom he saw sacrificing themselves for the nation on the front. He believed that the bond between soldiers could be used to rebuild his defeated nation. "What he wanted," notes the historian Ian Kershaw, "was a new 'warrior' elite whose actions and achievements had proved their right to rule." [1]

Röhm had served in a Free Corps unit during the revolutionary turmoil of 1919, and when he joined the Nazi Party he brought with him many battle-hardened, right-wing soldiers. He also had military connections that allowed the party to begin stockpiling weapons.[2] The failed Nazi coup of November 1923 led to Röhm's arrest and imprisonment, but by the end of 1924 he was out of prison and active once again in the party. In the mid-1920s, as the Nazi Party reorganized and began to aim at winning elections instead of organizing a coup, Röhm left the party and went to Bolivia to help train this South American country's national army. He returned to Germany in 1930, however, just in time to reap the political benefits that came to the Nazi Party during the Great Depression. In the following years, Röhm's SA would attack communist meetings, beat up individuals whom they perceived as being enemies of the German people, and otherwise contribute to an atmosphere of swelling violence by 1932.[3]

Röhm, though, was gay. Since the mid-1920s, there had been talk in homosexual circles that the high-ranking Nazi official had been spotted in Berlin's gay clubs and had had dealings with male prostitutes in Munich. He had even joined the BfM, though Friedrich Radszuweit kept quiet about this fact for some time.[4] In 1928 Karl-Günter Heimsoth, a young Berlin physician who was associated with Adolf Brand's circle and was also a friend of Ewald Tscheck's, wrote to Röhm hoping to convince him to lend his name to the effort to repeal Paragraph 175. Röhm, who was feeling lonely and rather homesick in Bolivia, replied in an extremely friendly fashion, and the two of them struck up a relationship, exchanging letters and even meeting in Berlin during one of Röhm's visits to the city.[5] In one of the letters, Röhm talked about his sexuality in a surprisingly open fashion. Heimsoth understood very well the sensitive nature of these letters, and he kept them locked in a safe in his office. He apparently told the wrong person about them, however, and when the police got wind of the letters in late 1931, they broke into Heimsoth's office and confiscated the correspondence.

Röhm was charged with breaking Paragraph 175 and underwent five trials in 1931 and 1932.[6] At the same time, a series of newspaper articles denouncing Röhm as a homosexual appeared in an SPD-affiliated Munich newspaper beginning in April 1932. The Social Democrats, as we have seen, had been fairly consistent opponents of Paragraph 175 since the end of the nineteenth century; however, as the Nazis won new ground with every election, they were not above taking advantage of popular prejudices against homosexuality in their political propaganda.[7] With titles such as "Warm Brotherhood in the Brown House," the SPD newspaper and others associated with the communists or the liberal parties used police reports and suggestive rumors to incriminate the leader and, by extension, the rest of the Nazi Party. Especially after Helmut Klotz, the SPD editor responsible for publishing the story, was assaulted by several Nazi members of the Reichstag while sitting in a Berlin coffeehouse, the Röhm scandal became a truly national affair. In front-page stories, major national newspapers repeated the accusations in the context of the attack on Klotz, thereby linking Nazi violence with Röhm's "immorality."[8]

Röhm had made himself vulnerable by his regular use of Munich's rent boys. It should be noted, however, that much of the evidence against him was either fabricated or based solely on unreliable informants, such as the ex-Nazi Otto Strasser, who had recently been kicked out of the party.[9] But then, in the spring of 1932, the first piece of indisputable evidence was published. As Hitler was pursuing his initial campaign to be elected president of Germany, the SPD editor Klotz went public with a photograph of Röhm's letter to Heimsoth, which apparently had been secretly taken while the letter was in police possession. Written in Röhm's own handwriting, it was a potentially devastating revelation, given that the presidential elections were just days away.

The information offered by the letter was not exactly news to Hitler. In fact, soon after Hitler had invited Röhm back into the Nazi fold, he had started receiving reports from various party officials of Röhm's adventures in the Berlin and Munich gay scenes.[10] Hitler, however, had been very clear from the beginning that such rumor mongering was not to be tolerated. "The private life," he stated, "cannot be an object of scrutiny unless it conflicts with basic principles of National Socialist ideology."[11] Then, in 1932, he once again defended Röhm in no uncertain terms. Within the party, he fended off suggestions that Röhm be quickly fired before the election took place. In public he denounced the "witch hunt" against Röhm as a bunch of socialist lies.[12]

The Röhm scandal of 1932 would lay the groundwork for a surprisingly long-lasting stereotype of the Nazi Party as a bunch of closeted homosexuals. Röhm's reputation would continue to haunt the party even after it took power in January 1933—and indeed after Röhm and his closest colleagues were brutally murdered by the Nazis during the 1934 "Night of Long Knives." The suggestion that the Nazi Party was thoroughly infiltrated with homosexuals remained a recurring motif during the 1930s in much of the communist propaganda coming out of Moscow as well as in the publicity material being produced by the SPD leadership in exile.[13] For at least some Germans, this propaganda rang true. After all, the party did place a very heavy emphasis on male bonding, especially in the SA and SS. It also patronized artists such as Arno Breker, Joseph Wackerle, Adolf Wamper, Sepp Hilz, and Leni Riefenstahl, who specialized in images of strong, attractive men, often nude or barely clothed. Officially, the Nazis might have held up such images as idealized portraits of masculine strength and racial health, but it would be very easy also to see this art as homoerotically charged (as evidenced by the fact that much of this art would reappear in the German gay magazines of the 1950s).[14] Over the years such evidence has been repeatedly cited as "proof" that the chief Nazis were at least latently homosexual.[15] Moreover, using the often bizarre logic of much Freudian reasoning, the violent assault on homosexuals underneath Hitler is twisted into further evidence to the claim.

To be clear, there are few reputable historians today who would argue that Hitler was gay, and their arguments have not been seen as persuasive.[16] Yes, there is a great deal of evidence that Hitler, Himmler, Goebbels, Rosenberg, and the rest of the chief Nazis remaining after Röhm's murder had some serious sexual hang-ups, to say the least. More important, Dagmar Herzog has recently offered an important challenge to the older historical interpretation, which largely emphasized Nazi prudishness. "What is clear," she writes, "is that all the manifestly brutal aspects of Nazi sexual politics were not embedded in a broader antisexual attitude but, rather, coexisted with injunctions and encouragements to the majority of Germans to seek and experience sexual pleasure."[17] Nevertheless, when it came to homosexuality, the Nazi regime was terrifyingly clear about its position from 1934 on. Homosexuals, from its point of view, were a danger to the German nation and had to be dealt with using all the means available to the Nazi police state.

THE NAZI TAKEOVER AND THE
CRACKDOWN ON WEIMAR "DECADENCE"

As the Nazis crushed the trade unions, arrested political enemies, burned books, and dissolved rival political parties in early 1933, the police were busy clearing the streets of "dangerous" characters and closing down areas of "ill repute." On February 23, 1933, the Prussian Ministry of the Interior issued an order to the Berlin police to shut down any remaining bars in the city "frequented solely or mainly by persons who indulge in *unnatural sexual practices*."[18] The order was soon circulated to other areas of the Reich. In Cologne the police put pressure on the city's gay bars, forcing nearly all of them to shut down or at least to change the "character" of the establishment.[19] Hannover's police also acted aggressively in carrying out "Operation Clean Reich," which led to nearly all of the city's gay bars shutting their doors within the next year.[20] In the port city of Hamburg, besides stepping up arrests of the "shameless prostitutes who offer themselves from windows of the streets that used to have brothels on them," the police also increased the number of raids against homosexual meeting places.[21] The result was a jump in the number of indictments under Paragraph 175 in Hamburg from 103 in 1932 to 370 in 1933 and 659 in 1934.[22] The Hamburg police executed raids around the central train station and certain notorious public bathrooms as well as in such homosexual bars as the Minella and the Billiard Hall Schmidt in St. Pauli.[23] In October 1934 the new chief of the vice squad bragged that "thanks to the energetic measures of the police, the situation in terms of both female and male prostitution had become remarkably better." The *Hamburger Tageblatt* also praised the police department and the new Nazi government, remarking that the "streets again offer a clean picture."[24]

Beginning in March 1933, Germany's police departments, acting according to directives from Berlin, began to confiscate any printed material dealing with homosexuality. They rounded up whatever products of the gay publishing industry had survived the heightened censorship laws of the late 1920s—including *Friendship, The Friendship Paper, The Girlfriend,* and *The Pages for Human Rights*—and pressured bookstores and newsstands to stop carrying these publications.[25] The publishers themselves were targeted for destruction. Friedrich Radszuweit had already died in 1932 from tuberculosis, so it was his life partner and heir, Martin Butzkow, who had the sad job of watching his press be shut down. Adolf Brand's house was searched by the police no fewer than five times, during which all of his photographs, six thousand copies of his various magazines, and numerous books were carried off. "I was completely plundered by these five confiscations," reported Brand in a letter written in February 1934 to the British Sexological Society. "I have nothing more to sell. My business is ruined. I have no idea how I or my family will continue to live."[26] Similar police actions were certainly also taken against the Radszuweit publishers in Berlin, though the fate of this company is less clear.[27] The police efforts were not limited to these magazines, though. Even more scientifically minded tracts, such as Magnus Hirschfeld's works, were included on police and censorship lists.

Hirschfeld himself was lucky enough to be out of the country when Hitler came to power. As both a Jew and a homosexual, he had in the course of the 1920s become a target for the hatred of the national right. As we have seen, he had already been the victim of attacks by anti-Semitic students three times. Fortunately, in 1933 he was out on a worldwide lecture tour with the World League for Sexual Reform (WLSR). With Hirschfeld out of reach, the Nazis had to be satisfied with the destruction of Hirschfeld's pride and joy, the Institute for Sexual Science. On the night of May 6, 1933, as a part of a larger effort to purge the nation of "un-German" books, Nazi students and stormtroopers plundered the extensive library and archive of the institute; more than 12,000 books and many more photographs were carried away. The institute was destroyed, along with the offices of the WLSR. Most of the confiscated works of the institute, along with a large bust of Magnus Hirschfeld, were marched down to the now-infamous public book burning at Berlin's Opernplatz on the night of May 10.[28]

The WhK survived not much longer. Richard Linsert died in February 1933; Kurt Hiller—both a socialist and a homosexual—found himself in the hands of the Gestapo, soon to be taken off to the Berlin concentration camp Oranienburg. A last meeting of the WhK was held on June 8, 1933, in the organization's offices on Prager Strasse, during which the group voted to dissolve itself. Not much is known about the proceedings of this last meeting, but it is likely that the members made plans for the foreseen persecution. Here, as in numerous other meetings held by other groups of the gay movement through the summer of 1933, it was probably decided to destroy membership lists, address books, and other documents that could possibly help the Nazis hunt out homosexuals and political dissidents. Participants in the Weimar gay movement also seem to have come to some sort of agreement to keep quiet about their activities and membership in order to hamper police efforts. We know that members largely stuck to their promise: there are a few known cases of individuals who had been quite active within the gay movement but who, when caught by the Gestapo or criminal police, mentioned nothing about their previous involvement.[29] What happened to most of the participants in the WhK, the Community of the Special, or the Federation for Human Rights remains unknown.

At least a few gay men and lesbians chose to go into exile, especially those with liberal or leftist leanings.[30] The Mann family left Germany in 1933; Thomas and much of his family moved first to Switzerland and later, after the outbreak of war, to the United States. Hoping not to interrupt his income, which continued to come from mostly German sources, Thomas Mann was noticeably quiet about the Nazi regime for several years.[31] Beginning in 1936, though, he began to accuse the Nazi government of waging a war against European humanism, which he defined as an "attitude" or a "frame of mind" with "ingredients of justice and freedom, knowledge and patience, charity and good humor. And also doubt."[32]

Erika Mann and her partner, the actress Therese Giehse, took a similar path, though they went to the United States a little earlier. They both entered into lavender marriages with British citizens (Erika to the poet W. H. Auden, Therese to the writer John Hampton) in order to get British citizenship.[33] Erika had already started writing anti-Nazi pieces in 1933 for her touring cabaret, the Peppermill, and during the next decade she took on an increasingly prominent role in the fight against fascism—as an observer of the Spanish Civil War, as an author of *School for Barbarians* (1938), about the Nazi education system, and eventually as a journalist for the BBC.[34] Klaus Mann was more nomadic for a few years, moving between Paris, Amsterdam, Cannes, Prague, Zurich, and other European cities. He also engaged the Nazi regime by starting a German-language journal for German émigré writers called *The Collection* (*Die Sammlung*) and by condemning his old friend Gustaf Gründgens for his compromises with the new German regime in his novel *Mephisto* (1936). Like his father and sister, Klaus eventually moved to the United States, where in 1942 he joined the army. During the war he wrote propaganda leaflets for the U.S. Air Force and served on the editorial staff of *Stars and Stripes,* the American military newspaper.[35]

Even some gay writers of a more conservative bent withdrew from public life after 1933. Stefan George was noticeably cool toward the new government, despite the Nazi government's hope of exploiting his prestige for its own benefit. He refused to accept the position of president of the Academy of Arts, offered to him by the Reich Ministry of Public Enlightenment and Propaganda. He also stayed away from a massive birthday celebration thrown in his honor. He retreated to Switzerland, where he died in December 1933.[36] Hans Blüher, on the other hand, initially welcomed the Nazi government and its anti-Semitic policies with open arms, but by the mid-1930s he was also distancing himself from the regime. He spent over a decade writing his next book, *The Axis of Nature* (*Die Achse von Natur*), which would not be published until 1949.[37]

THE NIGHT OF LONG KNIVES AND ITS AFTERMATH

Given the assault on the gay scene and homosexual movement, it is surprising to learn that not all homosexuals found their lives changed greatly by the events of 1933. Yes, the gay magazines as well as the best-known gay bars were gone. Yes, certain landmarks within the Weimar homosexual world such as Hirschfeld's institute were shut down. Yes, a tremendous amount of police pressure could be felt around some locations that used to be crowded with male prostitutes. Nevertheless, at first anyway, the roundup of homosexuals concentrated on the most obvious members and manifestations of the gay scene—transvestites, male prostitutes, and the leaders of the movement (who were in many cases simultaneously targeted for their socialist affiliations or Jewish backgrounds). For those who did not stand out, on the other hand, there were still opportunities to meet and have fun. Despite the police crackdown, some gay bars survived in Hamburg and other smaller cities. Even in Berlin, where the raids on gay bars were the worst, gay men and lesbians found locations where they could blend in with the crowd—for example, predominantly heterosexual bars in which small circles of gay friends could meet. Berlin especially, in the words of one scholar, "still offered all sorts of adventures at that time. Most homosexuals still moved relatively freely and practiced their same old habits. The great game of hide and seek had not yet begun, and the fear of the Gestapo which would later prevail everywhere did not yet hamper men seeking contact with other men."[38]

Some gay men felt reassured by Röhm's presence in the party. Although Röhm had not publicly confirmed his homosexuality during the 1932 scandal, the letter to Heimsoth leaked to the SPD press indicated Röhm's opposition to Paragraph 175 and his own pride in his sexuality.[39] Certainly in his well-known autobiography, *The Story of a Traitor* (*Die Geschichte eines Hochverräters,* 1928), he had taken a firm stance against prudery. "Nothing is more false," he wrote, "than the so-called morality of society."[40] And Röhm was not the only homosexual among the National Socialists. As Andrew Wackerfuss has shown, the SA in particular created a certain potential for homoeroticism through the life that the stormtroopers lived in their barracks, the "all-consuming lifestyle" of their daily activity, and the highly emotional bonds encouraged among these comrades in arms. We should not exaggerate this homoeroticism: it was generally balanced by real efforts within the SA leadership to root its members in family life and neighborhood social networks.[41] Still, a small number of homosexuals did find the all-male environment of the SA and other party organizations emotionally satisfying. We might safely guess that gay Nazis must have believed that the party embodied the male-bonding group that Hans Blüher had championed in his books. And as the party had picked up many new members and voters in 1932 and 1933, there were quite a number of conservative homosexuals who mistook Hitler's toleration of Röhm for tacit approval. Even Friedrich Radszuweit, who was certainly no Nazi, had ventured to make a very public overture to Hitler's party in the pages of *The Girlfriend* in 1932.

Willhart Schlegel, who would go on to be a prominent sexologist and advocate for the reform of Paragraph 175 during the 1960s, remembered his reaction to Nazism in his autobiographical novel, *Rolf* (1995).[42] Years afterward, he could still recall the "hypnotic voice" of Hitler and the visual impression that the party made back in the early 1930s.[43] As an eighteen-year-old, he joined the Hitler Youth and the party after attending a small meeting in a suburb of Frankfurt. The leader of the meeting, speaking confidently in the relatively intimate atmosphere of the hall, had a powerful, "almost sexual" effect on him. A fan of Hans Blüher, Schlegel believed that "a kind of homosexual atmosphere played a role in the development of the movement." He saw Röhm as someone who combined homosexuality, leadership, and organizational talent. Years later, he still believed—amazingly, really, considering Röhm's penchant for violence—that Röhm's sexuality lent the party a "certain humanity, even humaneness."[44]

Whatever security gay men felt disappeared very quickly in the summer of 1934, after the Night of Long Knives. The chief target of this night was Ernst Röhm, who was accused of nurturing a den of perversions within the party and of plotting to seize power for himself. The so-called Röhm Putsch was a fabrication of state propaganda, but there is no doubt that Hitler was concerned about Röhm's ambitions. After the 1933 takeover, Röhm dreamed of a more thoroughgoing integration of the SA with the state bureaucracy and military apparatus. Meanwhile, his followers hoped for a "second revolution" that might produce real financial benefits for the rank-and-file stormtroopers.[45] Also important for Hitler's anxieties about the SA was the unpopularity of these thugs among the German population. Although their random acts of violence had once been an asset to the Nazi Party, they became a major liability as the party tried to promote its reputation as a guardian of law and order. Discipline within the SA certainly had always been a problem, and now, with Röhm's personality cult being nurtured among its members, Hitler began to see the group as a serious threat to his hold on the party and the country. Hitler's fears were fed by Himmler, Göring, and the leaders of the military, each of whom had his own complaints against Röhm.[46]

The arrest and execution of Röhm, as well as other SA leaders and several individuals who had made the mistake of crossing Hitler at one point or another, came swiftly and with little apparent warning on June 30, 1934. In the days that followed the Night of Long Knives, Hitler justified his ruthless removal of a onetime favorite by pointing to Röhm's homosexuality. His well-known "unfortunate disposition" had supposedly become central to the "clique" that had formed in the SA, which in turn had driven a "wedge" between it and Hitler's state. In the report released by the government and published in all the major papers, much was made of the fact that one SA leader, Edmund Heines, had been found in bed with another young man on the morning of his capture. On the following day, the state propaganda machine praised Hitler for saving Germany from Röhm's treason and for cleaning up the "pigsty" (*Saustall*) in the party.[47]

The sexual proclivities of Röhm's clique were not central to the propaganda; much more important were the accusations of corruption and plotting with foreign powers.[48] Nevertheless, homosexuals living in Germany interpreted the Night of Long Knives as a sign that they were no longer safe. Many gay men simply stopped having sex with other men at this point; those who continued looking for sexual opportunities did so much more carefully.[49] Some conservative homosexuals in the party silently retreated from active participation. For his part, Schlegel recalled his "shock about all the developments after June 30." "Badly disappointed," he retreated into his university studies.[50]

The massive police assault did not begin right away. There were a number of well-publicized raids that took place in Bavaria in July, but in general the party focused at first at rooting out homosexuals in the party.[51] Still, the Night of Long Knives proved to be an important turning point in a number of ways. Homohostile propaganda became a recurring motif of the regime, especially during the trial of the serial murderer Adolf Seefeld and the so-called immorality trials (*Sittlichkeitsprozesse*) of several Catholic priests in 1937.[52] The accusation of homosexuality also played an important role in the 1938 Fritsch affair, when General Werner von Fritsch was faced with the (false) accusation of having had relations with a Berlin rent boy and was forced to step down from his position as head of the German army.[53] Most important, after 1934, as the country's many institutions of policing were gradually integrated and concentrated under the power of the SS chief Heinrich Himmler, homosexuality became the focus for new mechanisms of legal enforcement.

Himmler and his main SS lieutenant, Reinhard Heydrich, had supported the arrest of Röhm in part because it gave them the chance to break free from their subordination to the SA and to begin their construction of a large police-state apparatus under their control.[54] Personal issues played a role as well, however. Himmler had a strong puritanical streak, to say the least, which made Röhm's homosexuality extremely distasteful to him.[55] In a later speech given privately to high-ranking SS officers, he revealed his fear that organizations like the SS and the Hitler Youth, based as they were on male bonding, could become hothouses for homosexuality, thus rotting the movement from within.[56] Röhm no doubt embodied this fear for him. Röhm's death did not end the issue for Himmler, however. With Himmler's encouragement, the Nazi Party used the so-called Röhm Putsch as an opportunity to initiate a more extensive campaign against homosexuals in their own ranks and, soon thereafter, in the rest of German society.[57]

On June 28, 1935, the Nazi government modified Paragraph 175 so that it applied not only to sexual acts that resemble coitus (*beischlafsähnliche Handlungen*) but also to other sexual acts. Men could be prosecuted under the law "objectively when a general sense of shame is harmed and subjectively when there exists the lustful intention to excite either of the two men or a third party." The courts also convicted men who had masturbated simultaneously or even embraced each other. In short, the new version of Paragraph 175 required much less proof to convict a man of this crime.[58]

In addition, the Nazi government added an addendum to the law: Paragraph 175a, which specified the aggravated cases that had previously been considered part of the proposed E1927 criminal law code (as Paragraph 297). Male prostitution was made illegal, as were cases involving sex with young men under the age of twenty-one or instances in which an employer or teacher used his position to coerce sexual favors. Such a law, we saw, had been discussed in 1929 as a possible *replacement* for Paragraph 175. Under the Nazis this law was finally appended to the criminal law code as an *additional* means for suppressing same-sex acts between men. Whereas a conviction under Paragraph 175 brought a sentence length between a day and five years, a conviction under Paragraph 175a specified a sentence of no fewer than three months and as much as ten years.[59]

In the same year Reinhard Heydrich issued an order turning all homosexual cases over to the Gestapo. As early as October 1934—only months after the Röhm affair had defined homosexuals not only as perverse criminals but also as traitors to the Nazi state—a telegram had been sent by the Gestapo to the police departments of every major German city ordering them to create a list of all men who had ever been known to be active homosexuals. These lists were collected by the Special Commission for Homosexuality in Berlin, which after October 10, 1936, evolved into the "Reich Central for the Fight against Homosexuality and Abortions" and worked in close conjunction with the "Special Bureau II S" of the Gestapo.[60]

While focusing at first on suspected homosexuals within the Nazi Party, the Special Commission for Homosexuality gradually took over the job of coordinating a Germany-wide crackdown on homosexual meeting places in the course of 1936. In Hamburg, for example, the police closed down at least four more gay bars after rapid raids on the establishments, and quite possibly more.[61] They also watched restaurants such as the Alsterpavillon, known for serving a mixed heterosexual and homosexual public, as well as the busiest public toilets. These police operations had quite an effect. After a year in which the number of indictments in Hamburg under Paragraph 175 had dropped to 359, the number skyrocketed to 1,059 in 1936. In Germany overall, the number climbed from 948 in 1934 to 2,106 in 1935 and 5,320 in 1936.[62] Men who were not jailed or thrown in a concentration camp could still prove vulnerable to the SS in other ways. One man remembers entire private companies being "cleansed" of gay men. Gathering names from men arrested in the raids, the SS would eventually visit the personnel offices of the firms that employed these men and demand that they be fired.[63]

The trials that followed the wave of arrests in 1936 were carried out in an "expedited fashion" (*Schnellgericht*), and the accused men very often stood before the court with no legal defense. In contrast to court proceedings that had taken place before 1933, expert witnesses were rarely called. In many cases the police had already won a confession from the accused party, which made a conviction certain.[64] In his research on Hamburg, Stefan Micheler also observes a notable transformation in the language and procedures of everyone involved in the arrests and convictions of homosexuals. Whereas the police reports had been surprisingly free of prejudiced language and stereotypes through the Weimar period, focusing instead on the bare facts of a case, in the midst of the 1936 crackdown this attitude changed. Police officials, lawyers, and judges—as well as court doctors, social workers, and other involved government officials—began to reproduce much of the official Nazi ideology in their reports and decisions. In what one may easily argue was a critical step in the radicalization of the regime, a new political culture was clearly taking hold, as government officials bought into the regime's project of "stamping out the plague of homosexuality" (*die Seuche der Homosexualität auszurotten*).[65]

With the help of the new version of Paragraph 175 as well as the extensive resources of the SS police state at its disposal, the Nazi regime incarcerated thousands of gay men between 1933 and 1945. An unknown number found by Nazi courts to be certifiably unfit to stand trial were compulsorily confined to psychiatric institutions.[66] Many others were sentenced to years in prison, after which, beginning in 1937, it was common practice to send convicted homosexuals to concentration camps using the "preventive custody" (*Vorbeugungshaft*) power granted to Germany's police by the Nazi state. Even those not formally tried and convicted could still find themselves in a concentration camp under the Gestapo's powers of "protective custody" (*Schutzhaft*)—either as a means of inducing cooperation with the authorities before trial or simply because there was not enough evidence to yield a conviction.

The German police—both the state secret police (*Gestapo*) and the criminal investigation units of the regular police (*Kriminalpolizei*)—used every means at their disposal to carry out the hunt against homosexuals. Police raids in parks, around toilets, and in areas frequented by male prostitutes often produced many arrests. The police also depended a great deal on denunciations made by neighbors, relatives, coworkers, vengeful students or employees, and even angry or jealous boyfriends. Sometimes these came from random passersby who happened to oversee or overhear something they should not have, but there were also cases of Hitler Youth or other self-appointed "morality guardians" who took it upon themselves to ensnare homosexuals in traps that they had laid.[67] There were numerous other state and Nazi Party institutions that could also bring homosexual suspects to the attention of the police: railroad officials, social workers, and especially youth welfare officers, as well as party officials from the German Workers' Front (DAF), the SA, the SS, or the Hitler Youth.[68]

Once homosexual suspects were identified, the police had an arsenal of methods available to produce evidence and even confessions. Police officers generally assumed that those accused of being homosexual were guilty, especially if they had a previous conviction or if there were earlier police records of them pursuing same-sex contact, and so they pulled out the stops during the interrogation process.[69] At times the temporary detention facilities themselves, with their grim, forbidding cells, were enough to induce confessions. In these cells, gay men felt alone and "forgotten," as one inmate noted. Here there was nothing to do but worry about their uncertain future. Many found their appetites waning and their sleep becoming irregular. Here they could remain for three weeks, the time punctuated only by the terrible police interrogations. Confronted with screams, curses, threats, and endless questions, many would confess. Some even experienced mental breakdowns that led them to sign whatever was put in front of them. Others had to be exposed to harsher measures, which ranged from being thrown for days into a lightless cell to being beaten at the hands of a Gestapo officer. Alternatively, the police could simply lie to the accused, insisting that he would be released or perhaps receive a lighter sentence if he would simply confess. Otherwise, the accused could face long-term incarceration or an indefinite stay in a concentration camp.[70]

The Nazi police were experts at turning one arrest into many. Even before a man was arrested, he would often be extensively observed for a time to locate friends or acquaintances who might turn out to be homosexual themselves. Upon arrest, a man could count on having his house and personal belongings searched thoroughly—not only for gay magazines, pornography, and other pieces of evidence that could be used in a trial, but also for address books, personal correspondence, photographs, portraits, and any other material that could be used to identify additional suspects. On occasion, the police would release suspects for a time with the hope that they would then lead the police to others. And, if a suspect proved willing (which happened most often in the case of male prostitutes), he would be shown a photo album of previously arrested homosexuals that the Nazi police started to keep in the 1930s with the goal of arresting those who sought refuge behind false names or anonymous sexual encounters.[71]

Arrest for committing a homosexual act could also lead to castration. This state practice was based on two laws, both passed in the first year of the regime's existence. The earlier bill—the Law for the Prevention of Hereditary Diseases, passed July 14, 1933—was above all a eugenics measure using sterilization rather than castration. Originally it targeted not homosexuals at all but, rather, the congenitally blind, the deaf, the disabled, and those citizens with inheritable diseases. The second piece of legislation—the Law against Dangerous Habitual Criminals and Sex Offenders, enacted November 24, 1933—affected gay men only obliquely, that is, if they were convicted of sexually abusing children (Paragraph 176) or committing a heinous sexual offense publicly (Paragraph 183). This law was not a eugenics measure like the first but was aimed instead at "releasing" men from their "abnormal" sex drives. There was some discussion during the 1930s of extending this law to include men who violated Paragraphs 175 and 175a, but in the end most castrations of gay men were actually performed according to a revision of the first law, made on June 26, 1935—at roughly the same time, we should note, that Paragraph 175 was altered. According to the amendment, the Law for the Prevention of Hereditary Diseases also allowed the voluntary castration of men who had committed a crime "resulting from a degenerative sex drive." As much research has shown, though, the "voluntary" nature of many of the castrations done under this law is problematic at best: men often agreed to castration after false promises were made by police or SS officials that doing so would lead to lesser prison terms or even release from concentration camps. Either way, once performed, castration could have serious medical consequences ranging from excessive sweating and severe depression to heart irregularities.[72]

CONCENTRATION CAMPS AND THE PINK TRIANGLE

Gay men and lesbians who spent any time in the Nazi concentration camps experienced some of the worst conditions that humans have ever been forced to endure.[73] As has been well described in many classic accounts of life in the camps, the initiation of prisoners into the camp involved procedures designed to break their will and rob them of their identity: inmates were stripped of all their previous clothing, their bodies were shaved, they were driven naked into the showers to be washed and deloused, they were assigned numbers that were often painfully tattooed on their arms, and, finally, they were given new clothing and shoes that rarely fit.[74]

New prisoners faced one of the most difficult challenges—adapting themselves to their new lives: perpetual filth and stench, numerous prohibitions, rigid yet generally senseless routines, random acts of violence and cruelty committed by both SS guards and even fellow prisoners (especially the privileged *Kapos*), and, last but not least, the inability to control any aspect of their lives. Confronted with such conditions, many simply lost all will to cope and stay alive, which soon resulted in death; others failed to adapt quickly enough to their environment and were consequently taken advantage of by other inmates or were beaten for not living by the rules. Either possibility quickly lessened an inmate's chance of making it through another day. Homosexuals were not systematically exterminated, as the Jews were, but that fact does not mean that survival was easy. Even if they made it through the first few weeks of the camp, inmates faced threats on a daily basis. Hunger, thirst, and exhaustion provided a constant backdrop to life in the camp. Diseases spread quickly—especially diarrhea, dysentery, and so-called swollen feet brought on by infected foot wounds—and claimed many victims. The SS employed various forms of torturous punishment against the inmates—ranging from ruthless beatings and whippings to the unbearable pain of the "pole hanging," in which inmates' hands were tied behind their backs and then yanked up behind them, and they then were left to dangle for hours on end.

Surviving in these conditions depended a lot on luck, but a few strategies could increase one's chances. These included "conforming, not standing out, doing what was ordered to do, and in this way achieving the trust and favor of those who had power."[75] The *"Hundertfünfundsiebziger,"* or "175ers," as the homosexual inmates were known, faced some problems here since their homosexuality exposed them to the mockery and cruelty of the SS guards and other inmates. A few fortunate ones were classified as "BVers" (*Berufsverbrecher*, or career criminals) and given a green triangle to wear. Most, though, were clearly identified with the pink triangle (*Rosa Winkel*) as having been condemned according to Paragraph 175 or 175a.

There were two basic survival strategies for all inmates: either form bonds with other prisoners who could then help out in small but often crucial ways, or acquire a position of authority within the camp. Homosexuals unfortunately had a harder time taking advantage of either strategy. Several groups within the camp society managed to build elaborate bonds of solidarity that helped them through some of the worst times in the camps. Feelings of unity among the ordinary criminal inmates (identified with the green triangle) were fostered by a sense of being at the top of the prisoner hierarchy: they were often given the job of work commando captain (*Kapo*), which brought them authority over other inmates and certain privileges within the camp system. Political prisoners, normally communists or socialists identified with the red triangle, arrived with a sense of camaraderie built through previous political work; this feeling often transferred to camp life, despite the best efforts of the SS. Homosexual inmates, however, had difficulty establishing such bonds, given that they were rarely afforded any positions of authority and generally had no previous relationships to build on. Younger, attractive inmates could sometimes establish sexual relationships with *Kapos*, block wardens, or even SS guards that would bring them some rewards. Mostly, the 175ers fell victim to the diversity that existed within the group. Homosexual inmates actually included a range of individuals, from young, working-class prostitutes to effeminate "fairies" (*Tunten*) to more masculine-acting men from bourgeois families. There were even those who were not homosexual at all but had only been victims of homosexual accusations made by the Nazis during politically motivated attacks on the Catholic Church and the Weimar youth movement.[76]

And yet some studies have suggested that the earlier belief that homosexuals could *never* establish such bonds is exaggerated somewhat.[77] There are some rare but extraordinary examples of friendship and solidarity that have been documented by recent historical work—even in one of the worst concentration camps for homosexuals, Sachsenhausen. In one case, the inmate Max Juds found help from fellow inmates in getting his work done after repeatedly being subjected to the torturous pole hanging. Another involved a friendship between the businessman Ernst Haase and the cabaret actor Robert Odeman, who developed a close friendship shortly after their arrival in the camp in December 1944 and who remained lifelong friends after their release. The most common cases involved homosexuals who had been politically active before their arrests. The socialist artist Richard Grune, for instance, who had participated in the SPD youth movement of the 1920s, eventually found himself a camp inmate after his arrest in 1935. Here, with the help of his fellow inmates who assisted in smuggling in drawing material and then provided cover for his work, he illustrated a number of extremely moving portrayals of his experiences in the camp.[78]

Such examples are rare, though. Most homosexuals had to rely only on themselves to survive in the camps. The chances for survival were better in some camps than others. Conditions in Neuengamme, near Hamburg, for instance, seem to have been much more hospitable for homosexuals than those in Buchenwald, Dachau, or Sachsenhausen.[79] An inmate's chances for survival also varied greatly depending on when he or she arrived in the camp. The historian Andreas Sternweiler, as part of a larger group from Berlin's Gay Museum who has produced an extensive study of life and death in Sachsenhausen, suggests a rough periodization that allows a better understanding of the conditions that homosexuals faced in the camp. Sachsenhausen, a camp located north of Berlin, did not come into full operation until September 1936. Before this time, there were of course some gay inmates already in other camps, most notably Dachau. Among them were male prostitutes and transvestites, both of whom were targets of some of the earliest police actions against the gay scene.[80] Large numbers of gay inmates, however, did not arrive in the concentration camps until after 1935, by which time the earlier system of ad hoc camps the Nazis had set up soon after coming to power were being converted into the more extensive system that was based on large central camps, each with a gradually expanding number of satellite camps (*Aussenlager*).[81] Sachsenhausen was one of the most important of these central camps.

In the earliest phase of Sachsenhausen's existence, running between the fall of 1936 and the beginning of World War II, homosexuals found the best conditions that they ever were going to encounter in this camp. Not only could homosexuals realistically hope for some release from the camp during this period, they could also more easily blend in and mix with the other inmates. They were subjected to roughly the same conditions as everyone else and they had better chances at developing social relationships with other inmates that would further their survival. Effeminate inmates clearly had greater trouble than the more masculine-acting men, but the categorization of inmates by the infamous system of colored triangles and stars was not introduced until 1937, first in Dachau and a little later in the rest of the camp system.[82] Around the same time, the practice of isolating the homosexual prisoners from the rest of the inmate population was introduced, again first at Dachau and over the next few years gradually in the rest of the camp system.[83]

The situation for all the inmates got much worse once war arrived in September 1939. All the camps were flooded with new inmates: prisoners of war and resistance fighters from occupied areas of Europe, but also Jews. In fact, the population of Sachsenhausen doubled in the course of the year. At the same time that the camp became more crowded, new regulations established in the cold of the 1939–40 winter included the heating of bunkers only in the evening and a vast reduction of the bread ration.[84] Sick inmates and those unwilling to work even had their rations halved. All this helps partially explain the staggering increase of the camp mortality rates overall after 1939. Besides dying, the only hope that most homosexuals in Sachsenhausen had during this period was to be sent to another concentration camp where conditions might be slightly better. Those who remained faced the "torment and torture" of the camp's SS guards.[85]

During this second phase, "the men with the pink triangle" were isolated in separate barracks because of the growing concern among the Nazis that homosexuality would spread to other inmates in the camp. Here they had little contact with other categories of inmates, especially those who were also forced into isolation: Jehovah's Witnesses, political inmates who showed some potential for agitation or sabotage, and, finally, Jewish inmates convicted of breaking the Nazi laws regarding sexual contact with Germans. In these isolated barracks, the 175ers were exposed to an escalating "lust to kill" that overcame the SS after 1939.[86]

From 1940 onward, homosexuals in Sachsenhausen were routinely assigned to the "SK," which technically stood for "special commando" (*Sonderkommando*) but which was understood by the inmates to mean "penal regiment" (*Strafkompanie*). The SK was given the most dangerous and exhausting work to be found in the camp. Some were assigned to the "shoe runners" (*Schuhläufer*), who were given the seemingly innocuous task of testing various styles of shoes. The execution of this task could be murderous, however: inmates were given a pair of shoes, told to put them on whether they fit or not, and then ordered to run around for half an hour at a fast clip. Afterward the shoes would be changed, a new pair put on quickly (which could be torturous in the cold of winter), and the running again commenced—over and over again, for several hours every day of the week. The running quickly drained the half-starved inmates, and in addition the feet of the shoe runners soon developed painful blisters and sores that could easily become infected in camp conditions.[87]

Other members of the Sachsenhausen SK regiment were assigned to the dirty, grueling work at the wartime brick-making plant in the nearby town of Oranienburg, which produced massive numbers of deaths simply through exhaustion. Others, however, were murdered personally by SS guards, who enjoyed playing sadistic games with the prisoners. Near the brick-making plant was an SS shooting range, where inmates assigned to throwing targets into the air were frequently turned into targets themselves. But even when the inmates were in their barracks, they were not safe from SS cruelty. Guards found ways to disguise the murder of inmates: prisoners were hanged in the washroom in ways that made them look like suicides or were driven to hang themselves through various threats and torments. Heart attacks and lung inflammations could also be induced with repeated "cold water attacks."[88]

The death rate of 175ers during this period was so high that most who found themselves in the camps were dead before the end of 1942. From this point on, though, the conditions in the camp became steadily less murderous, as the Nazi government began to take more seriously the labor potential offered by camp inmates. In Sachsenhausen, anyway, the number of homosexual inmates climbed somewhat during the period simply because more were surviving. The isolation of the 175ers broke down, and increasingly they were reintegrated into the main prison population. Furthermore, the explosion in the number of foreign inmates in the camps forced the SS increasingly to turn to the remaining German prisoners to act as "camp officers"—among them even a few "men with the pink triangle" who previously had only rarely been allowed access to such positions of authority. There were certainly still horrible crimes committed during this period. Some inmates continued to work in the SKs. It was in this period also that the notorious Nazi medical experiments were conducted on homosexuals. The best-known of these were the hormonal experiments aimed at "curing" homosexuals carried out in 1944 by the endocrinologist Carl Vaernet at Buchenwald, which had terrible consequences for the health of the human subjects; less well known are the experiments in Buchenwald with various treatments for typhus, as well as the research in Sachsenhausen with opiates and therapies for phosphorus wounds, all of which involved largely Jewish and homosexual inmates.[89]

DEBATES ABOUT NAZI MOTIVES

The exact motive behind the Nazi persecution of homosexuals has been much debated. There is no easy answer, mainly because there were many different reasons that the Nazis gave to justify it. Perhaps this confusion is not surprising, though, given what we know about the Nazi Party. Although there were certainly some governing ideas that held the party together, its membership comprised many different groups: rabid anti-Semites, eugenics devotees, radicalized students, violent thugs, World War I veterans, nationalists with pronounced socialist tendencies, but also more traditional cultural conservatives. All of them believed the Nazi Party would provide an efficient path toward achieving their goals.[90] They all seemed to see in the party what they wanted to see.

Probably the most common explanation over the years for the Nazi obsession with homosexuality has been that it was an expression of traditional middle-class prudishness. Among the Nazis "mediocrity predominated—respectable petty bourgeois mediocrity," wrote Hans Peter Bleuel in his early account of Nazi attitudes toward sexuality.[91] The movement was described as a violent reaction against Weimar's sexual liberalism, but it was perhaps rooted in much deeper German tendencies toward self-denial and political subordination.[92] George Mosse, thankfully, relied less on German stereotypes, but he still described fascist morality as the culmination of a Europe-wide tendency to fuse nationalism with respectability. Nationalism "absorbed and sanctioned middle-class manners and morals and played a crucial part in spreading respectability to all classes of the population, however much these classes hated and despised one another." Although the attitude of fascism toward sexuality "was not one of simple oppression," Mosse acknowledged, its emphasis on healthy families and public order, masculine strength and feminine maternity, reiterated the major themes of nineteenth-century bourgeois morality.[93]

For social historians an equation between Nazism and bourgeois morality was relatively straightforward, since it was the middle class broadly defined that provided most of the electoral support for the Nazi victories of the 1930s. For Marxist historians it was even easier, since for them all varieties of fascism were rooted in the capitalist class's desire to maintain social control. Other scholars, though, have tried to ground Nazi hostility to sexuality in Freudian psychoanalysis. As long ago as 1933, Wilhelm Reich argued in his book *The Mass Psychology of Fascism* that Nazism represented an intensification of the sexual repression created in the forges of the "authoritarian" bourgeois family. In the midst of social and economic crisis, the threat to order awakened the authoritarian instincts: a desire for dictatorship, an attraction to Nazi symbols, and a lust for violence. Nazism ultimately channeled immense amounts of brutal hostility to nonnormative forms of sexuality while at the same time harboring various forms of repressed sexuality, especially homoeroticism, within its midst.[94] A similar argument was made by members of the Frankfurt School in their work on the authoritarian family and then repeated often during the 1960s among the literature of the New Left.[95]

An alternative was offered in 1977 by Klaus Theweleit in his influential (but admittedly eccentric) work *Male Fantasies*. The Nazi anxiety about sexuality, he argued, was rooted not in familial dynamics exactly but more fundamentally in weaknesses of the male ego as it developed in the West. What fascist men (who did not disappear in 1945, he makes clear) desire above all are firmer boundaries. For them, sexuality becomes symbolic for the powerful psychic forces that have to be carefully controlled if they are not to overwhelm their fragile egos. Sexual pleasure can be experienced, but only insofar as it is channeled into violence: "These men look for ecstasy not in embraces, but in explosions, in the rumbling of bomber squadrons or in brains being shot to flames."[96] Violence against homosexuals is part of a larger defense mechanism against the "feminine" that lurks within all men, the erotic "flowing" interior that must be carefully contained by the "masculine" armor of the ego.[97] And yet, in a contradictory manner, many fascist men experience homoerotic, or even fully homosexual, urges that often take on sadomasochistic forms. The love of men allows them to escape the dangers of exposure to the feminine while simultaneously being bound to the movement: "Thou shalt do what is forbidden, yet still be punished, if those in power so desire."[98] A similar argument has been made more recently by the equally unconventional Nicolaus Sombart, except that he believed that German masculinity was particularly vulnerable to fascism thanks to the pervasiveness of all-male social institutions such as the army and the bureaucracy. Such institutions invoked homoerotic desire to cement male bonding while simultaneously suppressing conscious homosexual feelings as feminine. The result was an unusual level of aggression and rigidity among German men.[99]

At some level, though, historians have long known that there are difficulties with the assertion that Nazis were simply prudish.[100] What to do with the numerous nude statues and paintings that the party endorsed as images of the "healthy race"? The injunctions to have lots of children for the German race? The German military brothels? Such doubts came into clear focus in 2005, when Dagmar Herzog published her important work *Sex after Fascism*. Compiling the many ways that Nazism included "sexually inciting elements," she argued that in crucial ways Hitler's state "brought with it not only a redefinition but also a perpetuation, expansion, and intensification of preexisting liberalizing trends."[101] If it is too simplistic, then, to portray Nazism as anti-erotic across the board, how do we understand the Nazis' extreme hostility to homosexuality?

Nazi racism seems to offer one possible explanation. Perhaps the key is to connect the Nazi persecution of homosexuals with the Jewish Holocaust. Was homosexual persecution not simply part of a larger Nazi effort to cleanse the Aryan race? Or, putting it slightly differently, might violence aimed at both Jews and homosexuals be understood as the logical outcome of "modernity's nationalizing project" premised on a view of the nation as an "ethnically homogenous and intrinsically masculinist entity"?[102] Much research has pursued this possibility, documenting how Nazi high officials justified the persecution of homosexuals with language drawn from the German racial hygiene movement. Taking a cue from these eugenics experts, Nazis expressed concern about the effect that homosexuality would have on Germany's birth rate and the health of its people in general. Heinrich Himmler in particular made statements suggesting that gay men were considered a threat to Germans as a whole and were, like the Jewish race, to be exterminated as a whole: "Homosexual men are traitors and are to be treated as such. We are dealing here with the health of the body of the German people, with the maintenance and strengthening of the energy of the German people [*deutsche Volkskraft*]." "If I assume there are one to two million homosexuals, that means around 7, 8, or even 10 percent of the men in Germany are homosexual. If this stays the same, it can only mean that our people will die from this epidemic."[103] Such sentiments were echoed in the official SS newspaper, *Das Schwarze Korps,* by the SS officer Karl August Eckhardt, who wrote in his 1935 article "The Unnatural Vice Warrants Death" that homosexuals deserved to have their "aberrant life" not punished but "simply extinguished."[104] And the legal student Rudolf Klare argued in his Nazi-rhetoric-saturated dissertation "Homosexuality and Criminal Law" that homosexuality was an "Asiatic" racial degeneration that was inherently hated by the Nordic-Germanic people, except where the insidious effects of Christianity and French intellectuals made themselves felt.[105]

Although articulated by many scholars during the 1970s and 1980s, the most famous presentation of the eugenics-oriented position is Michael Burleigh and Wolfgang Wippermann's *The Racial State* (1991), which tried to tie all aspects of Nazi barbarity to the murderous logic of Nazi racism.[106] Recently, however, a group of scholars has begun to suggest that this book perhaps went too far. Other categories of identity such as religion, class, gender, and even ethnicity were just as important for the Nazis. Even when the Nazis confused these categories with race in their frequently muddled thinking, these identities did not lose their power to influence policy or public debate. And when it came to conquering Europe, Nazis were very often driven by primarily economic or political motives, even when these efforts might have acquired a "superficial racial gloss" in some of the propaganda. Moreover, the category of race itself was not a clear-cut concept even under the Nazi racial state: sometimes it was defined as a narrowly biological concept, sometimes as more of a cultural concept, and sometimes in other murkier metaphorical ways.[107]

This last point can be illustrated very well with the Nazi treatment of homosexuality. According to the eugenics-based science put to use by the state, homosexuality was a genetically acquired problem that could be solved only by sterilization or other, more radical methods. More commonly, however, when Nazi leaders talked about homosexuality as a "disease," they did not mean the term in a narrow medical or biological sense. Instead, what was invoked was the notion of the national or racial body (*Volkskörper*), a central concept for the Nazis that used the metaphor of the living body to imagine an ideal national or racial community (*Volksgemeinschaft*). According to this framework, the lives of individuals were supposed to be strictly subordinated to the needs of the whole, much as a living cell plays a role within the functioning of an organism. Homosexuals were "viruses" or "cancers" in the racial-national body insofar as they supposedly threatened the strength of the nation.

In the case of homosexuals, both kinds of racial logic were important for the practices of the Nazi state, but it was generally the second that won out. The SS became committed in the course of 1937 to the idea that there were actually two types of homosexuals, a minority who had acquired it genetically and a vast majority who had acquired it through experiences, most frequently through seduction. The former certainly had to be partitioned off from the rest of society (probably in a concentration camp) because they had the capability of spreading their "disease" to millions if the state let them. The others, however, were capable of "reeducation," which in the Nazi worldview would come from a prison term or, even better, experience in a concentration camp. Either way, though, the solution was the same—the only difference was that the second group could eventually be released, whereas the internment of the first group would theoretically be permanent.[108]

In practice, racial language proved so useful when it came to dealing with homosexuality because of its ability to refer to so many well-established prejudices. Homosexuality's alleged weakening of men was likened to a "sickness." Its potential to spread through society by means of the seduction of youth was compared to an "infection." The tendency of homosexuals to clump up into "cliques" that plotted against the state was described as "cancerous." Racism, however, was just one of the "dimensions of homophobia," to borrow a term from the historian Geoffrey Giles. The "homosexual panic" of the Nazi state had numerous underpinnings, Giles suggests: cultural, ideological, political, and social. Their "immorality," their alleged shiftiness, and their refusal to produce children also made them easy targets for the regime.[109]

At least one of these dimensions had an important gender component, as much recent research has suggested. Hostility to homosexuality proved to play an important role in policing gender norms in the country. Just as women were supposed to be mothers above all else, giving birth to a new generation of German soldiers, so men were supposed to combine strength, discipline, physical beauty, and moral purity.[110] The women's movement, though, had contributed to the breakdown of gender norms and the proliferation of homosexuals. As Himmler himself said to a group of his chief SS officers: "I regard it as a catastrophe when women's organizations, women's societies, women's associations get involved in a field of activity which destroys all feminine charm, all feminine grace and dignity. I regard it as a catastrophe when we so masculinize women that over time the gender difference or polarity disappears. Then the road to homosexuality is not far off."[111] The perceived weakness of homosexual males was also a symptom of the military and political impotence of the country in the wake of World War I.[112] It had to be eradicated if the country was ever going to rise again from the ashes.

The Nazis believed that their band of warriors would return proper gender order to the nation. They were haunted, however, by the anxiety that their own intense emphasis on male bonding and their clear admiration for the male physique could accidentally attract homosexuals into their midst.[113] As Geoffrey Giles puts it, "There was but a fine line" between the intense camaraderie of men in the party and "actual homosexual behavior. This line was frequently crossed, not least by some of the leaders of the youth movement."[114] Equally dangerous was the possibility that the wider population could misunderstand these qualities. There were in fact German citizens who expressed their resentments against local representatives of the Nazi regime by accusing them of being homosexual. Some people even dared to spread the rumor that Hitler himself was homosexual.[115] Especially after the Night of Long Knives, the Nazis were clearly paranoid about policing homosexuality within the party, particularly in the Hitler Youth, the SA, and the SS.[116] Violence against homosexuals, then, could serve the dual function of both punishing men who failed to live up to Nazi norms and clarifying the meaning of Nazi propaganda for the wider population.

HOMOSEXUAL LIFE AFTER 1934

The "multiple dimensions" of Nazi hostility to homosexuality, combined with the fragmented nature of the Nazi Party and the simple realities of legal enforcement, meant that there were some real inconsistencies when it came to how the Nazi state handled homosexuality. Within the German army and even the SS—a group that was supposed to set high standards (from a Nazi perspective, of course) with regard to sexual behavior and that, consequently, threatened serious penalties for members who broke these norms—there were examples of leniency shown by both the Nazi hierarchy and Nazi courts.[117]

The police crackdown was managed by the Gestapo on an intensive level in major cities such as Berlin, Hamburg, and Cologne but much less so in small towns or rural areas.[118] And as the Nazis expanded their reach with the conquest of Europe, they were largely uninterested in homosexuals who were not Germans—a noticeable contrast with their attitude toward Jews, who were determinedly sought out and arrested wherever they lived.[119]

Another inconsistency was that the Nazis were clearly more obsessed with male homosexuals than they were with lesbians. Although ideologically Nazis were certainly not tolerant of sex acts between women, in practice lesbians were not targeted for police persecution at anywhere close to the same level as men. Paragraph 175 remained aimed at men, although there were some debates among jurists about possibly extending the law to include women. Rudolf Klare, in particular, was an outspoken advocate for legal protections to guard girls against being seduced by adult lesbians. Hans Frank, the Nazi Party's chief jurist, as well as many of his supporters in the German Law Academy also argued persistently through the 1930s that lesbians had a potentially "race-corroding" effect. Interestingly, both arguments failed to convince key people in the Reich Justice Ministry. A majority of the legal experts believed that the threat of homosexual seduction was much weaker in the case of women. Revising Paragraph 175 would have little effect and might even lead to a flood of unwarranted denunciations. Women, after all, were naturally more "tender" with one another, argued Edmund Mezger, the foremost criminologist in the Third Reich. More important, measures taken to shore up the so-called proper gender order were seen as the most decisive factors when it came to preventing female homosexuality. The destruction of the women's movement, the removal of women from government positions and other positions of power, and the enrollment of women in the League of German Girls, the National Socialist Women's League, or other party-directed organizations would help guide women toward their "natural" destiny, procreation.[120]

Lesbians were certainly affected by the dissolution of lesbian organizations, the destruction of the lesbian press, and the closure of lesbian nightclubs, cafés, and other meeting places. The police did not entirely ignore them, especially if they had been well known previously as leaders in the old Weimar movement. Furthermore, several party organizations that dealt with women and government offices such as the Race Policy Bureau gathered denunciations when they came in.[121] The lesbians who were in the most danger, though, were those targeted by the regime for reasons entirely disconnected from their sexuality. Annette Eick, a young Jewish-German woman who had been a regular visitor in Berlin's lesbian scene and had written poetry for *The*

Love of Women, found her life ruined after 1933. Her parents lost their store; her hope of becoming a journalist was forgotten. She narrowly escaped the concentration camps, managing to flee to England.[122]

Most non-Jewish lesbians who were arrested faced charges of being prostitutes, political criminals, or "asocial." Hilde Radusch was arrested in April 1933 because of her membership in the Communist Party and the Revolutionary Trade Union Opposition and held in so-called protective custody in a women's prison for several months. Released in September, she was watched by the Gestapo for the next couple of years. She eked out a living in Berlin, and even managed to meet a new love in 1939 that turned into a long relationship. She stayed away from all the old meeting places, however, and in 1944 she narrowly escaped being thrown into a concentration camp by hiding with her partner in a small shed in a village outside the city.[123] Lotte Hahm, the most prominent woman in the BfM, was arrested in 1933 for having sex with a minor after being denounced by the father of her girlfriend. After spending some time in prison, she was eventually taken into custody by the SS and sent to the women's camp of Moringen in 1935, where she was kept until 1938.[124] Hahm is a good example of a lesbian who was probably arrested because of her sexual orientation but was accused of some other crime as a legal pretext. Claudia Schoppmann, the historian who has done the most work on the fate of lesbians under Nazism, has found a few other such cases. Elli S., arrested in 1940, was classified as a "political" criminal. Several others were accused of "subversion of the war effort."[125]

Even if they were not affected by Paragraph 175, lesbians understood the danger that they were in. Like their male counterparts, they withdrew from many of their old associations, sometimes retreating into small circles of friends, but very often breaking off all contact with former associates.[126] Those who could make some accommodation with the regime normally did so. Anna Sprüngli (aka Anna Rüling), who during the First World War had given up her feminist activism and become active in right-wing nationalist politics, joined the Reich Chamber of Music and began to produce music criticism for the German press.[127] Ruth Röllig, who wrote one of the most famous descriptions of the Weimar lesbian scene in 1928, joined the Reich Literature Association and continued to publish popular books. She had to give up writing lesbian literature, and several of her novels after 1933 were littered with anti-Semitic language and stereotypes. One that was set during the Russian Revolution had an overall anticommunist tone. Her mystery novel *The Other* (*Der Andere*, 1935), however, included a main character, described as possessing a "girl-like enthusiasm" but also "deep, dark secrets." Another character was a strong female, with a "penchant for riding and smoking," with whom the author obviously sympathized.[128] Clearly, this one at least was not normal Nazi fiction.

Gay men also did what they could to fit in. Gay men and lesbians had frequently gotten married before 1933, but now there was an added impetus to do so. If the thought did not occur to them on their own, they probably had a concerned friend, doctor, business associate, or priest who planted the idea. A number of gay men seem to have arranged lavender marriages with lesbians they knew from the gay scene who were also looking for "concealment" (*Tarnung*). Others found relationships with the help of straight friends or relatives. Such marriages were rarely happy and never caused the urges to have sex with other men to disappear. If arrest records are an indication, many continued to seek sexual contact with men on the side. There could also be dangers involved if an unhappy wife decided to denounce a man to arrange for a convenient separation. Still, for many it was a route that was difficult to resist given the threat of being discovered.[129]

For those who could not blend in, life was very difficult. The historian Andreas Sternweiler has uncovered the story of Fritz Kitzing, whom we would identify today as a transwoman, who was thirty years old when the Nazis came to power. She continued for a time to try to make a living as a prostitute in Berlin, until she was summoned to the police station and eventually arrested for indecent conduct.[130] After some time in prison, she got out of Germany and fled to London but then was arrested there and, sadly, deported back to her home country. In Berlin she went back to wearing men's clothing and tried to pass in an unassuming way, but she could not avoid looking for sexual partners on the streets. On June 5, 1935, Kitzing accidentally hit on an SA man who was out of uniform. Surprisingly, the police let her go with a warning that if she was accused again, she would find herself in a concentration camp. Kitzing was not so lucky the next year, when the Gestapo arrested her after she was denounced as a transvestite by one of her neighbors. At first, Kitzing tried to deny it, but eventually she confessed after women's clothes were found during an apartment search. In Mary 1936 she was taken to the Lichtenburg concentration camp. In October she was transferred to Sachsenhausen. Kitzing was released in April 1937 but arrested again in 1938 after a blackmailer who had known her from Sachsenhausen used her name. After that incident, the paper trail runs out. It is hard to say what happened to her. The best guess is that she died in the camp.[131]

A few gay clubs persisted into the 1930s—Hamburg's Stadtcasino amazingly, stayed open until 1938—but generally gay men who continued to associate with old friends met in mixed company. In Berlin men sometimes still risked dancing with one another in bars frequented by artists or well-to-do (but apparently tolerant) socialites. The police and SS watched these locations, but they did not shut them down since they were primarily used by heterosexual couples. There were baths near Kreuzberg where gay men sought out sexual partners as well as a number of movie theaters on Münzstrasse where darkness offered cover for quick encounters.[132] And in every city men continued to cruise streets, parks, and areas around public bathrooms for chance meetings. From arrest records, it is clear that in Berlin Alexanderplatz and the Friedrichstrasse persisted as locations where gay men went hunting for sexual partners, even under the Nazis.[133] Men who sought longer-lasting relationships combed personal ads in major newspapers for hints of men seeking "friendship."[134]

Whatever remnants of homoerotic socialization remained in Nazi Germany were much more fleeting and less visible than they had been earlier in the century. A small number might have felt some continued solidarity among themselves against the regime, but the vast majority watched sadly as their scenes fell apart and as relationships were torn apart by the fear of being accused by friends should those friends ever find themselves in the hands of the police. Many complained about feeling lonely and abandoned.[135] Their self-images suffered accordingly. Surrounded by anti-Röhm propaganda, unable to proclaim their sexuality confidently in any setting, and forced to deny who they were on a regular basis, gay men found it very difficult to think anything positive about themselves.[136] "On the inside," remembered one man, "I knew from the beginning that there was nothing to do about it. It is as it is, and stays that way. But on the outside I naturally acted, and even pretended to myself, that I could change it."[137]

As much as they were persecuted by a regime that hated them, gay men and lesbians who were successful at "camouflaging" themselves also fit into that large gray area between victims and perpetrators that historians have been busy exploring since the end of the 1980s.[138] As Manfred Herzer writes, they "belonged to the willing subjects and beneficiaries of the Nazi state just like other German men and women."[139] It is known that there were gay men in the ranks of the Nazi Party, even in the SS, in which such desires were supposedly entirely forbidden. There might have been some among the enthusiastic "Old Fighters" (Alte Kämpfer) in the party, but like most Germans who joined it after 1933, they did so out of professional reasons or to otherwise get ahead socially.[140] Many gay men served in the German military after the Second World War started, thereby helping to subordinate countries, and participated in the brutal war of aggression on the Eastern Front. And although we have fewer stories to verify this idea, we can guess that lesbians played their part as well. Like other women, they would have supported the war effort through their work in party associations, as nurses and secretaries, as auxiliary personnel for the military, and—during the final "Total War" phase, as the Nazis became desperate—as workers in industry. Claire Waldoff, the famous cabaret performer from the 1920s, might serve as an example. Although her career came to a halt in 1933, after she was banned from public performance as a suspected lesbian and communist, she was able to resume singing in 1935, and during World War II she gave performances for German troops. Some of her songs were broadcast on the radio, although they were not loved by Nazi leaders. In January 1942 she even sang in occupied Paris.[141]

NAZISM, SCIENCE, AND HOMOSEXUALITY

The Nazi takeover represented a significant crisis for the science of sexuality in Germany. The Institute for Sexual Science was destroyed. The Medical Society for Sexual Science and Eugenics, which already had moved away from the sex reformers at the end of the 1920s, as Hirschfeld began to focus on the WLSR, dissolved for political reasons in 1933.[142] The Berlin Psychoanalytic Institute found itself under siege, denounced as a purveyor of "Jewish poison" not only by Nazis such as Alfred Rosenberg and Julius Streicher but also by rival psychiatrists who saw an opportunity to rid themselves of competitors. As we have seen, many of the most prominent proponents of psychoanalysis had been either Jewish or leftists, and so many of them simply fled the country in the early 1930s. Max Eitingon, the director of the institute, left Germany in 1933, eventually moving to Palestine; the next year, Wilhelm Reich escaped to Norway. By 1934 only around twelve of sixty-five analysts were left in the institute.[143] The General Medical Society for Psychotherapy went through a massive restructuring. Ernst Kretschmer, who had no sympathy for Nazism, resigned from the society's presidency in 1933 and returned to a less visible position at the University of Marburg.[144] Most of what was left of the society after the mass exodus was renamed the German Medical Society for Psychotherapy and taken over by Matthias Heinrich Göring, a cousin of the Nazi Reich minister. Göring also headed up the new Göring Institute (formally the German Institute for Psychological Research and Psychotherapy), which by the end of the 1930s gathered up the remnants of Berlin's and Vienna's psychoanalytic tradition.[145]

Traditional psychiatry, with its orientation toward biological explanations of mental illness, experienced much less turbulence in 1933. Emil Kraepelin had died in 1926, but his students held many positions in the most important universities and research institutions of the day. Like their teacher, most of them had rejected (or simply ignored) Hirschfeld's sex reform movement during the 1920s, so the transition for them into the Nazi era was not a difficult one in this regard.[146] Interestingly, though, many of Kraepelin's students moved away from his emphasis on seduction as they were drawn into the young field of genetics.[147] Genetic science had appeared around 1900 and then had been further developed and popularized in the following decades by the British biologist William Bateson and the American biologist Thomas Hunt Morgan.[148] By the 1920s genetics in Germany had become closely associated with the right wing of the eugenics movement, known as racial hygiene.[149]

Under the Nazi regime, genetics research was pursued at two major institutes: the German Psychiatric Institute (*Deutscher Forschungsanstalt für Psychiatrie*) in Munich, led by the eugenics expert Ernst Rüdin after the death of Kraepelin; and the Kaiser Wilhelm Institute for Anthropology, Human Genetics, and Eugenics in Berlin, headed by the racial hygienist Eugen Fischer. Both institutes offered many services and professional advice to the new Nazi regime. Rüdin joined the Nazi Party, sat on Himmler's Task Force of Heredity Experts, and helped write the 1933 Sterilization Law. Fischer's institute provided expert advice to Nazi courts and government offices, as well as training to SS doctors and others in racial hygiene.[150]

After a brief period of quiet in 1933 and early 1934, when the scientific community waited to see what the exact position of the Nazis toward homosexuality would be, genetics researchers jumped at the opportunity offered by the Röhm Putsch and the intensification of policing that followed in the mid-1930s.[151] As the police made arrests, the authorities gathered information on family relationships, medical issues, and other details that looked like a gold mine to genetics researchers. Hans Habel, a student of the eugenicist Otmar Freiherr von Verschuer in Berlin, began working with a small sample of homosexual twins that he found in Prussian jails. Although the final results would not be published until 1950, he began to put together an argument that homosexuals tended to be weak at birth, to have families with other psychiatric problems, and to show signs of being indecisive and unstable.[152] It was very easy for Habel's teacher Verschuer to argue that this research fit well with Nazi goals: "The research done on twins . . . by taking into consideration their biological condition serves the direct goal of supporting the continued extension of the hereditary and racial care of the current state."[153]

As we have seen, though, Nazi attitudes toward homosexuals were multi-faceted and often contradictory, which meant that the party did not lend its full support to this genetic research, as one might expect. In fact, the lingering connection in people's minds between genetic research and Hirschfeld's earlier arguments left this scientific approach vulnerable to attacks, as the historian Susanne zur Nieden has shown in her research on Theo Lang. Lang is an interesting case, since he had joined the Nazi party back in 1923, several years before he became a researcher at Munich's German Psychiatric Institute. By the early 1930s he had become one of the leading advocates for uniting the institute's research with Nazi racial goals. In the middle of the decade, he began to exploit criminal files from Munich and Hamburg to make a claim on being the nation's leading expert on the genetic basis of homosexuality.[154] Borrowing Richard Goldschmidt's theory of intersexuality, he suggested that male homosexuals were actually "transformed men" (*Umwandlungsmännchen*), that is, men who had started their lives as girls but were then transformed into boys in the course of their fetal development. He based his argument on a statistical abnormality that he found in the files, namely, that the gay men that he looked at had fewer sisters than average (124.6 brothers for every 100 sisters, as opposed to the normal ratio of 106 boys for every 100 girls).[155] His results were partially confirmed at the Psychiatric Clinic in Leipzig in 1940 by Klaus Jensch, who examined the families of over two thousand men in Silesia and Saxony.[156]

Lang, however, had left the Nazi party in January 1933, probably because he was disillusioned with the party's shift away from the socially radical elements of their early party platform. Considered by some party members to be "politically unreliable," he came under attack by a number of doctors and psychiatrists, including the leading psychoanalysts, representatives of phenomenological psychiatry, and even a number from the biological school who had adhered a little more closely to Kraepelin's old argument that homosexuality could be explained only by taking into account both physical and environmental factors.[157] In fact, two leading endocrinal scientists carrying on Eugen Steinach's line of inquiry—Rudolf Lemke, a leading figure at the University of Jena's Psychiatric and Nerve Clinic, and Julius Deussen, a colleague of Lang's at the German Psychiatric Institute—came out against Lang's work.[158] Increasingly isolated in the psychiatric profession by the early 1940s, Lang left Germany for Switzerland. He continued to publish but became openly critical of the Nazi policies toward homosexuals. Nevertheless, he remained a racist, an anti-Semite, and a proponent of eugenic methods until the end.[159]

In their professional attacks against Lang's work, German psychoanalysts were no doubt at least partially motivated by their own anxieties about the future of their profession. Rooted as it was in the thinking of the Jew Sigmund Freud, this school of thought certainly stood to lose a lot under the Nazis. Even if the international organization was led at that time by the very German Carl Jung, many prominent Nazis still inveighed tirelessly against what they considered the un-German and sex-obsessed ideas of psychoanalysis. Still, the Nazis were, amazingly, not successful in completely silencing this school of thought in Germany, as is often assumed. At the Göring Institute a number of analysts continued their work in Jungian, Adlerian, and even Freudian therapy, though they certainly learned to avoid much of the traditional psychoanalytic language.[160]

As we have seen, many high-ranking Nazi leaders were not convinced that most forms of homosexuality were inborn. Although Freud himself had questioned whether most cases of homosexuality were "curable," even if they were not inborn, German psychoanalysts at the Göring Institute now offered their services to party members looking for treatment of individuals in their charge. The Hitler Youth and League of German Girls, in particular, sent "troubled" youths to the institute, hoping to have them cured. Even the SS apparently referred a few convicts to the institute after they were released from concentration camps.[161] By 1938 therapists working for the Göring Institute claimed to have seen 510 homosexual patients and cured 341. In 1944 they took credit for 500 instances of successful treatment.[162] They also occasionally intervened to mitigate the harsh sentences passed by Nazi courts.[163]

The psychiatric school to make the most headway during the 1930s was the phenomenological school. An increasingly important figure in this field in the 1930s and 1940s was Hans Bürger-Prinz, a leading psychiatrist at the University of Hamburg and director of the university's psychiatric clinic after 1936. A Nazi Party and SA member after 1933, he has been severely criticized by Karl Heinz Roth and others for putting unknown numbers of shell-shocked and otherwise psychologically disturbed veterans through a series of horrible electroshock and insulin treatments while sending others to the war courts to be executed simply because they supposedly showed no desire to be healed. Furthermore, Bürger-Prinz's denials notwithstanding, he was probably partially responsible for the many mentally ill inmates who were sent out from the hospital to be murdered as part of the Nazis' euthanasia program.[164] All these activities suggest the ways that the phenomenological school could be made to fit in with key aspects of the Nazi worldview.

Bürger-Prinz's view of homosexuality is a case in point. With regard to this issue, his most significant contribution was expanding on Gebsattel's rather vague notion that "perversions" were related to a self-destructive drive. From Bürger-Prinz's perspective, homosexuality was more or less a character flaw, a failure of courage. He characterized it as marked by a desire to stay "in one own's bodily sphere without the risk [*Einsatz*] and self-discipline that pursuing a heterosexual relationship always demands from a man." Homosexuality was always a danger for men, therefore, that only "pedagogically sound leadership" in the course of a man's maturation could hope to avoid.[165]

Certain factors such as alcohol use and lack of intelligence could encourage men to ignore ethical demands and have their first sexual encounter with a man. Bürger-Prinz insisted, however, that a personal decision was necessary to make this first encounter the basis for the entire "style of life" that surrounded homosexuals. This life was supposedly characterized by the destructive, addictive behavior that Gebsattel had theorized as the root of perversion.[166] Instead of finding a permanent mate, homosexuals tended to find themselves locked into a cycle of promiscuity and a search for new sexual partners that absorbed more and more of their lives. To understand why an individual chose such a life, one had to examine the individual's history for the influence that his "milieu in the widest sense" had on him, which included his "family situation, personal encounters, the mental-spiritual atmosphere of the time and place [in which he lived]."[167]

Bürger-Prinz had some connections with Paul Schröder, having been taught by him at the University of Leipzig. Schröder was not himself from the phenomenological school and instead continued to work in the tradition of his teacher Emil Kraepelin. Like Kraepelin, Schröder argued that homosexuals were psychopaths who were victims of their overdeveloped sex drives. Together, Schröder and Bürger-Prinz were the most outspoken critics of the hereditary explanation of homosexuality during the Nazi period. In a 1940 essay Schröder roundly criticized the scientific research of Steinach and Hirschfeld as well as that of the hormonal researchers Lang and Deussen.[168] Bürger-Prinz took a more indirect line of attack, insisting that heredity research would be possible only after a more thorough examination of the phenomenological "structures of existence" in general. Until then, such research presented only statistics that gave no insight into the heart of the matter: "We are nowhere close to delimiting the very distinct forms of homosexual being-in-the-world [Dasein] and having their structures clear and unequivocally in sight. Only then will it be possible to define carefully the question of its hereditary factors."[169]

This skepticism of genetic research did not at all put either Bürger-Prinz or Schröder at odds with the Nazi Party. As Geoffrey Giles notes, Schröder "welcomed the expansion of the scope of Section 175 in 1935 to cover the 'most common' manifestations of homosexuality, namely 'embracing, hugging, kissing, touching and above all else mutual masturbation.' "[170] And Bürger-Prinz's ideas, as Peter von Rönn has thoroughly shown, fit in very well with the emphasis placed on the seduction thesis by the SS after 1937. He agreed with the Nazis' "firm" measures against homosexuality, which he believed would keep this acquired sexual abnormality from spreading throughout German society. Bürger-Prinz's work, after all, accentuated the role of the homosexual seducer of young men, who took advantage of fearful or impressionable adolescents at a time in their lives when they need to be mustering their courage for heterosexuality.[171] Young men, therefore, needed strong laws and rigorous police enforcement to control the public manifestations of homosexuality that might divert them from their prescribed roles as husbands and fathers.[172]

Despite the differences in opinions within the field, psychiatrists and doctors active professionally in Germany under the new regime all agreed on one thing: homosexuality was a political-criminal matter to be handled by state and Nazi Party intervention. Silenced were those voices that suggested that homosexuality was a natural sexual variation, or at worst a psychological illness that deserved medical treatment rather than legal punishment. With the power of Himmler's SS and police institutions to back it up, the German state now declared itself to have the sole competency to effectively handle this problem. Homosexuality was now *both* an illness and a criminal-political problem.[173]

HOMOSEXUALS DURING THE SECOND WORLD WAR

In September 1939 Germany went to war with Poland, Britain, and France. The war quickly widened. The Nazi war machine overran Denmark, Norway, Belgium, the Netherlands, and France quickly in the course of 1940. By 1941 Eastern Europe was also involved, as Germany invaded Yugoslavia and Greece and found allies in Romania and Bulgaria. On June 22, 1941, came the German invasion of the Soviet Union, and at the end of the year, only a few days after the Japanese bombing of Pearl Harbor, Germany declared war on the United States, too. Life on the German home front did not fundamentally change at first, as the Nazi government ensured that the German economy continued to run smoothly by exploiting conquered countries and importing forced labor.

Homosexual men, of course, would have been among those absorbed into the Nazi war machine. In the army, they could sometimes find opportunities for sexual contact with other men. Even among normally heterosexual men, sexual gratification with other men could sometimes arise from sharing close physical quarters or from the intimate relationships commonly found among soldiers. Some men might have engaged in mutual masturbation or sex between the partner's thighs out of sexual frustration without entirely understanding that this might open them up to charges of being a homosexual, as Geoffrey Giles suggests in his examination of one Waffen-SS soldier.[174] The penalties were serious for men who were caught.

Sex with men outside the military was another matter. The occupation of much of the Continent by 1940 brought opportunities for travel and for sexual contact with men in other cities. Especially in cities like Paris and Amsterdam, which already had thriving gay scenes, German soldiers could look for male prostitutes while they were off duty or cruise streets and parks for chance encounters. Much more negatively, however, homosexual activity in occupied territory could happen in the form of rape or sexual abuse of fellow soldiers, subordinates, subjected peoples, so-called racial inferiors, or inmates. In these instances, homosexual sex became part of the brutalization of war that took place everywhere, but especially on the Eastern Front.[175] Again, this activity could be found among "heterosexuals" as well as self-identified homosexuals.

Back in Germany, legal and social order gradually broke down, especially beginning in early 1943, as the general mood of the country was negatively affected by the military loss at Stalingrad and by the sharply escalating bombing raids. The effect on homosexual men was somewhat contradictory. On the one hand, the regime became increasingly savage toward its own population as it tried desperately to keep control of the country. New drumhead courts given the power of summary execution were established in the military in January 1943 to deal with armed personnel, and by 1945 these courts were extended to deal with anyone who was considered a danger to Germany's ability to continue fighting the war.[176] Criminals of all types were increasingly executed by 1945, and men caught having sex with other men—especially those in the military or the SS—were certainly not spared such brutal sentencing.

The collapse of order in the cities, however, also created opportunities for sexual encounters that had been missing since the mid-1930s. The city blackouts that became routine during the Allied raids were occasionally used as cover for gay men to meet and have sex. Encounters in public bathrooms, the most spontaneous, anonymous, and fleeting manifestation of the gay scene, had always been difficult for the Nazis to suppress, and some evidence suggests that these encounters became more frequent during the final stages of the war.

We should be careful, though, not to emphasize the sexuality of the last years of the war too much. Like all Germans, gay men suffered and died. As the bombs came down and the Allied armies advanced on both the Eastern and Western fronts, homosexual soldiers were shot, captured by the Allied forces, and put into POW camps. Those left on the home front suffered along with everyone else as buildings were destroyed, food and coal shortages became common, and escape from the cities into the countryside became necessary. They watched with some mixture of remorse, fear, grief, and relief as their nation lost yet another world war.

In the twelve years that they ruled Germany, the Nazis arrested perhaps as many as 100,000 homosexuals, of whom around half served some time in prison.[177] Thousands died; countless others had their lives destroyed. Although lesbians were not persecuted with nearly the same intensity as gay men were, the lives that many had created in the Weimar era were uprooted by the Nazi hunt against so-called perversion and by this party's emphasis on reproduction and traditional families. The Nazi Party was riven by divisions and inconsistencies, both ideologically and when it came to government practice, which meant that there were gay men and lesbians who managed to get through the era relatively unscathed, especially if they were willing to suppress their sexual lives and to find jobs that made contributions to Nazi goals. Still, even conservative and nationalist homosexuals who might have hoped in 1933 that Röhm's prominent position in the party would guarantee a degree of tolerance were sorely disappointed. After Röhm's murder in 1934, the SS, the Gestapo, and the local police cooperated to use a greatly strengthened Paragraph 175 to destroy the institutions and social networks of the gay scene and homosexual movement.

After the fall of Nazism, memories of the Nazi era lingered for some time and tended to reinforce prejudices against homosexuality well into the 1950s. In their propaganda and through their police persecution, the Nazis had reinforced public associations among homosexuality, criminality, and medical illness. The new governments of East and West Germany would do little at first to cause people to question these associations. Nazi-era convictions were upheld by postwar courts. Those men who tried to register with the West German government as official victims of Nazism, thereby receiving compensation payments for their suffering, were at first all told that as "mere criminals" they did not qualify. Even after 1957, when a new law was passed that did allow them to register, such severe limits were put on the process that only fourteen ended up applying.[178] In both East and West Germany, Paragraph 175 would remain in force (though in slightly different versions). Well into the 1950s, Röhm would still be publicly cited as evidence that gay men were politically unreliable and tended toward conspiracies. Parents would remind their children of neighborhood men who had disappeared one day as a warning of the fate that awaited homosexuals.[179]

Very few of the men who had survived the camps went on to tell their stories afterward. The conservative climate of the 1950s was not at all hospitable to this. The main media outlets never discussed such topics, except by the vaguest allusions, until the second half of the 1960s, and even the few homosexual publications that appeared after 1945 rarely did so. A few men might have unburdened themselves to close friends or relatives, but most seem to have agreed tacitly to leave such unpleasantness behind them.[180] But the memories of persecution were not entirely gone, and in the 1960s they would be revived as part of a larger New Left critique about the sexually repressive nature of life in the capitalist West.

Many changes did take place after 1945, of course. The concentration camps were gone. In the East, "antifascism" became the watchword of the day. In the West, the limitations that accompanied the "legal state" (*Rechtsstaat*) were restored. Many gay men and lesbians were hopeful that the postwar world would once again create the possibility for more tolerance and real legal change.

CONCLUSION

Gay and Lesbian Life after 1945

CHAPTER SUMMARY

This chapter considers the evolution of LGBTQ life and politics after the demise of the Nazi regime. In both East Germany and West Germany, the long history of LGBTQ life and politics continued to be felt—in the gay scenes that reemerged after the war, in the various political movements that eventually reappeared, in the scientific theories of sexuality that continued to evolve, and in the different sexual identities that LGBTQ individuals adopted.

OVERVIEW

This chapter serves as an epilogue to the book; it considers the evolution of LGBTQ life and politics after the demise of the Nazi regime. The abilities to find relationships, to organize socially and politically, and to develop a sexual identity were very much affected by whether one lived in East Germany or West Germany. In the latter, the government for a long time actually retained the Nazi-era version of Paragraph 175, meaning that prior convictions were upheld and thousands more found themselves arrested in the coming decades. New gay scenes and a new homosexual movement did emerge, but it took some time before they had the vitality of their 1920s counterparts. In East Germany, on the other hand, the law against male homosexuality was initially less stringent and was rarely enforced after 1957. The conditions of communism, however, made it impossible to build gay scenes as vibrant as those that existed in West Germany or to organize a movement that could fight for homosexual rights. Moreover, East German sexual culture remained focused on high birth rates, "healthy" families, and a conservative vision of socialist manhood in a way that left little room for public LGBTQ life.

In the 1960s much began to change. Both countries removed their laws against consensual adult male homosexuality. The sexual revolution generated a new openness toward sexual relationships that did not fit the norm. By the 1980s homosexual activists in both East Germany and West Germany began to memorialize homosexual victims of Nazi persecution, suggesting that this era of brutality was being reclaimed and refashioned into an emblem of survival and strength. The unification of Germany in 1990 and the creation of the European Union shortly afterward laid the groundwork for achieving new rights and protections for LGBTQ people in Germany.

KEY TERMS

Hans Giese; homosexuality in West German history; homosexuality in East German history; sexual revolution in Germany; memorials to homosexual victims of Nazi persecution

Whisnant, Clayton J.

Queer Identities and Politics in Germany: A History 1880–1945

dx.doi.org/10.17312/harringtonparkpress/2016.08.qipg.00b

© Harrington Park Press, LLC, New York, NY 10011

FIGURE 18 **HANS GIESE**

The phenomenological psychiatrist and sexologist Hans Giese became one of the most famous personalities in the post–World War II struggle against Paragraph 175. His opposition to pornography laws and his studies on student sexuality also made him a well-known spokesman for the 1960s sexual revolution. This chapter considers the evolution of LGBTQ life and politics after the demise of the Nazi regime. The abilities to find relationships, to organize socially and politically, and to develop a sexual identity were very much affected by whether one lived in East or West Germany. On both sides of the divide, though, the long history of LGBTQ life and politics in Germany continued to be felt—in the gay scenes that reemerged after the war, in the various political movements that eventually reappeared, in the scientific theories of sexuality that continued to evolve, and in the different sexual identities that were adopted by LGBTQ individuals. Source: Courtesy of Gunter Schmidt, Hamburg

In April 1949 a twenty-eight-year-old doctor and aspiring sexologist from Frankfurt named Hans Giese (Figure 18) founded the new Institute for Sexual Research. Though clearly inspired by Hirschfeld, Giese's new institute was much more modest, to say the least: no palatial mansion, no clinical staff, no medical facilities to carry out research, certainly no museum to attract tourists. In fact, it really was just a small psychiatric practice, housed in his parents' apartment building, that Giese hoped to use as a springboard to do his own research. Surprisingly, Giese had been a member of the Nazi Party. The exact level of his engagement with the party is not yet known, though we can say at least that he was acquitted by the local tribunal (*Spruchkammer*) put in charge of the denazification process.[1] He first got a degree in philosophy and then, under pressure from his parents, pursued medicine. According to his sister, he probably had had homosexual encounters during puberty, and the medical dissertation that he completed in 1946 was entitled "The Forms of Male Homosexuality" (*Die Formen männlicher Homosexualität*).[2] It was hard to get a permanent position with this degree, but his father—who held a prominent chair in the law school of Frankfurt's Goethe University—had connections that allowed him to eke out a living for the next few years.

By 1949 Giese had clearly set his mind on trying to step into the big shoes left by Hirschfeld. Besides the Institute for Sexual Research, he also contacted *The Circle* (*Der Kreis*), a gay magazine that was published in Switzerland but had readers across Europe (and eventually worldwide), with a notice that he was trying to refound the WhK. This effort was stillborn, but in 1950 he organized the first major postwar conference for sexology in Germany and soon afterward became the chair for a newly created German Society for Sexual Research. He established a new academic journal, the *Journal of Sexual Research* (*Zeitschrift für Sexualforschung*) and, in 1953, a new monograph series entitled Contributions toward Sexual Research (*Beiträge zur Sexualforschung*). He published his first major work, *The Homosexual Man in the World* (*Der homosexuelle Mann in der Welt*), in 1958, which allowed him to find a more permanent academic position at the University of Hamburg. By the end of the 1960s, he had catapulted into the public eye as both a prominent voice in favor of liberal legal reform and a researcher documenting the changing sexual behaviors and attitudes of the decade.[3]

Giese might have seen himself as inheriting Hirschfeld's mantle, but he was a very different person. Struggling with depression much of his life, he was attracted early on to the angst-ridden philosophy of Martin Heidegger rather than the self-assured Enlightenment exhibited by Hirschfeld's works. His own research, in fact, was derived not from biologically based psychiatry at all but instead from the phenomenological psychotherapy of Viktor von

Gebsattel and Hans Bürger-Prinz. It fused together the sociological methods being championed in the United States, which were often based on extensive questionnaires circulated among the population and which he was then studying, with a phenomenological attention to language and an interest in letting his subjects "speak for themselves." Like Gebsattel and Bürger-Prinz, he was a little skeptical of the "destructive tendencies" exhibited by many forms of sexuality. Unlike many in the phenomenological school, though, he firmly believed that these tendencies could be countered by a loving commitment between two individuals, whether they were homosexual or heterosexual.[4]

Needless to say, many things had indeed changed after 1945. In every imaginable dimension, Germany was left in ruins. Cities had been leveled, industries and ports bombed repeatedly. Over seven million Germans had died, and much of the remaining population was uprooted by the physical destruction. Occupied by the victor nations, Germany was divided into East and West by 1949. In the eastern German Democratic Republic, the Communist Party emerged as dominant and by the early 1950s had begun the country's transformation toward a Soviet-style economic and political regime. In the Western-aligned Federal Republic of Germany a democratic constitution was written. The country began to rebuild, thanks to aid from the United States and massive cooperation with other European countries. By the early 1950s, evidence of the so-called economic miracle was clearly evident, paving the way for Germany to become the world economic power that it is today. It is easy, however, to forget how long evidence of the earlier destruction remained in many of the cities, especially Berlin. Even in the mid-1950s, vast, empty spaces where buildings had once stood and burnt-out government offices and train stations remained in Berlin to remind people of the recent past.[5]

In Berlin this landscape was haunted by memories of days gone by—not only of the war and Nazi oppression, but also of the chaotic times of the 1920s and even earlier. Such memories informed the lives of leaders and average Berliners alike, as Jennifer Evans has shown in her fascinating study *Life among the Ruins*.[6] Gay men and lesbians generally hoped for a return to the exciting time of the 1920s, and they were no doubt encouraged briefly in 1946 and 1947 by the difficulties of legal enforcement, the administrative confusion, and the opportunities for sexual contact amid the rubble, even with occupying Allied soldiers.[7] Such hopes, however, were quickly stifled by the return to economic and political stability. Anxieties about marital stability, birth rates, the mental state of Germans coming out of years of fascism and war, and dangerous "fraternizations" with occupying soldiers infused much public discussion during the late 1940s, which paved the way for a sexually conservative culture to take shape in West Germany in the following decade.[8] In East Germany the weakness of the Christian churches and the Communist Party's efforts to expand women's rights meant that this country's sexual norms would look very different. Here too, though, various social anxieties, along with the communist belief that "sexual decadence" was linked with fascism and capitalist oppression, produced a less-than-adventurous sexual climate.[9]

The related fields of psychiatry and sexology changed in subtle but significant ways. The biological school remained dominant in the 1950s, and there were a few voices out there—most notably East Germany's Rudolf Klimmer, director of Dresden's Polyclinic—who argued against the criminalization of homosexuality by suggesting that it had natural causes.[10] Phenomenological psychiatry had clearly gained in strength over the past two decades, however, and after 1945 Freudian-based psychoanalysis also made a slow comeback. American-based social psychology, as well as the social-scientific-based research of Alfred Kinsey, also got much attention. The result was that biologically based psychiatry faced many new challengers. In the gay scene, there were individuals who tried to revive Hirschfeld's old arguments. But signs were visible that a decade of abuse under National Socialism had taken a toll on the faith that many gay men and lesbians once attached to science. Quite a number voiced some skepticism about whether medical research could produce legal reform or end prejudice. This doubt is not surprising given the way that medical language had been worked into the popular vernacular by midcentury, linking homosexuality in many people's minds with illness. Certainly many men and women who experienced homosexual desires to some considerable degree continued to seek out medical advice and psychiatric treatment with the hope of overcoming their urges. Hirschfeld's work, however, with its Darwinian language and eugenic sympathies, seemed very out of place in the post-Nazi era. Those who looked to science for self-understanding increasingly preferred psychoanalytic, phenomenological, and social-psychological arguments.[11]

Very few of the familiar faces of the Weimar-era homosexual movement reemerged after 1945. Many were—quite simply—dead. Friedrich Radszuweit, as we mentioned earlier, had passed away in 1932. Linsert died of an illness in 1933. Hirschfeld had finished his world tour and then moved about Europe for a few years, eventually settling down in southern France. He remained close to his assistant and lover, Karl Giese (no relation to Hans Giese). He also developed an intimate relationship with a young Chinese medical student named Tao Li. Hirschfeld continued writing and otherwise kept busy with people he loved and who loved him back until he died from a heart attack in 1935.[12] Adolf Brand, amazingly, made it through most of the Nazi era alive, despite losing his business. He died in 1945 during an Allied bombing raid.[13]

Those who did survive sometimes remained active but with less success than they had had previously. Hans Blüher was still alive and crankier than ever. Continuing to believe that he was fundamentally misunderstood, he wrote one last work that was largely ignored and an autobiography before dying in Berlin in 1955. Lotte Hahm was also still in Berlin. She led a small women's group in the city, and in 1958 she was connected with a failed attempt to refound the BfM.[14] Claire Waldoff had left Berlin and settled in Bavaria. She lost all her savings during the currency reform of 1948. Her performances could still draw in huge crowds, but her health kept her from working regularly. Haunted by financial troubles, she died of a stroke in early 1957.[15] Kurt Hiller, despite his socialist affiliations and Jewish background, had also survived the Nazi era. He had been released from the concentration camps in 1934 and had wisely left Germany. After a period in exile in Czechoslovakia and then Britain, he returned in 1955 to live the last days of his life in Hamburg. He was involved with two short-lived attempts to revive the WhK—one in the early 1950s, and a second in the early 1960s. In both cases, though, Hiller proved to be a divisive factor. One of the men involved in the second effort recalled with some frustration, "I was familiar with Kurt Hiller's activism even before 1933 and I respected him greatly. . . . But Hiller was monstrously contentious his entire life."[16] Neither attempt got very far.

It was generally younger men who came to the fore in the decades after the war. Giese might have failed in his attempt to rebuild the WhK, but others would dive into the effort to build a new homosexual movement. Giese had some contact with one of the earliest organizations, Frankfurt's Association for a Humane Way of Life (*Verein für humanitäre Lebensgestaltung*), established by Heinz Meininger and modeled quite clearly on the friendship clubs that had been so prominent during the 1920s. In West Berlin the Society for the Reform of Sexual Law (*Gesellschaft für Reform des Sexualrechts*) registered with the city authorities in July 1951. Hamburg's Club of Friends (*Club der Freunde*) was organized by Johannes Dörrast, who simultaneously began to publish one of the first postwar homosexual magazines, *The Friends* (*Die Freunde*). In Bremen several anti-Nazi resistance activists established the International Friendship Lodge (*Internationale Freundschaftsloge*), which was connected with its own magazine, *The Island* (*Die Insel*)—a name clearly designed to remind people of Friedrich Radszuweit's entertainment magazine with the same title. The most successful of the organizations, though, was the Society for Human Rights (*Gesellschaft für Menschenrechte*), which by 1953 was led by Erwin Haarmann, the editor for another one of West Germany's gay magazines.[17] These "homophile" organizations—to use a word that picked up traction in homosexual circles in the 1950s and 1960s—were similar to the Mattachine Society in the United States and other groups internationally insofar as they generally advocated winning social acceptance through a strategy of respectability. Historians have generally seen this strategy as a response to the conservative, family-oriented climate of the Cold War years, but in Germany at least there is another story involved. As we have seen, it was already a strategy being championed by Radszuweit's press during the 1920s.

The magazines associated with the homophile movement were similar in many ways to those of the 1920s. *The Friends, The Island, The Path (Der Weg), The Fellows (Die Gefährten), The Ring (Der Ring)*, and *The Voice (Vox)* all included a mix of essays, romantic stories, poems, pictures, and personal ads. Only *Humanitas* stood out as something different—more serious and political and containing very little fluff. Readers who were old enough to remember the 1920s would have found much to make them nostalgic. References to Thomas Mann, Stefan George, and other figures of the "gay canon" were not uncommon. Even many of the photographs were taken in natural settings that made clear classical references to Wilhelm von Gloeden and Adolf Brand. Whether readers were disturbed at all by the amount of Nazi-era art (especially by Arno Breker and Leni Riefenstahl) that was reproduced in these postwar periodicals is harder to say. The clearest departures were the bodybuilder photographs and American-style "beefcake" drawings that became increasingly common by the middle of the decade.[18]

Unfortunately, hardly any of the West German homophile organizations lasted more than a few years, and none of the magazines ever had the success that Radszuweit's press had enjoyed. The revival of the old Law to Protect Youth against Trash and Smut in the form of the 1953 Law against the Distribution of Written Material Endangering Youth made it very difficult for any of the new homosexual publishers to get a toehold in the market.[19] Only *The Path to Friendship and Tolerance (Der Weg zu Freundschaft und Toleranz)* survived through the 1960s. In its final year *The Path* had a print run of only about four hundred copies per issue. Nevertheless, what is easy to miss if we focus too much on the weakness of the German homophile movement is that, at an international level, a network of associations and publications was finally appearing, led by the International Congress of Sexual Equality and encompassing groups across Western Europe and the United States. It had taken some time, but Hirschfeld's dream of an international movement for sexual reform was finally taking shape.[20]

Women, however, were noticeably less visible in the postwar movement than they had been during the 1920s, at least in Germany. There were some brief attempts to reestablish lesbian periodicals. The publisher of *The Friends* put out a sister magazine, *We Girlfriends (Wir Freundinnen)*, edited by Mary

Roland, who had been a regular in the 1920s Berlin scene. Very much modeled on 1920s publications such as *Girlfriend* and *The Bachelor Girl*, the magazine included poems, romance stories, personal ads, beauty advice, and photographs of nude and semi-nude women. In 1956 there was also a cheap insert called *Aphrodite* that was included briefly with *The Ring* (*Der Ring*), another of the short-lived gay magazines of the 1950s.[21] From the evidence available, though, none of the homophile organizations made as concerted an effort to organize women as Radszuweit's BfM had during the 1920s. The lesbian scenes were also noticeably less well developed than they had been before 1933.

In contrast, the male gay scenes reemerged rapidly. Berlin's scene was quieter, certainly, given the extent of the city's destruction and the Cold War pressure that its citizens lived under. Hamburg's scene, on the other hand, took off. From the red-light district of St. Pauli to the bars and hotels near the central train station, to the somewhat classier area around Grossneumarkt square, gay men were able to find plenty of restaurants, bars, and nightclubs. By 1954 there were no fewer than seventeen gay establishments in Hamburg.[22] This number grew to twenty-four in 1959, and then to thirty by 1964.[23] Whether it was the city's reputation for tolerance that turned Hamburg into the nation's center for gay life for about a decade and half or simply the fact that most of the country's gay publishing was located in the city is hard to say.[24] We should note that Hannover and Cologne also saw their gay scenes revive, and Munich, Frankfurt, and Stuttgart each developed a livelier scene than had existed even in the 1920s. By the end of the 1960s, West Berlin's scene had also picked up; the police estimated that there were at least thirty-eight gay bars, cafés, and nightclubs operating in this sector of the city.[25] Berlin was fast reestablishing its reputation as being one of the metropoles of European gay life.

By this point, West Germany was in the midst of the sexual revolution— or what Germans call the "sex wave" (*Sexwelle*). After the relatively conservative decade of the 1950s, public norms about sexuality began to be challenged on a number of levels around 1962. A major censorship case involving a German-language edition of Jean Genet's *Our Lady of the Flowers* (*Notre Dame des Fleurs*) paved the way for sexually explicit material to be published as long as it had artistic or educational worth.[26] Popular magazines such as *Quick* and *Revue* took the chance to begin printing articles on sex education, nudism, and topless sunbathing, often with risqué photos to attract readers. Building on her earlier success in the mail order business, Beate Uhse opened up her first brick-and-mortar "marital aid" store in Flensburg in 1962.[27] Public debates about the utility and morality of maintaining criminal laws banning certain kinds of sexual behavior picked up: lawyers, scientists, writers, and even prominent church figures spoke up for the modernization of the West German criminal code. New, youthful styles of dress, behavior, music, and language that subtly accentuated physical attractiveness and sexuality gradually worked their way into the culture. And by the mid-1960s the student movement and the youth counterculture were just the most obvious signs that many young people in general were taking on a more relaxed attitude toward birth control, premarital sex, and public nudity.[28]

East Germany was also going through a sexual revolution of sorts by the 1960s. State-controlled media and the lack of a free market meant that this revolution was necessarily less commercialized than the one that happened in the West. The near impossibility of organizing political and social institutions free from party control also meant that there could be no East German version of the homophile movement. Still, nude sunbathing became a common sight on East German beaches, and nude photos began to be printed in state-sponsored publications. The Communist Party embraced "healthy" sexuality as a natural part of young life and one of the freedoms that could be safely enjoyed by a socialist population.[29] And when it came to the criminal prosecution of homosexuality, East Germany was far ahead of its western counterpart. A revision to the criminal code in 1957 made Paragraph 175 for all practical purposes null and void; it was finally repealed entirely in July 1968.[30] The East German Communist Party, however, remained focused on birth rates, "healthy" family life, and "socialist manhood," so that the country was still not a very welcoming place for gay men and lesbians. As Josie McLellan puts it in her recent book, *Love in the Time of Communism*, "gay men . . . had won the right to have sex in private, but faced sometimes insurmountable difficulties in meeting potential partners, finding suitable living space, building a social life, and coming out to family and friends."[31]

In West Germany, Paragraph 175 lasted a little longer. Surprisingly, perhaps, it was the Nazi-era version of Paragraph 175 (along with its 1935 addendum, 175a) that had continued to be enforced during the 1950s and 1960s. It was one of the few Nazi-era laws that was not overturned or rewritten shortly after the war. Even East Germany originally reverted to the earlier version of the law.[32] The West German government made no apology to the homosexual men and women who had been incarcerated in Nazi camps; the legal establishment viewed them as criminals who had been justly punished. Homophile activists made much of this fact in their arguments against criminalization. A leader of Bremen's International Friendship Lodge insisted that the law's survival was a clear sign that "the century-old spirit of blind obedience and standing-at-attention [*Strammstehergeist*], as well as the dictatorship of uniforms and bureaucratic stamp-wielders, has not yet come to an end."[33] The concentration camps might have been gone, but the police still used whatever legal methods were at their disposal to catch offenders. The result was that West German arrest rates were much higher through most of the 1950s and 1960s than they had been during the Weimar era.[34] Nevertheless, in the early 1960s a considerable debate broke out in political and professional circles about the value of Paragraph 175. By the end of the decade, even many members of the conservative Christian Democratic Union (CDU) were turning against the law. As part of a larger effort to revise the criminal code to bring it in line with modern standards of justice, the German government revised the law on June 25, 1969, to make consensual sex between two adult men legal.[35] (The aggravated cases previously contained in Paragraph 175a were maintained for the time being, though.) It was further revised in 1973 to lower the age of consent, remove the penalization of male prostitution, and rewrite the prejudiced language of the earlier version. The last vestiges were finally repealed for good in 1994, in the wake of German reunification.

There is no doubt that the 1969 reform of Paragraph 175 proved to be an important turning point for gay life in West Germany. Gay scenes flourished; gay bathhouses appeared almost overnight, and by the mid-1970s gay pornography shops, gay and lesbian bookstores, and gay discos became prominent features. Gay neighborhoods comparable to San Francisco's Castro district appeared: Schöneberg and Kreuzberg in West Berlin, St. Georg in Hamburg, the Glockenbachviertel in Munich. Gay scenes have changed in ways that not everyone has seen as positive. As these scenes became larger and more commercialized, some older gay men and lesbians may have grown nostalgic about the more intimate opportunities for mixing and community that existed in the pre-1969 era.[36] These scenes certainly became more thoroughly "gay," as the sexual revolution, along with the growing attention paid to homosexuality in the public media, made it actually less likely that "heterosexual" boys would go cruising for the occasional release. And some men who, like the group in Adolf Brand's circle of friends, had previously been defined as homosexual but who really sought sex only with teenage boys have been redefined as pedophiles and marginalized to a significant degree.

The year 1969 was also a turning point when it came to gay and lesbian politics. Gay student groups emerged in the universities. Young radicals, inspired by student activism and the news of the Stonewall Riots in New York City, found themselves energized. They founded a new gay liberation movement in the 1970s to champion gay pride, fight for gay rights, and build community infrastructure. A decade of demonstrations set the stage for the institutionalization of Christopher Street Day parades in Berlin, Hamburg,

Cologne, and other major German cities beginning in 1979.[37] Lesbian activism also reemerged as a powerful political current, although it became much more closely allied with the feminist movement than it had been even at the turn of the century. By the mid-1970s, lesbians were an integral aspect of "autonomous" feminism, as the historian Myra Ferree calls it. Loving women emotionally and physically seemed a logical extension of the project to build autonomous social and political institutions that affirmed women's collective power and freed them from male influence.[38]

Gay and lesbian activism in East Germany was naturally more subdued, but even here there were small groups that began to organize, at first quietly, but in the 1980s more openly, with the support of the East German Protestant church.[39] Public treatment of homosexuality in the East German press became more tolerant and liberal. Roadblocks erected by the state to halt public demonstrations of gay identity, however, not to mention constant secret police surveillance of even private social gatherings, demonstrated the real challenges to coming out in East Germany.[40]

In both East and West Germany, the politics of memory became an important focus for gay and lesbian activists by the 1980s. In West Germany a cadre of historians connected with the gay liberation movement began to do work on gay and lesbian history. Understanding the persecution of homosexuals under Nazism became an especially important aspect of this work. Beginning with the 1972 publication of Heinz Heger's memoir, *The Men with the Pink Triangle,* the pink triangle was increasingly used by gay liberation activists as an important symbol of collective identity, a reminder of the dangers of remaining silent in the face of oppression.[41] In East Germany separate groups laid wreaths at the Buchenwald camp memorial in July 1983 and the Ravensbrück camp memorial in March 1984. A more coordinated ceremony planned for June 1984—to coincide with West German Christopher Street Day celebrations—was all but smothered by the intervention of the secret police.[42] In West Germany memorial stones and plaques were set up at the sites of the old concentration camps of Dachau and Neuengamme in the mid-1980s, and in Berlin at Nollendorfplatz subway station in 1989. The Frankfurt Angel was inaugurated in 1994, Cologne's Pink Triangle memorial stone in 1995. Berlin's Memorial to Homosexuals Persecuted under Nazism—a large concrete block with a window that viewers can look through to see a film of two men or two women kissing—was unveiled in 2008.[43] Similar memorials have gone up in Amsterdam, Bologna, Turin, Barcelona, San Francisco, New York, Montevideo, and quite recently Tel Aviv. These memorials are good evidence for the continuing power of the memory of Nazi persecution for the LGBTQ community worldwide. As the historian Erik

Jensen has suggested, however, this memory has acquired different inflections in different national contexts. And even within Germany, the effort to honor those persecuted under Nazism has often proved quite divisive, highlighting just some of the fractures that exist within the contemporary LGBTQ community.[44]

For example, issues of identity, so contentious in the years between 1880 and 1945, as we have seen, have not grown any simpler. If anything, they have perhaps become more complex. The appearance of leathermen in the early 1950s was a portent of the changes that would be wrought by consumerism and the influence of American popular culture.[45] Immigration has created racial and ethnic diversity at a level difficult to imagine in Germany before 1945, while the lingering effects of a nation long divided into two countries can also be felt. For several decades after the war, medical science and modern psychiatry continued to leave a powerful mark on both the prejudices and identities attached to same-sex desire, but since the early 1970s sociology, psychoanalysis, poststructuralist theory, and more recently queer theory have taken their place.

During the 1990s, many radical activists carrying on the legacy of 1970s gay liberation watched with some concern as the impetus for thoroughgoing social change began to fade from the movement. The Marxism that had served as the basis for the earlier social radicalism lost much of its appeal with the collapse of communism in East Germany, and the broader "alternative milieu" that had channeled so much energy into the gay liberation movement became professionalized and increasingly pragmatic, cooperating more and more with other organizations and institutions.[46] The result was that the politics of respectability, pioneered by Friedrich Radszuweit's BfM in the 1920s and championed by homophiles in the 1950s, began to reemerge as a viable option. The fight for gay marriage, which in Germany had its first step toward success with the Life Partnership Law of 2001, has been the most visible aspect of what Lisa Duggan and others have called the new "homonormativity." Underneath, however, critics have seen deeper forces at work: businesses that are excited to target so-called pink money, and neoliberals in search of safe social compromises that can stabilize a new post–Cold War economic order.[47]

Such leftist criticism has been increasingly marginalized, however, by some real political achievements in gaining new rights and protections for LGBTQ people. European Union politics has been very important in this respect. The ratification of the Amsterdam Treaty in 1999 signaled the European Union's willingness to champion gay and lesbian rights, echoing a larger shift that was taking place at the cultural level. What the anthropologist Matti Bunzl observes about 1990s Austria could easily be said about Germany, namely, that "a set of criminalizing and pathologizing stereotypes" was gradually replaced by an "assemblage of affirmative representations."[48] Given the public affirmations of the European LGBTQ community, it is unfortunately too easy to ignore the prejudice and everyday violence that LGBTQ persons can still suffer. As Matt Cook and Jennifer Evans have recently argued, the public image of the European Union as a sexually progressive paradise may be "more myth than reality."[49] Still, to return to Bunzl's argument, there is no doubt that the public affirmations have fundamentally changed the conditions in which LGBTQ persons have formed their identities, announced those identities to the world around them, and interacted with people afterward.[50]

This book began with a set of questions rather than a thesis. Since it is a survey rather than a monograph—and none of the questions are ones that have easy answers—I do not want to answer them for you now. I do hope that the material presented has given you a chance to think about important issues: How are identities formed? How can LGBTQ politics be pursued? How can LGBTQ communities be formed, and then how do they function afterward? How can challenges such as persecution and violence be faced? These are just some of the questions that were integral to queer German history during the formative years of the homosexual movement and urban scenes, and they are, of course, critical questions that are still with us today. It is an era of LGBTQ history that is often remembered as a warning—"Beaten to Death, Silenced to Death" (*Totgeschlagen, Totgeschweigen*), as it says on the Sachsenhausen Memorial Plaque. But there is also much here to be proud of and to take as an inspiration.

NOTES

NOTES TO THE INTRODUCTION

1   The "Q" in LGBTQ is also sometimes taken to mean "questioning."

2   Since I will discuss works on Germany later on, I will list only non-German books here. An exhaustive list would take up pages at this point, but good places to begin for English-language readers include George Chauncey, *Gay New York: Gender, Urban Culture, and the Makings of the Gay Male World, 1890–1940* (New York: Basic Books, 1994); Charles Kaiser, *The Gay Metropolis, 1940–1996* (Boston: Houghton Mifflin, 1997); Nan Boyd, *Wide-Open Town: A History of Queer San Francisco to 1965* (Berkeley: University of California Press, 2003); Lillian Faderman and Stuart Timmons, *Gay L.A.: A History of Sexual Outlaws, Power Politics, and Lipstick Lesbians* (New York: Basic Books, 2006); Michael Bronski, *A Queer History of the United States* (Boston: Beacon Press, 2011); Jeffrey Weeks, *Coming Out: Homosexual Politics in Britain from the Nineteenth Century to the Present* (London: Quartet Books, 1977); Matt Cook, *London and the Culture of Homosexuality, 1885–1914* (Cambridge: Cambridge University Press, 2003); Matt Houlbrook, *Queer London: Perils and Pleasures in the Sexual Metropolis, 1918–1957* (Chicago: University of Chicago Press, 2005); Dan Healey, *Homosexual Desire in Revolutionary Russia: The Regulation of Sexual and Gender Dissent* (Chicago: University of Chicago Press, 2001); Scott Gunther, *The Elastic Closet: A History of Homosexuality in France, 1942–Present* (New York: Palgrave Macmillan, 2008); Julian Jackson, *Living in Arcadia: Homosexuality, Politics, and Morality in France from the Liberation to AIDS* (Chicago: University of Chicago Press, 2009); Richard Cleminson and Francisco Vasquez Garcia, *"Los Invisibles": A History of Male Homosexuality in Spain, 1850–1939* (Cardiff: University of Wales Press, 2007); Matt Cook and Jennifer Evans, eds., *Queer Cities, Queer Cultures: Europe since 1945* (London: Bloomsbury, 2014); David Greenberg, *The Construction of Homosexuality* (Chicago: University of Chicago Press, 1988); K. J. Dover, *Greek Homosexuality* (Cambridge: Harvard University Press, 1978); David Halperin, *One Hundred Years of Homosexuality and Other Essays on Greek Love* (New York: Routledge, 1990); Dror Ze'evi, *Producing Desire: Changing Sexual Discourse in the Ottoman Middle East, 1500–1900* (Berkeley: University of California Press, 2006); Khaled El-Rouayheb, *Before Homosexuality in the Arab-Islamic World, 1500–1800* (Chicago: University of Chicago Press, 2005); Wu Cuncun, *Homoerotic Sensibilities in Late Imperial China* (New York: Routledge, 2004).

3   Joanne Meyerowitz, *How Sex Changed: A History of Transsexuality in the United States* (Cambridge: Harvard University Press, 2002); Susan Stryker, *Transgender History* (Berkeley: Seal Press, 2008).

4   James Steakley, *The Homosexual Emancipation Movement in Germany* (New York: Arno Press, 1975); Richard Plant, *The Pink Triangle: The Nazi War against Homosexuals* (New York: Henry Holt, 1986); Günter Grau, "Persecution, 'Re-education' or 'Eradication' of Male Homosexuals between 1933 and 1945: Consequences of the Eugenic Concept of Assured Reproduction," in *Hidden Holocaust? Gay and Lesbian Persecution in Germany, 1933–45*, ed. Günter Grau, trans. Patrick Camiller (Chicago: Fitzroy Dearborn, 1993), 1–7; Michael Burleigh and Wolfgang Wippermann, *The Racial State: Germany, 1933–1945* (Cambridge: Cambridge University Press, 1991), 182–97; Geoffrey Giles, "The Institutionalization of Homosexual Panic in the Third Reich," in *Social Outsiders in Nazi Germany*, ed. Robert Gellately and Nathan Stoltzfus (Princeton: Princeton University Press, 2001), 233–355; Stefan Micheler, "Homophobic Propaganda and the Denunciation of Same-Sex-Desiring Men under National Socialism," in *Sexuality and German Fascism*, ed. Dagmar Herzog (New York: Berghahn Books, 2005), 95–130; Robert Beachy, *Gay Berlin: Birthplace of a Modern Identity* (New York: Alfred A. Knopf, 2014); Laurie Marhoefer, *Sex and the Weimar Republic: German Homosexual Emancipation and the Rise of the Nazis* (Toronto: University of Toronto Press, 2015).

5   Martina Schuler, "Frauenarchive und Frauenbibliotheken," *Bibliothek: Forschung und Praxis* 20, no. 2 (1996): 348–64.

6   Douglas Blair Turnbaugh, "The Schwules Museum," *Journal of Performance and Art* 22, no. 2 (2000): 48.

7   Gisela Bleibtreu-Ehrenberg, *Tabu Homosexualität* (Frankfurt: Fischer, 1978); Bernd-Ulrich Hergemöller, *Sodom and Gomorrah: On the Everyday Reality and Persecution of Homosexuals in the Middle*

Ages, trans. John Phillips (London: Free Association Books, 2001). Though I will not discuss it any further here, I should mention in this context that there is also a quickly growing literature on gay and lesbian life as it existed in East Germany.

8   Outside a few earlier essays, the first major scholarly treatment of this topic came in 1977 with several essays in Rüdiger Lautmann, ed., *Seminar: Gesellschaft und Homosexualität* (Frankfurt am Main: Suhrkamp, 1977). Another classic in the field is Plant, *The Pink Triangle.* The number of works since the 1990s are too many to list here, but a good sampling is provided in Burkhard Jellonnek and Rüdiger Lautmann, eds., *Nationalsozialistischer Terror gegen Homosexuelle* (Paderborn: Ferdinand Schöningh, 2002).

9   Pathbreaking works include John Lauritson and David Thorstad, *The Early Homosexual Rights Movement (1864–1935)* (New York: Times Change, 1974); Steakley, *The Homosexual Emancipation Movement;* and Jonathan Katz, ed., *Documents of the Homosexual Rights Movement in Germany, 1836–1927* (New York: Arno Press, 1975). For more recent work on Ulrichs, see Hubert Kennedy, *Ulrichs: The Life and Works of Karl Heinrich Ulrichs, Pioneer of the Modern Gay Movement* (Boston: Alyson Publications, 1988); or Volkmar Sigusch, *Karl Heinrich Ulrichs: Der erste Schwule der Weltgeschichte* (Berlin: Rosa Winkel, 2000).

10 Steakley, *The Homosexual Emancipation Movement;* Manfred Baumgardt, "Die Homosexuellen-Bewegung bis zum Ende des Ersten Weltkrieges," in *Eldorado: Homosexuelle Frauen und Männer in Berlin, 1850–1950: Geschichte, Alltag und Kultur,* ed. Michael Bollé (Berlin: Frölich and Kaufmann, 1984), 17–27; Joachim Hohmann, ed., *Der Eigene: Ein Querschnitt durch die erste Homosexuellen-zeitschrift der Welt* (Berlin: Foerster, 1981); and the essays on the movement by Manfred Herzer and Andreas Sternweiler in *Goodbye to Berlin? 100 Jahre Schwulenbewegung,* ed. Schwules Museum (Berlin: Rosa Winkel, 1997).

11 This topic has not been as richly researched for Germany as it has been in the Anglo-American world, but it still has produced some interesting works: see Wolfgang Theis and Andreas Sternweiler, "Alltag im Kaiserreich und in der Weimarer Republik," in Bollé, *Eldorado,* 48–73; the essays in Cornelia Limpricht, Jürgen Müller, and Nina Oxenius, eds., *"Verführte" Männer: Das Leben der Kölner Homosexuellen im dritten Reich* (Cologne: Volksblatt, 1991); those in Kristof Balser, Mario Kramp, Jürgen Müller, and Joanna Gotzmann, eds., *"Himmel und Hölle": Das Leben der Kölner Homosexuellen, 1945–1969* (Cologne: Emons, 1994); Adele Meyer, *Lila Nächte: Die Damenklubs im Berlin der zwanziger Jahre* (Berlin: Lit Europe, 1994); Clayton Whisnant, "Hamburg's Gay Scene in the Era of Family Politics, 1945–1969" (PhD diss., University of Texas at Austin, 2001); Florence Tamagne, *A History of Homosexuality in Europe: Berlin, London, Paris, 1919–1939* (New York: Algora Publishing, 2004), 37–61; Heike Schader, *Virile, Vamps und wilde Veilchen: Sexualität, Begehren und Erotik in den Zeitschriften homosexueller Frauen im Berlin der 1920er Jahre* (Königstein: Helmer, 2004). For a good introduction to subcultural theory, see Ken Gelder and Sarah Thornton, eds., *The Subcultures Reader* (New York: Routledge, 1997).

12 An early Foucault-influenced work that, while technically dealing with Britain, still discusses the wide influence of German sexology is Jeffrey Weeks's *Sex, Politics, and Society: The Regulation of Sexuality since 1800,* 2nd ed. (New York: Longman, 1989). See also Greenberg, *The Construction of Homosexuality;* Jörg Hutter, *Die gesellschaftliche Kontrolle des homosexuellen Begehrens: Medizinische Definitionen und juristische Sanktionen im 19. Jahrhundert* (Frankfurt: Campus, 1992); Jonathan Ned Katz, *The Invention of Heterosexuality* (New York: Dutton, 1995); Gert Hekma, " 'A Female Soul in a Male Body': Sexual Inversion as Gender Inversion in Nineteenth-Century Sexology," in *Third Sex, Third Gender: Beyond Sexual Dimorphism in Culture and History,* ed. Gilbert Herdt (New York: Zone Books, 1996), 213–40; Gert Hekma, "Same-Sex Relations among Men in Europe, 1700–1990," in *Sexual Cultures in Europe: Themes in Sexuality,* ed. Franz X. Eder, Lesley Hall, and Gert Hekma (Manchester, U.K.: Manchester University Press, 1999), 79–103; or Tamagne, *A History of Homosexuality in Europe,* 207–84. For works that look at the cultural effect of the medical model of homosexuality on Germany, see James W. Jones, *"We of the Third Sex": Literary Representations of Homosexuality in Wilhelmine Germany* (New York: Peter Lang, 1990); and Klaus Müller, *Aber in meinem Herzen sprach eine Stimme so laut: Homosexuelle Autobiographien und medizinische Pathographien im neunzehnten Jahrhundert* (Berlin: Rosa Winkel, 1991). For an important recent

revision see Harry Oosterhuis, "Medical Science and the Modernisation of Sexuality," in Eder et al., *Sexual Cultures in Europe,* 221–41.

13   Harry Oosterhuis, "Homosexual Emancipation in Germany before 1933: Two Traditions," in *Homosexuality and Male Bonding in Pre-Nazi Germany: The Youth Movement, the Gay Movement, and Male Bonding before Hitler's Rise,* ed. Harry Oosterhuis, trans. Hubert Kennedy (New York: Haworth, 1991), 1–34.

14   Paul Weindling, *Health, Race, and German Politics between National Unification and Nazism, 1870–1945* (Cambridge: Cambridge University Press, 1989). Other works that emphasize the scientific and medical roots of Nazi policies toward homosexuality include Burleigh and Wippermann, *The Racial State;* and Grau, "Persecution, 'Re-education' or 'Eradication' of Male Homosexuals."

15   For example, see Christiane von Lengerke, " 'Homosexuelle Frauen': Tribaden, Freundinnen, Urninden," in Bollé, *Eldorado,* 125–48. Influential for this line of criticism were two English-language works: Lillian Faderman, *Surpassing the Love of Men: Romantic Friendship and the Love between Women from the Renaissance to the Present* (New York: William Morrow, 1981), and Esther Newton, "The Mythic Mannish Lesbian: Radclyffe Hall and the New Woman," in *Hidden from History: Reclaiming the Gay and Lesbian Past,* ed. Martin Duberman, Martha Vicinus, and George Chauncey (New York: New American Library, 1989), 281–93.

16   For a work that analyzes the slow influence of the discursive turn on the German historical profession, see Peter Jelavich, "Contemporary Literary Theory: From Deconstruction Back to History," *Central European History* 22, nos. 3/4 (1989): 374–80, as well as the other essays in this special edition.

17   Groundbreaking here was George Mosse, *Nationalism and Sexuality: Respectability and Abnormal Sexuality in Modern Europe* (New York: Howard Fertig, 1985). The bulk of this work, though, has come since 1990. A complete list would be quite enormous, but a few examples include John Fout, "Sexual Politics in Wilhelmine Germany: The Male Gender Crisis, Moral Purity, and Homophobia," in *Forbidden History: The State, Society, and the Regulation of Sexuality in Modern Europe,* ed. John Fout (Chicago: University of Chicago Press, 1992), 259–92; Harry Oosterhuis, "Medicine, Male Bonding and Homosexuality in Nazi Germany," *Journal of Contemporary History* 32, no. 2 (1997): 187–205; Hubert Kennedy, *Der Kreis: Eine Zeitschrift und ihr Programm* (Berlin: Rosa Winkel, 1999); Micheler, "Homophobic Propaganda and the Denunciation of Same-Sex-Desiring Men"; Jennifer Evans, "*Bahnhof* Boys: Policing Male Prostitution in Post-Nazi Berlin," *Journal of the History of Sexuality* 12, no. 4 (2003): 605–36; Claudia Bruns, "The Politics of Masculinity in the (Homo-) Sexual Discourse (1880–1920)," *German History* 23, no. 3 (2005): 306–20; and Clayton Whisnant, "Styles of Masculinity in the West German Gay Scene, 1950–1965," *Central European History* 39, no. 3 (2006): 359–93.

18   Good introductions to queer theory include the essays in Michael Warner, ed., *Fear of a Queer Planet: Queer Politics and Social Theory* (Minneapolis: University of Minnesota Press, 1993); Iain Morland and Annabelle Willox, *Queer Theory* (New York: Palgrave Macmillan, 2005); and Lois Tyson, *Critical Theory Today: A User-Friendly Guide* (New York: Garland, 1999), 317–61.

19   Mosse, *Nationalism and Sexuality;* and George Mosse, *The Image of Man: The Creation of Modern Masculinity* (Oxford: Oxford University Press, 1996).

20   Alan Bray, *Homosexuality in Renaissance England* (London: Gay Men's Press, 1982); Randolph Trumbach, "The Birth of the Queen: Sodomy and the Emergence of Gender Equality in Modern Culture, 1660–1750," in Duberman et al., *Hidden from History,* 129–40; Michael Rey, "Police and Sodomy in Eighteenth-Century Paris: From Sin to Disorder," in *The Pursuit of Sodomy: Male Homosexuality in Renaissance and Enlightenment Europe,* ed. Kent Gerard and Gert Hekma (New York: Harrington Park Press, 1989), 129–46; Theo van der Meer, "The Persecution of Sodomites in Eighteenth-Century Amsterdam: Changing Perceptions of Sodomy," in Gerard and Hekma, *The Pursuit of Sodomy,* 263–307; George Chauncey, "From Sexual Inversion to Homosexuality: Medicine and the Changing Conceptualization of Female Deviance," *Salmagundi* 58/59 (1982): 114–46.

21   Eve Kosofsky Sedgwick, *Epistemology of the Closet* (Berkeley: University of California Press, 1990), 1–63.

22　Helmut Puff, "After the History of (Male) Homosexuality," in *After the History of Sexuality: German Genealogies with and beyond Foucault,* ed. Scott Spector, Helmut Puff, and Dagmar Herzog (New York: Berghahn Books, 2012), 20.

23　Judith Halberstam, *Female Masculinity* (Durham: Duke University Press, 1998), 50.

24　David M. Halperin, *How to Do the History of Homosexuality* (Chicago: University of Chicago Press, 2002), 107.

25　Laura Doan, *Disturbing Practices: History, Sexuality, and Women's Experience of Modern War* (Chicago: University of Chicago Press, 2013).

26　Spector et al., *After the History of Sexuality.*

27　Marti Lybeck, *Desiring Emancipation: New Women and Homosexuality in Germany, 1890–1933* (Albany: SUNY Press, 2014), 11.

28　Scott Spector, introduction to Spector et al., *After the History of Sexuality,* 5.

29　Denise Riley, *"Am I That Name?" Feminism and the Category of "Women" in History* (Minneapolis: University of Minnesota Press, 1988), 6.

30　Clayton Whisnant, *Male Homosexuality in West Germany: Between Persecution and Freedom, 1945– 69* (New York: Palgrave Macmillan, 2012), 5–6.

31　Robert Stephens also employs the term *scene* in his book *Germans on Drugs: The Complications of Modernization in Hamburg* (Ann Arbor: University of Michigan Press, 2007).

NOTES TO CHAPTER 1

1　Charlotte Wolff, *Magnus Hirschfeld: A Portrait of a Pioneer in Sexology* (London: Quartet Books, 1986), 22–23; Manfred Herzer, *Magnus Hirschfeld: Leben und Werk eines jüdischen, schwulen und sozialistischen Sexologen* (Frankfurt: Campus, 1992), 16–18.

2　Wolff, *Magnus Hirschfeld,* 27.

3　Beachy, *Gay Berlin,* 85–86.

4　Elena Mancini, *Magnus Hirschfeld and the Quest for Sexual Freedom: A History of the First International Sexual Freedom Movement* (New York: Palgrave Macmillan, 2010), 36.

5　Ibid., 52.

6　Manfred Herzer, "Das Wissenschaftlich-humanitäre Komitee," in *Goodbye to Berlin? 100 Jahre Schwulenbewegung,* ed. Schwules Museum (Berlin: Rosa Winkel, 1997), 37–39; Wolff, *Magnus Hirschfeld,* 42–43; Herzer, *Magnus Hirschfeld,* 56.

7　John Boswell, *Christianity, Social Tolerance, and Homosexuality: Gay People in Western Europe from the Beginning of the Christian Era to the Fourteenth Century* (Chicago: University of Chicago Press, 1980).

8　See especially R. I. Moore, *The Formation of a Persecuting Society: Power and Deviance in Western Europe, 950–1250* (Oxford: Blackwell, 1987), but also Boswell, *Christianity.*

9　Anna Clark, *Desire: A History of European Sexuality* (London: Routledge, 2008), 74–75; Manfred Herzer, "Ursprünge der Homosexuellenverfolgung," in *Goodbye to Berlin?* 19–20; Hull, *Sexuality, State, and Civil Society in Germany,* 78.

10　Clark, *Desire,* 114.

11　For the complicated case of Bavaria, see Hull, *Sexuality, State, and Civil Society in Germany,* 359–65.

12　Klaus Müller, "Die unmittelbare Vorgeschichte: Heinrich Hössli," in *Homosexualität: Handbuch der Theorie- und Forschungsgeschichte,* ed. Rüdiger Lautmann (Frankfurt: Campus, 1993), 1318; Robert

D. Tobin, "Early Nineteenth-Century Sexual Radicalism: Heinrich Hössli and the Liberals of His Day," in Spector et al., *After the History of Sexuality,* 76–89.

13   Karoly Maria Kertbeny, "Paragraph 143 and the Prussian Penal Code," in *Sodomites and Urnings: Homosexual Representations in Classic German Journals,* ed. and trans. Michael A. Lombardi-Nash (New York: Harrington Park Press, 2006), 51.

14   Ibid., 52–53.

15   Beachy, *Gay Berlin,* 4–25; Vern L. Bullough, introduction to Karl Heinrich Ulrichs, *The Riddle of "Man-Manly" Love,* trans. Michael A. Lombardi-Nash, 2 vols. (New York: Prometheus Books, 1994), 1:21–27; Steakley, *The Homosexual Emancipation Movement in Germany,* 3–5.

16   Bullough, introduction to Ulrichs, *The Riddle of "Man-Manly" Love,* 1:22–25.

17   Ulrichs, *The Riddle of "Man-Manly" Love,* 1:36.

18   Ibid., 301.

19   Ibid., 306.

20   Ibid., 53.

21   Manfred Herzer and Jean-Claud Féray, "Karl Maria Kertbeny," in Lautmann, *Homosexualität,* 44–45.

22   Karl Maria Kertbeny, "Letter to Karl Heinrich Ulrichs in Würzburg from Karl Marie Kertbeny in Hanover," in Lombardi-Nash, *Sodomites and Urnings,* 83–84.

23   For a good recent account, see Harry Oosterhuis, *Stepchildren of Nature: Krafft-Ebing, Psychiatry, and the Making of Sexual Identity* (Chicago: University of Chicago Press, 2000), 25–36.

24   Clark, *Desire,* 107.

25   Oosterhuis, *Stepchildren of Nature,* 32.

26   Ibid., 33.

27   Klaus Müller, "Johan Ludwig Casper," in Lautman, *Homosexualität,* 29.

28   Clark, *Desire,* 143–44.

29   Greenberg, *The Construction of Homosexuality,* 406.

30   Carl Westphal, "Contrary Sexual Feeling: Symptom of a Neuropathic (Psychopathic) Condition," in Lombardi-Nash, *Sodomites and Urnings,* 107.

31   Jörg Hutter, "Carl Friedrich Otto Westphal, in Lautmann, *Homosexualität,* 39.

32   Oosterhuis, *Stepchildren of Nature,* 52–54.

33   Ibid., 87, 95.

34   Ibid., esp. 100–112.

35   Ibid., 48.

36   Ibid., 117.

37   Ibid., 118–25.

38   Quoted ibid., 114.

39   Ibid., 130.

40   Ibid., 139.

41   Quoted in Bullough's introduction to Ulrichs, *The Riddle of "Man-Manly" Love,* 1:25.

42   Oostherhuis, *Stepchildren of Nature,* 164–65.

43 Ibid., 172–73.

44 Ibid., 66–67; Chandak Sengoopta, *Otto Weininger: Sex, Science, and Self in Imperial Vienna* (Chicago: University of Chicago Press, 2000), 92–93.

45 Oosterhuis, *Stepchildren of Nature*, 275–78.

46 Albert Moll, *Libido Sexualis: Studies in the Psychosexual Laws of Love Verified by Clinical Sexual Case Histories,* trans. David Berger (New York: American Ethnological Press, 1933).

47 Greenberg, *The Construction of Homosexuality,* 411.

48 Iwan Bloch, *The Sexual Life of Our Time and Its Relation to Modern Civilization,* trans. M. Eden Paul (London: Rebman, 1908).

49 Mancini, *Magnus Hirschfeld,* 61.

50 Thomas Odell Haakenson, "Grotesque Visions: Art, Science, and Visual Culture in Early Twentieth-Century Germany" (PhD diss., University of Minnesota, 2006), 188.

51 Mancini, *Magnus Hirschfeld,* 61.

52 Otto Weininger, *Sex and Character: An Investigation of Fundamental Principles,* trans. Ladislaus Löb (Bloomington: Indiana University Press, 2005), 79–81.

53 Ibid., 29. See also Allan Janik and Stephen Toulmin, *Wittgenstein's Vienna* (New York: Simon and Schuster, 1973), 71–72.

54 J. Edgar Bauer, "Magnus Hirschfeld's Doctrine of Sexual Intermediaries and the Transgender Politics of (No-)Identity," 6, www.iisg.nl/~womhist/hirschfeld.doc, accessed July 30, 2015.

55 Wolff, *Magnus Hirschfeld,* 107–9.

56 Magnus Hirschfeld, *Transvestites: The Erotic Drive to Cross-Dress,* trans. Michael A. Lombardi-Nash (Buffalo, N.Y.: Prometheus Books, 1991), 219.

57 Magnus Hirschfeld, *The Homosexuality of Men and Women,* trans. Michael A. Lombardi-Nash (Amherst, N.Y.: Prometheus Books, 2000), esp. part 1. This translation is actually based on the second edition of the book, published in 1919.

58 Benjamin Carter Hett, *Death in the Tiergarten: Murder and Criminal Justice in the Kaiser's Berlin* (Cambridge: Harvard University Press, 2004), 181, 194–213.

59 Wolff, *Magnus Hirschfeld,* 67.

60 Beachy, *Gay Berlin,* 170–72.

61 Herzer, "Das Wissenschaftlich-humanitäre Komitee," 41–42.

62 Steakley, *The Homosexual Emancipation Movement in Germany,* 30–31; Hans-Georg Stümke, *Homosexuelle in Deutschland: Eine politische Geschichte* (Munich: C. H. Beck, 1989), 36–38.

63 Carl Schorske, *Fin-de-Siècle Vienna: Politics and Culture* (New York: Alfred A. Knopf, 1979), 116–20.

64 David Blackbourn, *History of Germany, 1780–1918: The Long Nineteenth Century,* 2nd ed. (Oxford: Blackwell, 2003), 316.

65 Ibid., 255–56.

66 Michael Hau, *The Cult of Health and Beauty in Germany: A Social History, 1890–1930* (Chicago: University of Chicago Press, 2003).

67 Herzer, *Magnus Hirschfeld,* 30–31.

68 Ibid., 36–37; Plant, *The Pink Triangle,* 35–36.

69 Eduard Bernstein, "Die Beurteilung des widernormalen Geschlechtsverkehrs," *Die neue Zeit* 13 (1895): 228–33. See also Plant, *The Pink Triangle,* 36–37.

70   Plant, *The Pink Triangle,* 37–38; Hubert Kennedy, "Johan Baptist von Schweitzer: The Queer Marx Loved to Hate," in *Gay Men and the Sexual History of the Political Left,* ed. Gert Hekma, Harry Oosterhuis, and James Steakley (Binghamton, N.Y.: Haworth Press, 1995), 69–96.

71   Herzer, *Magnus Hirschfeld,* 35–36.

72   Mancini, *Magnus Hirschfeld,* 88.

73   Ulrichs, *The Riddle of "Man-Manly" Love,* 1:306.

74   Peter Gay, *The Bourgeois Experience: Victoria to Freud,* vol. 2, *The Tender Passion* (New York: Oxford University Press, 1986), 237–49.

75   The term *masculinist* is suggested by Bruns, "The Politics of Masculinity," 307.

76   *Encyclopedia Britannica,* 11th ed., s.v. "Jäger, Gustav."

77   Bruns, "The Politics of Masculinity," 310.

78   Hubert Kennedy, *Anarchist of Love: The Secret Life of John Henry Mackay,* 2nd rev. ed. (San Francisco: Peremptory Publications, 2002).

79   Benedict Friedlaender, quoted in Steakley, *The Homosexual Emancipation Movement in Germany,* 43.

80   Claudia Bruns, "Der homosexuelle Staatsfreund: Von der Konstruktion des erotischen Männerbund bei Hans Blüher," in *Homosexualität und Staatsräson: Männlichkeit, Homophobie und Politik in Deutschland, 1900–1945,* ed. Susanne zur Nieden (Frankfurt: Campus, 2005), 101.

81   Bruns, "The Politics of Masculinity," 310–11.

82   Friedlaender, quoted in Steakley, *The Homosexual Emancipation Movement in Germany,* 44; emphasis in original.

83   Bernd-Ulrich Hergemöller, "Benedict Friedlaender," in Lautmann, *Homosexualität,* 82–85; Herzer, "Das Wissenschaftlich-humanitäre Komitee," 43–44.

84   Quoted in Kennedy, *Anarchist of Love,* 15.

85   John Henry Mackay, *The Hustler,* trans. Hubert Kennedy (Bloomington, Ind.: Xlibris, 2002), 183–84.

86   Hubert Kennedy first pointed out this connection with Stiner's text. See his notation in Oosterhuis, "Homosexual Emancipation in Germany before 1933," 22n.

87   Manfred Herzer, "Adolf Brand und *Der Eigene,*" in *Goodbye to Berlin?* 49; Oosterhuis, "Homosexual Emancipation in Germany before 1933," 1–34.

88   Oosterhuis, "Homosexual Emancipation in Germany before 1933," 3.

89   Beachy, *Gay Berlin,* 94–95, 113–14.

90   Harry Oosterhuis, "Homosexual Emancipation in Germany before 1933," 4.

91   Ibid., 8.

92   Ibid., 8–9.

93   Glenn Ramsey, "The Rites of *Artgenossen:* Contesting Homosexual Political Culture in Weimar Germany," *Journal of the History of Sexuality* 17, no. 1 (January 2008): 87.

94   Marita Keilson-Lauritz, "Tante, Kerle und Skandale: Die Geburt des 'modernen Homosexuellen' aus den Flügelkämpfen der Emanzipation," in Suzanne zur Nieden, *Homosexualität und Staatsräson,* 82–83. See also her more extended treatment: Marita Keilson-Lauritz, *Die Geschichte der eigenen Geschichte: Literatur und Literaturkritik in den Anfangen der Schwulenbewegung* (Berlin: Rosa Winkel, 1997).

95   Mancini, *Magnus Hirschfeld,* xi.

NOTES TO CHAPTER 2

1   Ulrike Krettmann, "Johanna Elberskirchen," in Lautmann, *Homosexualität,* 111; Lybeck, *Desiring Emancipation,* 90.

2   Ute Frevert, *Women in German History: Bourgeois Emancipation to Sexual Liberation,* trans. Stuart McKinnon-Evans (New York: Berg, 1989).

3   Krettmann, "Johanna Elberskirchen," 113.

4   Ibid., 111–15.

5   Lybeck, *Desiring Emancipation,* 92.

6   Quoted ibid., 98.

7   Ibid., 95–98.

8   Ibid., 33–34.

9   Ibid., 19, 35–36.

10   Ibid., especially chaps. 2 and 3.

11   Sedgwick, *Epistemology of the Closet,* 2.

12   Ibid., 45.

13   Laura Doan, *Fashioning Sapphism: The Origins of a Modern English Lesbian Culture* (New York: Columbia University Press, 2001), xx.

14   Chauncey, *Gay New York,* esp. chap. 4.

15   Whisnant, *Male Homosexuality in West Germany,* 153–54.

16   Detlef Grumbach, "Die Linke und das Laster," in *Die Linke und das Laster: Schwule Emanzipation und linke Vorurteile,* ed. Detlef Grumbach (Hamburg: MännerschwarmSkript, 1995), 26; Claudia Bruns, "Skandale im Beraterkreis um Kaiser Wilhelm II: Die homoerotische 'Verbündelung' der 'Liebenberger Tafelrunde' als Politikum," in Nieden, *Homosexualität und Staatsräson,* 56; Weindling, *Health, Race, and German Politics,* 118.

17   Heike I. Schmidt, "Colonial Intimacy: The Rechenberg Scandal and Homosexuality in German East Africa," *Journal of the History of Sexuality* 17, no. 1 (January 2008): 33–36.

18   Ibid., 39.

19   Ibid., 37–38.

20   Ibid., 39–43.

21   Ibid., 44–47.

22   Ibid., 49.

23   Michael Balfour, *The Kaiser and His Times* (1964; repr., New York: W. W. Norton, 1972), 89–90; Peter Winzen, *Das Ende der Kaiserherrlichkeit: Die Skandalprozesse um die homosexuellen Berater Wilhelms II, 1907–1909* (Cologne: Böhlau, 2010), 14–15.

24   Beachy, *Gay Berlin,* 122.

25   Both quotes from Isabel V. Hull, *The Entourage of Kaiser Wilhelm II, 1888–1918* (New York: Cambridge University Press, 1982), 130–31. The statement of the doctor was taken down by Chancellor Bernard von Bülow in his journal.

26   Claudia Bruns, "Masculinity, Sexuality, and the German Nation: The Eulenburg Scandals and Kaiser Wilhelm II in Political Cartoons," in *Pictorial Cultures and Political Iconographies: Approaches, Perspectives, Case Studies from Europe and America,* ed. Udo J. Hebel and Christoph Wagner (Berlin: Walter de Gruyter, 2011), 122–23.

27 Jeffrey Alan Schneider, "Militarism, Masculinity and Modernity in Germany" (PhD diss., Cornell University, 1997), 153–54.

28 For a history of the Moltke family, see Olaf Jessen, *Die Moltkes: Biographie einer Familie* (Munich: C. H. Beck, 2010).

29 Winzen, *Das Ende der Kaiserherrlichkeit,* 17.

30 Ibid., 22–24.

31 Quoted in Wolfgang J. Mommsen, "Homosexualität, aristokratische Kultur und Weltpolitik: Die Herausforderung des wilhelminischen Establishments durch Maximilian Harden 1906–1908," in *Große Prozesse: Recht und Gerechtigkeit in der Geschichte,* ed. Uwe Schultz (Munich: C. H. Beck, 2001), 281.

32 Schneider, "Militarism, Masculinity and Modernity in Germany," 142.

33 Bruns, "Masculinity, Sexuality, and the German Nation," 135.

34 Schneider, "Militarism, Masculinity and Modernity in Germany," 144–47.

35 Bruns, "Masculinity, Sexuality, and the German Nation," 125.

36 Winzen, *Das Ende der Kaiserherrlichkeit,* 9.

37 Helmuth Rogge, *Holstein und Harden: Politisch-publizistisches Zusammenspiel zweier Außenseiter des Wilhelminischen Reichs* (Munich: C. H. Beck, 1959).

38 Winzen, *Das Ende der Kaiserherrlichkeit,* 38–65; Hull, *The Entourage of Kaiser Wilhelm II,* 126–30.

39 Balfour, *The Kaiser and His Times,* 274; Hull, *The Entourage of Kaiser Wilhelm II,* 137.

40 Schneider, "Militarism, Masculinity and Modernity in Germany," 153–56.

41 Beachy, *Gay Berlin,* 129–31.

42 Peter Winzen, *Das Ende der Kaiserherrlichkeit,* 193–98.

43 Hull, *The Entourage of Kaiser Wilhelm II,* 138.

44 Winzen, *Das Ende der Kaiserherrlichkeit,* 273–93.

45 Ibid., 333–37.

46 Mommsen, "Homosexualität, aristokratische Kultur und Weltpolitik," 284, 286.

47 Bruns, "Masculinity, Sexuality, and the German Nation," 129–30.

48 Winzen, *Das Ende der Kaiserherrlichkeit,* 345.

49 Isabel V. Hull, "Kaiser Wilhelm II and the 'Liebenberg Circle,'" in *Kaiser Wilhelm II: New Interpretations,* ed. John C. G. Röhl and Nicolaus Sombart (New York: Cambridge University Press, 1982), 212; Hull, *The Entourage of Kaiser Wilhelm II,* 237–65, 296–300.

50 James Steakley, "Iconography of a Scandal," in Duberman et al., *Hidden from History,* 233–63; Bruns, "Masculinity, Sexuality, and the German Nation."

51 Susanne zur Nieden, "Homophobie und Staatsräson," in Nieden, *Homosexualität und Staatsräson,* 17–51.

52 Quoted in Bruns, "Masculinity, Sexuality, and the German Nation," 124.

53 Steakley, "Iconography of a Scandal," 251.

54 Mancini, *Magnus Hirschfeld,* 100.

55 Kennedy, *Anarchist of Love,* 18.

56 Herzer, *Magnus Hirschfeld,* 74.

57 Ibid., 75.

58 Kennedy, *Anarchist of Love*, 15–16.

59 Stephen Mitchell and Margaret Black, *Freud and Beyond: A History of Modern Psychoanalytic Thought* (New York: Basic Books, 1995), 2–3.

60 Edward Shorter, *A History of Psychiatry: From the Era of the Asylum to the Age of Prozac* (New York: John Wiley and Sons, 1997), 154–59. For the development of the profession of psychotherapy alongside the classic psychiatric profession in Germany, see Geoffrey Cocks, *Psychotherapy in the Third Reich: The Göring Institute*, 2nd ed. (New Brunswick, N.J.: Transaction, 1997), 43–49.

61 Cocks, *Psychotherapy in the Third Reich*, 31–34. For the classic study that places Freud's theory of the unconscious into a more general revolt against positivism at the turn of the twentieth century, see H. Stuart Hughes, *Consciousness and Society: The Reorientation of European Social Thought, 1890–1930*, rev. ed. (New York: Vintage Books, 1977).

62 Sigmund Freud, *Three Essays on the Theory of Sexuality*, trans. James Strachey (New York: Basic Books, 1975), 3.

63 Sigmund Freud, "Certain Neurotic Mechanisms in Jealousy, Paranoia and Homosexuality," in *Sexuality and the Psychology of Love*, ed. Philip Rieff (New York: Collier Books, 1963), 167–69.

64 Jung's conception of homosexuality must be pieced together from a number of his works. See Carl Jung, "Concerning the Archetypes with Special Reference to the Anima Concept" and "Psychological Aspects of the Mother Archetype," in *The Archetypes and the Collective Unconscious*, trans. R. F. C. Hull, 2nd ed. (Princeton: Princeton University Press, 1980), 54–91; and Carl Jung, *Psychological Types*, trans. H. G. Baynes, rev. by R. F. C. Hull (1971; repr., Princeton: Princeton University Press, 1976), 471. For a short summary, see Friedrich Wilhelm Doucet, *Homosexualität* (Munich: Lichtenberg, 1967), 33–35.

65 Herzer, *Magnus Hirschfeld*, 94.

66 Ibid., 75.

67 Wolff, *Magnus Hirschfeld*, 100–101.

68 Sigmund Freud, "Leonardo da Vinci and a Memory of His Childhood," trans. James Strachey, in *The Freud Reader*, ed. Peter Gay (New York: W. W. Norton, 1989), 455.

69 Ibid., 462–63.

70 Herzer, *Magnus Hirschfeld*, 110–11.

71 Ernst Falzeder, ed. and trans., *The Complete Correspondence of Sigmund Freud and Karl Abraham, 1907–1925* (London: Karnac Books, 2002), 140.

72 Quoted in Herzer, *Magnus Hirschfeld*, 112.

73 Ibid., 116–17.

74 Edward Ross Dickinson, *Sex, Freedom, and Power in Imperial Germany, 1880–1914* (New York: Cambridge University Press, 2014), 164–65.

75 John Hoenig, "Sexology," in *Handbook of Psychiatry*, vol. 1, *General Psychopathology*, ed. Michael Shepherd and O. L. Zangwill (New York: Cambridge University Press, 1983), 50.

76 Wolff, *Magnus Hirschfeld*, 130–31; Dickinson, *Sex, Freedom, and Power in Imperial Germany*, 249.

77 Dickinson, *Sex, Freedom, and Power in Imperial Germany*, 281–303.

78 Florian Mildenburger, *"In der Richtung der Homosexualität verdorben": Psychiater, Kriminalpsychologen und Gerichtsmediziner über männliche Homosexualität, 1850–1970* (Hamburg: MännerschwarmSkript, 2002), 53.

79 Vern Bullough, *Science in the Bedroom: A History of Sex Research* (New York: Basic Books, 1994), 47.

80 Sengoopta, *Otto Weininger*, 88.

81 Havelock Ellis, *Studies in the Psychology of Sex,* vol. 2, *Sexual Inversion* (Philadelphia: F. A. Davis, 1915), 83.

82 Ibid., 47.

83 Sengoopta, *Otto Weininger,* 89.

84 Florian Mildenberger, "Kraepelin and the 'Urnings': Male Homosexuality in Psychiatric Discourse," *History of Psychiatry* 18, no. 3 (2007): 324.

85 Quoted in Christiane Leidinger, "Anna Rüling: A Problematic Foremother of Lesbian History," *Journal of the History of Sexuality* 13, no. 4 (October 2004): 480.

86 Ibid., 488.

87 Ibid., 477.

88 Anna Rüling, "What Interest Does the Women's Movement Have in Solving the Homosexual Problem?" in Lombardi-Nash, *Sodomites and Urnings,* 34.

89 Kirsten Leng, "Anna Rüling, Michel Foucault, and the 'Tactical Polyvalence' of the Female Homosexual," in Spector et al., *After the History of Sexuality,* 95–108.

90 Rüling, "What Interest Does the Women's Movement Have?" 30.

91 Ibid., 36, 38.

92 Though it had the same name (*Bund für Menschenrecht*), this is not the same organization as the homosexual group led by Friedrich Radszuweit, which will be discussed later. I translate *Bund* in this case as "League" but in the latter case as "Federation" to make the difference clear.

93 Leidinger, "Anna Rüling," 495.

94 Ibid.

95 Lybeck, *Desiring Emancipation,* 109.

96 Quoted ibid.

97 Wolff, *Magnus Hirschfeld,* 86; Stümke, *Homosexuelle in Deutschland,* 23.

98 Myra Marx Ferree, *Varieties of Feminism: German Gender Politics in Global Perspective* (Stanford: Stanford University Press, 2012), 37; Cornelie Usborne, *The Politics of the Body in Weimar Germany: Women's Reproductive Rights and Duties* (Ann Arbor: University of Michigan Press, 1992), 9.

99 Ann Taylor Allen, "Mothers of the New Generation: Adele Schreiber, Helene Stöcker, and the Evolution of a German Idea of Motherhood, 1900–1914," *Signs* 10, no. 3 (Spring 1985): 424.

100 Weindling, *Health, Race and German Politics,* 250.

101 Allen, "Mothers of the New Generation," 419–22.

102 Ibid., 425.

103 Ibid., 426.

104 Ibid., 428; Wolff, *Magnus Hirschfeld,* 92.

105 Wolff, *Magnus Hirschfeld,* 89.

106 Herzer, "Das Wissenschaftlich-humanitäre Komitee," 47.

107 Wolff, *Magnus Hirschfeld,* 89.

108 Ibid., 93.

109 Ibid., 94.

110 Ibid., 95.

111 Lybeck, *Desiring Emancipation,* 110–11.

112 Ibid., 113–14; Elena Mancini, *Magnus Hirschfeld*, 110.

113 Edwin Bab, "The Women's Movement and Male Culture," in Oosterhuis, *Homosexuality and Male Bonding in Pre-Nazi Germany*, 144. Original version is Edwin Bab, "Frauenbewegung und männliche Kultur," *Der Eigene* (June 1903): 406–7.

114 Bruns, "The Politics of Masculinity," 312.

115 Quoted ibid.

116 For a history of the youth movement, see Walter Laqueur, *Young Germany: A History of the German Youth Movement* (New York: Basic Books, 1962).

117 Ibid., 16.

118 Ibid., 19.

119 George Mosse, *The Crisis of German Ideology: The Intellectual Origins of the Third Reich,* new ed. (New York: Schocken Books, 1981), 172.

120 Laqueur, *Young Germany,* 28; John R. Gillis, *Youth and History: Tradition and Change in European Age Relations, 1770–Present,* expanded ed. (New York: Academic Press, 1981), 152.

121 Elizabeth Heineman, "Gender Identity in the Wandervogel Movement," *German Studies Review* 12 (1989): 251.

122 Ibid., 252.

123 Mosse, *The Crisis of German Ideology,* 84.

124 Jost Hermand, "Meister Fidus: Vom Jugendstil-Hippie zum Germanenschwärmer," in *Der Schein des schönen Lebens: Studien zur Jahrhundertwende,* ed. Jost Hermand (Frankfurt: Athenäum, 1972), 127.

125 Hans Bethge, "Fidus," originally published in *Der Eigene* (June 1903): 419–23. This translation is from Oosterhuis, *Homosexuality and Male Bonding in Pre-Nazi Germany,* 115–18.

126 Angel Millar, "Bohemian Groves: The Nineteenth Century Roots of the Hippie Movement," *People of Shambhala,* June 8, 2008, http://peopleofshambhala.com/bohemian-groves-the-19th-century-roots-of-the-hippie-movement, accessed December 2, 2015.

127 Hans Blüher, *Wandervogel: Geschichte einer Jugendbewegung,* 5th ed., 3 vols. (Frankfurt am Main: Dipa, 1976), 2:57.

128 Ibid., 49.

129 Hans Blüher, *Werke und Tage: Geschichte eines Denkers* (Munich: Paul List, 1953), 232–33.

130 Ibid., 236.

131 Ibid., 118–22.

132 Ibid., 238–39.

133 Ibid.

134 Quoted in Martin Lichtmesz, "Autorenportrait Hans Blüher," *Sezession* 15 (October 2006): 3.

135 Ibid.

136 Blüher, *Wandervogel,* 2:110–11.

137 Originally published as Hans Blüher, *Die deutsche Wandervogelbewegung als erotischen Phänomen: Ein Beitrag zur Erkenntnis der sexuellen Inversion* (Berlin: Bernhard Weise, 1912). My citation comes from a 1957 edition: Blüher, *Wandervogel,* 3:42.

138 Mosse, *The Crisis of German Ideology,* 176–77.

139 Bernd-Ulrich Hergemöller, "Hans Blüher," in Lautmann, *Homosexualität,* 152–53.

140 Hans Blüher, *Die Rolle der Erotik in der männlichen Gesellschaft: Eine Theorie der menschlichen Staats-bildung nach Wesen und Wert*, 2 vols. (Jena: Eugen Diederichs, 1919), 1:226.

141 Ibid., 235–36.

142 Ibid., 239.

143 Ibid., 2, pt. 1.

144 Ibid., pt. 2.

145 Claudia Bruns, "The Politics of Eros: The German Männerbund between Anti-Feminism and Anti-Semitism in the Early Twentieth Century," in *Masculinity, Senses, Spirit*, ed. Katherine M. Faull (Lewisburg, Pa.: Bucknell University Press, 2011), 174.

146 Ibid., 170.

147 Herzer, "Das Wissenschaftlich-humanitäre Komitee," 46–47.

148 Magnus Hirschfeld, *The Sexual History of the World War* [1930] (1934; repr., Honolulu, Hawaii: University Press of the Pacific, 2006).

149 Jason Crouthamel, *An Intimate History of the Front: Masculinity, Sexuality, and German Soldiers in the First World War* (New York: Palgrave Macmillan, 2014), 129.

150 Ibid., 125.

151 Ibid., 126.

152 Peter Gay, *Weimar Culture: The Outsider as Insider* (New York: Harper and Row, 1968), xiv.

NOTES TO CHAPTER 3

1 For more on the Roland cabaret, see Peter Jelavich, *Berlin Cabaret* (Cambridge: Harvard University Press, 1993), 95–96.

2 Ibid., 102.

3 Claudia Schoppmann, *The Days of Masquerade: Life Stories of Lesbians during the Third Reich* (New York: Columbia University Press, 1996), 57.

4 Quoted in Jelavich, *Berlin Cabaret,* 102.

5 Quoted in Schoppmann, *Days of Masquerade,* 61.

6 Ibid., 61–62.

7 Alan Lareau, "Lavender Songs: Undermining Gender in Weimar Cabaret and Beyond," *Popular Music and Society* 28, no. 1 (February 2005): 22.

8 This is my translation. I make no attempt to keep the rhythm or rhyme of the song. Much thanks to Geoffrey Giles for some assistance with this translation.

9 Jelavich, *Berlin Cabaret,* 103.

10 Ibid., 104.

11 Modris Eksteins, *Rites of Spring: The Great War and the Birth of the Modern Age* (Boston: Houghton Mifflin, 1989), 55–94; Hew Strachan, *The First World War* (New York: Penguin Books, 2003), 59.

12 Marhoefer, *Sex and the Weimar Republic,* 26–31.

13 Eksteins, *Rites of Spring,* 208–38.

14 Christopher Isherwood, *Christopher and His Kind, 1929–1939* (New York: Farrar, Straus and Giroux, 1976), 2.

15 Hirschfeld, *The Homosexuality of Men and Women,* 787.

16   Quoted ibid., 778.

17   Wilhelm Stieber, *Die Prostitution in Berlin und ihre Opfer,* 2nd ed. (Berlin: Hofmann, 1846), 209.

18   Alexandra Richie, *Faust's Metropolis: A History of Berlin* (New York: Carroll and Graf, 1998), 95.

19   Ibid., 138–39.

20   Blackbourn, *History of Germany,* 72, 86–88.

21   Richie, *Faust's Metropolis,* 206–8.

22   David Clay Large, *Berlin* (New York: Basic Books, 2000), 85–88.

23   Jelavich, *Berlin Cabaret,* 14.

24   Quoted in Large, *Berlin,* 93.

25   Ibid., 94–95.

26   See Manfred Herzer's caption to the photo of the Panopticum in Magnus Hirschfeld, *Berlins Drittes Geschlecht: Schwule und Lesben um 1900* (Berlin: Rosa Winkel, 1991), 20.

27   Jelavich, *Berlin Cabaret,* esp. 10–35.

28   Richie, *Faust's Metropolis,* 181–87.

29   On the first report of such a costume ball in Germany, see Ulrichs, *The Riddle of "Man-Manly" Love,* 394. See also Jens Dobler, *Zwischen Duldungspolitik und Verbrechensbekämpfung: Homosexuellenverfolgung durch die Berliner Polizei von 1848 bis 1933* (Frankfurt: Polizeiwissenschaft, 2008), 350–51.

30   Dobler, *Zwischen Duldungspolitik und Verbrechensbekämpfung,* 360.

31   Steakley, *The Homosexual Emancipation Movement in Germany,* 27.

32   Staatsarchiv Hamburg, Medizinalkollegium, IIP3, "Der erste Siegfriedsruf," Ausschnitt aus *Deutsch-Soziale Blätter,* no. 21.

33   Steakley, *The Homosexual Emancipation Movement in Germany,* 27.

34   Hirschfeld, *The Homosexuality of Men and Women,* 802–3.

35   See, for example, Weeks, *Sex, Politics, and Society,* 13; Greenberg, *The Construction of Homosexuality,* 330–31.

36   Roland Barthes, *The Pleasure of the Text,* trans. Richard Miller (New York: Hill and Wang, 1975).

37   Jean-Ulrick Désert, "Queer Space," in *Queers in Space: Communities, Public Spaces, Sites of Resistance,* ed. Gordon Brent Ingram, Anne-Marie Bouthillette, and Yolanda Retter (Seattle: Bay Press, 1997), 21.

38   Lawrence Knopp, "Sexuality and Urban Space: A Framework for Analysis," in *Mapping Desire: Geographies of Sexualities,* ed. David Bell and Gill Valentine (New York: Routledge, 1995), 149.

39   Peter Fritzsche, *Reading Berlin 1900* (Cambridge: Harvard University Press, 1996), 51–58.

40   Beachy, *Gay Berlin,* 20.

41   Ibid., 90.

42   Eric Weitz, *Weimar Germany: Promise and Tragedy* (Princeton: Princeton University Press, 2007), 285.

43   Dorothy Rowe, *Representing Berlin: Sexuality and the City in Imperial and Weimar Germany* (Burlington, Vt.: Ashgate, 2003), 147–79; Maria Tatar, *Lustmord: Sexual Murder in Weimar Germany* (Princeton: Princeton University Press, 1995).

44   Devin Fore, "Döblin's Epic: Sense, Document, and the Verbal World Picture," *New German Critique* 33, no. 3 (2006): 171–207.

45   Weitz, *Weimar Germany,* 170.

46 Large, *Berlin,* 211–12.

47 Weitz, *Weimar Germany,* 228.

48 Ibid., 302.

49 Atina Grossmann, *Reforming Sex: The German Movement for Birth Control and Abortion Reform, 1920–1950* (Oxford: Oxford University Press, 1995), 15.

50 Ibid., especially chap. 3.

51 Cocks, *Psychotherapy in the Third Reich.*

52 Weitz, *Weimar Germany,* 297–301.

53 Curt Moreck, "We Will Show You Berlin," in *The Weimar Republic Sourcebook,* ed. Anton Kaes, Martin Jay, and Edward Dimendberg (Berkeley: University of California Press, 1994), 564.

54 Weitz, *Weimar Germany,* 313.

55 Jelavich, *Berlin Cabaret,* 176.

56 Lareau, "Lavender Songs," 18–24.

57 Hau, *The Cult of Health and Beauty in Germany;* Chad Ross, *Naked Germany: Health, Race and the Nation* (New York: Berg, 2005).

58 Houlbrook, *Queer London,* 9.

59 For a fascinating discussion of this sex tourism to the city, see Robert *Gay Berlin,* 187–219.

60 Theis and Sternweiler, "Alltag im Kaiserreich und in der Weimarer Republik," 63.

61 Beachy, *Gay Berlin,* 70.

62 Ibid., 59.

63 Ibid., 61.

64 Ibid., 59.

65 Hirschfeld, *The Homosexuality of Men and Women,* 785.

66 Ibid.

67 Paul Näcke, "Ein Besuch bei den Homosexuellen in Berlin," republished as an appendix to Hirschfeld, *Berlins Drittes Geschlecht,* 170. All translations are mine unless otherwise noted.

68 Hirschfeld, *Berlins Drittes Geschlecht,* 90.

69 Näcke, "Ein Besuch bei den Homosexuellen in Berlin," 171.

70 Ibid., 172.

71 Isherwood, *Christopher and His Kind,* 30.

72 Hirschfeld, *The Homosexuality of Men and Women,* 785–86.

73 Ibid.

74 Tamagne, *A History of Homosexuality in Europe,* 1:51.

75 Theis and Sternweiler, "Alltag im Kaiserreich und in der Weimarer Republik," 59.

76 Hirschfeld, *Homosexuality of Men and Women,* 785.

77 Tamagne, *A History of Homosexuality in Europe,* 1:54.

78 Hirschfeld, *Homosexuality of Men and Women,* 787.

79 Ruth Margarete Röllig, quoted in Tamagne, *A History of Homosexuality in Europe,* 1:54.

80 Hirschfeld, *Homosexuality of Men and Women,* 787.

81 Tamagne, *A History of Homosexuality in Europe,* 1:55.

82 Ibid., 54.

83 Lybeck, *Desiring Emancipation,* 156–57.

84 Ibid., 164.

85 Ibid., 167.

86 Oscar Méténier, *Vertus et Vices allemands, les Berlinois chez eux,* cited in Hirschfeld, *The Homosexuality of Men and Women,* 787.

87 Hirschfeld, *The Homosexuality of Men and Women,* 788.

88 "Miss R," quoted in Hirschfeld, *Homosexuality of Men and Women,* 789.

89 For works on this topic in other national contexts, see Chauncey, *Gay New York;* Cook, *London and the Culture of Homosexuality;* Houlbrook, *Queer London;* Gert Hekma, "Queer Amsterdam 1945–2010," in Cook and Evans, *Queer Cities, Queer Cultures,* 118–34.

90 Chauncey, *Gay New York,* 195–201; Houlbrook, *Queer London,* 61–62; Dan Healey, "Moscow," in *Queer Sites: Gay Urban Histories since 1600,* ed. David Higgs (New York: Routledge, 1999), 51–52; Gert Hekma, "Amsterdam" in Higgs, *Queer Sites,* 67; David Higgs, "Lisbon," in Higgs, *Queer Sites,* 134; Marc Stein, *City of Sisterly and Brotherly Loves: Lesbian and Gay Philadelphia, 1945–1972* (2000; repr., Philadelphia: Temple University Press, 2004), 101–5.

91 Hirschfeld, *The Homosexuality of Men and Women,* 800.

92 Ibid.

93 Ibid. 795

94 Ibid., 792–93.

95 Theis and Sternweiler, "Alltag im Kaiserreich und in der Weimarer Republik," 55.

96 Hirschfeld, *The Homosexuality of Men and Women,* 793.

97 Otto de Joux, quoted in Wolfgang Voigt, "Geschichte der Schwulen in Hamburg," in *Hamburg ahoi! Der schwule Lotse durch die Hansestadt,* ed. Wolfgang Voigt and Klaus Weinriech (Berlin: Rosa Winkel, 1982), 14.

98 Abraham Flexner, *Prostitution in Europe* (New York: Century, 1914), 31.

99 Wolfgang Voigt, "Geschichte der Schwulen in Hamburg," in *Hamburg ahoi! Der schwule Lotse durch die Hansestadt,* ed. Wolfgang Voigt and Klaus Weinrich (Berlin: Rosa Winkel, 1982), 27; Bernhard Rosenkranz and Gottfried Lorenz, *Hamburg auf anderen Wegen: Die Geschichte des schwulen Lebens in der Hansestadt,* 2nd ed. (Hamburg: Lambda, 2005), 20–26.

100 Stephen Spender, *The Temple: A Novel* (New York: Grove Press, 1988), 74.

101 Rainer Hoffschildt, *Olivia: Die bisher geheime Geschichte des Tabus Homosexualität und der Verfolgung der Homosexuellen in Hannover* (Hannover: Selbstverlag, 1992), 64–65.

102 Ibid., 65–66.

103 Theodor Lessing, *Haarmann: Die Geschichte eines Werwolfs* (Berlin: Schmeide, 1925), 15.

104 Hans Hyan, *Massenmörder Haarmann,* quoted in Hoffschildt, *Olivia,* 67.

105 Jürgen Müller and Helge Schneberger, "Schwules Leben in Köln," in Limpricht et al., *"Verführte" Männer.*

106 Frank Sparing, *Wegen Vergehen nach §175 verhaftet: Die Verfolgung der Düsseldorfer Homosexuellen während des Nationalsozialismus* (Düsseldorf: Grupello, 1997), 15–25.

107 Laurie Marhoefer, *Sex and the Weimar Republic,* 49–50.

108 Stephan Heiß and Albert Knoll, "Übrigens komme derlei im Hofbräuhaus fast jede Woche vor," in *München und Bayern von hinten,* ed. Ralf Waldau (Berlin: Bruno Gmünder, 1995), 15; Stephan Heiß, "Das Dritte Geschlecht und die Namenlose Liebe: Homosexuelle im München der Jahrhundertwende," in *MannBilder: Ein Lese- und Quellenbuch zur historischen Männerforschung,* ed. Wolfgang Schmale (Berlin: Arno Spitz, 1998), 189.

109 Dobler, *Zwischen Duldungspolitik und Verbrechensbekämpfung,* 308.

110 For a history of Hamburg's police department, see Wolfgang Schult, "Geschichte der Hamburger Polizei, 1814–1964" (Hamburg, 1964), manuscript in Staatsarchiv Hamburg.

111 For the modernization of Berlin's police procedures, see Dobler, *Zwischen Duldungspolitik und Verbrechensbekämpfung,* 145–76.

112 Ibid., 308–10.

113 Beachy, *Gay Berlin,* 54–59.

114 Hirschfeld, *The Homosexuality of Men and Women,* 786.

115 Dobler, *Zwischen Duldungspolitik und Verbrechensbekämpfung,* 527–43.

116 Sparing, *Wegen Vergehen nach §175 verhaftet,* 18–19.

117 Edward Ross Dickinson, "Policing Sex in Germany, 1882–1982: A Preliminary Analysis," *Journal of the History of Sexuality* 16 (2007): 224–25.

118 Tamagne, *A History of Homosexuality in Europe,* 2:328. Munich seems to have stood out as a major exception to this rule, which may at least partially explain how small the gay scene remained in Munich during the 1920s.

119 For some of the problems of equating the notion of *Rechtsstaat* with "rule of law," see Gustavo Gozzi, "Rechtsstaat and Individual Rights in German Constitutional History," in *The Rule of Law: History, Theory, and Criticism,* ed. Pietro Costa and Danilo Zolo (Dordrecht: Springer, 2007), 237–59.

120 Hirschfeld, *The Homosexuality of Men and Women,* 776, 780.

121 Ibid., 781.

122 Ibid.

123 Hirschfeld, *Berlins Drittes Geschlecht,* 80–81.

124 Lybeck, *Desiring Emancipation,* 104–5.

125 Andreas Sternweiler, "Die Freundschaftsbünde—eine Massenbewegung," in Schwules Museum, *Goodbye to Berlin?* 97. See also Stümke, *Homosexuelle in Deutschland,* 54–55.

126 Rosenkranz and Lorenz, *Hamburg auf anderen Wegen,* 13–14.

127 Stefan Micheler, "Zeitschriften, Verbände und Lokale: Gleichgeschlechtlich gebehrender Menschen in der Weimarer Republik," August 1, 2008, www.stefanmicheler.de/wissenschaft/stm_zvlggbm .pdf, 26, accessed September 2, 2014.

128 Ibid., 26–27; Jens Dobler, *Von anderen Ufern: Geschichte der Berliner Lesben und Schwulen in Kreuzberg und Friedrichshain* (Berlin: Gmünder, 2003), 72–73.

129 Stefan Micheler, *Selbstbilder und Fremdbilder der "Anderen": Eine Geschichte Männer begehrender Männer in der Weimarer Republik und der NS-Zeit* (Konstanz: UVK, 2005), 195.

130 Micheler, "Zeitschriften, Verbände und Lokale," 58–59.

131 Lybeck, *Desiring Emancipation,* 152.

132 Schader, *Virile, Vamps und wilde Veilchen,* 76.

133 Lybeck, *Desiring Emancipation,* 163–64.

134 Katharina Vogel, "Zum Selbstverständnis lesbischer Frauen in der Weimarer Republik: Eine Analyse der Zeitschrift 'Die Freundin' 1924–1933," in Bollé, *Eldorado,* 166.

135 Marhoefer, *Sex and the Weimar Republic,* 62.

136 The *Lex Heinze* was inspired by the trial of the pimp Hermann Heinze and his prostitute wife, who were ultimately convicted of murdering a night guard during a robbery gone wrong. The trial attracted much press attention and ultimately raised a great deal of public concern about the moral and physical conditions that prostitutes lived in. The *Lex Heinze* both made pimping illegal and broadened the country's censorship laws. For the effect of the *Lex Heinze* on imperial censorship, see Gary D. Stark, "Pornography, Society, and the Law in Imperial Germany," *Central European History* 14, no. 3 (1981): 216–19.

137 Micheler, "Zeitschriften, Verbände und Lokale," 3–4.

138 Ibid., 23.

139 Ibid., 6–7.

140 Claus Nordbruch, *Sind Gedanken noch frei? Zensur in Deutschland* (Munich: Universitas, 1998), 31.

141 Micheler, "Zeitschriften, Verbände und Lokale," 11–14.

142 Ibid., 8.

143 Sternweiler, "Die Freundschaftsbünde—eine Massenbewegung," 96.

144 Stümke, *Homosexuelle in Deutschland,* 53–54. This number is probably based on Radszuweit's own statement, which Micheler observes there is good reason to doubt. Unfortunately, coming up with a more reliable number is difficult. See Micheler, "Zeitschriften, Verbände und Lokale," 32.

145 There was an earlier version of *The Third Sex* published by Radszuweit in late 1928 and early 1929 that focused on sensational stories of (hetero)sexual crimes of various sort. It was shut down after only a few issues. Except for the title, it had nothing in common with the transvestite magazine that was published by Radszuweit during the early 1930s. See Micheler, "Zeitschriften, Verbände und Lokale," 32.

146 Andreas Sternweiler, "Die Freundschaftsbünde—eine Massenbewegung," 103.

147 Schader, *Virile, Vamps und wilde Veilchen,* 74–76; Marhoefer, *Sex and the Weimar Republic,* 57.

148 Micheler, "Zeitschriften, Verbände und Lokale," 33.

149 Margaret Stieg, "The 1926 German Law to Protect Youth against Trash and Dirt: Moral Protectionism in a Democracy," *Central European History* 23, no. 1 (March 1990): 22–56.

150 Quoted in Schader, *Virile, Vamps, und wilde Veilchen,* 50.

151 Ibid., 48–51, 142.

152 Ibid., 54–60.

153 Micheler, "Zeitschrifen, Verbände, und Lokale," 35–36.

154 Michael Warner, *Publics and Counterpublics* (New York: Zone Books, 2002), 65–124.

155 Martin Meeker, *Contacts Desired: Gay and Lesbian Communications and Community, 1940s–1970s* (Chicago: University of Chicago Press, 2006), 12–13. See also Marhoefer, *Sex and the Weimar Republic,* 65–71.

156 Matt Houlbrook makes a similar argument about the attraction that London had on British provincials. See Houlbrook, *Queer London,* 9.

157 Hirschfeld, *Berlins Drittes Geschlecht,* 74.

158 Kirsten Plötz, *Einsame Freundinnen? Lesbisches Leben während der zwanziger Jahre in der Provinz* (Hamburg: MännerschwarmScript, 1999).

159 Benedict Anderson, *Imagined Communities: Reflections on the Origin and Spread of Nationalism* (New York: Verso, 1991), 9–36. The term *imagined community* was developed by Benedict Anderson as a model for understanding nationalism; however, the relationship it establishes between cultural material and social groups has proved very useful for thinking about the other kinds of social categories.

160 Micheler, *Selbstbilder und Fremdbilder,* 83–84.

161 Marhoefer, *Sex and the Weimar Republic,* 114.

162 Meeker, *Contacts Desired,* 16–29.

NOTES TO CHAPTER 4

1 Anthony Heilbut, *Thomas Mann: Eros and Literature* (New York: Alfred A. Knopf, 1996), 41.

2 Ibid., 43.

3 James W. Jones, "Mann, Thomas (1875–1955)," *GLBTQ: An Encyclopedia of Gay, Lesbian, Bisexual, Transgender, and Queer Culture,* www.glbtq.com/literature/mann_t.html, accessed November 7, 2014.

4 Andrew O'Hehir, "Just How Gay Is 'Death in Venice'?" *Salon,* August 10, 2004, www.salon.com /2004/08/10/venice_2/, accessed November 6, 2014.

5 Heilbut, *Thomas Mann,* 247.

6 Andrea Weiss, *In the Shadow of the Magic Mountain: The Erika and Klaus Mann Story* (Chicago: University of Chicago Press, 2008), 10.

7 Harry Oosterhuis, "The Dubious Magic of Male Beauty: Politics and Homoeroticism in the Lives and Works of Thomas and Klaus Mann," trans. Ton Brouwers, in *Queering the Canon: Defying Sights in German Literature and Culture,* ed. Christoph Lorey and John L. Plews (Columbia, S.C.: Camden House, 1998), 181.

8 Weiss, *In the Shadow of the Magic Mountain,* 62.

9 Doan, *Fashioning Sapphism,* 62.

10 Ibid., 162–63.

11 Oosterhuis, *Stepchildren of Nature,* 15.

12 Faderman, *Surpassing the Love of Men,* 178.

13 Matti Bunzl, *Jews and Queers: Symptoms of Modernity in Late-Twentieth-Century Vienna* (Berkeley: University of California Press, 2004), 13.

14 Mosse, *Nationalism and Sexuality,* 13.

15 Judith Butler, *Gender Trouble: Feminism and the Subversion of Identity* (New York: Routledge, 1990).

16 For an introduction to *Alltagsgeschichte,* see Alf Lüdtke, ed. *The History of Everyday Life: Reconstructing Historical Experiences and Ways of Life,* trans. William Templar (Princeton: Princeton University Press, 1995).

17 The influence of queer theory, with its more fluid take on identity construction, can clearly be seen in Micheler, *Selbstbilder und Fremdbilder der "Anderen."* For my own effort at using Judith Butler's conception of "performance" to reconstruct identities in a slightly later period, see Whisnant, "Styles of Masculinity in the West German Gay Scene."

18 Michael Warner, introduction to *Fear of a Queer Planet,* xv.

19 Claude Lévi-Strauss, *The Savage Mind* (Chicago: University of Chicago Press, 1966), 16–18.

20 Lybeck, *Desiring Emancipation,* esp. chap. 5.

21 Interestingly, this appears to have been true even in some countries where homosexuality was not a crime. For the case of France, see Victoria Thompson, "Creating Boundaries: Homosexuality and the Changing Social Order in France, 1830–1870," in *Homosexuality in Modern France,* ed. Jeffrey Merrick and Bryant T. Ragan Jr. (New York: Oxford University Press, 1996), 113–17.

22 On the turn-of-the-century media explosion, see Fritzsche, *Reading Berlin 1900.*

23 Jody Skinner, *Warme Brüder, Kesse Väter: Lexikon mit Ausdrücken für Lesben, Schwule und Homosexualität* (Essen: Blaue Euele, 1997), 172–73. See also Jim Steakley's remarks in a contribution to the H-Histsex list on May 16, 2004, http://h-net.msu.edu/cgi-bin/logbrowse.pl?trx=vx&list=H-Histsex&month=0405&week=c&msg=mwEyMln/687UCcM6ac364w&user=&pw=, accessed December 7, 2015.

24 Skinner, *Warme Brüder, Kesse Väter,* 146.

25 Works that support the priority of gay scenes over medical discourse include Trumbach, "The Birth of the Queen"; Vernon A. Rosario, "Pointy Penises, Fashion Crimes, and Hysterical Mollies," in Merrick and Ragan, *Homosexuality in Modern France,* 146–76; and Meer, "The Persecution of Sodomites in Eighteenth-Century Amsterdam."

26 John Fout, "Sexual Politics in Wilhelmine Germany: The Male Gender Crisis, Moral Purity, and Homophobia," *Journal of the History of Sexuality* 2, no. 3 (January 1992): 259–92.

27 Faderman, *Surpassing the Love of Men,* 29.

28 Ibid., 43–45.

29 James W. Jones, *"We of the Third Sex": Literary Representations of Homosexuality in Wilhelmine Germany* (New York: Peter Lang, 1990), 174–75.

30 Aimée Duc, *Sind Es Frauen? Roman über das dritte Geschlecht* (Berlin: Gabriele Meixner, 1976).

31 Jones, *"We of the Third Sex,"* 150.

32 Hughes, *Consciousness and Society.*

33 Oosterhuis, *Stepchildren of Nature,* 260.

34 On the so-called discovery of adolescence, see Gillis, *Youth and History,* 95–131.

35 Bram Dijkstra, "The Androgyne in Nineteenth-Century Art and Literature," *Comparative Literature* 26, no. 1 (Winter 1974): 63.

36 Peter Jelavich, *Munich and Theatrical Modernism: Politics, Playwriting, and Performance, 1890–1914* (Cambridge: Harvard University Press, 1985), 89–90.

37 Ibid., 82.

38 Schader, *Virile, Vamps und wilde Veilchen,* 139.

39 Siegfried Kracauer, *From Caligari to Hitler: A Psychological History of the German Film* (Princeton: Princeton University Press, 1947), 226.

40 Richard Dyer, "Less and More Than Women and Men: Lesbian and Gay Cinema in Weimar Germany," *New German Critique* 51 (Autumn 1990): 35–36.

41 Kracauer, *From Caligari to Hitler,* 227.

42 Dyer, "Less and More Than Women and Men," 41.

43 Ibid., 33.

44 Jones, *"We of the Third Sex,"* 150.

45 Dyer, "Less and More Than Women and Men," 34.

46 Quoted in Rosi Kreische, "Lesbische Liebe im Film bis 1950," in Bollé, *Eldorado,* 195–96.

47 Jones, *"We of the Third Sex,"* 206–7.

48   Ibid., 215–16.

49   Gay, *The Bourgeois Experience: Victoria to Freud,* vol. 2, *The Tender Passion,* 238.

50   Winckelmann and Platen were, by today's definition, almost certainly homosexual. The case of Goethe is more debatable. See Karl Hugo Pruys, *The Tiger's Tender Touch: The Erotic Life of Goethe* (Carol Stream, Ill.: Edition Q, 1999); Robert Tobin, *Warm Brothers: Queer Theory and the Age of Goethe* (Philadelphia: University of Pennsylvania Press, 2000); Robert Aldrich, *The Seduction of the Mediterranean: Writing, Art and Homosexual Fantasy* (New York: Routledge, 1993).

51   Mosse, *The Crisis of German Ideology,* 209.

52   Michael Winkler, "Master and Disciple: The George Circle," in *A Companion to the Works of Stefan George,* ed. Jens Rieckmann (Rochester, N.Y.: Camden House, 2005), 145.

53   Karl Wolfskehl, quoted in Robert E. Norton, *Secret Germany: Stefan George and His Circle* (Ithaca: Cornell University Press, 2002), 434.

54   Norton, *Secret Germany,* 687.

55   Ibid., 119–21.

56   Ibid., 339–41.

57   Marita Keilson-Lauritz, "Stefan George's Concept of Love and the Gay Emancipation Movement," in Rieckmann, *A Companion to the Works of Stefan George,* 207.

58   Ibid., 208.

59   Norton, *Secret Germany,* 266.

60   Ibid., 510–11.

61   Keilson-Lauritz, "Stefan George's Concept of Love," 210–15.

62   Theodor Lessing, quoted in Norton, *Secret Germany,* 153.

63   Norton, *Secret Germany,* 154.

64   Ibid., 298–301.

65   Ibid., 420–22.

66   Emmanuel Cooper, *The Sexual Perspective: Homosexuality and Art in the Last 100 Years in the West* (New York: Routledge and Kegan Paul, 1986), 24–43.

67   Ibid., 63–85.

68   Hirschfeld, *The Homosexuality of Men and Women,* 102; Andreas Sternweiler, "Kunst und schwuler Alltag," in Bollé, *Eldorado,* 75–79.

69   Sternweiler, "Kunst und schwuler Alltag," 81–82.

70   Ibid., 82–86.

71   Ulrich Pohlmann, *Wilhelm von Gloeden: Taormina* (Munich: Schirmer/Mosel, 1998), 7–8.

72   Wilhelm von Gloeden, "Kunst in der Photographie," *Photographische Mitteilungen* 36 (1898): 4.

73   Pohlmann, *Wilhelm von Gloeden,* 8–10.

74   Ibid., 17, 19–20.

75   Kenneth R. Dutton, *The Perfectible Body: The Western Ideal of Male Physical Development* (New York: Continuum, 1995), 95.

76   Andreas Sternweiler, "Kunstbetrieb und Homosexualität," in Schwules Museum, *Goodbye to Berlin?* 59.

77   Rowe, *Representing Berlin.*

78   Jones, *"We of the Third Sex,"* 137.

79   For a lengthier analysis of Kästner's, Döblin's, and Keun's novels, see Katie Sutton, *The Masculine Woman in Weimar Germany* (New York: Berghahn Books, 2011), 159–67.

80   Faderman, *Surpassing the Love of Men,* 254–76.

81   Thompson, "Creating Boundaries," 120.

82   Ibid., 118–19.

83   Jelavich, *Munich and Theatrical Modernism,* 106–10.

84   Kreische, "Lesbische Liebe im Film bis 1950," 190–91.

85   Margaret Schäfer, "Theater, Theater!" in Bollé, *Eldorado,* 180–81.

86   Marti Lybeck, "Gender, Sexuality, and Belonging: Female Homosexuality in Germany, 1890–1933" (PhD diss., University of Michigan at Ann Arbor, 2008), 229.

87   Ibid., 235.

88   For a similar interpretation of turn-of-the-century Expressionism, see Edward Timms, "Expressionists and Georgians: Demonic City and Enchanted Village," in *Unreal City: Urban Experience in Modern European Literature and Art,* ed. Edward Timms and David Kelley (New York: St. Martin's Press, 1985), 111–27.

89   Weiss, *In the Shadow of Magic Mountain,* 42.

90   Klaus Mann, *The Pious Dance: The Adventure Story of a Young Man*, trans. Laurence Senelick (New York: PAJ, 1987), 145.

91   Schader, *Virile, Vamps und wilde Veilchen,* 147–48.

92   Mackay, *The Hustler,* 35.

93   Ibid., 42.

94   Quoted in Hubert Kennedy, afterword to Mackay, *The Hustler,* 302.

95   Ibid., 305.

96   Mackay, *The Hustler,* 254.

97   Sutton, *The Masculine Woman in Weimar Germany,* 155.

98   Ibid., 156–57.

99   The first two volumes are available in English as Anna Elisabet Weirauch, *The Scorpion,* trans. Whittaker Chambers (New York: Greenberg, 1932). The last volume is translated as Anna Elisabet Weirauch, *The Outcast,* trans. Guy Endore (New York: Greenberg, 1933).

100   Nancy P. Nenno, "Bildung and Desire: Anna Elisabet Weirauch's *Der Skorpion,*" in Lorey and Plews, *Queering the Canon,* 209.

101   Sutton, *The Masculine Woman in Weimar Germany,* 171.

102   Vibek Rützou Petersen, *Women and Modernity in Weimar Germany: Reality and Its Representation in Popular Fiction* (New York: Berghahn Books, 2001), 97.

103   Beachy, *Gay Berlin,* 106.

104   Micheler, *Selbstbilder und Fremdbilder,* 130–34.

105   Ibid., 163–66.

106   This is my translation of the original, German-language lyrics written by Kurt Schwabach, not the English version composed by Jeremy Lawrence and made famous by Ute Lemper with her 1996 recording of the song.

107 Micheler, *Selbstbilder und Fremdbilder*, 117.

108 Beachy, *Gay Berlin,* 106, 111–12 .

109 Schader, *Virile, Vamps und wilde Veilchen,* 114–15.

110 Micheler, *Selbtsbilder und Fremdbilder,* 157.

111 Ibid., 154.

112 Quoted ibid., 154–55.

113 Ibid., 184.

114 Ibid., 197.

115 Ibid., 199.

116 Dr. R. Schild, quoted ibid., 186.

117 Micheler, *Selbtsbilder und Fremdbilder,* 184.

118 Ibid., 171–73.

119 Ramsey, "The Rites of *Artgenossen,*" 97–98.

120 Micheler, *Selbstbilder und Fremdbilder,* 143.

121 Ramsey, "The Rites of *Artgenossen,*" 99.

122 Micheler, *Selbstbilder und Fremdbilder,* 146.

123 Ibid., 156.

124 Ibid., 145.

125 Schader, *Virile, Vamps und wilde Veilchen,* 84–85.

126 Katie Sutton, *The Masculine Woman in Weimar Germany,* 117.

127 Ibid.

128 Schader, *Virile, Vamps und wilde Veilchen,* 110.

129 Sutton, *The Masculine Woman in Weimar Germany,* 28.

130 Ibid., 40.

131 For a queer analysis of the "breeches role" in Weimar film, see ibid., especially chap. 4. For an analysis of the role as it was revived in 1950s film, see Alison Guenther-Pal, "Projecting Deviance/Seeing Queerly: Homosexual Representations and Queer Spectatorship in 1950s West Germany" (PhD diss., University of Minnesota, 2007), especially chap. 5.

132 Sutton, *The Masculine Woman in Weimar Germany,* 6.

133 Ruth Röllig, quoted in Katie Sutton, *The Masculine Woman in Weimar Germany,* 48.

134 Schader, *Virile, Vamps und wilde Veilchen,* 123–26.

135 Quoted in Vogel, "Zum Selbstverständnis lesbischer Frauen in der Weimarer Republik," 165.

136 Both quoted ibid.

137 Quoted in Sutton, *The Masculine Woman in Weimar Germany,* 100.

138 Ibid., 101.

139 Schader, *Virile, Vamps und wilde Veilchen,* 109–14.

140 Sutton, *The Masculine Woman in Weimar Germany,* 98.

141 Schader, *Virile, Vamps und wilde Veilchen,* 114–19.

142 Ibid., 119–21; Katie Sutton, *The Masculine Woman in Weimar Germany,* 95–96.

143 Schader, *Virile, Vamps und wilde Veilchen,* 122–36.

144 Vogel, "Zum Selbstverständnis lesbischer Frauen in der Weimarer Republik," 165.

145 Schader, *Virile, Vamps und wilde Veilchen,* 98.

146 Ibid., 96–98.

147 Micheler, *Selbstbilder und Fremdbilder,* 230–31.

NOTES TO CHAPTER 5

1 Seth Taylor, *Left-Wing Nietzscheans: The Politics of German Expressionism, 1910–1920* (New York: de Gruyter, 1990), 64.

2 Ibid., 63.

3 Kurt Hiller, *Leben gegen die Zeit,* vol. 1, *Logos* (Reinbek bei Hamburg: Rowohlt, 1969), 71.

4 Ibid., 72.

5 Ibid., 80.

6 Taylor, *Left-Wing Nietzscheans,* 40–41.

7 Steven E. Aschheim, *The Nietzsche Legacy in Germany, 1890–1990* (Berkeley: University of California Press, 1992), 69–70.

8 Hiller, *Leben gegen die Zeit,* 1:80.

9 Ibid., 98.

10 Taylor, *Left-Wing Nietzscheans,* 70–72.

11 Stümke, *Homosexuelle in Deutschland,* 76.

12 Tamagne, *A History of Homosexuality in Europe,* 2:90.

13 Willem Melching, "'A New Morality': Left-Wing Intellectuals on Sexuality in Weimar Germany," *Journal of Contemporary History* 25 (1990): 69–85.

14 Manfred Baumgardt, "Das Institut für Sexualwissenschaft und die Homosexuellenbewegung in der Weimarer Republik," in Bollé, *Eldorado,* 31. On the experience of homosexuals in the early period of the Soviet Union, see Simon Karlinsky's "Russia's Gay Literature and Culture," in Duberman et al., *Hidden from History,* 347–64; Healey, *Homosexual Desire in Revolutionary Russia.*

15 Marhoefer, *Sex and the Weimar Republic,* 38–40; Crouthamel, *An Intimate History of the Front,* 128–29.

16 Crouthamel, *An Intimate History of the Front,* 130–34.

17 Micheler, "Homophobic Propaganda and the Denunciation of Same-Sex-Desiring Men," 102.

18 Quoted in Mancini, *Magnus Hirschfeld,* 114.

19 Ian Kershaw, *Hitler,* vol. 1, *Hubris, 1889–1936* (New York: W. W. Norton, 1998), 159.

20 Weitz, *Weimar Germany,* 89, 92–94.

21 For a history of the morality leagues, see Dickinson, *Sex, Freedom and Power in Imperial Germany,* 13–133.

22 Usborne, *The Politics of the Body in Weimar Germany,* 69–75.

23 Sabdste Schleiermacher, "Racial Hygiene and Deliberate Parenthood: Two Sides of Demographer Hans Harmsen's Population Policy," *Reproductive and Genetic Engineering: Journal of International Feminist Analysis* 3, no. 3 (1990): 201–10.

24   Kracauer, *From Caligari to Hitler*, 44.

25   Usborne, *The Politics of the Body in Weimar Germany*, 76; Kracauer, *From Caligari to Hitler*, 46–47.

26   Marhoefer, *Sex and the Weimar Republic*, 33–35.

27   Ursula von Keitz, *Filme vor Gericht: Theorie und Praxis der Filmprüfung in Deutschland, 1920 bis 1938* (Frankfurt: Deutsches Institut für Filmkunde, 1999).

28   Marhoefer, *Sex and the Weimar Republic*, 36–37.

29   Thomas Wehrling, "Berlin Is Becoming a Whore," in Kaes et al., *The Weimar Republic Sourcebook*, 721.

30   Ludwig Finckh, "The Spirit of Berlin," in Kaes et al., *The Weimar Republic Sourcebook*, 414.

31   Quoted in Wolfgang D. Berude, "Das Ende der 'Blütenfeste': Zum Vorgehen der nationalsozialistischen Polizei gegen Homosexuellenlokale," in *Das sind Volksfeinde! Die Verfolgung von Homosexuellen an Rhein und Ruhr, 1933–1945*, ed. Centrum Schwule Geschichte (Cologne: Centrum Schwule Geschichte, 1998), 47.

32   Stefan Zweig, *The World of Yesterday: An Autobiography* (New York: Viking Press, 1943), 313.

33   For a short version of the Redl affair, see Alan Sked, "Colonel Redl and a Question of Identity," *History Today* 36 (July 1986): 9–14. A longer history is offered by Georg Markus, *Der Fall Redl* (Vienna: Amalthea, 1984).

34   Wolfgang Theis, "Verdrängung und Travestie: Das vage Bild der Homosexualität im deutschen Film (1917–1957)," in Bollé, *Eldorado*, 104.

35   Tamagne, *A History of Homosexuality in Europe*, 2:37.

36   Tihamér Tóth, *Reine Jugendreife* (Freiburg im Breisgau: Herder, 1923).

37   Quoted in Tamagne, *A History of Homosexuality in Europe*, 2:39.

38   Hoffschildt, *Olivia*, 69–76.

39   Tamagne, *A History of Homosexuality in Europe*, 2:46.

40   Tatar, *Lustmord*, 3.

41   Lessing, *Haarmann*.

42   Hoffschildt, *Olivia*, 76–78.

43   Wolff, *Magnus Hirschfeld*, 196.

44   Ibid., 197–98.

45   Ibid., 218.

46   Detlev J. K. Peukert, *The Weimar Republic: The Crisis of Classical Modernity* (New York: Hill and Wang, 1987), xiii.

47   Dickinson, *Sex, Freedom and Power in Imperial Germany*, 310.

48   Peukert, *The Weimar Republic*, 280.

49   Mancini, *Magnus Hirschfeld*, 83.

50   Isherwood, *Christopher and His Kind*, 15.

51   Wolff, *Magnus Hirschfeld*, 177.

52   Beachy, *Gay Berlin*, 179–80.

53   Wolff, *Magnus Hirschfeld*, 181–82.

54   Beachy, *Gay Berlin*, 176–77.

55   Wolff, *Magnus Hirschfeld*, 181–82.

56   Grossmann, *Reforming Sex,* 16.

57   Isherwood, *Christopher and His Kind,* 16.

58   Wolfgang Jacobsen, "Oswald, Richard," in *Neue Deutsche Biographie* (Berlin: Duncker and Humblot, 1999), 19:637–38.

59   Wolfgang Theis, "Anders als die Andern: Geschichte eines Filmskandals," in Bollé, *Eldorado,* 28–30; Stümke, *Homosexuelle in Deutschland,* 63–64.

60   Tamagne, *A History of Homosexuality in Europe,* 1:88; Dyer, "Less and More Than Women and Men," 9.

61   Tamagne, *A History of Homosexuality in Europe,* 1:88.

62   Steakley, *The Homosexual Emancipation Movement in Germany,* 92; Stümke, *Homosexuelle in Deutschland,* 63.

63   Atina Grossmann, "The New Woman and the Rationalization of Sexuality in Weimar Germany," in *Powers of Desire: The Politics of Sexuality,* ed. Ann Snitow, Christine Stansell, and Sharon Thompson (New York: Monthly Review Press, 1983), 153–71.

64   Ralf Dose, "The World League for Sexual Reform: Some Possible Approaches," *Journal of the History of Sexuality* 12, no. 1 (2003): 1–15.

65   Herzer, *Magnus Hirschfeld,* 13.

66   Weindling, *Health, Race, and German Politics,* 375.

67   Ibid., 6–7.

68   Michael Schwartz, *Sozialistische Eugenik: Eugenische Sozialtechnologien in Debatten und Politik der deutschen Sozialdemokratie, 1890–1933* (Bonn: J. H. W. Dietz, 1995); Ingrid Richter, *Katholizismus und Eugenik in der Weimarer Republik und im Dritten Reich: Zwischen Sittlichkeitsreform und Rassenhygiene* (Paderborn: Ferdinand Schöningh, 2001).

69   For a history of eugenics in different national and political contexts, see Alison Bashford and Philippa Levine, eds., *The Oxford Handbook of the History of Eugenics* (Oxford: Oxford University Press, 2010).

70   Grossmann, *Reforming Sex,* esp. 46–77.

71   Wolff, *Magnus Hirschfeld,* 249–50.

72   Laurie Marhoefer, "Degeneration, Sexual Freedom, and the Politics of the Weimar Republic," *German Studies Review* 34, no. 3 (2011): 541–42.

73   Magnus Hirschfeld, *Geschlechtskunde,* 5 vols. (Stuttgart: J. Püttmann, 1926–30), 2:653.

74   Wolff, *Magnus Hirschfeld,* 251.

75   Marhoefer, "Degeneration, Sexual Freedom, and the Politics of the Weimar Republic," 532.

76   Grossmann, *Reforming Sex,* 136.

77   Christopher Koehler, "The Sex Problem: Thomas Hunt Morgan, Richard Goldschmidt, and the Question of Sex and Gender in the Twentieth Century" (PhD diss., University of Florida, 1998), 199–230.

78   Doucet, *Homosexualität,* 27.

79   Beachy, *Gay Berlin,* 173–75.

80   Dickinson, *Sex, Freedom, and Power,* 303.

81   Emil Kraepelin, *Psychiatrie: Ein Lehrbuch für Studierende und Ärzte,* 4 vols. (Leipzig: Johann Ambrosius Barth, 1909–15), 4:1966.

82   Mildenberger, "Kraepelin and the 'Urnings,'" 325–26.

83   Volkmar Sigusch, "The Sexologist Albert Moll: Between Sigmund Freud and Magnus Hirschfeld," *Medical History* 56 (2012): 193–95.

84   Wolff, *Magnus Hirschfeld,* 194.

85   Sigusch, "The Sexologist Albert Moll," 195–96.

86   Ernst Kretschmer, *Physique and Character: An Investigation of the Nature of Constitution and of the Theory of Temperament,* 2nd ed., trans. W. J. H. Sprott (New York: Cooper Square Publishers, 1970), 17–36. See also Thaddeus E. Weckowicz and Helen P. Liebel-Weckowicz, *A History of Great Ideas in Abnormal Psychology* (Amsterdam: North-Holland, 1990), 213–21, and Michael H. Stone, *Healing the Mind: A History of Psychiatry from Antiquity to the Present* (New York: W. W. Norton, 1997), 148.

87   Mildenberger, "Kraepelin and the 'Urnings,' " 328.

88   On the reception of Kretschmer in Sweden, see Jens Rydström, *Sinners and Citizens: Bestiality and Homosexuality in Sweden, 1880–1950* (Chicago: University of Chicago Press, 2003), 279.

89   Florian Mildenberger, "Diskursive Deckungsgleichheit—Hermaphroditismus und Homosexualität im medizinischen Diskurs (1850–1960)," in *Medizin, Geschichte und Geschlecht: Körperhistorische Rekonstruktionen von Identitäten und Differenzen,* ed. Frank Stahnisch and Florian Steger (Stuttgart: Franz Steiner, 2005), 272.

90   Ernst Kretschmer, *A Text-Book of Medical Psychology,* trans. E. B. Strauss (London: Oxford University Press, 1934), 132.

91   Kretschmer, *Physique and Character*, 92.

92   Veronika Fuechtner, *Berlin Psychoanalytic: Psychoanalysis and Culture in Weimar Republic Germany and Beyond* (Berkeley: University of California Press, 2011), 8.

93   Wolff, *Magnus Hirschfeld,* 201.

94   Fuechtner, *Berlin Psychoanalytic,* 11.

95   Joseph Schwartz, *Cassandra's Daughter: A History of Psychoanalysis* (New York: Viking, 1999), 176–77; Mitchell and Black, *Freud and Beyond,* 62–63.

96   Fuechtner, *Berlin Psychoanalytic,* 7.

97   Schwartz, *Cassandra's Daughter,* 247.

98   Mitchell and Black, *Freud and Beyond,* 87.

99   Paul Robinson, *The Freudian Left: Wilhelm Reich, Geza Roheim, Herbert Marcuse* (New York: Harper and Row, 1969), 40–46.

100 Sigmund Freud, "The Psychogenesis of a Case of Homosexuality in a Woman," in Freud, *Sexuality and the Psychology of Love,* ed. Philip Rieff (New York: Collier Books, 1963), 144.

101 Ibid., 143.

102 Ibid., 156.

103 Ibid., 137.

104 Quoted in Wolff, *Magnus Hirschfeld,* 256.

105 Weckowicz and Liebel-Weckowicz, *A History of Great Ideas in Abnormal Psychology,* 327–28.

106 Rollo May, "The Origins and Significance of the Existential Movement in Psychology," in *Existence: A New Dimension in Psychiatry and Psychology,* ed. Rollo May, Ernest Angel, and Henri F. Ellenberger (New York: Basic Books, 1958), 5.

107 Ludwig Binswanger, *Being-in-the-World: Selected Papers of Ludwig Binswanger,* ed. Jacob Needleman (New York: Basic Books, 1963), 166.

108 Burkhard Stefan Schieble, "Viktor Emil von Gebsattel: Leben und Werk" (PhD diss., University of Tübingen, 2008).

109   See W. Stark's introduction to Max Scheler, *The Nature of Sympathy* (1954; repr., Hamden, Conn.: Archon Books, 1970), xv. On Scheler's work in general, see Herbert Spiegelberg, *Phenomenology in Psychology and Psychiatry: A Historical Introduction* (Evanston, Ill.: Northwestern University Press, 1972), 16–18.

110   Viktor Erich von Gebsattel, "Süchtiges Verhalten im Gebiet sexueller Verirrungen" (1932), in *Prolegomena einer Medizinischen Anthropologie* (Berlin: Springer, 1954), 161–212.

111   Viktor Erich von Gebsattel, "Daseinsanalytische und anthropologische Auslegung der sexuellen Perversionen" (1950), in *Prolegomena einer Medizinischen Anthropologie,* 219. For a discussion of Gebsattel's perversion theory, see Spiegelberg, *Phenomenology in Psychology and Psychiatry,* 257–58.

112   Max Radin, "The Proposed German Penal Code," *California Law Review* 15, no. 5 (July 1927): 378.

113   Anton-Hermann Croust, "The Philosophy of Law of Gustav Radbruch," *Philosophical Review* 53, no. 1 (1944): 23–45.

114   Ibid.

115   Radin, "The Proposed German Penal Code," 379.

116   Hiller, *Leben gegen die Zeit,* 1:208.

117   Ibid.

118   Kartell für Reform des Sexualstrafrechts, *Gegen-Entwurf zu den Strafbestimmungen des Amtlichen Entwurfs eines Allgemeinen Deutschen Strafgesetzbuchs über geschlechtliche und mit dem Geschlechtsleben im Zusammenhang stehende Handlungen* (Berlin: Neuen Gesellschaft, 1927), 38.

119   Ibid., 56.

120   Kurt Hiller, *Leben gegen die Zeit,* vol. 2, *Eros* (Reinbek bei Hamburg: Rowohlt, 1973), 99.

121   Ibid., 94.

122   Marhoefer, *Sex and the Weimar Republic,* 6.

123   Hiller, *Leben gegen die Zeit,* 2:87.

124   Ibid., 87–88; Dobler, *Von anderen Ufern,* 102.

125   For more on Linsert's role in establishing the Munich Friendship League, see Marhoefer, *Sex and the Weimar Republic,* 20

126   Hiller, *Leben gegen die Zeit,* 2:87–88.

127   Ibid., 88–89.

128   Ibid., 94.

129   Dobler, *Von anderen Ufern,* 101.

130   Hiller, *Leben gegen die Zeit,* 2:104.

131   Tamagne, *A History of Homosexuality in Europe,* 1:58–59.

132   On the sexual politics of the Communist Party, see W. U. Eissler, *Arbeiterparteien und Homosexuellenfrage: Zur Sexualpolitik von SPD und KPD in der Weimarer Republik* (Berlin: R. Winkel, 1980).

133   Magnus Hirschfeld and Richard Linsert, *Empfängnisverhütung: Mittel und Methoden* (Berlin: Neuer Deutsches, 1928); Magnus Hirschfeld and Richard Linsert, *Liebesmittel: Eine Darstellung der geschlechtlichen Reizmittel* (Berlin: Man, 1930).

134   Hubert Kennedy, "Brand, Adolf (1874–1945)," *GLBTQ: An Encyclopedia of Gay, Lesbian, Bisexual, Transgender, and Queer Culture,* www.glbtqarchive.com/ssh/brand_a_S.pdf, accessed October 16, 2015.

135   Magnus Herzer, "Die Gemeinschaft der Eigenen," in Schwules Museum, *Goodbye to Berlin?* 89.

136   Micheler, "Zeitschriften, Verbände und Lokale."

137 Herzer, "Die Gemeinschaft der Eigenen," 91.

138 Crouthamel, *An Intimate History of the Front,* 130–31.

139 Micheler, "Zeitschriften, Verbände und Lokale," 24.

140 Crouthamel, *An Intimate History of the Front,* 136–37.

141 Micheler, "Zeitschriften, Verbände und Lokale," 24.

142 Herzer, "Die Gemeinschaft der Eigenen," 91; Micheler, "Zeitschriften, Verbände und Lokale," 13.

143 Herzer, "Die Gemeinschaft der Eigenen," 90.

144 Ibid., 89–90.

145 Ramsey, "The Rites of *Artsgenossen,*" 89.

146 Dobler, *Von anderen Ufern,* 89.

147 Bruns, "The Politics of Eros," 167.

148 Ibid., 166–67.

149 Ibid., 175.

150 Kershaw, *Hitler,* 1:100.

151 Hiller, *Leben gegen die Zeit,* 1:115.

152 Bruns, "The Politics of Eros," 175.

153 Hans Blüher, *Secessio Judaica* (Berlin: Weiße Ritter, 1922), 49.

154 Bruns, "The Politics of Eros," 172, 177.

155 Dobler, *Von anderen Ufern,* 91.

156 Ibid., 92.

157 St. Ch. Waldecke, "Die Homosexualität vor dem Staatsanwalt," *Der Eigene* 9 (1925): 391–98, reprinted in Hohmann, *Der Eigene.* For more on Oskar Nerlinger, see Andreas Sternweiler, "Das Lusthaus der Knaben—Homosexualität und Kunst," in Schwules Museum, *Goodbye to Berlin?* 122.

158 Herzer, "Die Gemeinschaft der Eigenen," 91. See also Harry Oosterhuis, "Homosexual Emancipation in Germany before 1933," 6.

159 Crouthamel, *An Intimate History of the Front,* 137.

160 Micheler, "Zeitschriften, Verbände und Lokale," 45.

161 Micheler, *Selbstbilder und Fremdbilder,* 144.

162 Quoted in Sternweiler, "Die Freundschaftsbünde," 95.

163 Stümke, *Homosexuelle in Deutschland,* 58.

164 Quoted in Micheler, *Selbstbilder und Fremdbilder,* 144.

165 Ramsey, "The Rites of *Artgenossen,*" 100.

166 Micheler, *Selbstbilder und Fremdbilder,* 142.

167 Ibid., 144.

168 Micheler, "Zeitschriften, Verbände und Lokale," 38.

169 Ibid.

170 Ibid., 44.

171 Ibid., 46.

172 Ibid., 45.

173   Ibid., 45–46.

174   Quoted in Steakley, *The Homosexual Emancipation Movement in Germany*, 82.

175   Marhoefer, "Degeneration, Sexual Freedom, and the Politics of the Weimar Republic," 539.

176   Christian Müller, *Verbrechensbekämpfung im Anstaltsstaat: Psychiatrie, Kriminologie und Strafrechtsreform in Deutschland, 1871–1933* (Göttingen: Vandenhoek and Ruprecht, 2004), 196–97.

177   Hiller, *Leben gegen die Zeit*, 2:99–100.

178   Marhoefer, "Degeneration, Sexual Freedom, and the Politics of the Weimar Republic," 539.

179   Marhoefer, *Sex and the Weimar Republic*, 120.

180   Marhoefer, "Degeneration, Sexual Freedom, and the Politics of the Weimar Republic," 538.

181   Sebastian, "Als Homosexualität noch strafbar war: '§175 StGB—Unzucht zwischen Männern,'" JuraForum, February 20, 2005, www.juraforum.de/forum/t/als-homosexualitaet-noch-strafbar-war-175-stgb-unzucht-zwischen-maennern.15965/, accessed October 20, 2014.

182   Micheler, "Zeitschriften, Verbände und Lokale," 47.

183   Quoted in Wolff, *Magnus Hirschfeld*, 227.

184   Marhoefer, *Sex and Weimar Germany*, 116–17.

185   Ibid., 129–33.

186   Herzer, *Magnus Hirschfeld*, 89; Mancini, *Magnus Hirschfeld*, 124.

187   Wolff, *Magnus Hirschfeld*, 229.

188   Herzer, *Magnus Hirschfeld*, 90.

189   Marhoefer, *Sex and the Weimar Republic*, 131.

190   Kurt Hiller, writing in the WhK newsletter, quoted in Armin Schäfer, *Biopolitik des Wissens: Hans Henny Jahnns literarisches Archiv des Menschen* (Würzburg: Königshausen and Neumann, 1996), 116.

191   Marhoefer, *Sex and the Weimar Republic*, 133.

192   Ibid., 134.

193   Tamagne, *A History of Homosexuality in Europe*, 1:59; Marhoefer, *Sex and the Weimar Republic*, 116–17.

194   Hiller, *Leben gegen die Zeit*, 2:55.

195   Ibid., 57.

196   Wolff, *Magnus Hirschfeld*, 227.

197   Andreas Pretzel, "Homosexuality in the Sexual Ethics of the 1930s: A Values Debate in the Culture Wars between Conservatism, Liberalism, and Moral-National Renewal," in Spector et al., *After the History of Sexuality*, 204.

198   Kershaw, *Hitler*, 1:315–427.

199   Pretzel, "Homosexuality in the Sexual Ethics of the 1930s," 210.

200   For a longer analysis of this historiography, see Marhoefer, *Sex and the Weimar Republic*, 194–98.

201   For an excellent overview of this emerging view of Weimar, see the essays in Anthony McElligott, ed., *Weimar Germany* (New York: Oxford University Press, 2009).

202   Marhoefer, *Sex and the Weimar Republic*, especially chap. 6.

203   McElligott, introduction to McElligott, *Weimar Germany*, 20.

204   Pretzel, "Homosexuality in the Sexual Ethics of the 1930s," 204.

205 McElligott, "Political Culture," in McElligott, *Weimar Germany,* 40–44.

206 Micheler, *Selbstbilder und Fremdbilder,* 287–88.

207 Kershaw, *Hitler,* 1:360–91.

208 Ibid., 413–27; McElligott, "Political Culture," 43.

209 Kershaw, *Hitler,* 1:431.

210 Beachy, *Gay Berlin,* 230.

NOTES TO CHAPTER 6

1 Kershaw, *Hitler,* 1:173.

2 Ibid., 174.

3 Richard Bessel, *Political Violence and the Rise of Nazism: The Storm Troopers in Eastern Germany, 1925–1934* (New Haven: Yale University Press, 1984).

4 Baumgardt, "Das Institut für Sexualwissenschaft," 41.

5 Ibid., 154–55.

6 Eleanor Hancock, " 'Only the Real, the True, the Masculine Held Its Value': Ernst Röhm, Masculinity, and Male Homosexuality," *Journal of the History of Sexuality* 8, no. 4 (1998): 628.

7 Burkhard Jellonnek, *Homosexuelle unter dem Hakenkreuz: Die Verfolgung von Homosexuellen im Dritten Reich* (Paderborn: Ferdinand Schöningh, 1990), 63.

8 Marhoefer, *Sex and the Weimar Republic,* 146–48.

9 Jellonnek, *Homosexuelle unter dem Hakenkreuz,* 65.

10 Ibid., 61.

11 Plant, *The Pink Triangle,* 61.

12 Suzanne zur Nieden, "Aufstieg und Fall des virilen Männerhelden: Der Skandal um Ernst Röhm und seine Ermordung," in Nieden, *Homosexualität und Staatsräson,* 174–75.

13 Manfred Herzer, "Communists, Social Democrats, and the Homosexual Movement in the Weimar Republic," in Hekma et al., *Gay Men and the Sexual History of the Political Left,* 197–226; Alexander Zinn, "Die soziale Konstruktion des homosexuellen Nationalsozialisten im antifaschistischen Exil," in Grumbach, *Die Linke und das Laster,* 38–84.

14 For a queer reading of Nazi art, see Tim Pursell, "Queer Eyes and Wagnerian Guys: Homoeroticism in the Art of the Third Reich," *Journal of the History of Sexuality* 17, no. 1 (January 2008): 110–37.

15 For a discussion of the long-standing association between Nazism and sexual perversity, see Dagmar Herzog, *Sex after Fascism: Memory and Morality in Twentieth-Century Germany* (Princeton: Princeton University Press, 2005), 11–13.

16 Lothar Machtan's *The Hidden Hitler* (New York: Basic Books, 2001) has not generally been well received by historians.

17 Herzog, *Sex after Fascism,* 11.

18 "Second Directive of the Prussian Minister of the Interior, 23 February 1933," quoted in Grau, *Hidden Holocaust?* 28; emphasis in original.

19 Müller and Schneberger, "Schwules Leben in Köln" in Limpricht et al., *"Verführte" Männer.*

20 Hoffschildt, *Olivia,* 89–93.

21 Staatsarchiv Hamburg, Polizeibehörde I, 461 Band 2, Befehlsheft II no. 72, April 6, 1933.

22 Rudolf Klare, *Homosexualität und Strafrecht* (Hamburg: Hanseatische Verlagsanstalt, 1937), 146.

23 Hans-Georg Stümke, "Von 'unausgeglichenen Geschlechtshaushalt': Zur Verfolgung Homosexueller," in *Verachtet, Verfolgt, Vernichtet: Zu den "vergessenen" Opfern des NS-Regimes,* ed. Projektgruppe für die vergessenen Opfer des NS-Regimes (Hamburg: VSA, 1988), 51–53.

24 Quoted in Helmut Fangmann, Udo Reifner, and Norbert Steinborn, *"Parteisoldaten": Hamburger Polizei im "3. Reich"* (Hamburg: VSA, 1987), 80.

25 Hoffschildt, *Olivia,* 84.

26 Quoted in Karl-Heinz Steinle, *Der Literarische Salon bei Richard Schultz* (Berlin: Schwules Museum, 2002), 48.

27 Manfred Herzer, "Die Zerschlagung der Schwulenbewegung," in Schwules Museum, *Goodbye to Berlin?* 158–59.

28 Stümke, *Homosexuelle in Deutschland,* 102; Manfred Baumgardt, "Das Institut für Sexualwissenschaft," 35–38.

29 Andreas Sternweiler, " 'Nachteiliges über ihn konnte nicht festgestellt werden': Mitstreiter aus der Schwulenbewegung," in *Homosexuelle Männer im KZ Sachsenhausen,* ed. Joachim Müller and Andreas Sternweiler (Berlin: Rosa Winkel, 2000), 150–51.

30 Andreas Sternweiler, "Exil," in Schwules Museum, *Goodbye to Berlin?* 169–73.

31 Weiss, *In the Shadow of the Magic Mountain,* 102–3.

32 Thomas Mann, "Humanism and Europe," *New Republic,* April 28, 1937, 349.

33 Weiss, *In the Shadow of the Magic Mountain,* 114–16.

34 Ibid., 159–73.

35 Ibid., 189–99.

36 Norton, *Secret Germany,* 727–37.

37 Hergemöller, "Hans Blüher," 150–51.

38 Andreas Sternweiler, *Liebe, Forschung, Lehre: Der Kunsthistoriker Christian Adolf Isermeyer* (Berlin: Rosa Winkel, 1998), 35.

39 Hancock, "Only the Real, the True, the Masculine," 626.

40 Quoted ibid., 623.

41 Andrew Wackerfuss, *Stormtrooper Families: Homosexuality and Community in the Early Nazi Movement* (New York: Harrington Park Press, 2015).

42 For Willhart Schlegel's later career, see Whisnant, *Male Homosexuality in West Germany,* 172–74.

43 Willhart Schlegel, *Rolf: Eine Zeitgeschichtliche Erzählung* (Frankfurt: R. G. Fischer, 1995), 41.

44 Ibid., 43–45.

45 Kershaw, *Hitler,* 1:503.

46 The full story of the Night of Long Knives is told ibid., 500–524.

47 Micheler, *Selbstbilder und Fremdbilder,* 305–6.

48 Ibid., 304–5.

49 Ibid., 392–93.

50 Schlegel, *Rolf,* 46.

51 Micheler, *Selbstbilder und Fremdbilder,* 294.

52 Ibid., 309–14.

53 Kershaw, *Hitler,* 2:54–56.

54 Ibid., 1:506.

55 Giles, "The Institutionalization of Homosexual Panic in the Third Reich," 235.

56 This speech is discussed in Oosterhuis, "Medicine, Male Bonding and Homosexuality in Nazi Germany," 201.

57 Kershaw, *The "Hitler Myth": Image and Reality in the Third Reich* (New York: Oxford University Press, 1987), 85; Jellonnek, *Homosexuelle unter dem Hakenkreuz*, 95–100.

58 Stümke, *Homosexuelle in Deutschland*, 8–9; Christian Schulz, *Paragraph 175. (abgewickelt) Homosexualität und Strafrecht im Nachkriegsdeutschland: Rechtsprechung, juristische Diskussionen und Reformen seit 1945* (Hamburg: MännerschwarmSkript, 1994), 109–10.

59 Schulz, *Paragraph 175*, 9.

60 Stümke, "Vom 'unausgeglichenen Geschlechtshaushalt,'" 54; Jellonnek, *Homosexuelle unter dem Hakenkreuz*, 100–110, 122–24.

61 Micheler, *Selbstbilder und Fremdbilder*, 324–25.

62 Georg Stümke, "Vom 'unausgeglichenen Geschlechtshaushalt,'" 53–54.

63 Ibid., 58.

64 Micheler, *Selbstbilder und Fremdbilder*, 330–31.

65 Ibid., 340–65.

66 Sparing, *Wegen Vergehen nach §175 verhaftet*, 168–72.

67 Andreas Pretzel, "Als Homosexueller in Erscheinung getreten: Anzeigen und Denunciationen," in *Wegen der zu erwartenden hohen Strafe: Homosexuellenverfolgung in Berlin, 1933–1945*, ed. Andreas Pretzel and Gabriele Roßbach (Berlin: Rosa Winkel, 2000), 25–31; Sparing, *Wegen Vergehen nach §175 verhaftet*, 128–32; Micheler, "Homophobic Propaganda and the Denunciation of Same-Sex-Desiring Men under National Socialism," 117–24.

68 Pretzel, "Als Homosexueller in Erscheinung getreten," 32–39.

69 Gabriele Roßbach, "Sie sahen das Zwecklose ihres Leugnens ein: Verhöre bei Gestapo und Kripo," in Pretzel and Roßbach, *Wegen der zu erwartenden hohen Strafe*, 74.

70 Ibid.; Sparing, *Wegen Vergehen nach §175 verhaftet*, 132–46.

71 Andreas Pretzel, "Erst dadurch wird eine wirksame Bekämpfung ermöglicht: Polizeiliche Ermittlungen," in Pretzel and Roßbach, *Wegen der zu erwartenden hohen Strafe*, 43–54.

72 Geoffrey Giles, "'The Most Unkindest Cut of All': Castration, Homosexuality and Nazi Justice," *Journal of Contemporary History* 27, no. 1 (January 1992): 46–61; Joachim Müller, "'Um von meinem Trieb befreit zu werden': Kastrationen im Krankenrevier," in Müller and Sternweiller, *Homosexuelle Männer im KZ Sachsenhausen;* Frank Sparing, "'Daß er es der Kastration zu verdanken hat, daß er überhaupt in die Volksgemeinschaft entlassen wird': Die Entmannung von Homosexuellen im Bereich der Kriminalbiologischen Sammelstelle Köln," in *Das sind Volksfeinde! Die Verfolgung von Homosexuellen an Rhein und Ruhr, 1933–1945*, ed. Centrum Schwule Geschichte (Cologne: Centrum Schwule Geschichte, 1998), 160–81; Albert Knoll, "Totgeschlagen-totgeschwiegen: Die homosexuellen Häftlinge im KZ Dachau," *Dachauer Hefte* 14 (November 1998): 99–100.

73 As one might guess, inmates in German prisons were actually better off than those kept in Nazi concentration camps. Andreas Sternweiler even notes some cases of men in concentration camps who volunteered statements about their homosexual activity within the camps, hoping that this would lead to a formal prison sentence. See Andreas Sternweiler, "Chronologischer Versuch zur Situation der Homosexuellen im KZ Sachsenhausen," in *Homosexuelle Männer im KZ Sachsenhausen*, ed. Joachim Müller and Andreas Sternweiler (Berlin: Rosa Winkel, 2000), 39. Rainer Hoffschildt rightly remarks, though, that we know very little about conditions within Nazi prisons (*Gefängnisse*) and penitentiaries (*Zuchthäuser*), which have not been traditionally seen as "significant sites of confinement, pain, and death," despite evidence that they too produced increasing numbers of deaths in the

course of the Nazi period. See Rainer Hoffschildt, *Die Verfolgung der Homosexuellen in der NS-Zeit: Zahlen und Schicksale aus Norddeutschland* (Berlin: Rosa Winkel, 1999), 143.

74   There are numerous accounts of life in the concentration camps. The most famous ones generally treat the Jewish experience of the death camps, usually Auschwitz, but much of these descriptions can be generalized to the larger work camps in Germany and Austria (Buchenwald, Dachau, Flossenbürg, Mauthausen, Neuengamme, and Sachsenhausen). Four of the best-known are Primo Levi, *Survival in Auschwitz: The Nazi Assault on Humanity* (1958; repr., New York: Simon and Schuster, 1996); Terrence Des Pres, *The Survivor: An Anatomy of Life in the Death Camps* (New York: Oxford University Press, 1976); Elie Wiesel, *Night* (1955; repr., New York: Hill and Wang, 2006); and Eugene Heimler, *Night of the Mist* (New York: Vanguard Press, 1960).

75   Knoll, "Totgeschlagen-Totgeschwiegen," 85.

76   For a hint at the range of inmates in Sachsenhausen, see Andreas Sternweiler, " 'Er ging mit ihm alsbald ein sogenanntes "Festes Verhältnis" ein': Ganz normale Homosexuelle," in Müller and Sternweiler, *Homosexuelle Männer im KZ Sachsenhausen,* 58–78. For some examples of nonhomosexual inmates who were nonetheless classified as 175ers, see Andreas Sternweiler, " 'Wegen dringenden Verdachts homosexueller und bündischer Betätigung festgenommen: Homosexuelle aus der Jugendbewegung," in Müller and Sternweiler, *Homosexuelle Männer im KZ Sachsenhausen,* 109–44; and Karl-Heinz Steinle, " 'Auf verlorenem Posten': Der sudetendeutsche Politiker Walter Brand," in Müller and Sternweiler, *Homosexuelle Männer im KZ Sachsenhausen,* 277–82.

77   This claim was above all made by Plant, *The Pink Triangle,* 165–66.

78   Andreas Sternweiler, " 'Als ein Beweis, daß wir zusammenhalten': Freundschaft und Solidarität," in Müller and Sternweiler, *Homosexuelle Männer im KZ Sachsenhausen,* 316–30; Andreas Sternweiler, " 'Er habe sich zeichnend am Leben erhalten': Der Künstler Richard Grune," in Müller and Sternweiler, *Homosexuelle Männer im KZ Sachsenhausen,* 190–206.

79   For a comparison of Neuengamme with Sachsenhausen, see Andreas Sternweiler, "Nachteiliges über ihn konnte nicht festgestellt werden," 155.

80   For example, Egon Wüst, a dancer at the Eldorado, was taken to Dachau for "reeducation measures" in 1933. See Sternweiler, " 'Er ging mit ihm alsbald ein sogenanntes "Festes Verhältnis" ein,' " 59–60.

81   For a good English-language overview of the expansion and systematization of the Nazi camp system in the course of 1935 and 1936, see Robert Gellately, *Backing Hitler: Consent and Coercion in Nazi Germany* (New York: Oxford University Press, 2001), 61–67.

82   Even before the Dachau system of identification began being used, though, many camps appear to have been making some more basic visual distinctions by 1936. In Dachau, one Social Democratic exile noted that gay inmates wore a large "175" on their clothing. At the same time in Sachsenhausen, several categories of prisoners were already being identified with different colored stripes (and a yellow spot if they were Jewish), though it is unclear if homosexuals were included in this earlier system. See Knoll, "Totgeschlagen-totgeschwiegen," 88–89; and Sternweiler, "Chronologischer Versuch," 34–35.

83   Knoll, "Totgeschlagen-totgeschiegen," 89–90; Sternweiler, "Chronologischer Versuch," 39–40.

84   Sternweiler, "Chronologischer Versuch," 42.

85   Heinz Heger, *The Men with the Pink Triangle,* 2nd ed., trans. David Fernbach (Boston: Alyson Books, 1994), 40.

86   Joachim Müller, " 'Wohl dem, der hier nur eine Nummer ist': Die Isolierung der Homosexuellen," in Müller and Sternweiler, *Homosexuelle Männer im KZ Sachsenhausen,* 89–108.

87   Joachim Müller, " 'Wie die Bewegung, so die Verpflegung': Die Strafkompanie Schuhläufer," in Müller and Sternweiler, *Homosexuelle Männer im KZ Sachsenhausen,* 181–89.

88   Joachim Müller, " 'Unnatürliche Todesfälle': Vorfälle in den Außenbereichen Klinkerwerk, Schießplatz und Tongrube," in Müller and Sternweiler, *Homosexuelle Männer im KZ Sachsenhausen,* 216–63.

89 Plant, *The Pink Triangle,* 175–79; Sternweiler, "Chronologischer Versuch," 50; Knoll, "Totgeschlagen-totgeschwiegen," 99.

90 Kershaw, *Hitler,* 1:154, 316.

91 Hans Peter Bleuel, *Sex and Society in Nazi Germany,* trans. J. Maxwell Brownjohn (1972; repr., New York: Dorset Press, 1996), 6.

92 Udo Pini, *Leibeskult und Liebeskitsch: Erotik im Dritten Reich* (Munich: Klinkhardt and Biermann, 1992), 9–11.

93 Mosse, *Nationalism and Sexuality,* 9, 153–80.

94 Wilhelm Reich, *The Mass Psychology of Fascism,* 3rd ed., trans. V. R. Carfagno (New York: Farrar, Straus and Giroux, 1970). This argument is also implicit in Bleuel, *Sex and Society in Nazi Germany.*

95 Elizabeth Heineman, "Sexuality and Nazism: The Doubly Unspeakable," in *Sexuality and German Fascism,* ed. Dagmar Herzog (New York: Berghahn Books, 2005), 26; Herzog, *Sex after Fascism,* 152–62.

96 Klaus Theweleit, *Male Fantasies,* trans. Erica Carter, Stephen Conway, and Chris Turner, 2 vols. (Minneapolis: University of Minnesota Press, 1987), 1:41.

97 Ibid., 2:338.

98 Ibid., 339.w

99 Nicolaus Sombart, *Die Deutschen Männer und ihre Feinde: Carl Schmitt, ein deutsches Schicksal zwischen Männerbund und Matriarchatmythos* (Munich: Hanser, 1991), 51–53.

100 For an excellent overview of the literature, see Heineman, "Sexuality and Nazism."

101 Herzog, *Sex after Fascism,* 15–16. See also her summary in Herzog, *Sexuality in Europe: A Twentieth-Century History* (New York: Cambridge University Press, 2011), 67–75.

102 Bunzl, *Symptoms of Modernity,* 16.

103 Both passages quoted in Stümke, *Homosexuelle in Deutschland,* 113.

104 Quoted in Erhard Vismar, "Perversion und Verfolgung unter dem deutschen Faschismus," in Lautmann, *Seminar,* 320.

105 Klare, *Homosexualität und Strafrecht,* 13, 33–34.

106 Burleigh and Wippermann, *The Racial State.* See also Stümke, *Homosexuelle in Deutschland,* 92–94; and Günter Grau, "Persecution, 'Re-education' or 'Eradication' of Male Homosexuals."

107 For a longer discussion of these critiques of the "racial state" paradigm, see Patrick Gilner, "Beyond the Racial State: Rethinking Nazi Germany," *GHI Bulletin* 46 (Spring 2010): 163–70.

108 Peter von Rönn, "Politische und psychiatrische Homosexualitätskonstruktion im NS-Staat. Teil II: Die soziale Genese der Homosexualität als defizitäre Heterosexualität," *Zeitschrift für Sexualforschung* 11 (1998): 243–46.

109 Geoffrey Giles, "The Institutionalization of Homosexual Panic in the Third Reich," 237–42. See also William Spurlin's argument that "homophobia seldom operated alone, but operated in conjunction with other axes of power . . . including race, gender and particular national policies, which under the Third Reich included eugenics and population policies." William J. Spurlin, *Lost Intimacies: Rethinking Homosexuality under National Socialism* (New York: Peter Lang, 2009), 7.

110 Mosse, *The Image of Man.*

111 Quoted in Claudia Schoppmann, "The Position of Lesbian Women in the Nazi Period," in Grau, *Hidden Holocaust?* 11.

112 Jellonnek, *Homosexuelle unter dem Hakenkreuz,* 23–24.

113 Oosterhuis, "Medicine, Male Bonding and Homosexuality in German Nationalism"; Pursell, "Queer Eyes and the Wagnerian Guys."

114 Giles, "The Institutionalization of Homosexual Panic in the Third Reich," 238.

115 Micheler, *Selbstbilder und Fremdbilder,* 320–22.

116 Jellonnek, *Homosexuelle unter dem Hakenkreuz,* 100–110.

117 Geoffrey J. Giles, "The Denial of Homosexuality: Same-Sex Incidents in Himmler's SS and Police," in *Sexuality and German Fascism,* ed. Dagmar Herzog (New York: Berghahn Books, 2005), 256–90.

118 Jellonnek, *Homosexuelle unter dem Hakenkreuz,* 330.

119 Heineman, "Sexuality and Nazism," 35.

120 Schoppmann, "The Position of Lesbian Women in the Nazi Period," 8–12.

121 Ibid., 13.

122 Schoppmann, *Days of Masquerade,* 102–14. Some of Annette Eick's story can also be heard in the film *Paragraph 175.*

123 Schoppmann, *Days of Masquerade,* 31–37.

124 Schader, *Virile, Vamps und wilde Veilchen,* 77.

125 Schoppmann, "The Position of Lesbian Women in the Nazi Period," 13.

126 Schoppmann, *Days of Masquerade,* 11.

127 Leidinger, "Anna Rüling," 488–92.

128 Ibid., 139.

129 Micheler, *Selbstbilder und Fremdbilder,* 412–19.

130 Fritz was biologically male, but I will assume, given what we know about her, that she would have preferred the use of the feminine pronoun.

131 Sternweiler, "'Er ging mit ihm alsbald ein sogenanntes "Festes Verhältnis" ein,'" 59–62.

132 Carola Gerlach, "Außerdem habe ich dort mit meinem Freund getanzt," in Pretzel and Roßbach, *Wegen der zu erwartenden hohen Strafe,* 309–13.

133 Ibid., 322–27.

134 Micheler, *Selbstbilder und Fremdbilder,* 398–406.

135 Ibid., 420–21.

136 Ibid., 437–39.

137 Rudolf E., quoted ibid., 438.

138 The best-known work in this vein is Daniel Goldhagen's *Hitler's Willing Executioners: Ordinary Germans and the Holocaust* (New York: Alfred A. Knopf, 1996). It has, however, been severely criticized on many accounts by numerous historians. For some key works that have been better received by the historical community, see Claudia Koonz, *Mothers in the Fatherland: Women, the Family, and Nazi Politics* (New York: St. Martin's Press, 1987); Omer Bartov, *Hitler's Army: Soldiers, Nazis, and War in the Third Reich* (New York: Oxford University Press, 1991); Christopher Browning, *Ordinary Men: Reserve Police Battalion 101 and the Final Solution in Poland* (New York: HarperCollins, 1992); Eric A. Johnson, *Nazi Terror: The Gestapo, Jews, and Ordinary Germans* (New York: Basic Books, 1999); and Gellately, *Backing Hitler.*

139 Quoted in Elizabeth Heineman, "Sexuality and Nazism," 37.

140 Micheler, *Selbstbilder und Fremdbilder,* 420.

141 Schoppmann, *Days of Masquerade,* 65–71.

142 Volkmar Sigusch and Günter Grau, *Geschichte der Sexualwissenschaft* (Frankfurt: Campus, 2008), 93.

143 Cocks, *Psychotherapy in the Third Reich,* 90.

144 Ibid., 109.

145 Ibid., 90–91.

146 Mildenberger, "Kraepelin and the 'Urnings,'" 327.

147 Ibid., 330–31.

148 Weckowicz and Liebel-Weckowicz, *A History of Great Ideas in Abnormal Psychology,* 209–10.

149 Weindling, *Health, Race and German Politics,* 328–31; Robert Proctor, *Racial Hygiene: Medicine under the Nazis* (Cambridge: Harvard University Press, 1988), 35.

150 Weckowicz and Liebel-Weckowicz, *A History of Great Ideas in Abnormal Psychology,* 210; Shorter, *A History of Psychiatry,* 240–43; Proctor, *Racial Hygiene,* 40–43; Weindling, *Health, Race, and German Politics,* 309–10.

151 Susanne zur Nieden, "Erbbiologische Forschungen zur Homosexualität an der Deutschen Forschungsanstalt für Psychiatrie während der Jahre des Nationalismus: Zur Geschichte von Theo Lang," Ergebnisse 25 for the Research Program "History of the Kaiser Wilhelm Society in the National Socialist Era" (2008), www.mpiwg-berlin.mpg.de/KWG/Ergebnisse/Ergebnisse25.pdf, 11–13, accessed December 6, 2014.

152 Hans Habel, "Zwillingsuntersuchungen an Homosexuellen," *Zeitschrift für Sexualforschung* 1 (1950): 168–80. See also Barbara Zeh, "Der Sexualforscher Hans Giese: Leben und Werk" (PhD diss., Johann Wolfgang Goethe University, 1988), 59.

153 Verschuer to Ministry of Interior, quoted in Zeh, "Der Sexualforscher Hans Giese," 61.

154 Nieden, "Erbbiologische Forschungen zur Homosexualität an der Deutschen Forschungsanstalt für Psychiatrie während der Jahre des Nationalismus," 15–17.

155 Theo Lang, "Über die erbliche Bedingtheit der Homosexualität und die grundsätzliche Bedeutung der Intersexualitätsforschung für die menschliche Genetik," *Allgemeine Zeitschrift für Psychiatrie und ihre Grenzgebiet* 112 (1939: 237–54. For a discussion of Lang's research, see Rudolf Klimmer, *Die Homosexualität als biologisch-soziologische Zeitfrage* (Hamburg: Kriminalistik, 1958), 47–49; Giles, "'The Most Unkindest Cut of All,'" 51.

156 Klaus Jensch, "Zur Genealogie der Homosexualität," *Archiv für Psychiatrie und Nervenkrankheiten* 112, no. 4 (February 1941): 527–40. See also Jellonnek, "Homosexuellenforschung im Dritten Reich," 223.

157 Nieden, "Erbbiologische Forschungen zur Homosexualität an der Deutschen Forschungsanstalt für Psychiatrie während der Jahre des Nationalismus," 25–27.

158 For more on Deussen and Lemke, see Marc Dupont, "Biologische und psychologische Konzepte im 'Dritten Reich' zur Homosexualitaet," in Jellonnek and Lautman, *Nationalsozialistischer Terror gegen Homosexuelle,* 197–99.

159 Nieden, "Erbbiologische Forschungen zur Homosexualität an der Deutschen Forschungsanstalt für Psychiatrie während der Jahre des Nationalismus," 37–39.

160 Cocks, *Psychotherapy in the Third Reich.*

161 Ibid., 207–9.

162 Ibid., 209–10.

163 Giles, "The Denial of Homosexuality," 271.

164 Karl-Heinz Roth, "Großhungern und Gehorchen: Das Universitätskrankenhaus Eppendorf," in *Heilen und Vernichten im Mustergau Hamburg: Bevölkerungs- und Gesundheitspolitik im Dritten*

Reich, ed. Angelika Ebbinghaus, Heidrun Kaupen-Haas, and Karl Heinz Roth (Hamburg: Konkret, 1984), 130–34.

165 Hans Bürger-Prinz, "Betrachtungen über einen Homosexualitätsprozeß," *Monatsschrift für Kriminalbiologie und Strafrechtsreform* 29 (1938): 335.

166 Hans Bürger Prinz, "Gedanken zum Problem der Homosexualität," *Monatsschrift für Kriminalbiologie und Strafrechtsreform* 30 (1939): 433–35.

167 Ibid., 437.

168 Dupont, "Biologische und psychologische Konzepte im 'Dritten Reich' zur Homosexualität," 201–2; Giles, " 'The Most Unkindest Cut of All,' " 50–51.

169 Bürger-Prinz, "Gedanken zum Problem der Homosexualität," 431.

170 Giles, " 'The Most Unkindest Cut of All,' " 50.

171 Bürger-Prinz, "Gedanken zum Problem der Homosexualität," 435.

172 For a more thorough treatment of the ways that Bürger-Prinz's ideas fit well with the Nazi worldview, see Peter von Rönn, "Das Homosexualitätskonzept des Psychiaters Hans Bürger-Prinz im Rahmen der NS-Verfolgungspolitik," in Jellonek and Lautmann, *Nationalsozialistischer Terror gegen Homosexuelle,* 237–60.

173 Rönn, "Politische und psychiatrische Homosexualitätskonstruktion im NS-Staat," 240–45.

174 Giles, "The Denial of Homosexuality," 273–77.

175 On the brutality of war on the Eastern Front, see Bartov, *Hitler's Army.*

176 Gellately, *Backing Hitler,* 230–31.

177 This is according to current estimates of the U.S. Holocaust Museum: www.ushmm.org/learn /students/learning-materials-and-resources/homosexuals-victims-of-the-nazi-era/persecution-of -homosexuals, accessed December 9, 2015.

178 Whisnant, *Male Homosexuality in West Germany,* 46–47.

179 Ibid., 43–44.

180 Ibid., 46.

NOTES TO THE CONCLUSION

1 Zeh, "Der Sexualforscher Hans Giese," 18–19.

2 Ibid., 13–14, 22–25.

3 Whisnant, *Male Homosexuality in West Germany,* 70–78, 170–72.

4 Ibid., 75.

5 The photographer Erich Lessing took a number of photographs of Berlin in 1955; they are currently available online at Magnum Photos, www.magnumphotos.com/Catalogue/Erich-Lessing/1955 /WEST-BERLIN-NN133768.html, accessed December 9, 2015.

6 Jennifer Evans, *Life among the Ruins: Cityscape and Sexuality in Cold War Berlin* (New York: Palgrave Macmillan, 2011).

7 Whisnant, *Male Homosexuality in West Germany,* 22–25.

8 Herzog, *Sex after Fascism,* esp. chaps. 2 and 3.

9 Jennifer V. Evans, "Decriminalization, Seduction, and 'Unnatural Desire' in East Germany," *Feminist Studies* 36, no. 3 (2010): 555–60.

10 Ibid., 555.

11 Whisnant, *Male Homosexuality in West Germany*, 36–43.

12 Wolff, *Magnus Hirschfeld*, 365–415.

13 Kennedy, "Brand, Adolf (1874–1945)."

14 Dobler, *Von anderen Ufern*, 228.

15 Schoppmann, *The Days of Masquerade*, 72.

16 Sternweiler, *Liebe, Forschung, Lehre*, 104–22.

17 Whisnant, *Male Homosexuality in West Germany*, 70–91.

18 Clayton Whisnant, "Images of Masculinity in the West German Homophile Magazines of the 1950s," paper presented at the Thirty-sixth Annual Conference of the German Studies Association, panel titled "Restrained, Regulated or Rampant? The History of Masculinities and Sexuality in 20th Century Germany" (October 6, 2012), www.academia.edu/2020977/GSA_2012_Images_of_Masculinity_in_the_Homophile_Magazines_of_the_1950s, accessed December 9, 2015.

19 Whisnant, *Male Homosexuality in West Germany*, 105–8.

20 Leila J. Rupp, "The Persistence of Transnational Organizing: The Case of the Homophile Movement," *American Historical Review* 116, no. 4 (October 2011): 1014–39.

21 Guenther-Pal, "Projecting Deviance/Seeing Queerly," 168–74.

22 Gerhard Kuhn, "Das Phänomen der Strichjungen in Hamburg" (PhD diss., University of Hamburg, 1955), 68.

23 Ernst Schramm, "Das Strichjungenwesen," in *Sittlichkeitsdelikte: Arbeitstagung im Bundeskriminalamt Wiesbaden von 20. April bis 25. April 1959 über die Bekämpfung der Sittlichkeitsdelikte*, ed. Bundeskriminalamt (Wiesbaden: Bundeskriminalamt, 1959), 95; letter from Polizeipräsident betr. Transvestiten-Unwesen, September 30, 1964, Hamburg Staatsarchiv, Behörde für Inneres, 1792.

24 Whisnant, *Male Homosexuality in West Germany*, 113–18.

25 "Nachtleben soll gesäubert warden . . . in Berlin," *Frankfurter Rundschau*, June 16, 1967.

26 Whisnant, *Male Homosexuality in West Germany*, 187–88.

27 For an extended treatment of Beate Uhse and her business, see Elizabeth Heineman, *Before Porn Was Legal: The Erotica Empire of Beate Uhse* (Chicago: University of Chicago Press, 2011).

28 Hermann Glaser, *Kulturgeschichte der Bundesrepublik Deutschland*, vol. 2, *Zwischen Grundgesetz und Großer Koalition, 1949–1967* (Munich: Carl Hanser, 1986), 98–107; Axel Schildt and Detlef Siegfried, *Deutsche Kulturgeschichte: Die Bundesrepublik von 1945 bis zur Gegenwart* (Munich: Carl Hanser, 2009), 260–65; Franz Eder, "The Long History of the 'Sexual Revolution' in West Germany," in *Sexual Revolutions*, ed. Gert Hekma and Alain Giami (New York: Palgrave Macmillan, 2014), 99–120.

29 Josie McLellan, *Love in the Time of Communism: Intimacy and Sexuality in the GDR* (New York: Cambridge University Press, 2011).

30 Evans, "Decriminalization, Seduction, and 'Unnatural Desire' in East Germany." One of the most detailed versions of this story in English is a very good senior honors thesis by Adam Amir, of the University of Florida, "The Persistence of Paragraph 175: Nazi-Style Justice in Postwar Germany" (May 2010), 13–20.

31 McLellan, *Love in the Time of Communism*, 114. See also Evans, "Decriminalization, Seduction, and 'Unnatural Desire' in East Germany," 557–60.

32 A little inconsistently, though, the East German government kept Paragraph 175a on the books until 1968.

33 International Friendship Lodge, "Wir und der demokratische Staat," *Die Insel* 2 (March 1952): 4–5.

34 Whisnant, *Homosexuality in West Germany*, 29–36.

35   Ibid., 166–203.

36   Matt Cook makes this observation in his recent essay "Capital Stories: Local Lives in Queer Lon-
      don," in Cook and Evans, *Queer Cities, Queer Cultures*, 36–54. Whether older Germans felt this way
      will need to be verified by other research.

37   Wolfgang Theis, "Mach dein Schwulsein öffentlich—Bundesrepublik," in Schwules Museum, *Good-
      bye to Berlin?* 279–93.

38   Ferree, *Varieties of Feminism*, 69–72.

39   McLellan, *Love in the Time of Communism*, 118–29.

40   Evans, "Decriminalization, Seduction, and 'Unnatural Desire' in East Germany," 560–69.

41   Erik N. Jensen, "The Pink Triangle and Political Consciousness: Gays, Lesbians, and the Memory of
      Nazi Persecution," *Journal of the History of Sexuality* 11, nos. 1/2 (January/April 2002): 319–49.

42   Josie McLellan, *Love in the Time of Communism*, 124–26.

43   Liam Johnson, "13 of the World's Most Inspiring Gay Monuments," *GayStarNews*, October 1,
      2013, www.gaystarnews.com/article/13-worlds-most-inspiring-gay-monuments011013, accessed
      December 9, 2015.

44   Jensen, "The Pink Triangle and Political Consciousness," 336–49. See also Jennifer V. Evans, "Harm-
      less Kisses and Infinite Loops: Making Space for Queer Place in Twenty-First Century Berlin," in
      Cook and Evans, *Queer Cities, Queer Cultures*, 75–94.

45   Whisnant, *Male Homosexuality in West Germany*, 148–51.

46   Dieter Rucht, "Das Alternative Milieu in der Bundesrepublik," in *Das Alternative Milieu: Antibür-
      gerlicher Lebensstil und linke Politik in der Bundesrepublik Deutschland und Europa, 1968–1983*, ed.
      Sven Reichardt and Detlef Siegfried (Göttingen: Wallstein, 2010), 78–80.

47   Lisa Duggan, "The New Homonormativity: The Sexual Politics of Neoliberalism," in *Materializ-
      ing Democracy: Toward a Revitalized Cultural Politics*, ed. Russ Castronova and Dana D. Nelson
      (Durham: Duke University Press, 2002), 173–94.

48   Bunzl, *Symptoms of Modernity*, 204.

49   Matt Cook and Jennifer Evans, introduction to Cook and Evans, *Queer Cities, Queer Cultures*, 9.

50   Bunzl, *Symptoms of Modernity*, 205–11.

BIBLIOGRAPHY

Aldrich, Robert. *The Seduction of the Mediterranean: Writing, Art and Homosexual Fantasy.* London and New York: Routledge, 1993.

Allen, Ann Taylor. "Mothers of the New Generation: Adele Schreiber, Helene Stöcker, and the Evolution of a German Idea of Motherhood, 1900–1914." *Signs* 10, no. 3 (Spring 1985): 418–38.

Anderson, Benedict. *Imagined Communities: Reflections on the Origin and Spread of Nationalism.* New York: Verso, 1991.

Aschheim, Steven E. *The Nietzsche Legacy in Germany, 1890–1990.* Berkeley: University of California Press, 1992.

Balfour, Michael. *The Kaiser and His Times.* 1964. Reprint, New York: W. W. Norton, 1972.

Balser, Kristof, Mario Kramp, Jürgen Müller, and Joanna Gotzmann, eds. *"Himmel und Hölle": Das Leben der Kölner Homosexuellen, 1945–1969.* Cologne: Emons, 1994.

Barthes, Roland. *The Pleasure of the Text.* Translated by Richard Miller. New York: Hill and Wang, 1975.

Bartov, Omer. *Hitler's Army: Soldiers, Nazis, and War in the Third Reich.* New York: Oxford University Press, 1992.

Bashford, Alison, and Philippa Levine, eds. *The Oxford Handbook of the History of Eugenics.* Oxford: Oxford University Press, 2010.

Baumgardt, Manfred. "Die Homosexuellen-Bewegung bis zum Ende des Ersten Weltkriegs." In *Eldorado: Homosexuelle Frauen und Männer in Berlin, 1850–1950,* edited by Michael Bollé, 17–27. Berlin: Frölich and Kaufmann, 1992.

———. "Das Institut für Sexualwissenschaft und die Homosexuellen-Bewegung in der Weimarer Republik." In *Eldorado: Homosexuelle Frauen und Männer in Berlin, 1850–1950,* edited by Michael Bollé, 31–43. Berlin: Frölich and Kaufmann, 1992.

Beachy, Robert. *Gay Berlin: Birthplace of a Modern Identity.* New York: Alfred A. Knopf, 2014.

———. "The German Invention of Homosexuality." *Journal of Modern History* 82, no. 4 (December 2010): 801–38.

Berude, Wolfgang D. "Das Ende der 'Blütenfeste': Zum Vorgehen der nationalsozialistischen Polizei gegen Homosexuellenlokale." In *Das sind Volksfeinde! Die Verfolgung von Homosexuellen an Rhein und Ruhr, 1933–1945,* edited by Centrum Schwule Geschichte, 47–61. Cologne: Centrum Schwule Geschichte, 1998.

Bessel, Richard. *Political Violence and the Rise of Nazism: The Storm Troopers in Eastern Germany, 1925–1934.* New Haven: Yale University Press, 1984.

Binswanger, Ludwig. *Being-in-the-World: Selected Papers of Ludwig Binswanger.* Edited by Jacob Needleman. New York: Basic Books, 1963.

Blackbourn, David. *History of Germany, 1780–1918: The Long Nineteenth Century.* 2nd edition. Oxford: Blackwell, 2003.

Bleibtreu-Ehrenberg, Gisela. *Tabu Homosexualität.* Frankfurt: Fischer, 1978.

Bleuel, Hans Peter. *Sex and Society in Nazi Germany.* Translated by J. Maxwell Brownjohn. 1972. Reprint, New York: Dorset Press, 1996.

Bloch, Iwan. *The Sexual Life of Our Time in Its Relation to Modern Civilization.* Translated by M. Eden Paul. London: Rebman, 1908.

Blüher, Hans. *Die Rolle der Erotik in der männlichen Gesellschaft: Eine Theorie der menschlichen Staatsbildung nach Wesen und Wert.* 2 vols. Jena: Eugen Diederichs, 1919.

———. *Secessio Judaica.* Berlin: Weiße Ritter, 1922.

———. *Wandervogel: Geschichte einer Jugendbewegung.* 5th edition. 3 vols. Frankfurt am Main: Dipa, 1957.

———. *Werke und Tage: Geschichte eines Denkers.* Munich: Paul List, 1953.

Bollé, Michael, ed. *Eldorado: Homosexuelle Frauen und Männer in Berlin, 1850–1950: Geschichte, Alltag und Kultur.* Berlin: Frölich and Kaufmann, 1984.

Boswell, John. *Christianity, Social Tolerance, and Homosexuality: Gay People in Western Europe from the Beginning of the Christian Era to the Fourteenth Century.* Chicago: University of Chicago Press, 1980.

Boyd, Nan. *Wide-Open Town: A History of Queer San Francisco to 1965.* Berkeley: University of California Press, 2003.

Bray, Alan. *Homosexuality in Renaissance England.* London: Gay Men's Press, 1982.

Bronski, Michael. *A Queer History of the United States.* Boston: Beacon Press, 2011.

Bruns, Claudia. "Der homosexuelle Staatsfreund: Von der Konstruktion des erotischen Männerbund bei Hans Blüher." In *Homosexualität und Staatsräson: Männlichkeit, Homophobie und Politik in Deutschland, 1900–1945,* edited by Susanne zur Nieden, 100–117. Frankfurt: Campus, 2005,.

———. "Masculinity, Sexuality, and the German Nation: The Eulenburg Scandals and Kaiser Wilhelm II in Political Cartoons." In *Pictorial Cultures and Political Iconographies: Approaches, Perspectives, Case Studies from Europe and America,* edited by Udo J. Hebel and Christoph Wagner, 119–41. Berlin: Walter de Gruyter, 2011.

———. "The Politics of Eros: The German Männerbund between Anti-Feminism and Anti-Semitism in the Early Twentieth Century." In *Masculinity, Senses, Spirit,* edited by Katherine M. Faull, 153–90. Lewisburg, Pa.: Bucknell University Press, 2011.

———. "The Politics of Masculinity in the (Homo-) Sexual Discourse (1880–1920)." *German History* 23, no. 3 (2005): 306–20.

———. "Skandale im Beraterkreis um Kaiser Wilhelm II: Die homoerotische 'Verbündelung' der 'Liebenberger Tafelrunde' als Politikum." In *Homosexualität und Staatsräson: Männlichkeit, Homophobie und Politik in Deutschland, 1900–1945,* edited by Suzanne zur Nieden, 52–80. Frankfurt: Campus, 2005.

Bullough, Vern. *Science in the Bedroom: A History of Sex Research.* New York: Basic Books, 1994.

Bunzl, Matti. *Symptoms of Modernity: Jews and Queers in Late-Twentieth-Century Vienna.* Berkeley: University of California, 2004.

Bürger-Prinz, Hans. "Betrachtungen über einen Homosexualitätsprozeß." *Monatsschrift für Kriminalbiologie und Strafrechtsreform* 29 (1938): 333–36.

———. "Gedanken zum Problem der Homosexualität." *Monatsschrift für Kriminalbiologie und Strafrechtsreform* 30 (1939): 430–38.

Burleigh, Michael, and Wolfgang Wippermann. *The Racial State: Germany, 1933–1945.* Cambridge: Cambridge University Press, 1991.

Butler, Judith. *Gender Trouble: Feminism and the Subversion of Identity.* New York: Routledge, 1990.

Centrum Schwule Geschichte, ed. *Das sind Volksfeinde! Die Verfolgung von Homosexuellen an Rhein und Ruhr, 1933–1945.* Cologne: Centrum Schwule Geschichte, 1998.

Chauncey, George. "From Sexual Inversion to Homosexuality: Medicine and the Changing Conceptualization of Female Deviance." *Salmagundi* 58/59 (1982): 114–46.

———. *Gay New York: Gender Urban Culture, and the Making of the Gay Male World, 1890–1940.* New York: Basic Books, 1994.

Clark, Anna. *Desire: A History of European Sexuality.* London: Routledge, 2008.

Cleminson, Richard, and Francisco Vasquez Garcia. *"Los Invisibles": A History of Male Homosexuality in Spain, 1850–1939.* Cardiff: University of Wales Press, 2007.

Cocks, Geoffrey. *Psychotherapy in the Third Reich: The Göring Institute.* 2nd edition. New Brunswick, N.J.: Transaction, 1997.

Cook, Matt. *London and the Culture of Homosexuality, 1885–1914.* Cambridge: Cambridge University Press, 2003.

Cook, Matt, and Jennifer Evans, eds. *Queer Cities, Queer Cultures: Europe since 1945*. London: Bloomsbury, 2014.

Cooper, Emmanuel. *The Sexual Perspective: Homosexuality and Art in the Last 100 Years in the West*. New York: Routledge and Kegan Paul, 1986.

Croust, Anton-Hermann. "The Philosophy of Law of Gustav Radbruch." *Philosophical Review* 53, no. 1 (1944): 23–45.

Crouthamel, Jason. *An Intimate History of the Front: Masculinity, Sexuality, and German Soldiers in the First World War*. New York: Palgrave Macmillan, 2014.

Désert, Jean-Ulrick. "Queer Space." In *Queers in Space: Communities, Public Spaces, Sites of Resistance,* edited by Gordon Brent Ingram, Anne-Marie Bouthillette, and Yolanda Retter, 17–26. Seattle: Bay Press, 1997.

Dickinson, Edward Ross. "Policing Sex in Germany, 1882–1982: A Preliminary Analysis." *Journal of the History of Sexuality* 16 (2007): 204–50.

———. *Sex, Freedom, and Power in Imperial Germany, 1880–1914*. New York: Cambridge University Press, 2014.

Dijkstra, Bram. "The Androgyne in Nineteenth-Century Art and Literature." *Comparative Literature* 26, no. 1 (Winter 1974): 62–73.

Doan, Laura. *Disturbing Practices: History, Sexuality, and Women's Experience of Modern War*. Chicago: University of Chicago Press, 2013.

———. *Fashioning Sapphism: The Origins of a Modern English Lesbian Culture*. New York: Columbia University Press, 2001.

Dobler, Jens. *Von anderen Ufern: Geschichte der Berliner Lesben und Schwulen in Kreuzberg und Friedrichshain*. Berlin: Gmünder, 2003.

———. *Zwischen Duldungspolitik und Verbrechensbekämpfung: Homosexuellenverfolgung durch die Berliner Polizei von 1848 bis 1933*. Frankfurt: Polizeiwissenschaft, 2008.

Dose, Ralf. "The World League for Sexual Reform: Some Possible Approaches." *Journal of the History of Sexuality* 12, no. 1 (2003): 1–15.

Doucet, Friedrich Wilhelm. *Homosexualität*. Munich: Lichtenberg, 1967.

Dover, K. J. *Greek Homosexuality*. Cambridge: Harvard University Press, 1978.

Duc, Aimée. *Sind Es Frauen? Roman über das dritte Geschlecht*. Berlin: Gabriele Meixner, 1976.

Duggan, Lisa. "The New Homonormativity: The Sexual Politics of Neoliberalism." In *Materializing Democracy: Toward a Revitalized Cultural Politics,* edited by Russ Castronova and Dana D. Nelson, 173–94. Durham: Duke University Press, 2002.

Dupont, Marc. "Biologische und psychologische Konzepte im 'Dritten Reich' zur Homosexualitaet." In *Nationalsozialistischer Terror gegen Homosexuelle,* edited by Burkhard Jellonnek and Rüdiger Lautmann, 189–207. Paderborn: Ferdinand Schöningh, 2002.

Dutton, Kenneth R. *The Perfectible Body: The Western Ideal of Male Physical Development.* New York: Continuum, 1995.

Dyer, Richard. "Less and More Than Women and Men: Lesbian and Gay Cinema in Weimar Germany." *New German Critique,* no. 51 (Autumn 1990): 5–60.

Eder, Franz. "The Long History of the 'Sexual Revolution' in West Germany." In *Sexual Revolutions,* edited Gert Hekma and Alain Giami, 99–120. New York: Palgrave Macmillan, 2014.

Eder, Franz X., Lesley Hall, and Gert Hekma, eds. *Sexual Cultures in Europe,* vol. 1, *National Histories.* Manchester: Manchester University, 1999.

———. *Sexual Cultures in Europe,* vol. 2, *Themes in Sexuality.* Manchester: Manchester University, 1999.

Eissler, W. U. *Arbeiterparteien und Homosexuellenfrage: Zur Sexualpolitik von SPD und KPD in der Weimarer Republik.* Berlin: R. Winkel, 1980.

Eksteins, Modris. *Rites of Spring: The Great War and the Birth of the Modern Age.* Boston: Houghton Mifflin, 1989.

Ellis, Havelock. *Studies in the Psychology of Sex,* vol. 2, *Sexual Inversion.* Philadelphia: F. A. Davis, 1915.

El-Rouayheb, Khaled. *Before Homosexuality in the Arab-Islamic World, 1500–1800.* Chicago: University of Chicago Press, 2005.

Evans, Jennifer. "*Bahnhof* Boys: Policing Male Prostitution in Post-Nazi Berlin." *Journal of the History of Sexuality* 12, no. 4 (2003): 605–36.

———. "Decriminalization, Seduction, and 'Unnatural Desire' in East Germany." *Feminist Studies* 36, no. 3 (2010): 553–77.

———. *Life among the Ruins: Cityscape and Sexuality in Cold War Berlin.* New York: Palgrave Macmillan, 2011.

Faderman, Lillian. *Surpassing the Love of Men: Romantic Friendship and the Love between Women from the Renaissance to the Present.* New York: William Morrow, 1981.

Faderman, Lillian, and Stuart Timmons. *Gay L.A.: A History of Sexual Outlaws, Power Politics, and Lipstick Lesbians.* New York: Basic Books, 2006.

Falzeder, Ernst, ed. and trans. *The Complete Correspondence of Sigmund Freud and Karl Abraham, 1907–1925.* London: Karnac Books, 2002.

Fangmann, Helmut, Udo Reifner, and Norbert Steinborn. *"Parteisoldaten": Hamburger Polizei im 3. Reich.* Hamburg: VSA, 1987.

Ferree, Myra Marx. *Varieties of Feminism: German Gender Politics in Global Perspective.* Stanford: Stanford University Press, 2012.

Flexner, Abraham. *Prostitution in Europe.* New York: Century, 1914.

Fore, Devin. "Döblin's Epic: Sense, Document, and the Verbal World Picture." *New German Critique* 33, no. 3 (2006): 171–207.

Fout, John. "Sexual Politics in Wilhelmine Germany: The Male Gender Crisis, Moral Purity, and Homophobia." In *Forbidden History: The State, Society, and the Regulation of Sexuality in Modern Europe,* edited by John Fout, 259–92. Chicago: University of Chicago Press, 1992.

Freud, Sigmund. "Certain Neurotic Mechanisms in Jealousy, Paranoia and Homosexuality." In *Sexuality and the Psychology of Love,* edited by Philip Rieff, 160–70. New York: Collier Books, 1963.

———. "Leonardo da Vinci and a Memory of His Childhood," translated by James Strachey. In *The Freud Reader,* edited by Peter Gay, 443–81. New York: W. W. Norton, 1989.

———. "The Psychogenesis of a Case of Homosexuality in a Woman." In Freud, *Sexuality and the Psychology of Love,* edited by Philip Rieff, 133–59. New York: Collier Books, 1963.

———. *Three Essays on the Theory of Sexuality.* Translated by James Strachey. New York: Basic Books, 1975.

Frevert, Ute. *Women in German History: Bourgeois Emancipation to Sexual Liberation.* Translated by Stuart McKinnon-Evans. New York: Berg, 1989.

Fritzsche, Peter. *Reading Berlin 1900.* Cambridge: Harvard University Press, 1996.

Fuechtner, Veronika. *Berlin Psychoanalytic: Psychoanalysis and Culture in Weimar Republic Germany and Beyond.* Berkeley: University of California Press, 2011.

Gay, Peter. *The Bourgeois Experience: Victoria to Freud,* vol. 2, *The Tender Passion.* New York: Oxford University Press, 1986.

———. *Weimar Culture: The Outsider as Insider.* New York: Harper and Row, 1968.

Gebsattel, Viktor Erich von. "Daseinsanalytische und anthropologische Auslegung der sexuellen Perversionen" (1950). In Gebsattel, *Prolegomena einer Medizinischen Anthropologie,* 212–20. Berlin: Springer, 1954.

———. "Süchtiges Verhalten im Gebiet sexueller Verirrungen" (1932). In Gebsattel, *Prolegomena einer Medizinischen Anthropologie,* 161–212. Berlin: Springer, 1954.

Gelder, Ken, and Sarah Thornton, eds. *The Subcultures Reader.* New York: Routledge, 1997.

Gellately, Robert. *Backing Hitler: Consent and Coercion in Nazi Germany.* New York: Oxford University Press, 2001.

Gerard, Kent, and Gert Hekma, eds. *The Pursuit of Sodomy: Male Homosexuality in Renaissance and Enlightenment Europe.* New York: Harrington Park Press, 1989.

Gerlach, Carola. "Außerdem habe ich dort mit meinem Freund getanzt." In *Wegen der zu erwartenden hohen Strafe: Homosexuellenverfolgung in Berlin, 1933–1945,* edited by Andreas Pretzel and Gabriele Roßbach, 305–32. Berlin: Rosa Winkel, 2000.

Giles, Geoffrey J. "The Denial of Homosexuality: Same-Sex Incidents in Himmler's SS and Police." In *Sexuality and German Fascism,* edited by Dagmar Herzog, 256–90. New York: Berghahn Books, 2005.

———. "The Institutionalization of Homosexual Panic in the Third Reich." In *Social Outsiders in Nazi Germany,* edited by Robert Gellately and Nathan Stotlzfus, 233–355. Princeton: Princeton University Press, 2001.

———. " 'The Most Unkindest Cut of All': Castration, Homosexuality and Nazi Justice." *Journal of Contemporary History* 27, no. 1 (January 1992): 46–61.

Gillis, John R. *Youth and History: Tradition and Change in European Age Relations, 1770–Present.* Expanded edition. New York: Academic Press, 1981.

Gilner, Patrick. "Beyond the Racial State: Rethinking Nazi Germany." *GHI Bulletin* 46 (Spring 2010): 163–70.

Glaser, Hermann. *Kulturgeschichte der Bundesrepublik Deutschland,* vol. 2, *Zwischen Grundgesetz und Großer Koalition, 1949–1967.* Munich: Carl Hanser, 1986.

Gloeden, Wilhelm von. "Kunst in der Photographie." *Photographische Mitteilungen* 36 (1898): 3–6.

Gozzi, Gustavo. "Rechtsstaat and Individual Rights in German Constitutional History." In *The Rule of Law: History, Theory, and Criticism,* edited by Pietro Costa and Danilo Zolo, 237–59. Dordrecht: Springer, 2007.

Grau, Günter, ed. *Hidden Holocaust? Gay and Lesbian Persecution in Germany, 1933–45.* Translated by Patrick Camiller. Chicago: Fitzroy Dearborn, 1993.

———. "Persecution, 'Re-education' or 'Eradication' of Male Homosexuals between 1933 and 1945: Consequences of the Eugenic Concept of Assured Reproduction." In *Hidden Holocaust? Gay and Lesbian Persecution in Germany, 1933–45,* edited by Günter Grau, translated by Patrick Camiller, 1–7. Chicago: Fitzroy Dearborn, 1993.

Greenberg, David. *The Construction of Homosexuality.* Chicago: University of Chicago Press, 1988.

Grossmann, Atina. "The New Woman and the Rationalization of Sexuality in Weimar Germany." In *Powers of Desire: The Politics of Sexuality,* edited by Ann Snitow, Christine Stansell, and Sharon Thompson, 153–71. New York: Monthly Review Press, 1983.

———. *Reforming Sex: The German Movement for Birth Control and Abortion Reform, 1920–1950.* Oxford: Oxford University Press, 1995.

Grumbach, Detlef. "Die Linke und das Laster." In *Die Linke und das Laster: Schwule Emanzipation und linke Vorurteile,* edited by Detlef Grumbach, 17–37. Hamburg: MännerschwarmSkript, 1995.

Guenther-Pal, Alison. "Projecting Deviance/Seeing Queerly: Homosexual Representations and Queer Spectatorship in 1950s West Germany." PhD dissertation, University of Minnesota, 2007.

Gunther, Scott. *The Elastic Closet: A History of Homosexuality in France, 1942–Present.* New York: Palgrave Macmillan, 2008.

Haakenson, Thomas Odell. "Grotesque Visions: Art, Science, and Visual Culture in Early Twentieth-Century Germany." PhD dissertation, University of Minnesota, 2006.

Hacker, Hanna. *Frauen und Freundinnen: Studien zur "weiblichen Homosexualität" am Beispiel Österreich, 1870–1938.* Weinheim: Beltz Verlag, 1987.

Halberstam, Judith. *Female Masculinity.* Durham: Duke University Press, 1998.

Halperin, David. *How to Do the History of Homosexuality.* Chicago: University of Chicago Press, 2002.

———. *One Hundred Years of Homosexuality and Other Essays on Greek Love.* New York: Routledge, 1990.

Hancock, Eleanor. "'Only the Real, the True, the Masculine Held Its Value': Ernst Röhm, Masculinity, and Male Homosexuality." *Journal of the History of Sexuality* 8, no. 4 (1998): 616–41.

Hau, Michael. *The Cult of Health and Beauty in Germany: A Social History, 1890–1930.* Chicago: University of Chicago Press, 2003.

Healey, Dan. *Homosexual Desire in Revolutionary Russia: The Regulation of Sexual and Gender Dissent.* Chicago: University of Chicago Press, 2001.

———. "Moscow." In *Queer Sites: Gay Urban Histories since 1600,* edited by David Higgs, 38–60. New York: Routledge, 1999.

Heger, Heinz. *The Men with the Pink Triangle.* 2nd edition. Translated by David Fernbach. Boston: Alyson Books, 1994.

Heilbut, Anthony. *Thomas Mann: Eros and Literature.* New York: Alfred A. Knopf, 1996.

Heineman, Elizabeth. *Before Porn Was Legal: The Erotica Empire of Beate Uhse.* Chicago: University of Chicago Press, 2011.

———. "Gender Identity in the Wandervogel Movement." *German Studies Review* 12 (1989): 249–70.

———. "Sexuality and Nazism: The Doubly Unspeakable." In *Sexuality and German Fascism,* edited by Dagmar Herzog, 22–66. New York: Berghahn Books, 2004.

Heiß, Stephan. "Das Dritte Geschlecht und die Namenlose Liebe: Homosexuelle im München der Jahrhundertwende." In *MannBilder: Ein Lese- und Quellenbuch zur historischen Männerforschung,* edited by Wolfgang Schmale, 183–219. Berlin: Arno Spitz, 1998.

Heiß, Stephan, and Albert Knoll. "Übrigens komme derlei im Hofbräuhaus fast jede Woche vor." In *München und Bayern von hinten,* edited by Ralf Waldau, 15–19. Berlin: Bruno Gmünder, 1995.

Hekma, Gert. "Amsterdam." In *Queer Sites: Gay Urban Histories since 1600,* edited by David Higgs, 61–88. London and New York: Routledge, 1999.

———. "'A Female Soul in a Male Body': Sexual Inversion as Gender Inversion in Nineteenth-Century Sexology." In *Third Sex, Third Gender: Beyond Sexual Dimorphism in Culture and History,* edited by Gilbert Herdt, 213–40. New York: Zone Books, 1996.

———. "Queer Amsterdam 1945–2010." In Cook and Evans *Queer Cities, Queer Cultures: Europe since 1945,* edited by Matt Cook and Jennifer V. Evans, 118–34. London: Bloomsbury, 2014.

———. "Same-Sex Relations among Men in Europe, 1700–1990." In *Sexual Cultures in Europe,* vol. 2, *Themes in Sexuality,* edited by Franz X. Eder, Lesley Hall, and Gert Hekma, 79–103. Manchester, U.K.: Manchester University Press, 1999.

Hergemöller, Bernd-Ulrich. "Benedict Friedlaender." In *Homosexualität: Handbuch der Theorie- und Forschungsgeschichte,* edited by Rüdiger Lautmann, 82–85. Frankfurt: Campus, 1993.

———. "Hans Blüher." In *Homosexualität: Handbuch der Theorie- und Forschungsgeschichte,* edited by Rüdiger Lautmann, 150–58. Frankfurt: Campus, 1993.

———. *Sodom and Gomorrah: On the Everyday Reality and Persecution of Homosexuals in the Middle Ages.* Translated by John Phillips. London: Free Association Books, 2001.

Hermand, Jost. "Meister Fidus: Vom Jugendstil-Hippie zum Germanenschwärmer." In *Der Schein des schönen Lebens: Studien zur Jahrhundertwende,* edited by Jost Hermand, 55–127. Frankfurt: Athenäum, 1972.

Herzer, Magnus. "Die Gemeinschaft der Eigenen." In *Goodbye to Berlin? 100 Jahre Schwulenbewegung,* edited by Schwules Museum, 89–94. Berlin: Rosa Winkel, 1997.

Herzer, Manfred. "Adolf Brand und *Der Eigene.*" In *Goodbye to Berlin? 100 Jahre Schwulenbewegung,* edited by Schwules Museum, 49–53. Berlin: Rosa Winkel, 1997.

———. "Communists, Social Democrats, and the Homosexual Movement in the Weimar Republic." In *Gay Men and the Sexual History of the Political Left,* edited by Gert Hekma, Harry Oosterhuis, and James Steakley, 197–226. New York: Harrington Park Press, 1995.

———. *Magnus Hirschfeld: Leben und Werk eines jüdischen, schwulen und sozialistischen Sexologen.* Frankfurt: Campus, 1992.

———. "Ursprünge der Homosexuellenverfolgung." In *Goodbye to Berlin? 100 Jahre Schwulenbewegung,* edited by Schwules Museum, 19–20. Berlin: Rosa Winkel, 1997.

———. "Das Wissenschaftlich-humanitäre Komitee." In *Goodbye to Berlin? 100 Jahre Schwulenbewegung,* edited by Schwules Museum, 37–47. Berlin: Rosa Winkel, 1997.

———. "Die Zerschlagung der Schwulenbewegung." In *Goodbye to Berlin? 100 Jahre Schwulenbewegung,* edited by Schwules Museum, 155–59. Berlin: Rosa Winkel, 1997.

Herzog, Dagmar. *Sex after Fascism: Memory and Morality in Twentieth-Century Germany.* Princeton: Princeton University Press, 2005.

———. *Sexuality in Europe: A Twentieth-Century History.* New York: Cambridge University Press, 2011.

Hett, Benjamin Carter. *Death in the Tiergarten: Murder and Criminal Justice in the Kaiser's Berlin.* Cambridge: Harvard University Press, 2004.

Higgs, David. "Lisbon." In *Queer Sites: Gay Urban Histories since 1600,* edited by David Higgs, 112–37. New York: Routledge, 1999.

———, ed. *Queer Sites: Gay Urban Histories since 1600.* New York: Routledge, 1999.

Hiller, Kurt. *Leben gegen die Zeit.* 2 vols. Reinbek bei Hamburg: Rowohlt, 1969–1973.

Hirschfeld, Magnus. *Berlins Drittes Geschlecht: Schwule und Lesben um 1900.* Berlin: Rosa Winkel, 1991.

———. *Geschlechtskunde.* 5 vols. Stuttgart: J. Püttmann, 1926–30.

———. *The Homosexuality of Men and Women.* Translated by Michael A. Lombardi-Nash. Amherst, N.Y.: Prometheus Books, 2000.

———. *The Sexual History of the World War.* [1930] 1934. Reprint, Honolulu: University Press of the Pacific, 2006.

———. *Transvestites: The Erotic Drive to Cross-Dress.* Translated by Michael A. Lombardi-Nash. Buffalo, N.Y.: Prometheus Books, 1991.

Hirschfeld, Magnus, and Richard Linsert. *Empfängnisverhütung: Mittel und Methoden.* Berlin: Neuer Deutsches, 1928.

———. *Liebesmittel: Eine Darstellung der geschlechtlichen Reizmittel.* Berlin: Man, 1930.

Hoenig, John. "Sexology." In *Handbook of Psychiatry,* vol. 1, *General Psychopathology,* edited by Michael Shepherd and O. L. Zangwill, 48–52. Cambridge: Cambridge University Press, 1983.

Hoffschildt, Rainer. *Olivia: Die bisher geheime Geschichte des Tabus Homosexualität und der Verfolgung der Homosexuellen in Hannover.* Hannover: Selbstverlag, 1992.

———. *Die Verfolgung der Homosexuellen in der NS-Zeit: Zahlen und Schicksale aus Norddeutschland.* Berlin: Rosa Winkel, 1999.

Hohmann, Joachim, ed. *Der Eigene: Das Beste aus der ersten Homosexuellenzeitschrift der Welt.* Frankfurt: Foerster, 1981.

Houlbrook, Matt. *Queer London: Perils and Pleasures in the Sexual Metropolis, 1918–1957.* Chicago: University of Chicago Press, 2005.

Hughes, H. Stuart. *Consciousness and Society: The Reorientation of European Social Thought, 1890–1930.* Revised edition. New York: Vintage Books, 1977.

Hull, Isabel V. *The Entourage of Kaiser Wilhelm II, 1888–1918.* New York: Cambridge University Press, 1982.

———. "Kaiser Wilhelm II and the 'Liebenberg Circle.'" In *Kaiser Wilhelm II: New Interpretations,* edited by John C. G. Röhl and Nicolaus Sombart, 193–200. Cambridge: Cambridge University Press, 1982.

———. *Sexuality, State, and Civil Society in Germany, 1700–1815.* Ithaca: Cornell University Press, 1996.

Hutter, Jörg. *Die gesellschaftliche Kontrolle des homosexuellen Begehrens: Medizinische Definitionen und juristische Sanktionen im 19. Jahrhundert.* Frankfurt: Campus, 1992.

Ingram, Gordon Brent, Anne-Marie Bouthillette, and Yolanda Retter, eds. *Queers in Space: Communities, Public Places, Sites of Resistance.* Seattle: Bay Press, 1997.

Isherwood, Christopher. *Christopher and His Kind, 1929–1939.* New York: Farrar, Straus and Giroux, 1976.

Jackson, Julian. *Living in Arcadia: Homosexuality, Politics, and Morality in France from the Liberation to AIDS.* Chicago: University of Chicago Press, 2009.

Jacobsen, Wolfgang. "Oswald, Richard." In *Neue Deutsche Biographie,* 19:637–38. Berlin: Duncker and Humblot, 1999.

Janik, Allan, and Stephen Toulmin. *Wittgenstein's Vienna.* New York: Simon and Schuster, 1973.

Jelavich, Peter. *Berlin Cabaret.* Cambridge: Harvard University Press, 1993.

———. "Contemporary Literary Theory: From Deconstruction Back to History." *Central European History* 22, nos. 3/4 (1989): 360–80.

———. *Munich and Theatrical Modernism: Politics, Playwriting, and Performance, 1890–1914.* Cambridge: Harvard University Press, 1985.

Jellonnek, Burkhard. "Homosexuellenforschung im Dritten Reich." In *Homosexualität: Handbuch der Theorie- und Forschungsgeschichte,* edited by Rüdiger Lautmann, 221–25. Frankfurt: Campus, 1993.

———. *Homosexuelle unter dem Hakenkreuz: Die Verfolgung von Homosexuellen im Dritten Reich.* Paderborn: Ferdinand Schöningh, 1990.

Jellonnek, Burkhard, and Rüdiger Lautmann, eds. *Nationalsozialistischer Terror gegen Homosexuelle.* Paderborn: Ferdinand Schöningh, 2002.

Jensch, Klaus. "Zur Genealogie der Homosexualität." *Archiv für Psychiatrie und Nervenkrankheiten* 112, no. 4 (February 1941): 527–40.

Jensen, Erik N. "The Pink Triangle and Political Consciousness: Gays, Lesbians, and the Memory of Nazi Persecution." *Journal of the History of Sexuality* 11, nos. 1/2 (January/April 2002): 319–49.

Jessen, Olaf. *Die Moltkes: Biographie einer Familie.* Munich: C. H. Beck, 2010.

Jones, James W. "Mann, Thomas (1875–1955)." *GLBTQ: An Encyclopedia of Gay, Lesbian, Bisexual, Transgender, and Queer Culture.* www.glbtq.com/literature/mann_t.html.

———. *"We of the Third Sex": Literary Representations of Homosexuality in Wilhelmine Germany.* New York: Peter Lang, 1990.

Jung, Carl. "Concerning the Archetypes with Special Reference to the Anima Concept." In *The Archetypes and the Collective Unconscious,* translated by R. F. C. Hull, 54–72. Princeton: Princeton University Press, 1981.

———. "Psychological Aspects of the Mother Archetype." In *The Archetypes and the Collective Unconscious,* translated by R. F. C. Hull, 2nd edition, 73–91. Princeton: Princeton University Press, 1981.

———. *Psychological Types.* Translated by H. G. Baynes and revised by R. F. C. Hull. 1971. Reprint, Princeton: Princeton University Press, 1976.

Kaes, Anton, Martin Jay, and Edward Dimendberg, eds. *The Weimar Republic Sourcebook.* Berkeley: University of California Press, 1994.

Kaiser, Charles. *The Gay Metropolis, 1940–1996.* Boston: Houghton Mifflin, 1997.

Karlinsky, Simon. "Russia's Gay Literature and Culture." In *Hidden from History: Reclaiming the Gay and Lesbian Past,* edited by Martin Duberman, Martha Vicinus, and George Chauncey, 347–64. New York: New American Library, 1989.

Kartell für Reform des Sexualstrafrechts. *Gegen-Entwurf zu den Strafbestimmungen des Amtlichen Entwurfs eines Allgemeinen Deutschen Strafgesetzbuchs über geschlechtliche und mit dem Geschlechtsleben im Zusammenhang stehende Handlungen.* Berlin: Neuen Gesellschaft, 1927.

Katz, Jonathan Ned, ed. *Documents of the Homosexual Rights Movement in Germany, 1836–1927.* New York: Arno Press, 1975.

———. *The Invention of Heterosexuality.* New York: Dutton, 1995.

Keilson-Lauritz, Marita. *Die Geschichte der eigenen Geschichte: Literatur und Literaturkritik in den Anfangen der Schwulenbewegung.* Berlin: Rosa Winkel, 1997.

————. "Stefan George's Concept of Love and the Gay Emancipation Movement." In *A Companion to the Works of Stefan George,* edited by Jens Rieckmann, 207–31. Rochester, N.Y.: Camden House, 2005.

————. "Tante, Kerle und Skandale: Die Geburt des 'modernen Homosexuellen' aus den Flügelkämpfen der Emanzipation." In *Homosexualität und Staatsräson: Männlichkeit, Homophobie und Politik in Deutschland, 1900–1945,* edited by Suzanne zur Nieden, 81–99. Frankfurt: Campus, 2005.

Keitz, Ursula von. *Filme vor Gericht: Theorie und Praxis der Filmprüfung in Deutschland, 1920 bis 1938.* Frankfurt: Deutsches Institut für Filmkunde, 1999.

Kennedy, Hubert. *Anarchist of Love: The Secret Life of John Henry Mackay.* 2nd revised edition. San Francisco: Peremptory Publications, 2002.

————. "Brand, Adolf (1874–1945)." *GLBTQ: An Encyclopedia of Gay, Lesbian, Bisexual, Transgender, and Queer Culture.* www.glbtqarchive.com/ssh/brand_a_S.pdf.

————. "Johan Baptist von Schweitzer: The Queer Marx Loved to Hate." In *Gay Men and the Sexual History of the Political Left,* edited by Gert Hekma, Harry Oosterhuis, and James Steakley, 69–96. New York: Harrington Park Press, 1995.

————. *Der Kreis: Eine Zeitschrift und ihr Programm.* Berlin: Rosa Winkel, 1999.

————. *Ulrichs: The Life and Works of Karl Heinrich Ulrichs, Pioneer of the Modern Gay Movement.* Boston: Alyson Publications, 1988.

Kershaw, Ian. *Hitler.* 2 vols. New York: W. W. Norton, 1998–2000.

————. *The "Hitler Myth": Image and Reality in the Third Reich.* New York: Oxford University Press, 1987.

Klare, Rudolf. *Homosexualität und Strafrecht.* Hamburg: Hanseatische Verlagsanstalt, 1937.

Klimmer, Rudolf. *Die Homosexualität als biologisch-soziologische Zeitfrage.* Hamburg: Kriminalistik, 1958.

Knoll, Albert. "Totgeschlagen-totgeschwiegen: Die homosexuellen Häftlinge im KZ Dachau." *Dachauer Hefte* 14 (November 1998): 77–101.

Knopp, Lawrence. "Sexuality and Urban Space: A Framework for Analysis." In *Mapping Desire: Geographies of Sexualities,* edited by David Bell and Gill Valentine, 149–61. New York: Routledge, 1995.

Koehler, Christopher. "The Sex Problem: Thomas Hunt Morgan, Richard Goldschmidt, and the Question of Sex and Gender in the Twentieth Century." PhD dissertation, University of Florida, 1998.

Kokula, Ilse. "Lesbisches Leben von Weimar bis zur Nachkriegszeit." In *Eldorado: Homosexuelle Frauen und Männer in Berlin, 1850–1950,* edited by Michael Bollé, 149–61. Berlin: Frölich and Kaufmann, 1992.

Kracauer, Siegfried. *From Caligari to Hitler: A Psychological History of the German Film.* Princeton: Princeton University Press, 1947.

Kraepelin, Emil. *Psychiatrie: Ein Lehrbuch für Studierende und Ärzte.* 4 vols. Leipzig: Johann Ambrosius Barth, 1909–15.

Kreische, Rosi. "Lesbische Liebe im Film bis 1950." In *Eldorado: Homosexuelle Frauen und Männer in Berlin, 1850–1950,* edited by Michael Bollé, 187–96. Berlin: Frölich and Kaufmann, 1992.

Kretschmer, Ernst. *Physique and Character: An Investigation of the Nature of Constitution and of the Theory of Temperament.* 2nd edition. Translated by W. J. H. Sprott. New York: Cooper Square, 1970.

———. *A Text-Book of Medical Psychology.* 4th edition. Translated by E. B. Strauss. London: Oxford University Press, 1934.

Krettmann, Ulrike. "Johanna Elberskirchen." In *Homosexualität: Handbuch der Theorie- und Forschungsgeschichte,* edited by Rüdiger Lautmann, 111–16. Frankfurt: Campus, 1993.

Kuhn, Gerhard. "Das Phänomen der Strichjungen in Hamburg." PhD dissertation, University of Hamburg, 1955.

Lang, Theo. "Beitrag zur Frage nach der genetischen Bedingtheit der Homosexualität." *Zeitschrift für die gesamte Neurologie und Psychiatrie* 155 (1936): 702–13.

———. "Über die erbliche Bedingtheit der Homosexualität und die grundsätzliche Bedeutung der Intersexualitätsforschung für die menschliche Genetik." *Allgemeine Zeitschrift für Psychiatrie und ihre Grenzgebiet* 112 (1939): 237–54.

Laqueur, Walter. *Young Germany: A History of the German Youth Movement.* New York: Basic Books, 1962.

Lareau, Alan. "Lavender Songs: Undermining Gender in Weimar Cabaret and Beyond." *Popular Music and Society* 28, no. 1 (February 2005): 15–33.

Large, David Clay. *Berlin.* New York: Basic Books, 2000.

Lauritson, John, and David Thorstad. *The Early Homosexual Rights Movement.* New York: Times Change, 1974.

Lautmann, Rüdiger, ed. *Homosexualität: Handbuch der Theorie- und Forschungsgeschichte.* Frankfurt: Campus, 1993.

———. "The Pink Triangle: The Persecution of Homosexual Males in Concentration Camps in Nazi Germany." *Journal of Homosexuality* 6, nos. 1/2 (Fall–Winter 1980–81): 141–60.

————, ed. *Seminar: Gesellschaft und Homosexualität.* Frankfurt am Main: Suhrkamp, 1977.

Leidinger, Christiane. "Anna Rüling: A Problematic Foremother of Lesbian History." *Journal of the History of Sexuality* 13, no. 4 (October 2004): 477–99.

Leng, Kirsten. "Anna Rüling, Michel Foucault, and the 'Tactical Polyvalence' of the Female Homosexual." In *After the History of Sexuality: German Genealogies with and beyond Foucault,* edited by Scott Spector, Helmut Puff, and Dagmar Herzog, 95–108. New York: Berghahn Books, 2012.

Lengerke, Christiane von. "'Homosexuelle Frauen': Tribaden, Freundinnen, Urninden." In *Eldorado: Homosexuelle Frauen und Männer in Berlin, 1850–1950,* edited by Michael Bollé, 125–48. Berlin: Frölich and Kaufmann, 1992.

Lessing, Theodor. *Haarmann: Die Geschichte eines Werwolfs.* Berlin: Schmeide, 1925.

Lévi-Strauss, Claude. *The Savage Mind.* Chicago: University of Chicago Press, 1966.

Lichtmesz, Martin. "Autorenportrait Hans Blüher." *Sezession* 15 (October 2006): 2–7.

Limpricht, Cornelia, Jürgen Müller, and Nina Oxenius, eds. *"Verführte" Männer: Das Leben der Kölner Homosexuellen im dritten Reich.* Cologne: Volksblatt, 1991.

Lombardi-Nash, Michael A., ed. and trans. *Sodomites and Urnings: Homosexual Representations in Classic German Journals.* Binghamton, N.Y.: Harrington Park Press, 2006.

Lüdtke, Alf, ed. *The History of Everyday Life: Reconstructing Historical Experiences and Ways of Life.* Translated by William Templar. Princeton: Princeton University Press, 1995.

Lybeck, Marti. *Desiring Emancipation: New Women and Homosexuality in Germany.* Albany: SUNY Press, 2014.

————. "Gender, Sexuality, and Belonging: Female Homosexuality in Germany, 1890–1933." PhD dissertation, University of Michigan at Ann Arbor, 2008.

Machtan, Lothar. *The Hidden Hitler.* New York: Basic Books, 2001.

Mackay, John Henry. *The Hustler.* Translated by Hubert Kennedy. Bloomington, Ind.: Xlibris, 2002.

Makela, Maria. "Rejuvenation and Regen(d)eration: Der Steinachfilm, Sex Glands, and Weimar-Era Visual and Literary Culture." *German Studies Review* 31, no. 1 (2015): 35–62.

Mancini, Elena. *Magnus Hirschfeld and the Quest for Sexual Freedom: A History of the First International Sexual Freedom Movement.* New York: Palgrave Macmillan, 2010.

Mann, Klaus. *The Pious Dance: The Adventure Story of a Young Man.* Translated by Laurence Senelick. New York: PAJ, 1987.

Mann, Thomas. "Humanism and Europe." *New Republic,* April 28, 1937, 349.

Marhoefer, Laurie. "Degeneration, Sexual Freedom, and the Politics of the Weimar Republic." *German Studies Review* 34, no. 3 (2011): 529–50.

———. *Sex and the Weimar Republic: German Homosexual Emancipation and the Rise of the Nazis.* Toronto: University of Toronto Press, 2015.

Markus, Georg. *Der Fall Redl.* Vienna: Amalthea, 1984.

May, Rollo. "The Origins and Significance of the Existential Movement in Psychology." In *Existence: A New Dimension in Psychiatry and Psychology,* edited by Rollo May, Ernest Angel, and Henri F. Ellenberger, 3–36. New York: Basic Books, 1958.

McElligott, Anthony. "Political Culture." In *Weimar Germany,* edited by Anthony McElligott, 26–49. New York: Oxford University Press, 2009.

———, ed. *Weimar Germany.* New York: Oxford University Press, 2009.

McLellan, Josie. *Love in the Time of Communism: Intimacy and Sexuality in the GDR.* New York: Cambridge University Press, 2011.

Meeker, Martin. *Contacts Desired: Gay and Lesbian Communications and Community, 1940s–1970s.* Chicago: University of Chicago Press, 2006.

Meer, Theo van der. "The Persecution of Sodomites in Eighteenth-Century Amsterdam: Changing Perceptions of Sodomy." In *The Pursuit of Sodomy: Male Homosexuality in Renaissance and Enlightenment Europe,* edited by Kent Gerard and Gert Hekma, 263–307. New York: Harrington Park Press, 1989.

Melching, Willem. "'A New Morality': Left-Wing Intellectuals on Sexuality in Weimar Germany." *Journal of Contemporary History* 25 (1990): 69–85.

Meyer, Adele. *Lila Nächte: Die Damenklubs im Berlin der zwanziger Jahre.* Berlin: Lit Europe, 1994.

Meyerowitz, Joanne. *How Sex Changed: A History of Transsexuality in the United States.* Cambridge: Harvard University Press, 2002.

Micheler, Stefan. "Homophobic Propaganda and the Denunciation of Same-Sex-Desiring Men under National Socialism." In *Sexuality and German Fascism,* edited by Dagmar Herzog, 95–130. New York: Berghahn Books, 2005.

———. *Selbstbilder und Fremdbilder der "Anderen": Eine Geschichte Männer begehrende Männer in der Weimarer Republik und der NS-Zeit.* Konstanz: UVK, 2005.

———. "Zeitschriften, Verbände und Lokale: Gleichgeschlechtliche gebehrender Menschen in der Weimar Republik." Hamburg, 2008. www.stefanmicheler.de/wissenschaft/stm_zvlggbm.pdf.

Mildenberger, Florian. "Diskursive Deckungsgleichheit—Hermaphroditismus und Homosexualität im medizinischen Diskurs (1850–1960)." In *Medizin, Geschichte und Geschlecht:*

Körperhistorische Rekonstruktionen von Identitäten und Differenzen, edited by Frank Stahnisch and Florian Steger, 259–83. Stuttgart: Franz Steiner, 2005.

————. *"In der Richtung der Homosexualität verdorben": Psychiater, Kriminalpsychologen und Gerichtsmediziner über männliche Homosexualität, 1850–1970.* Hamburg: MännerschwarmSkript, 2002.

————. "Kraepelin and the 'Urnings': Male Homosexuality in Psychiatric Discourse." *History of Psychiatry* 18, no. 3 (2007): 321–35.

Mitchell, Stephen, and Margaret Black. *Freud and Beyond: A History of Modern Psychoanalytic Thought.* New York: Basic Books, 1995.

Moll, Albert. *Libido Sexualis: Studies in the Psychosexual Laws of Love Verified by Clinical Sexual Case Histories.* Translated by David Berger. New York: American Ethnological Press, 1933.

Mommsen, Wolfgang J. "Homosexualität, aristokratische Kultur und Weltpolitik: Die Herausforderung des wilhelminischen Establishments durch Maximilian Harden 1906–1908." In *Große Prozesse: Recht und Gerechtigkeit in der Geschichte,* edited by Uwe Schultz, 279–88. Munich: C. H. Beck, 1996.

Moore, R. I. *The Formation of a Persecuting Society: Power and Deviance in Western Europe, 950–1250.* Oxford: Blackwell, 1987.

Morland, Iain, and Annabelle Willox. *Queer Theory.* New York: Palgrave Macmillan, 2005.

Mosse, George. *The Crisis of German Ideology: Intellectual Origins of the Third Reich.* New edition. New York: Schocken Books, 1981.

————. *The Image of Man: The Creation of Modern Masculinity.* New York: Oxford University Press, 1996.

————. *Nationalism and Sexuality: Respectability and Abnormal Sexuality in Modern Europe.* New York: Howard Fertig, 1985.

Müller, Christian. *Verbrechensbekämpfung im Anstaltsstaat: Pyschiatrie, Kriminologie und Strafrechtsreform in Deutschland, 1871–1933.* Göttingen: Vandenhoek and Ruprecht, 2004.

Müller, Joachim. "'Um von meinem Trieb befreit zu werden': Kastrationen im Krankenrevier." In *Homosexuelle Männer im KZ Sachsenhausen,* edited by Joachim Müller and Andreas Sternweiler, 283–99. Berlin: Rosa Winkel, 2000.

————." 'Unnatürliche Todesfälle': Vorfälle in den Außenbereichen Klinkerwerk, Schießplatz und Tongrube." In *Homosexuelle Männer im KZ Sachsenhausen,* edited by Joachim Müller and Andreas Sternweiler, 216–63. Berlin: Rosa Winkel, 2000.

————. "'Wie die Bewegung, so die Verpflegung': Die Strafkompanie Schuhläufer." In *Homosexuelle Männer im KZ Sachsenhausen,* edited by Joachim Müller and Andreas Sternweiler, 181–89. Berlin: Rosa Winkel, 2000.

———. "'Wohl dem, der hier nur eine Nummer ist': Die Isolierung der Homosexuellen." In *Homosexuelle Männer im KZ Sachsenhausen,* edited by Joachim Müller and Andreas Sternweiler, 89–108. Berlin: Rosa Winkel, 2000.

Müller, Joachim, and Andreas Sternweiler, eds. *Homosexuelle Männer im KZ Sachsenhausen.* Berlin: Rosa Winkel, 2000.

Müller, Jürgen, and Helge Schneberger. "Schwules Leben in Köln." In *"Verführte" Männer: Das Leben der Kölner Homosexuellen im dritten Reich,* edited by Cornelia Limpricht, Jürgen Müller, and Nina Oxenius, 10–22. Cologne: Volksblatt, 1991.

Müller, Klaus. *Aber in meinem Herzen sprach eine Stimme so laut: Homosexuelle Autobiographien und medizinische Pathographien im neunzehnten Jahrhundert.* Berlin: Rosa Winkel, 1991.

Näcke, Paul. "Ein Besuch bei den Homosexuellen in Berlin: Mit Bemerkungen über Homosexualität" (1904). Appendix to Magnus Hirschfeld, *Berlins Drittes Geschlecht: Schwule Lesben um 1900,* 165–94. Berlin: Rosa Winkel, 1991.

Nenno, Nancy P. "Bildung and Desire: Anna Elisabet Weirauch's *Der Skorpion.*" In *Queering the Canon: Defying Sights in German Literature and Culture,* edited by Christoph Lorey and John Plews, 207–21. Columbia, S.C.: Camden House, 1998.

Newton, Esther. "The Mythic Mannish Lesbian: Radclyffe Hall and the New Woman." In *Hidden from History: Reclaiming the Gay and Lesbian Past,* edited by Martin Duberman, Martha Vicinus, and George Chauncey, 281–93. New York: New American Library, 1989.

Nieden, Suzanne zur. "Aufstieg und Fall des virilen Männerhelden: Der Skandal um Ernst Röhm und seine Ermordung." In *Homosexualität und Staatsräson: Männlichkeit, Homophobie und Politik in Deutschland, 1900–1945,* edited by Suzanne zur Nieden, 147–92. Frankfurt: Campus, 2005.

———. "Erbbiologische Forschungen zur Homosexualität an der Deutschen Forschungsanstalt für Psychiatrie während der Jahre des Nationalsozialismus: Zur Geschichte von Theo Lang." Berlin: Research Program "History of the Kaiser Wilhelm Society in the National Socialist Era," 2008. www.mpiwg-berlin.mpg.de/KWG/Ergebnisse/Ergebnisse25.pdf.

———. "Homophobie und Staatsräson." In *Homosexualität un Staatsräson: Männlichkeit, Homophobie und Politik in Deutschland, 1900–1945,* edited by Suzanne zur Nieden, 17–51. Frankfurt: Campus, 2005.

———, ed. *Homosexualität und Staatsräson: Männlichkeit, Homophobie und Politik in Deutschland, 1900–1945.* Frankfurt: Campus, 2005.

Nordbruch, Claus. *Sind Gedanken noch frei? Zensur in Deutschland.* Munich: Universitas, 1998.

Norton, Robert E. *Secret Germany: Stefan George and His Circle.* Ithaca: Cornell University Press, 2002.

Oosterhuis, Harry. "The Dubious Magic of Male Beauty: Politics and Homoeroticism in the Lives and Works of Thomas and Klaus Mann," translated by Ton Brouwers. In *Queering the Canon: Defying Sights in German Literature and Culture,* edited by Christoph Lorey and John L. Plews, 181–206. Columbia, S.C.: Camden House, 1998.

———. "Homosexual Emancipation in Germany before 1933: Two Traditions." In *Homosexuality and Male Bonding in Pre-Nazi Germany: The Youth Movement, the Gay Movement, and Male Bonding before Hitler's Rise,* edited by Harry Oosterhuis, 1–34. New York: Haworth, 1991.

———, ed. *Homosexuality and Male Bonding in Pre-Nazi Germany: The Youth Movement, the Gay Movement, and Male Bonding before Hitler's Rise.* Translated by Hubert Kennedy. Binghamton, N.Y.: Haworth, 1991.

———. "Medical Science and the Modernisation of Sexuality." In *Sexual Cultures in Europe,* vol. 2, *Themes in Sexuality,* edited by Franz X. Eder, Lesley Hall, and Gert Hekma, 221–41. Manchester, U.K.: Manchester University Press, 1999.

———. "Medicine, Male Bonding and Homosexuality in Nazi Germany." *Journal of Contemporary History* 32, no. 2 (1997): 187–205.

———. *Stepchildren of Nature: Krafft-Ebing, Psychiatry, and the Making of Sexual Identity.* Chicago: University of Chicago Press, 2000.

Petersen, Vibeke Rützou. *Women and Modernity in Weimar Germany: Reality and Its Representation in Popular Fiction.* New York: Berghahn Books, 2001.

Peukert, Detlev J. K. *The Weimar Republic: The Crisis of Classical Modernity.* New York: Hill and Wang, 1987.

Pieper, Mecki. "Die Frauenbewegung und ihre Bedeutung für lesbische Frauen (1850–1920)." In *Eldorado: Homosexuelle Frauen und Männer in Berlin, 1850–1950,* edited by Michael Bollé, 116–24. Berlin: Frölich and Kaufmann, 1992.

Pini, Udo. *Leibeskult und Liebeskitsch: Erotik im Dritten Reich.* Munich: Klinkhardt and Biermann, 1992.

Plant, Richard. *The Pink Triangle: The Nazi War against Homosexuals.* New York: Henry Holt, 1986.

Plötz, Kirsten. *Einsame Freundinnen? Lesbisches Leben während der zwanziger Jahre in der Provinz.* Hamburg: MännerschwarmScript, 1999.

Pohlmann, Ulrich. *Wilhelm von Gloeden: Taormina.* Munich: Schirmer/Mosel, 1998.

Pretzel, Andreas. "Als Homosexueller in Erscheinung getreten: Anzeigen und Denunciationen." In *Wegen der zu erwartenden hohen Strafe: Homosexuellenverfolgung in Berlin, 1933–1945,* edited by Andreas Pretzel and Gabriele Roßbach, 18–42. Berlin: Rosa Winkel, 2000.

———. "Erst dadurch wird eine wirksame Bekämpfung ermöglicht: Polizeiliche Ermittlungen." In *Wegen der zu erwartenden hohen Strafe: Homosexuellenverfolgung in Berlin, 1933–1945,* edited by Andreas Pretzel and Gabriele Roßbach, 43–73. Berlin: Rosa Winkel, 2000.

———. "Homosexuality in the Sexual Ethics of the 1930s: A Values Debate in the Culture Wars between Conservatism, Liberalism, and Moral-National Renewal." In *After the History of Sexuality: German Genealogies with and beyond Foucault,* edited by Scott Spector, Helmut Puff, and Dagmar Herzog, 202–15. New York: Berghahn Books, 2012.

Pretzel, Andreas, and Gabriele Roßbach, eds. *Wegen der zu erwartenden hohen Strafe: Homosexuellenverfolgung in Berlin, 1933–1945.* Berlin: Rosa Winkel, 2000.

Proctor, Robert. *Racial Hygiene: Medicine under the Nazis.* Cambridge: Harvard University Press, 1988.

Pruys, Karl Hugo. *The Tiger's Tender Touch: The Erotic Life of Goethe.* Carol Stream, Ill.: Edition Q, 1999.

Puff, Helmut. "After the History of (Male) Homosexuality." In *After the History of Sexuality: German Genealogies with and beyond Foucault,* edited by Scott Spector, Helmut Puff, and Dagmar Herzog, 17–30. New York: Berghahn Books, 2012.

Pursell, Tim. "Queer Eyes and Wagnerian Guys: Homoeroticism in the Art of the Third Reich." *Journal of the History of Sexuality* 17, no. 1 (January 2008): 110–37.

Radin, Max. "The Proposed German Penal Code." *California Law Review* 15, no. 5 (July 1927): 378–80.

Ramsey, Glenn. "The Rites of *Artgenossen:* Contesting Homosexual Political Culture in Weimar Germany." *Journal of the History of Sexuality* 17, no. 1 (January 2008): 85–109.

Reich, Wilhelm. *The Mass Psychology of Fascism.* 3rd edition. Translated by V. R. Carfagno. New York: Farrar, Straus and Giroux, 1970.

Richie, Alexandra. *Faust's Metropolis: A History of Berlin.* New York: Carroll and Graf, 1998.

Richter, Ingrid. *Katholizismus und Eugenik in der Weimarer Republik und im Dritten Reich: Zwischen Sittlichkeitsreform und Rassenhygiene.* Paderborn: Ferdinand Schöningh, 2001.

Robinson, Paul. *The Freudian Left: Wilhelm Reich, Geza Roheim, Herbert Marcuse.* New York: Harper and Row, 1969.

Rogge, Helmuth. *Holstein und Harden: Politisch-publizistisches Zusammenspiel zweier Außenseiter des Wilhelminischen Reichs.* Munich: C. H. Beck, 1959.

Rönn, Peter von. "Das Homosexualitätskonzept des Psychiaters Hans Bürger-Prinz im Rahmen der NS-Verfolgungspolitik." In *Nationalsozialistischer Terror gegen Homosexuelle,* edited by Burkhard Jellonnek and Rüdiger Lautmann, 237–60. Paderborn: Ferdinand Schöningh, 2002.

———. "Politische und psychiatrische Homosexualitätskonstruktion im NS-Staat. Teil II: Die soziale Genese der Homosexualität als defizitäre Heterosexualität." *Zeitschrift für Sexualforschung* 11 (1998): 220–60.

Rosario, Vernon A. "Pointy Penises, Fashion Crimes, and Hysterical Mollies." In *Homosexuality in Modern France,* edited by Jeffrey Merrick and Bryant Ragan, 146–76. New York: Oxford University Press, 1996.

Rosenkranz, Bernhard, and Gottfried Lorenz. *Hamburg auf anderen Wegen: Die Geschichte der schwulen Lebens in der Hansastadt.* 2nd edition. Hamburg: Lambda, 2005.

Ross, Chad. *Naked Germany: Health, Race and the Nation.* New York: Berg, 2005.

Roßbach, Gabriele. "Sie sahen das Zwecklose ihres Leugnens ein: Verhöre bei Gestapo und Kripo." In *Wegen der zu erwartenden hohen Strafe: Homosexuellenverfolgung in Berlin, 1933–1945,* edited by Andreas Pretzel and Gabriele Roßbach, 74–98. Berlin: Rosa Winkel, 2000.

Roth, Karl Heinz. "Großhungern und Gehorchen: Das Universitätskrankenhaus Eppendorf." In *Heilen und Vernichten im Mustergau Hamburg: Bevölkerungs- und Gesundheitspolitik im Dritten Reich,* edited by Angelika Ebbinghaus, Heidrun Kaupen-Haas, and Karl Heinz Roth, 130–34. Hamburg: Konkret, 1984.

Rowe, Dorothy. *Representing Berlin: Sexuality and the City in Imperial and Weimar Germany.* Burlington, Vt.: Ashgate, 2003.

Rucht, Dieter. "Das Alternative Milieu in der Bundesrepublik." In *Das Alternative Milieu: Antibürgerlicher Lebensstil und linke Politik in der Bundesrepublik Deutschland und Europa, 1968–1983,* edited by Sven Reichardt and Detlef Siegfried, 61–86. Göttingen: Wallstein, 2010.

Rüling, Anna. "What Interest Does the Women's Movement Have in Solving the Homosexual Problem?" In *Sodomites and Urnings: Homosexual Representations in Classic German Journals,* edited and translated by Michael A. Lombardi-Nash, 25–40. New York: Harrington Park Press, 2006.

Rupp, Leila J. "The Persistence of Transnational Organizing: The Case of the Homophile Movement." *American Historical Review* 116, no. 4 (2011): 1014–39.

Rydström, Jens. *Sinners and Citizens: Bestiality and Homosexuality in Sweden, 1880–1950.* Chicago: University of Chicago Press, 2003.

Schader, Heike. *Virile, Vamps und wilde Veilchen: Sexualität, Begehren und Erotik in den Zeitschriften homosexueller Frauen im Berlin der 1920er Jahre.* Königstein: Helmer, 2004.

Schäfer, Armin. *Biopolitik des Wissens: Hans Henny Jahnns literarisches Archiv des Menschen.* Würzburg: Königshausen and Neumann, 1996.

Schäfer, Margaret. "Theater, Theater!" In *Eldorado: Homosexuelle Frauen und Männer in Berlin, 1850–1950,* edited by Michael Bollé, 180–86. Berlin: Frölich and Kaufmann, 1992.

Scheler, Max. *The Nature of Sympathy.* 1954. Reprint, Hamden, Conn.: Archon Books, 1970.

Schieble, Burkhard Stefan. "Viktor Emil von Gebsattel: Leben und Werk." PhD dissertation, University of Tübingen, 2008.

Schildt, Axel, and Detlef Siegfried. *Deutsche Kulturgeschichte: Die Bundesrepublik von 1945 bis zur Gegenwart.* Munich: Carl Hanser, 2009.

Schlegel, Willhart. *Rolf: Eine Zeitgeschichtliche Erzählung.* Frankfurt: R. G. Fischer, 1995.

Schleiermacher, Sabdste. "Racial Hygiene and Deliberate Parenthood: Two Sides of Demographer Hans Harmsen's Population Policy." *Reproductive and Genetic Engineering: Journal of International Feminist Analysis* 3, no. 3 (1990): 201–10.

Schlierkamp, Petra. "Die Garconne." In *Eldorado: Homosexuelle Frauen und Männer in Berlin, 1850–1950,* edited by Michael Bollé, 169–79. Berlin: Frölich and Kaufmann, 1992.

Schmidt, Heike I. "Colonial Intimacy: The Rechenberg Scandal and Homosexuality in German East Africa." *Journal of the History of Sexuality* 17, no. 1 (January 2008): 25–59.

Schneider, Jeffrey Alan. "Militarism, Masculinity and Modernity in Germany." PhD dissertation, Cornell University, 1997.

Schoppmann, Claudia. *The Days of Masquerade: Life Stories of Lesbians during the Third Reich.* New York: Columbia University Press, 1996.

———. "Ein Lesbenroman aus der Weimarer Zeit: 'Der Skorpion.' " In *Eldorado: Homosexuelle Frauen und Männer in Berlin, 1850–1950,* edited by Michael Bollé, 197–99. Berlin: Frölich and Kaufmann, 1992.

———. "The Position of Lesbian Women in the Nazi Period." In *Hidden Holocaust? Gay and Lesbian Persecution in Germany, 1933–45,* edited by Günter Grau, 8–15. Translated by Patrick Cammiller. Chicago: Fitzroy Dearborn, 1993.

Schorske, Carl. *Fin-de-Siècle Vienna: Politics and Culture.* New York: Alfred A. Knopf, 1979.

Schuler, Martina. "Frauenarchive und Frauenbibliotheken." *Bibliothek: Forschung und Praxis* 20, no. 2 (1996): 348–64.

Schult, Wolfgang. "Geschichte der Hamburger Polizei, 1814–1964." Manuscript in Staatsarchiv Hamburg. Hamburg, 1964.

Schulz, Christian. *Paragraph 175. (abgewickelt) Homosexualität und Strafrecht im Nachkriegsdeutschland: Rechtsprechung, juristische Diskussionen und Reformen seit 1945.* Hamburg: MännerschwarmSkript, 1994.

Schwartz, Joseph. *Cassandra's Daughter: A History of Psychoanalysis.* New York: Viking, 1999.

Schwartz, Michael. *Sozialistische Eugenik: Eugenische Sozialtechnologien in Debatten und Politik der deutschen Sozialdemokratie, 1890–1933.* Bonn: J. H. W. Dietz, 1995.

Schwules Museum, ed. *Goodbye to Berlin? 100 Jahre Schwulenbewegung.* Berlin: Rosa Winkel, 1997.

Sedgwick, Eve Kosofsky. *Epistemology of the Closet.* Berkeley: University of California Press, 1990.

Sengoopta, Chandak. *Otto Weininger: Sex, Science, and Self in Imperial Vienna.* Chicago: University of Chicago Press, 2000.

Shorter, Edward. *A History of Psychiatry: From the Era of the Asylum to the Age of Prozac.* New York: John Wiley and Sons, 1997.

Sigusch, Volkmar. *Karl Heinrich Ulrichs: Der erste Schwule der Weltgeschichte.* Berlin: Rosa Winkel, 2000.

———. "The Sexologist Albert Moll: Between Sigmund Freud and Magnus Hirschfeld." *Medical History* 56 (2012): 184–200.

Sigusch, Volkmar, and Günter Grau. *Geschichte der Sexualwissenschaft.* Frankfurt: Campus, 2008.

Sked, Alan. "Colonel Redl and a Question of Identity." *History Today* 36 (July 1986): 9–14.

Skinner, Jody. *Warme Brüder, Kesse Väter: Lexikon mit Ausdrücken für Lesben, Schwule, und Homosexualität.* Essen: Blaue Euele, 1997.

Sombart, Nicolaus. *Die deutschen Männer und ihre Feinde: Carl Schmitt, ein deutsches Schicksal zwischen Männerbund und Matriarchatmythos.* Munich: Hanser, 1991.

Sparing, Frank. " 'Daß er es der Kastration zu verdanken hat, daß er überhaupt in die Volksgemeinschaft entlassen wird': Die Entmannung von Homosexuellen im Bereich der Kriminalbiologischen Sammelstelle Köln." In *Das sind Volksfeinde! Die Verfolgung von Homosexuellen an Rhein und Ruhr, 1933–1945,* edited by Centrum Schwule Geschichte, 160–81. Cologne: Centrum Schwule Geschichte, 1998.

———. *Wegen Vergehen nach §175 verhaftet: Die Verfolgung der Düsseldorfer Homosexuellen während des Nationalsozialismus.* Düsseldorf: Grupello, 1997.

Spector, Scott, Helmut Puff, and Dagmar Herzog, eds. *After the History of Sexuality: German Genealogies with and beyond Foucault.* New York: Berghahn Books, 2012.

Spender, Stephen. *The Temple: A Novel.* New York: Grove Press, 1988.

Spiegelberg, Herbert. *Phenomenology in Psychology and Psychiatry: A Historical Introduction.* Evanston, Ill.: Northwestern University Press, 1972.

Spurlin, William J. *Lost Intimacies: Rethinking Homosexuality under National Socialism.* New York: Peter Lang, 2009.

Stark, Gary D. "Pornography, Society, and the Law in Imperial Germany." *Central European History* 14, no. 3 (1981): 200–229.

Steakley, James. *The Homosexual Emancipation Movement in Germany.* New York: Arno Press, 1975.

————. "Iconography of a Scandal." In *Hidden from History: Reclaiming the Gay and Lesbian Past,* edited by Martin Duberman, Martha Vicinus, and George Chauncey, 233–63. New York: New American Library, 1989.

Stein, Marc. *City of Sisterly and Brotherly Loves: Lesbian and Gay Philadelphia, 1945–1972.* 2000. Reprint, Philadelphia: Temple University Press, 2004.

Steinle, Karl-Heinz. "'Auf verlorenem Posten': Der sudetendeutsche Politiker Walter Brand." In *Homosexuelle Männer im KZ Sachsenhausen,* edited by Joachim Müller and Andreas Sternweiler, 277–82. Berlin: Rosa Winkel, 2000.

————. *Der Literarische Salon bei Richard Schultz.* Berlin: Schwules Museum, 2002.

Stephens, Robert. *Germans on Drugs: The Complications of Modernization in Hamburg.* Ann Arbor: University of Michigan Press, 2007.

Sternweiler, Andreas. "'Als ein Beweis, daß wir zusammenhalten': Freundschaft und Solidarität." In *Homosexuelle Männer im KZ Sachsenhausen,* edited by Joachim Müller and Andreas Sternweiler, 316–30. Berlin: Rosa Winkel, 2000.

————. "Chronologischer Versuch zur Situation der Homosexuellen im KZ Sachsenhausen." In *Homosexuelle Männer im KZ Sachsenhausen,* edited by Joachim Müller and Andreas Sternweiler, 29–55. Berlin: Rosa Winkel, 2000.

————. "'Er ging mit ihm alsbald ein sogenanntes "Festes Verhältnis" ein': Ganz normale Homosexuelle." In *Homosexuelle Männer im KZ Sachsenhausen,* edited by Joachim Müller and Andreas Sternweiler, 58–78. Berlin: Rosa Winkel, 2000.

————. "'Er habe sich zeichnend am Leben erhalten': Der Künstler Richard Grune." In *Homosexuelle Männer im KZ Sachsenhausen,* edited by Joachim Müller and Andreas Sternweiler, 190–206. Berlin: Rosa Winkel, 2000.

————. "Exil." In *Goodbye to Berlin? 100 Jahre Schwulenbewegung,* edited by Schwules Museum, 169–73. Berlin: Rosa Winkel, 1997.

————. "Die Freundschaftsbünde—eine Massenbewegung." In *Goodbye to Berlin? 100 Jahre Schwulenbewegung,* edited by Schwules Museum, 95–104. Berlin: Rosa Winkel, 1997.

————. "Kunstbetrieb und Homosexualität." In *Goodbye to Berlin? 100 Jahre Schwulenbewegung,* edited by Schwules Museum, 59–69. Berlin: Rosa Winkel, 1997.

————. "Kunst und schwuler Alltag." In *Eldorado: Homosexuelle Frauen und Männer in Berlin, 1850–1950,* edited by Michael Bollé, 74–92. Berlin: Frölich and Kaufmann, 1992.

————. *Liebe, Forschung, Lehre: Der Kunsthistoriker Christian Adolf Isermeyer.* Berlin: Rosa Winkel, 1998.

————. "Das Lusthaus der Knaben—Homosexualität und Kunst." In *Goodbye to Berlin? 100 Jahre Schwulenbewegung,* edited by Schwules Museum, 110–22. Berlin: Rosa Winkel, 1997.

———. "'Nachteiliges über ihn konnte nicht festgestellt werden': Mitstreiter aus der Schwulenbewegung." In *Homosexuelle Männer im KZ Sachsenhausen*, edited by Joachim Müller and Andreas Sternweiler, 150–71. Berlin: Rosa Winkel, 2000.

———. "'Wegen dringenden Verdachts homosexueller und bündischer Betätigung festgenommen: Homosexuelle aus der Jugendbewegung." In *Homosexuelle Männer im KZ Sachsenhausen*, edited by Joachim Müller and Andreas Sternweiler, 109–44. Berlin: Rosa Winkel, 2000.

Stieber, Wilhelm. *Die Prostitution in Berlin und ihre Opfer*. 2nd edition. Berlin: Hofmann, 1846.

Stieg, Margaret. "The 1926 German Law to Protect Youth against Trash and Dirt: Moral Protectionism in a Democracy." *Central European History* 23, no. 1 (March 1990): 22–56.

Stone, Michael H. *Healing the Mind: A History of Psychiatry from Antiquity to the Present*. New York: W. W. Norton, 1997.

Strachan, Hew. *The First World War*. New York: Penguin Books, 2003.

Stryker, Susan. *Transgender History*. Berkeley: Seal Press, 2008.

Stümke, Hans-Georg. *Homosexuelle in Deutschland: Eine politische Geschichte*. Munich: C. H. Beck, 1989.

———. "Von 'unausgeglichenen Geschlechtshaushalt': Zur Verfolgung Homosexueller." In *Verachtet, Verfolgt, Vernichtet: Zu den "vergessenen" Opfern des NS-Regimes*, edited by Projektgruppe für die vergessenen Opfer des NS-Regimes, 46–63. Hamburg: VSA, 1988.

Sutton, Katie. *The Masculine Woman in Weimar Germany*. New York: Berghahn Books, 2011.

Tamagne, Florence. *A History of Homosexuality in Europe, 1919–1939*. 2 vols. New York: Algora Publishing, 2004.

Tatar, Maria. *Lustmord: Sexual Murder in Weimar Germany*. Princeton: Princeton University Press, 1995.

Taylor, Seth. *Left-Wing Nietzscheans: The Politics of German Expressionism, 1910–1920*. New York: de Gruyter, 1990.

Theis, Wolfgang. "Anders als die Andern: Geschichte eines Filmskandals." In *Eldorado: Homosexuelle Frauen und Männer in Berlin, 1850–1950*, edited by Michael Bollé, 28–30. Berlin: Frölich and Kaufmann, 1992.

———. "Verdrängung und Travestie: Das vage Bild der Homosexualität im deutschen Film (1917–1957)." In *Eldorado: Homosexuelle Frauen und Männer in Berlin, 1850–1950*, edited by Michael Bollé, 102–13. Berlin: Frölich and Kaufmann, 1992.

Theis, Wolfgang, and Andreas Sternweiler. "Alltag im Kaiserreich und in der Weimarer Republik." In *Eldorado: Homosexuelle Frauen und Männer in Berlin, 1850–1950,* edited by Michael Bollé, 48–73. Berlin: Frölich and Kaufmann, 1992.

Theweleit, Klaus. *Male Fantasies.* Translated by Erica Carter, Stephen Conway, and Chris Turner. 2 vols. Minneapolis: University of Minnesota Press, 1987–89.

Thompson, Victoria. "Creating Boundaries: Homosexuality and the Changing Social Order in France, 1830–1870." In *Homosexuality in Modern France,* edited by Jeffrey Merrick and Bryant Ragan, 102–27. New York: Oxford University Press, 1996.

Timms, Edward. "Expressionists and Georgians: Demonic City and Enchanted Village." In *Unreal City: Urban Experience in Modern European Literature and Art,* edited by Edward Timms and David Kelley, 111–27. New York: St. Martin's Press, 1985.

Tobin, Robert Deam. "Early Nineteenth-Century Sexual Radicalism: Heinrich Hössli and the Liberals of His Day." In *After the History of Sexuality: German Genealogies with and beyond Foucault,* edited by Scott Spector, Helmut Puff, and Dagmar Herzog, 76–93. New York: Berghahn Books, 2012.

———. *Warm Brothers: Queer Theory and the Age of Goethe.* Philadelphia: University of Pennsylvania Press, 2000.

Tóth, Tihamér. *Reine Jugendreife.* Freiburg im Breisgau: Herder, 1923.

Trumbach, Randolph. "The Birth of the Queen: Sodomy and the Emergence of Gender Equality in Modern Culture, 1660–1750." In *Hidden from History: Reclaiming the Gay and Lesbian Past,* edited by Martin Duberman, Martha Vicinus, and George Chauncey, 129–40. New York: New American Library, 1989.

Turnbaugh, Douglas Blair. "The Schwules Museum." *Journal of Performance and Art* 22, no. 2 (2000): 48–49.

Tyson, Lois. *Critical Theory Today: A User-Friendly Guide.* New York: Garland, 1999.

Ulrichs, Karl Heinrich. *The Riddle of "Man-Manly" Love.* Translated by Michael A. Lombardi-Nash. 2 vols. New York: Prometheus Books, 1994.

Usborne, Cornelie. *The Politics of the Body in Weimar Germany: Women's Reproductive Rights and Duties.* Ann Arbor: University of Michigan Press, 1992.

Verschuer, Freiherr von Otmar. *Rassenhygiene als Wissenschaft und Staatsaufgabe.* Frankfurt: H. Bechhold, 1936.

Vismar, Erhard. "Perversion und Verfolgung unter dem deutschen Faschismus." In *Seminar: Gesellschaft und Homosexualität,* edited by Rüdiger Lautmann, 308–25. Frankfurt am Main: Suhrkamp, 1977.

Vogel, Katharina. "Zum Selbstverständnis lesbischer Frauen in der Weimarer Republik: Eine Analyse der Zeitschrift 'Die Freundin,' 1924–1933." In *Eldorado: Homosexuelle Frauen und Männer in Berlin, 1850–1950,* edited by Michael Bollé, 162–68. Berlin: Frölich and Kaufmann, 1992.

Voigt, Wolfgang. "Geschichte der Schwulen in Hamburg." In *Hamburg ahoi! Der schwule Lotse durch die Hansestadt,* edited by Wolfgang Voigt and Klaus Weinrich, 5–45. Berlin: Rosa Winkel, 1982.

Wackerfuss, Andrew. *Stormtrooper Families: Homosexuality and Community in the Early Nazi Movement.* New York: Harrington Park Press, 2015.

Warner, Michael. *Fear of a Queer Planet: Queer Politics and Social Theory.* Minneapolis: University of Minnesota Press, 1993.

———, ed. *Publics and Counterpublics.* New York: Zone Books, 2002.

Weckowicz, Thaddeus E., and Helen P. Liebel-Weckowicz. *A History of Great Ideas in Abnormal Psychology.* Amsterdam: North-Holland, 1990.

Weeks, Jeffrey. *Coming Out: Homosexual Politics in Britain from the Nineteenth Century to the Present.* London: Quartet Books, 1977.

———. *Sex, Politics and Society: The Regulation of Sexuality since 1800.* 2nd edition. London: Longman, 1989.

Weindling, Paul. *Health, Race, and German Politics between National Unification and Nazism, 1870–1945.* Cambridge: Cambridge University Press, 1989.

Weininger, Otto. *Sex and Character: An Investigation of Fundamental Principles.* Translated by Ladislaus Löb. Bloomington: Indiana University Press, 2005.

Weirauch, Anna Elisabet. *The Outcast.* Translated by Guy Endore. New York: Greenberg, 1933.

———. *The Scorpion.* Translated by Whittaker Chambers. New York: Greenberg, 1932.

Weiss, Andrea. *In the Shadow of the Magic Mountain: The Erika and Klaus Mann Story.* Chicago: University of Chicago Press, 2008.

Weitz, Eric. *Weimar Germany: Promise and Tragedy.* Princeton: Princeton University Press, 2007.

Whisnant, Clayton. "Hamburg's Gay Scene in the Era of Family Politics, 1945–1969." PhD dissertation, University of Texas at Austin, 2001.

———. *Male Homosexuality in West Germany: Between Persecution and Freedom, 1945–69.* New York: Palgrave Macmillan, 2012.

———. "Styles of Masculinity in the West German Gay Scene, 1950–1965." *Central European History* 39, no. 3 (2006): 359–93.

Winkler, Michael. "Master and Disciple: The George Circle." In *A Companion to the Works of Stefan George,* edited by Jens Rieckmann, 145–59. Rochester, N.Y.: Camden House, 2005.

Winzen, Peter. *Das Ende der Kaiserherrlichkeit: Die Skandalprozesse um die homosexuellen Berater Wilhelms II, 1907–1909.* Cologne: Böhlau, 2010.

Wolff, Charlotte. *Magnus Hirschfeld: A Portrait of a Pioneer in Sexology.* London: Quartet Books, 1986.

Wu, Cuncun. *Homoerotic Sensibilities in Late Imperial China.* New York: Routledge, 2004.

Ze'evi, Dror. *Producing Desire: Changing Sexual Discourse in the Ottoman Middle East, 1500–1900.* Berkeley: University of California Press, 2006.

Zeh, Barbara. "Der Sexualforscher Hans Giese: Leben und Werk." PhD dissertation, Johann Wolfgang Goethe University, 1988.

Zinn, Alexander. "'Die Bewegung der Homosexuellen': Die soziale Konstruktion des homosexuellen Nationalsozialisten im antifaschistischen Exil." In *Die Linke und das Laster: Schwule Emanzipation und linke Vorurteile,* edited by Detlef Grumbach, 38–84. Hamburg: MännerschwarmSkript, 1995.

Zweig, Stefan. *The World of Yesterday: An Autobiography.* New York: Viking Press, 1943.

alternative milieu: the network of associations, stores, businesses, and other institutions that emerged from the counterculture in the 1970s.

anarchism: a political philosophy that advocates destruction of the state, which it sees as an oppressive and ultimately unnecessary system of control.

BfM: see the Federation for Human Rights.

cabaret: a form of nightclub entertainment that typically mixes singing, dancing, skits, comedy, and sometimes storytelling.

Center Party: the Catholic political party in Germany, founded in 1870 and merged into the Christian Democratic Party (CDU) after the Second World War.

classicism: styles or ideas, especially in art and literature, that are associated with ancient Greece and Rome.

communism: a variety of revolutionary socialism based on Marxism and V. I. Lenin's theories of party organization and practice. By the 1930s communist parties generally looked to the example of Soviet dictatorship and economic modernization as offering the best path toward a future socialist world.

Community of the Special (*Gemeinschaft der Eigenen,* GdE): a society of men who were all readers of Adolf Brand's magazine *The Special One,* this group served as the institutional framework for the masculinist wing of the homosexual movement.

counterpublic: a term developed by Michael Warner to describe the alternative public spheres sometimes formed by various marginalized groups in society.

DFV: see German Friendship Alliance.

Federation for Human Rights (*Bund für Menschenrecht,* BfM): a federation of friendship clubs led by Friedrich Radszuweit from 1923 until it disbanded in 1933.

friendship club: a general term for a series of homosexual social clubs that emerged in twentieth-century Germany.

GdE: see Community of the Special.

German Friendship Alliance (*Deutsche Freundschafts-Verband,* DFV): a federation of friendship clubs formed in 1920; it was renamed the Federation for Human Rights (BfM) after Radszuweit took over its leadership in 1923. In 1925 a new German Friendship Alliance was reorganized by several friendship clubs that had left the Federation for Human Rights because of dissatisfaction with Radszuweit's leadership.

German National People's Party (*Deutschnationale Volkspartei,* DNVP): the chief conservative party of the Weimar era.

German People's Party (*Deutsche Volkspartei,* DVP): the right-liberal party of the Weimar era. It was dedicated to democratic politics, although it was not always excited about democracy. In contrast with left-liberalism, it was generally opposed to the welfare state and labor politics.

Gestapo (short for *Geheime Staatspolizei*): the secret state police. Under Hitler the Gestapo became intertwined (though never identical) with the Nazi SS.

homonormativity: a term introduced by Lisa Duggan to describe what many see as an emerging assimilationist trend in gay and lesbian life since the 1990s that emphasizes sexual monogamy, domesticity, consumerism, and depoliticization.

League for the Protection of Motherhood (*Bund für Mutterschutz*): originally a third organization within the wider German feminist movement made up primarily of left-liberals and independent socialists (that is, those not aligned with the SPD). By the turn of the century, it was quickly emerging as a major proponent of sex reform in Germany.

liberal: in the European context, a political position defined by a belief in constitutions, personal freedoms guaranteed by civil rights, and capitalist free enterprise.

male-bonding community (*Männerbund*): a community of men focused on creating intense and close emotional bonds among its members. Borrowed from the ethnologist Heinrich Schurtz, this concept was further developed by Benedict Friedlaender and Hans Blüher to suggest that homosexuality (or at least homoeroticism) might play an important role in generating the intensity and intimacy of these emotional bonds.

masculinism: advocating a more masculine understanding of male homosexuality, one very much opposed to the idea advocated by Karl Heinrich Ulrichs, Magnus Hirschfeld, and many psychiatrists that homosexuality was caused by a biological mixture of male and female gender characteristics. The masculinists looked instead to ancient Greece for their understanding of male homosexuality, arguing that sexuality served as an important instrument for creating male bonds.

National Socialism (*Nationalsozialismus*): the political ideology of the Nazi party, which fused together radical nationalism, racial anti-Semitism, and anti-Marxism in an effort to rejuvenate German society after the First World War.

neo-Romanticism: a wave of artistic and philosophical figures, especially from the late nineteenth and early twentieth centuries, which combined many of the traditional Romantic themes (especially an appreciation of nature, skepticism toward rationality, and an emphasis on human emotional life) with more recent developments in philosophy and the arts, such as Friedrich Nietzsche's critique of reason and Sigmund Freud's theories of sexuality.

Night of Long Knives: a bloody purge of Ernst Röhm, many of his supporters, and several other individuals who had made an enemy of Hitler over the years, which took place on June 30, 1934.

Paragraph 175: Germany's sodomy law, adopted in 1871, shortly after unification. It was modified by the Nazi government in 1935 to make it easier to enforce. The East German government reformed the law in 1968, the West German government in 1969, making sex between two consenting adult males legal in both countries by the 1970s. The law was removed entirely from the criminal code in 1994.

Paragraph 175a: an addendum to Paragraph 175 appended by the Nazi government in 1935 that specified certain aggravating cases, including male prostitution, coercion, and sex with a minor. All were included in the rewritten version of Paragraph 175 of 1969, so that they continued to be illegal in West Germany in the early 1970s. In 1973 Paragraph 175 was further revised in West Germany, leaving only sex with a minor illegal.

phenomenology: a philosophical movement of the early twentieth century that aimed at the investigation of consciousness itself by examining its structures and the ways that objects were constituted within it.

Prussia: a northern German state whose strong economy and military tradition enabled it to unify Germany in 1871. Its culture was stereotypically described as militaristic, authoritarian, and strictly disciplined.

psychoanalysis: a set of psychological theories and treatment originally developed by Sigmund Freud in the 1890s and later expanded in distinct directions by other researchers. It generally assumes that the human psyche is fundamentally influenced by unconscious impulses and mental structures.

queer theory: a new wave of gay and lesbian scholarship that emerged in the early 1990s that took inspiration from both poststructural linguistic theory and recent critiques of gender. This body of theory above all assumes that both sexuality and gender are fluid constructions rather than fixed or stable entities.

Romanticism: an artistic and philosophical movement from the late eighteenth and early nineteenth century that was skeptical of Enlightenment rationalism. It saw nature as an elemental force that humans could never fully understand. Humanity was valued less for its power of rationality and more for its creative abilities and depth of feeling.

SA (*Sturmabteilung*): the so-called stormtroopers of the Nazi Party. A branch of the party originally designed to enable a coup against the Weimar government, the SA evolved to take on the role of orchestrating street fights against communists and other enemies of Nazism during the 1930s. After the 1933 takeover, the SA often assisted the police in their crackdown against "dangerous elements."

Scientific-Humanitarian Committee (*Wissenschaftlich-humanitäres Komitee,* WhK): an organization founded by Magnus Hirschfeld in 1897, which dedicated itself to the scientific study of homosexuality, the elimination of Germany's prejudices against homosexuality, and the repeal of Germany's sodomy law (Paragraph 175).

sexology: a branch of science dedicated to the study of sexuality.

Social Democratic Party (*Sozialdemokratische Partei Deutschlands,* SPD): Germany's longest-lasting socialist party, founded in 1875 when two previously organized socialist groups merged. Although technically a Marxist party until the 1950s, the party gradually accepted more mainstream democratic practices. By the 1920s it was considered by many less revolutionary than the Soviet-aligned Communist Party of Germany (KPD).

socialism: a broad political movement aimed at the creation of a world that is based on social equality and economic cooperation. For much of the twentieth century, socialism was divided between Soviet-style communism and the democratic socialism that evolved in western Europe.

SPD: see Social Democratic Party.

The Special One (*Der Eigene*): the world's first magazine to address an explicitly male homosexual audience. It was also the chief publication of the masculinist wing of the German homosexual movement.

SS (*Schutzstaffel*): a major division of the Nazi Party that after 1933 was closely integrated with the nation's police force and in charge of enforcing Nazi racial policy.

transgender: a term used broadly to apply to individuals whose gender identity does not match the identity that we would normally connect with the physical sexual attributes that they were born with. A transwoman identifies as woman (though is or was physically male), while a transman identifies as male (though is or was physically female).

transvestite: a person who enjoys wearing clothes commonly associated with the opposite sex. Although today we increasingly distinguish between transvestites and transgender individuals, at the turn of the twentieth century the term was used broadly to include a variety of different cross-dressers.

Uranian (*Urning*): a nineteenth-century term for a man who is sexually attracted to other men. It was introduced by Karl Heinrich Ulrichs and for a time adopted by other researchers and writers in Germany and elsewhere. Uranians were generally assumed to have bodies with largely male characteristics but at least traces of female psychic or behavioral tendencies. See also Urninde.

Urninde (*Urninde*): a nineteenth-century term for a woman who is sexually attracted to other women. It was introduced by Karl Heinrich Ulrichs and for a time adopted by other writers. *Urninden* were generally assumed to have bodies with largely female characteristics but at least traces of male psychic or behavioral tendencies. See also Uranian.

Waffen-SS: units of armed SS soldiers who fought alongside the regular armed forces (*Wehrmacht*) during the Second World War.

Wandervogel: a youth movement that emerged in Germany during the late 1890s. The organization was infused with a back-to-nature ethos, and its members enjoyed hiking, singing folksongs, and rediscovering what they imagined was a lost Germanic way of life. Many hoped that their activities would rejuvenate a society that they saw as overly authoritarian, materialistic, and hypocritical. Although the organization fragmented after 1904, various Wandervogel groups continued to operate in the 1920s and early 1930s under the larger umbrella of the Youth Alliance (*Bündische Jugend*). They were officially disbanded (or in a few cases merged with the Hitler Youth) shortly after the Nazis came to power, though some carried on secretly despite official persecution.

Weimar Republic: a constitutional democracy founded in Germany after the First World War and lasting until the Nazis took over in 1933. It was named after the eastern German city of Weimar, where the constitution was signed in 1919.

WhK: see Scientific-Humanitarian Committee.

WLSR: see World League for Sexual Reform.

World League for Sexual Reform (*Weltliga für Sexualreform,* WLSR): an international organization that in 1928 brought together sex reformers from Europe and the United States. It advocated the liberalization of marriage laws, free access to contraception, the repeal of laws against homosexuality, the toleration of nonmarital sexual relationships, and some eugenic controls over births.

INDEX

Page references given in *italics* indicate illustrations or material contained in their captions.

European Union, 242, 253–54
Evans, Jennifer, 245, 254
evolutionary theory, 23
exhibitionism, 103
Expressionism, 164, 165

Fabian: The Story of a Moralist (Kästner), 145
Faderman, Lillian, 126, 130
Fairy, The (*Special One* special issue), 192
Fanfare (magazine), 116, 117
farmers' leagues, 31
fascist men, 224–25
fashion, 158
Fashioning Sapphism (Doan), 47
Federation for Human Rights (*Bund für Men-schenrecht;* BfM): Berlin HQs of, 119; establishment of, 80, 109, 114; female members of, 230, 249; Hiller and, 186; membership of, 109, 194; Nazi shutdown of, 210; as politically unaffiliated, 194; post–WWII reestablishment attempt, 247; publicity/education focus of, 194–95; Radszuweit as head of, 80, 109–11, *110;* Röhm as member of, 206; social clubs united in, 80; WhK vs., 192–93
Federation for Ideal Female Friendship, 111
Fellows, The (homophile magazine), 248
Female Masculinities (Halberstam), 8
female prostitution, *87,* 92, 98, 99, 104, 209
femininity, 26–27, 28, 131, 225
feminism: conservative view of, 170; Elberskirchen as, 44; homosexual activism and, 42, *43,* 47; lesbianism and, 66, 126; WhK alliance with, 68–69. *See also* antifeminism; women's movement
Ferenczi, Sándor, 62
Ferree, Myra, 252
fetishism, 27, 62, 92, 183
Fidus (Hugo Höppener), 72
film, 91; censorship of, 168–69, 175, 179–80; female cross-dressing in, 158; lesbian, 133–34; Redl affair as portrayed in, 170; Stonewall Riots in, 4
Film Review Board, 179–80
Fischer, Eugen, 234
Fischer, Karl, 70, 71, 72–73, 74
Flandrin, Jean-Hippolyte, 139
Flato, Fritz, 186, 187
Flensburg, 249

Flexner, Abraham, 100
Forel, Auguste, 176
Forward (socialist newspaper), 48
Foucault, Michel, 7–8, 38, 47, 122, 125, 161, 177
Foundation for Scientific Sexual Research, 167, 173
Fout, John, 6
foxtrot (dance), 91
France, 184, 200, 238
franchise, expansion of, 30–31
Franco-Prussian War (1870), 55
Frank, Hans, 229
Frankfurt, 213, 247, 249, 252
Frankfurt Angel, 252
Frankfurt School, 224
Franz Ferdinand (Austrian archduke), 78
Frederick the Great, 100, 152
Free Corps, 167, 206
Free Germans, 165
"free unions," 67–68
French pornography, 129
Freud, Sigmund: Academic Workshop discussions about, 191; as anti–Paragraph 175 petition signatory, 166; Blüher and, 74, 78; European vs. U.S. acceptance of ideas of, 180; fin-de-siècle interest in sex and, 131; *Girls in Uniform* and, 134; Hirschfeld and, 59, 61–62; homosexuality theories of, 60, 181–82; humanity as viewed by, 183; intellectual influences on, 64; Krafft-Ebing and, 25; Nazi psychoanalytic studies and, 235–36; publications of, 59, 61–62; scientific debate over homosexuality and, 154. *See also* psychoanalysis
Freudianism. *See* psychoanalysis
Friedlaender, Benedict: Blüher and, 74; Elberskirchen and, 44; intellectual influence of, 157; intellectual influences on, 35; Jansen and, 72, 73; as masculinist, 14, 34–35, 36, 74, 76, 135; publications of, 35, 59, 70; scholarship on, 38; secession from WhK, 58–59, 66, 72; suicide of, 59; as WhK chief intellectual, 14; women devalued by, 66, 70; youth movement and, 72
Friends, The (homophile magazine), 248
Friendship (magazine): circulation statistics, 112, 114; editorship of, 112, 116–17; establishment of, 112; homosexual identity and, 152, 154, 155–56; influence of, *113;* interrupted publi-

cation of, 114, 116; Nazi shutdown of, 209; on Paragraph 175 repeal efforts, 199; as *Special One* competition, 188; target audience of, 112, 116; WhK-masculinist rivalry and, 194

friendship, use of term, 153–54

Friendship and Freedom (magazine), 188–89

friendship clubs, 108–11, *115,* 116, 165–66, 186, 189

friendship magazines, 149, 152, 154–56, 157. *See also Friendship* (magazine); *specific magazine*

Friendship Paper (magazine), 118, 119, 209

friendship press, 132, 149, 154

Fries, Jakob Friedrich, 164

Fritsch, Werner von, 214

Fuchs, Hanns, 134–35

Future, The (Berlin weekly), 51, 52, 56

Gainsborough, Thomas, 140

Gala of Girlfriends, The (von Bern), 118

Galton, Francis, 177

gambling, 104

garçonne, use of term, 154

Gaupp, Robert, 198

Gautier, Théophile, 145–46

Gay, Peter, 79, 135

gay, use of term, 11–12

gay and lesbian bookstores, 251

gay and lesbian history, 7–8, 252

gay and lesbian liberation movement, 6, 38, 251–52, 253

Gay Appetite (Hannover), 101

gay balls, 88, 97–98, 101

gay bars: advertising for, 112; in Berlin, 92–96, 209; cross-dressing acts in, *3;* Nazi crackdown on, 204, 209, 212, 216; outside Berlin, 100–103, 209, 216; policing of, 201; post–WWII, 249; as sign of modern decadence, 144; social networks in, 107; Weimar-era flourishing of, 79, 120. *See also* Eldorado Club (Berlin); *specific bar*

gay bathhouses, 251

Gay Berlin (Beachy), 104, 160

gay discos, 251

gay identity, 90

gay marriage, 253

Gay Museum (Berlin), 6, 221

gay neighborhoods, 251

Gay New York (Chauncey), 47

gay pornography, 103, 251

gay social clubs, 79, 80, 107–11, 155, 191

GdE. *See* Community of the Special (*Die Gemeinschaft der Eigenen;* GdE)

Gebsattel, Viktor Emil von, 183, 236–37, 244–45

Geleng, Otto, 140–41

Gemeinschaft der Eigenen, Die. See Community of the Special (*Die Gemeinschaft der Eigenen;* GdE)

gender, 11, 226

gender ambiguity, 158

gender history, 8

gender identity, 61

gender inversion, 21–22, 25, 26, 60

gender norms, 227–28

gender transgression, 130, 159

Gender Trouble (Butler), 127

General Medical Society for Psychotherapy, 233

General Psychopathology (Jaspers), 182

Genet, Jean, 249

genetics, 234

genital inversion, 182

George, Stefan, 122, 136–39, 211, 248

George circle, 136, 137

German Army, 53

German Catastrophe, The (Meinecke), 200

German Communist Party, 187, 195, 196, 206, 230

German Democratic Party, 195

German East Africa, 42, 48–50

German East African Newspaper, 48, 49

German Empire, 86

German Foreign Office, 53

German Friendship Alliance (*Deutsche Freundschafts-Verband;* DFV), 109–11, 116, 166, 186. *See also* Federation for Human Rights (*Bund für Menschenrecht;* BfM)

German-Hanoverian Party, 168

German Institute for Psychological Research and Psychotherapy, 233

German Law Academy, 229

German League for Human Rights, 185

German masculinity, 224–25

German Medical Society for Psychotherapy, 233

German National People's Party, 117, 162, 167, 194, 195–96

German People's Party, 168

German Psychiatric Institute (Munich), 234, 235

German Revolution (1918), 79, 83, 153, 162, 167–68, 200

German Romanticism, 71, 72
German Society for Sexual Research, 244
German Workers' Front (DAF), 217
Germany: gay scene history in, 85; LGBTQ rights in, 242, 253–54; queer history overview, 6–9; unification of (1990), 242
Germany, East, 240, 241, 242, 245–46, 250, 252, 253
Germany, pre–WWI: court system in, 29–30; homosexual activism in, 18–22, 38–40; scientific debate over homosexuality in, 22–27; turn-of-the-century politics in, 30–33; women's movement in, 44. *See also* homosexual rights movement; homosexual scandals
Germany, West: establishment of, 245; gay/lesbian activism in, 6, 251–52; homophile movement in, 247–48; homosexual/heterosexual distinction in, 47; lesbian magazines in, 248–49; male gay scene in, 249; Paragraph 175 retained/enforced in, 242, 250–51; Paragraph 175 revisions (1969/1973), 251; politics of memory in, 252–53; post–WWII rebuilding of, 245; sexually conservative society in, 240–41, 245; sexual revolution in, 249–50
Gestapo, 210, 212, 215, 217, 229, 230, 240
Gide, André, 131, 136
Giehse, Therese, 211
Giese, Hans, *243,* 244–45, 247
Giese, Karl, 174, 246
Giles, Geoffrey, 6, 227, 228, 237, 238
Girlfriend, The (magazine): advertising in, *115;* bisexuality debated in, 160; censorship of, *115,* 118; competing publications, 116; establishment of, 114; film reviews in, 133–34; Nazi Party and, 213; Nazi shutdown of, 209; post–WWII magazines modeled after, 249; scientific research on homosexuality in, 193; target audience of, 114, *115;* transvestism supplement included in, 157
Girls in Uniform (film; 1931), 122, 133–34, 145
Glockenbachviertel (Munich), 103, 251
Glöckner, Ernst, 137
Gloeden, Wilhelm von, 122, 140–44, *142,* 248
Goebbels, Joseph, 208
Goethe, Johann Wolfgang von, 124, 135, 139, 140, 153
Goethe University (Frankfurt), 244
Goldschmidt, Richard, 178, 235
Göring, Hermann, 213

Göring, Matthias Heinrich, 233
Göring Institute, 233, 236
gothic novels, 131–32
Grans, Hans, 171
Grau, Günter, 6
Great Bell, The (Berlin newspaper), 108
Great Britain, 238
Great Depression, 169, 199, 201, 206
Greco-Roman heritage, 122, 124, 135, 161
Greece, 238
Greek antiquity, 72, 73, 139
"Greek love," revival of, 14, 34, 35, 44, 76, 135–39
green triangle, 219
Grey, Joel, 200
Griesinger, Wilhelm, 23, 24
Gropius, Walter, 90–91
Grossmann, Anita, 91
Grosz, George, 90
Grotjahn, Alfred, 168
Gründgens, Gustaf, 125, 211
Grune, Richard, 220–21

Haarmann, Erwin, 247
Haarmann, Fritz, 105, 171–72
Haase, Ernst, 220
Habel, Hans, 234
Haeckel, Ernst, 17
Hahm, Lotte, 111, *115,* 230, 247
hairstyles, 158
Halberstam, Judith, 8
Hall, Radclyffe, 47, 151
Halperin, David, 8
Hamburg: gay scene in, 80, *81,* 100–101, 109, 209, 212, 231; Hirschfeld assaulted in, 172, 175; LGBTQ historical research in, 6; Nazi persecution in, 209, 216, 229; population statistics, 100; post–WWII gay/lesbian activism in, 251–52; post–WWII gay scene in, 247, 249, 251; socioeconomic development of, 86, 100; Wandervogel branch in, 189; WhK branch in, 30
Hamburger Tageblatt, 209
Hamburg Society for Sexual Research, 109
Hamecher, Peter, 137
Hampton, John, 211
"Hannelore" (song), 82–83
Hannover: gay scene in, 101–2, 209; homosexual publishing in, 166; legal reforms in, 19;

LGBTQ historical research in, 6; Nazi perse-
cution in, 209; policing of homosexuality in,
105, 172; post–WWII gay scene in, 249;
WhK branch in, 30
Harden, Maximilian, 51–56
Harmsen, Hans, 168
Heartfield, John, 90
Hegel, G. W. F., 77
Heger, Heinz, 252
Heidegger, Martin, 244
Heilbut, Anthony, 124
Heimsoth, Karl-Günther, 206–7, 212
Heine, Heinrich, 135
Heineman, Elizabeth, 71
Heines, Edmund, 214
Hellenic Messenger, The (magazine), 114, 117
Hergt, Oskar, 195
hermaphroditism, 21–22, 25, 26, 45, 146, 174,
198
Herzer, Manfred, 6, 39, 232
Herzog, Dagmar, 208, 225
heterosexual bars, 212, 231–32
heterosexuality: homosexual identity vs., 7–8, 9,
47, 157; masculinists and, 36; in Uranian
theory, 21; WhK-masculinist rivalry and
support from, 193–94
Heydrich, Reinhard, 214, 215
Hiller, Kurt: Blüher and, 190; Brand vs., 192;
Hirschfeld and, 164, 184, 185, 197–98; as homo-
sexual, 199; homosexuality theories of,
185–86; legal reform bill and, 197–98, 199;
Linsert and, 186–87; masculinists and, 186;
Nazi arrest/incarceration of, 210, 247; as New
Club cofounder, 164–65; post–WWII life of,
247; publications of, 166; as WhK officer, *163,*
165–66, 185, 198
Hilz, Sepp, 208
Himmler, Heinrich, 208, 213, 214–15, 228, 234
Hindenburg, Paul von, 201
Hirschfeld, Magnus: on Berlin as gay metropole,
119–20; on Berlin's gay scene, 84, 88–89, 92,
93, 94, 96, 99, 106–7, 108; birth of, 16;
Blüher and, 62; death of, 246; as eugenics a
dvocate, 176–78, 246; Eulenberg scandal and,
54, 56–58; exile of, 210; family/educational
background, 16; film appearance of, 175;
Foundation for Scientific Sexual Research
founded by, 167; Freud and, 59, 61–63,
182; Giese and, 244; Hiller and, 164, 184,

185, 197–98; as homosexual, 16–17, 210;
homosexuality theories of, 17, 27–30, 33, 36,
39, 61–63, 64, 76, 154, 155, 157, 174, 192,
193, 198; influence of, 34, 36; Institute for
Sexual Science founded by, 173–75; as Jew,
210; masculinist criticisms of, 192; as medical
expert in trials, 29–30, 54, 56–58; Nazi shutdown of institutions/publications of, 210, 233;
Paragraph 175 repeal efforts of, 162, 167;
policing of homosexuality and, 104–5;
political activity of, 30–33, 167; populariza-
tion of, 154; post–WWII attempts to revive
ideas of, 246; post–WWII life of, 246; psychi-
atric/sexological criticism of, 178–83, 233–34;
publications of, 17, 28, 29, 36, 61, 79, 90,
107, 178, 181; as publisher, 112; Radszuweit
vs., 111, 192–93, 197; retirement of, as WhK
chair, *163,* 198; right-wing violence against,
162, 172, 173; scholarship on, 6–7, 39; sexological conference organized by (1921),
176; as WhK chair, 14, *15,* 17–18, 30, 32–33,
58, 64–65; WhK–women's movement alliance
and, 68–69; as WLSR founder, 176; WWI as
viewed by, 166. *See also* Scientific-Humanitarian Committee (*Wissenschaftlich-humanitäres
Komitee;* WhK); sex reform movement
History of Sexuality (Foucault), 47
Hitler, Adolf: appointed chancellor (1933),
201–2; electoral campaigning of, 207; homo-
sexual stereotypes used by, 78; in Munich, 167;
Night of Long Knives ordered by, 213–14;
Röhm scandal and, 207–8; rumored to be
homosexual, 228; SA and, 213; WWI military
service of, 206
Hitler Youth, 213, 215, 217, 228, 236
Höch, Hannah, 90
Hoffschildt, Rainer, 6
Hofmannsthal, Hugo von, 131, 166
Hohenlohe, Chlodwig von, 50
Holocaust, 225–28
Holstein, Friedrich von, 53
Holy Roman Empire, 18
Holzmann, Johannes, 66
Homer, 141
"Homoerotic Friendship Party" (unrealized
concept), 194
homoeroticism: in classical/classically inspired art,
139–44, *142;* effeminacy and, 198; in Greco-
Roman heritage, 135–39; homosexual scandals

and, 54; in Mann's works, 124; Nazism and, 208, 212–13, 224–25, 232; use of term, 153

homonormativity, 253

homophile movement, 247–48, 253

homophile strategy, 156

homophobia, 28, 227

homosexual circles/informal networks, 106–7

Homosexual Emancipation Movement, The (Steakley), 4–5

homosexual identity, 90; heterosexuality vs., 157; homosexual publishing and, 119–20, 122, *123,* 152–60, 161; lesbian identity, 126, 151, 157–60; scholarship on, 7–9; terminology, 152–54

homosexuality: as biologically rooted, 17, 20–21, 44, 59, 66; Blüher's theories of, 74–78; coining of term, 4, 20, 46; criminalization of, 18–21, 26, 32, 47, 103–6, 128, 160, 182, 196–97, 246; fin-de-siècle reevaluation of, 131–35; as hereditary, 22, 157; Hirschfeld's theories of, 17, 27–30, 76; independent women and, 45–46; masculinist ideas of, 33–39, 44; medicalization of, 39, 130–31, 136; modernity and, 144–52; Nazi views of, 233–38; policing of, 103–6; prejudices about, 128–29, 240–41; psychoanalytic view of, 59–62, 76, 181–83; psychological roots of, 179; in public discourse, 56–58, *57;* schizophrenia and, 180; scientific debate over, 19–20, 22–27, 59–63, 161, 204, *205,* 233–38; transvestism vs., 29; trials involving, 29–30; Uranian theory, 21–22, 33–34, 36, 154. *See also* gay *entries;* homosexual identity; homosexuality—literary/ artistic representations of; homosexuals

"Homosexuality and Criminal Law" (dissertation; Klare), 226

homosexuality—literary/artistic representations of: in classical/classically inspired art, 139–44, *142;* film portrayals, 133–34; in fin-de-siècle works, 130–35; homosexual identity and, 126–28; in modernist works, 144–52, *148;* in neo-Romantic literature, 135–39, 161

Homosexuality of Men and Women, The (Hirschfeld), 29

Homosexual Man in the World, The (Giese), 244

"homosexual panic," 42, 46–47, 58, 89–90, 227

homosexual press/publishing industry: advertising by, 101–2; art/literature in, 132, 152; first periodical issued by, 7; gay magazines, *113;* homosexual identity and, 122; homosexual

identity debated in, 152–60, 161; lesbian magazines, *115;* Nazi shutdown of, 204, 209–10, 212; Paragraph 175 and, 196; post–WWII, 247, 248; Radszuweit as figure in, *110;* terminology used in, 154; Weimar-era flourishing of, 79, 80, 112–20

homosexual rights movement: academic views of, 38–40; alliances of, 42, *43,* 47, 64–74; first, 6, 14; German Revolution and, 162; Hirschfeld and, *15;* maturation of, 47; media coverage of, 56–58; Nazi crackdown on, 209–10, 212, 233; Nazi electoral victories and, 199; polarization of, 58–59, 162, 187–95; post–WWII remnants of, 246–47; scandals and, 39–40, 42, *43,* 47, 56–58, 78; Weimar downfall and, 200; Weimar-era interest in, 166–67; women's movement and, 64–70; WWI and, 162, 166. *See also* Community of the Special (*Die Gemeinschaft der Eigenen;* GdE); Federation for Human Rights (*Bund für Menschenrecht;* BfM); Scientific-Humanitarian Committee (*Wissenschaftlich-humanitäres Komitee;* WhK)

homosexuals: castrations of, 218; as child predators, 170–72, 193; in concentration camps, 4, 216–17, 219–23; conservative, 213, 214, 240; effeminate stereotype, 33–34, 52, 54, 56, 58, 76–77, 129, 144, 155–56, 193, 220, 221; "enemy of the state" stereotype, 56, 78, 170; honorary, "ancestral gallery" of, 152; Jungian view of, 61; lives of, in post-1934 Nazi Germany, 228–33; Nazi arrests/trials of, 215–18; in Nazi Party, 201, 204, *205,* 206–8, 212, 213–15, 228; political/social awareness of, 120; use of term, 11–12, 152–53; WWI military service of, 78–79, 166; WWII military service of, 232

homosexual scandals: Eulenberg scandal, 42, 50–58, *57,* 59, 67, 78, 108, 137, 170; George sexuality rumors and, 137; homosexual activism and, 39–40, 42, *43,* 47, 56–58, 78; "homosexual panic" caused by, 42; Krupp scandal, 48, 140; media coverage of, 55–58, *57;* Rechenberg scandal, 48–50

homosexual social clubs, 107–11

homosexual squads, 103–5

Höppener, Hugo, 72

Horney, Karen, 181

Hössli, Heinrich, 14, 19–20

hotels, as sex sites, 99
How to Do the History of Homosexuality (Halperin), 8
Hubertine (Düsseldorf transvestite entertainer), 102
Hubertusstock (Kaiser's hunting lodge), 51
Hull, Isabel, 55
Humanitas (homophile magazine), 248
Huret, Jules, 86–88
Hustler, The (Mackay), 35–36, 149–50
hyperinflation, 114, 173, 184, 200

Ibsen, Henrik, 16
I Lay in the Deep Night of Death (Vacano), 145
Images of Self and Images of Others (Micheler), 156–57
"imagined community," 119–20, 153
immorality trials (1937), 214
Incident in Lohwinckel, An (Baum), 150–51
Individuals' League, 191
Institute for Sexual Science (Berlin), 181; establishment of, 173–75; Hirschfeld finances and, 198; Hirschfeld residence in, 174–75; Linsert and, 187; Nazi shutdown of, 210, 212, 233; post–WWII reestablishment of, 244; sexological conference held at (1921), 176; WhK HQs in, 174
International Congress for Sex Reform on the Basis of Sexual Science (Berlin; 1921), 176
International Congress of Sexual Equality, 248
International Friendship Lodge (Bremen), 247, 250–51
International Psychoanalytical Association, 59, 62
International Psychoanalytic Congress (Nuremberg; 1910), 61
International Society for Sexual Research, 179
Interpretation of Dreams, The (Freud), 59, 74
intersexuality, 27–30, 39, 154, 155, 178–79, 192, 193, 198, 235
inversion, 60, 76, 153, 154
Isherwood, Christopher, 84, 92, 94, 173
Island, The (post–WWII homophile magazine), 247, 248
Island, The (Weimar-era gay literary/entertainment magazine), 116, 247
Italian Journey (Goethe), 140
Italian Renaissance art, 139–40
Italy, 48

Jäger, Gustav, 34, 191
Jansen, Wilhelm, 38, 72–74, 78
Japan, 238
Jasmine Blossoms (Dilsner), 130
Jaspers, Karl, 182
jazz, 91
Jelavich, Peter, 132, 146
Jellonnek, Burkhard, 6
Jensch, Klaus, 235
Jensen, Erik, 252–53
Jews, 190–91, 221–22, 225–28. *See also* anti-Semitism
Jones, James, 130, 131
Jordan, Friedrich, 187–88
jouissance, 89
Journal for Sexual Science, The, 61, 63, 68
Journal of Sexual Research, 244
Judaism and Socialism (Blüher), 190
Juds, Max, 220
Jugend (journal), *57*
Juliusburger, Otto, 198
Jung, Carl G., 61, 62, 235–36
Justinian (Roman emperor), 18

Kahl, Wilhelm, 69, 195, 196, 197–98
Kant, Immanuel, 164
Kapos (privileged concentration camp inmates), 219, 220
Kapp Putsch (1920), 167, 200
Karsch-Haack, Ferdinand, *113,* 152
Kassel, 109
Kästner, Erich, 145
Kautsky, Karl, 33
Keilson-Lauritz, Marita, 39, 138
Kennedy, Hubert, 4
Kershaw, Ian, 206
Kertbeny, Karl Maria, 20, 21–22
Keun, Irmgard, 145
King of Prussia (Hamburg), 100–101
Kinsey, Alfred, 27, 246
Kisch, Egon, 170
Kitzing, Fritz, 231
Klare, Rudolf, 226, 229
Klein, Julius, 49–50
Klein, Melanie, 181
Klimmer, Rudolf, 246
Klimt, Gustav, 131
Klotz, Helmut, 207
Kracauer, Siegfried, 133, 168

LGBTQ identities, *243,* 253
LGBTQ rights, 242, 253–54
Li, Tao, 246
libel suits, 108
libido, 60, 62, 181
Libido Sexualis (Moll), 27, 64
Liebenberg castle, 51
Life among the Ruins (Evans), 245
Life Partnership Law (2001), 253
life reform movement, 14, 31–32, 34
Linsert, Richard, *163,* 186–87, 197–98, 199, 210, 246
Lipps, Theodor, 183
literacy, 30–31
Little Corn Flower (Düsseldorf), 102
Logos, 77, 190
Lohengrin Club, 108
Lombardi-Nash, Michael, 4
Lombroso, Cesare, 24
London (England), gay scene in, 85
Love in the Time of Communism (McLellan), 250
Love of the Third Sex, The (Elberskirchen), *43,* 44
Love of Women, The (magazine), 117, 118–19, 229–30
Löwenstein, Hans Otto, 170
Luise Dorothea (duchess of Saxony and Gotha), 152
Lybeck, Marti, 9, 44, 45, 46, 96–97, 111, 127, 147

Mackay, John Henry, 34, 35–36, 58, 59, 73, 122, 149–50
Magic Mountain, The (T. Mann), 124
Magnan, Valentin, 24
male-bonding community, 35, 38, 72, 78, 190, 191, 212–13, 228
Male Club, 191
"Male Eros in the Work of Stefan George" (Hamecher), 137
Male Fantasies (Theweleit), 224–25
male prostitution: in Berlin, 85, *87,* 88–89, 92, 93, 98, 99, 100; among concentration camp inmates, 221; criminalization of, 184, 196–97, 215; eugenics and, 178; female prostitution and, 98; in Hamburg, 100, 101; in Hannover, 105, 171; Linsert's sociological survey of, 187, 199; literary portrayals of, 150; Nazi crackdown on, 209, 212, 217; policing

of, 103; post–WWII decriminalization of, 251; Röhm as client of, 206; serial killings involving, 105, 171; during WWII, 239
Mallarmé, Stéphane, 136
Maly and Jugel, The (Berlin), 96
Mammen, Jeanne, 147, *148*
Mancini, Elena, 28, 39
Mann, Erika, *123,* 124–25, 128, 211
Mann, Klaus, 122, *123,* 124–25, 128, 147–49, 211
Mann, Thomas, *123,* 124, 125, 128, 130, 136, 189, 211, 248
Marcuse, Max, 179
Marhoefer, Laurie, 5, 120, 178, 197, 200
Marienkasino (Berlin), 92, 150
marriage, 67
Marx, Karl, 33
Marx, Wilhelm, 195
Marxism, 9, 32, 224, 253
Masculine Woman in Weimar Germany, The (Sutton), 145
masculinism/masculinists: academic views of, 38–39; in art/literature, 149–50; Blüher as, *75,* 78, 166; Brand as, *37;* in GdE, 134, 166; Hiller and, 186; Hirschfeld vs., 59, 192–93; homosexuality theories of, 33–38, 44, 135, 156–57; homosexual publishing and, 116, 156–57; nationalism and, 126; Nazi racism and, 225–26; Nazi regime as viewed by, 202; Radszuweit vs., 156, 193; Tscheck as ideologue of, 191–92; WhK and, 59, 66, 166, 193–94; youth movement and, 70–74
masculinity: effeminate homosexual stereotype and, 34, 155; of fascist men, 224–25; Krafft-Ebing on malleability of, 26–27; of lesbians, 131, 144, 151, 154, 158–60; nationalism and, 126; socialist, in East Germany, 242; Weininger on, 28; youth movement and, 71
masculinity complex, 182
masochism, 27
Mass Psychology of Fascism, The (Reich), 224
mass suffrage, 31
masturbation, 22, 23, 89, 179, 215
matriarchy, 45
"Maximin" poems (George), 137, 139
May, Karl, 140
Mayer, Eduard von, 140
McLellan, Josie, 250

natural law theory, 19

nature, escape into, 132–33, 135

Navy League, 31

Nazi art, 208, 248

Nazi Germany: eugenics and, 176–77; gay bars in, 103, 231; gay/lesbian "camouflaging" in, 232–33; homoerotic association in, 232; homosexual life in (post-1934), 228–33; homosexual stereotypes in, 56; scholarship on, 5

Nazi Party, 162, 167, 172; assumption of power (1933), 201–2, 204, 209; coup attempt (1923), 206; electoral successes of, 199, 201, 207, 224; fragmented nature of, 228; Giese (Hans) as member of, 244; homosexuals in, 201, 204, 205, 206–8, 212, 213–15, 228; ideology of, 38, 191, 207, 216; as male-bonding community, 212–13, 228; membership of, 223–24; moral prudishness of, 200, 208, 224–25; reorganization of, 206

Nazi persecution, 4, 5; in concentration camps, 204, 216–17, 219–23; Holocaust and, 225–28; inconsistencies in, 228–29; legal measures, 215, 218, 234; lesbians and, 229–31, 240; memorialization of victims of, 242, 252–53; motives behind, 204, 205, 223–28; after Nazi takeover (1933), 209–12; Night of Long Knives and aftermath, 213–18; pink triangle, 219–20; scholarship on, 6; scientific view of homosexuality and, 233–38, 246; during WWII, 239–40

neo-Kantians, 164, 184

neo-Romanticism, 135–39

Nerlinger, Oskar, 192

Netherlands, 6, 191, 238

Nettesheim Casino (Cologne), 102

Neuberger, Ernst, 116

Neuengamme concentration camp, 221, 252

Neustädter Guest House (Hannover), 102

New Club, 164–65

New Friendship, The (magazine), 117, 152

New Generation, The (feminist magazine), 69

New Left, 224, 241

"New Reich" (George), 136

newspapers, 31

New Woman, 44, 45, 125, 126, *148,* 158

New Women's Community, 108

New York City, 92, 99, 100, 251, 252

Nieden, Suzanne zur, 234–35

Nietzsche, Friedrich, 67, 153, 164–65, 191

Night of Long Knives (1934), *205,* 208, 213–18, 228

Nordau, Max, 24

Norway, 238

Noster's Cottage (Berlin), 94

nude photography, 140–44

nudism, 35, 72, 73, 92, 249, 250

Nun, The (Diderot), 130

Nuremberg, 61

Oberg, Eduard, 17

obscenity laws, 114, 117–18, 120, 143–44, 168–69, *243. See also* Law to Protect Youth against Trash and Smut (1926)

Odeman, Robert, 220

Old Wandervogel, 72–74

O'Montis, Paul, 92

175ers (homosexual concentration camp inmates), 219–20, 223

Oosterhuis, Harry, 6, 22, 24–25, 26, 38, 39, 125, 126

Operation Clean Reich, 209

Oranienburg concentration camp, 210

Organization for the Reform of Marriage Law, 185

Oswald, Richard, 153, 175

Other, The, 130

Other, The (Röllig), 230–31

Our Lady of the Flowers (Genet), 249

outing, 54

Pabst, G. W., 146

Pages for Human Rights, The (BfM magazine), 114, 119, 157, 193, 194, 209

Pages of Ideal Female Friendship, The (magazine), 116

Pandora's Box (film; 1929), 146–47

Pandora's Box (Wedekind), 146–47

"pansy baiting," 155–56

Papen, Franz von, 201

Paragraph 175: East German revisions, 250; Freud vs., 182; friendship clubs and repeal of, 109; George poetry and, 137; Hiller as activist against, 166; Hirschfeld and, 27, 162, 167; historical background, 18–21, 67; homosexuality debate and, 27; homosexual publishing and repeal of, 120; Krupp scandal and,

Sachsenhausen concentration camp, 220, 221–23, 231, 254
sadism, 27, 92
sadomasochism, 225
Salome (Wilde), 143
San Francisco, 252
Sappho, 129, 135, 154
Sappho and Socrates (pamphlet; Hirschfeld), 17, 36, 90
scandals, 74, 78. *See also* homosexual scandals
scene, use of term, 11. *See also* Berlin gay scene; Weimar Republic—urban gay scene
Schad, Christian, 147
Schader, Heike, 132, 154, 158, 160
Scheler, Max, 183
Scherl Publishing, 65
Scheunenviertel (Berlin), 92
Schiele, Egon, 131
Schiller, Friedrich, 124, 153
schizophrenia, 180
Schlegel, Willhart, 213, 214
Schmalbach Inn (Düsseldorf), 102–3
Schmidt, Heinke, 48
Schneider, Jeffrey, 52
Schneider, Sascha, 140
Schnitzler, Arthur, 131
Schöneberg (Berlin), 251
School for Barbarians (E. Mann), 211
Schoppmann, Claudia, 230
Schrenck-Notzing, Albert von, 64
Schröder, Paul, 237
Schuler, Alfred, 138
Schultz, Karl, 112
Schurtz, Heinrich, 35
Schutzstaffel. See SS (*Schutzstaffel*)
Schwabe, Toni, 69
Schwarz, Friedel, 101
Schwarze Korps, Das (SS newspaper), 226
Schwarzfischer (Munich), 103
Schweinereien, 55, 128
schwul (gay), use of term, 12, 128–29
Scientific-Humanitarian Committee (*Wissenschaft-lich-humanitäres Komitee;* WhK): alliance with women's movement, 64–65, 67–69, 78; Berlin gay scene and, 119; BfM vs., 192–93; conference (1923), 157; Eulenberg scandal and, 42, 58; executive board, 165, 198; female members of, *43*, 44–45, 65, 68–69; female speaker at annual assembly of (1904), 65–66; feminist

criticism of, 68; Flato as conference delegate representing, 186; founding of, 14, 17–18; Friedlaender as officer in, 35; friendship clubs vs., 108–9; GdE and, 38, 39, 166, 192; goals of, 14, 78; Hiller as officer in, *163*, 165–66, 185; Hirschfeld as chair of, 14, *15*, 17–18, 30, 32–33, 64–65; Hirschfeld's retirement as chair of, *163*, 198; Jordan as member of, 187; Juliusburger as chair of, 198; leadership crisis in, 197–98; Linsert as chair of, *163*; literary bent of, 152; masculinists and, 38–39, 192, 193–94; Nazi shutdown of, 210; Nazi takeover and, 201; Operations Committee, 165–66, 192–93; Paragraph 175 repeal efforts of, 14, 18, 30, 32, 36, 56, 67, 78, 162, 182, 184; Paragraph 297 opposed by, 199; post–WWII reestablishment attempts, 247; propaganda shift in, 198–99; publications of, 30, 39, 90; scholarship on, 6–7; scientific bent to, 108; secessions from, 58, 66, 72. *See also* Hirschfeld, Magnus
Scorpion, The (Weirauch), 151–52
scouting movement, 70–71
Secessio Judaica (Blüher), 190, 191
"Secession of the Scientific-Humanitarian Committee" (manifesto; Friedlaender), 59
Sedgwick, Eve Kosofsky, 8, 42, 46–47
seduction, 179
Seefeld, Adolf, 214
serial killers, 105, 171–72, 214
Seventh Ring, The (George), 137
Sex, Freedom, and Power in Imperial Germany (Dickinson), 63
Sex and Character (Weininger), 28
Sex and the Weimar Republic (Marhoefer), 120
sex crimes, 218
sex education, 177, 249
sexology: conferences (1921/1928), 176; effeminate homosexual stereotype and, 33–34; emergence of, 24, 27; eugenics and, 177–78; Eulenberg scandal as publicity for, 58; forensic, 174; Hirschfeld critics, 178–83; homosexual police squads and, 104; homosexual publishing and, 90, 153, 157; independent women and, 46; lesbian scholarship and, 7; masculinized lesbian and, 151; post–WWII conference for (1950), 244; psychoanalysis vs., 180–81; public interest in, 45; publishers focusing on,

90; sexual identity and, 125–26; social effect of, 125–26; women's movement and, 64–70. *See also* Hirschfeld, Magnus; intersexuality; Krafft-Ebing, Richard von; Ulrichs, Karl Heinrich; *specific sexologist*

sex-reassignment surgery, 174

sex reform movement: Berlin Freudians and, 181; conservative view of, 169; eugenics and, 177–78; goals of, 91; Hirschfeld as figure in, 162, 167, 175; nudism and, 92; opponents of, 64, 162, 167, 179–80, 233–34; Paragraph 175 criticisms of, 64; Paragraph 175 revisions and, 70; post–WWII resurgence of, 248; Weimar-era flourishing of, 91

sex tourism, 92, *95*

sexual experimentation, 91–92, 200

sexual history, 8–9

Sexual History of the World War, The (Hirschfeld), 79

sexual identity, 11, 122, 125–28, *243*

"sexual intermediaries" theory, 27–30, 33

Sexual Inversion (Ellis), 27

sexuality, 11; congenital nature of, 17; of fascist men, 224–25; furtive forms of, 89; lesbian, 145; sublimated, 74–76

sexual libido, 60, 62, 181

Sexual Life of Our Times and Its Relations to Modern Culture, The (Bloch), 27

sexual orientation, 61

Sexual Pathology (Hirschfeld), 181

sexual perversion, 183, 236–37

sexual revolution, 242, *243,* 249–50

Sexual Science (Hirschfeld), 178

Sexual Transitions (Hirschfeld), 28

Shakespeare, William, 138

shoe runners, 222

Sie Representiert (painting; Mammen), *148*

Simmel, Georg, 164

Single Women (magazine), 118

Sizilianischer Jüngling (photograph; Gloeden), *142*

SK (*Sonderkommando;* penal regiment), 222–23

Sleeping Beauty (Cologne), 102

social class, 226

social Darwinism, 35

Social Democratic Party (SPD): Bebel as head of, 32; elections (1912), 69–70, 78; exiled leadership of, 208; Hirschfeld and, 31–32, 39, 167; Krupp scandal and, 48; legal reform

bill and, 195; masculinists vs., 188; Paragraph 175 repeal efforts of, 30, 33; press representing, 29–30, 48, 207; Röhm and, 207, 212; Weimar government and, 83, 183–84; women's movement and, 44; youth movement, 220 socialism, 31–32, 33, 44, 67, 73, 162, 165, 177, 177–78, 220. *See also* Social Democratic Party (SPD)

social psychology, 246

Society for Human Rights, 247

Society for Sex Education, 185

Society for Sex Reform, 185

Society for the Reform of Sexual Law (West Berlin), 247

sociology, 253

sodomy laws, 14; early activism against, 20–22; history of, 18–21, 67. *See also* Paragraph 175

soldiers, 98

soldiers' bars, 93

Solomon, Simeon, 139

Sombart, Nicolaus, 225

Soviet Union, 162, 166, 208, 238, 239

Spanish Civil War, 211

SPD. *See* Social Democratic Party (SPD)

Special Commission for Homosexuality, 215–16

Special One, The (gay periodical; *Der Eigene*): book reviews in, 152; Brand as publisher of, 7; circulation statistics, 112, 188; competing publications, 188; as elitist, 156; Fidus artwork in, 72; Friedlaender manifesto published in, 59; George poetry published in, 137; homosexuality theories promoted by, 36, 90; interrupted publication of, 36, 58, 187, 188; limited viewpoint range in, 116; outing tactic employed by, 54; personal ads in, 188; readership of, 112; Tscheck and, 192; WhK authors published in, 39; women's movement alliance and, 70; as world's first gay periodical, 7; WWI as viewed in, 166

Spender, Stephen, 101

Spengler, Oswald, 170

Spinnboden archive, 6

Spohr, Max, 17, 44, 65, 90, 112, 152

Spring Awakening (Wedekind), 132

Sprüngli, Theodora Ana, 65–67, 230

SS (*Schutzstaffel*): as concentration camp guards, 219, 222–23; Göring Institute referrals of, 236; Hahm arrested by, 230; homosexuality theories of, 227; homosexuals in, 228;